Conflict at the Edge of the African State

Conflict at the Edge of the African State

The ADF Rebel Group in the Congo-Uganda Borderland

Lindsay Scorgie

LEXINGTON BOOKS
Lanham • Boulder • New York • London

Published by Lexington Books
An imprint of The Rowman & Littlefield Publishing Group, Inc.
4501 Forbes Boulevard, Suite 200, Lanham, Maryland 20706
www.rowman.com

86-90 Paul Street, London EC2A 4NE

Copyright © 2022 by The Rowman & Littlefield Publishing Group, Inc.

All rights reserved. No part of this book may be reproduced in any form or by any electronic or mechanical means, including information storage and retrieval systems, without written permission from the publisher, except by a reviewer who may quote passages in a review.

British Library Cataloguing in Publication Information available

Library of Congress Cataloging-in-Publication Data
Names: Scorgie-Porter, Lindsay, author.
Title: Conflict at the edge of the African state : the ADF rebel group in the Congo-Uganda borderland / Lindsay Scorgie.
Description: Lanham : Lexington Books, [2022] | Includes bibliographical references and index. | Summary: "This book looks at one of the oldest and most secretive rebel groups in the eastern Congo warscape: the Allied Democratic Forces (ADF). Moving away from traditional state-centric concepts of cross-border conflict, the author examines how their deeply embedded position in local borderland histories has fueled their surprising resiliency"— Provided by publisher.
Identifiers: LCCN 2021038123 (print) | LCCN 2021038124 (ebook) | ISBN 9781498561693 (hardback) | ISBN 9781498561709 (epub)
Subjects: LCSH: Allied Democratic Forces | Terrorism—Congo (Democratic Republic) | Terrorism—Uganda.
Classification: LCC HV6432.5.A45 S36 2022 (print) | LCC HV6432.5.A45 (ebook) | DDC 363.325096751—dc23
LC record available at https://lccn.loc.gov/2021038123
LC ebook record available at https://lccn.loc.gov/2021038124

ISBN 978-1-4985-6171-6 (paper)

Contents

Acknowledgments	vii
List of Abbreviations	ix
Chapter 1: An Introduction to One of the World's Most Mysterious Rebel Groups	1
Chapter 2: A Borderlands Conceptual Framework	27
Chapter 3: A Burgeoning Borderland in the Rwenzories	65
Chapter 4: Formations and Consolidations: The ADF 1996–2003	101
Chapter 5: Setbacks and Recoveries: The ADF 2004–2013	151
Chapter 6: Transformations or Continuities? The ADF 2014–2021	201
Chapter 7: Quelling Conflict at the Edge of the African State	239
References	249
Index	293
About the Author	305

Acknowledgments

To say that this book has been a long time in the making would be an understatement. Its germination stretches back to 2008 when I began my PhD at Cambridge University in the Department of Politics and International Studies, and work on it continued through my first six years of teaching at Huron College, Western University. I could not have completed this project without the help of family, friends, and colleagues, but a few in particular deserve special mention.

I would first like to express my sincere gratitude to my PhD supervisor, Dr. Devon Curtis, who encouraged, motivated, and reassured me throughout the whole of the PhD process. She was unwaveringly supportive, and pivotal in helping me to shape my initial thoughts on borderlands and rebellion. Profound thanks also go to my PhD examiners, Dr. Christopher Clapham and Dr. Jonathan Goodhand, whose in-depth feedback on my dissertation and enthusiasm for the idea of a dissertation-to-book transformation helped to get this project off the ground. Writing a PhD can be a lonely experience at times, but my Cambridge friends helped to make this considerably less so. Thank you to Joo Hee, Astrid, Serita, Kristine, Amel, and Einat for making the Cambridge experience a special one.

I would also like to thank my research assistants, beginning with my brother Jeff Scorgie, who accompanied me on one of my fieldwork trips to Uganda. Jeff's patience, calmness, and humor in even the most unpleasant of conditions, made him a superb travel companion. While at Huron College I had the good fortune of hiring two phenomenal undergraduates, Kris Kowalchuk and Mallory Dunlop, whose attention to detail and willingness to delve into some pretty obscure research tasks I greatly appreciated. I also need to acknowledge the tremendous support of my department chair, colleague, and mentor, Neil Bradford, who provided constant encouragement in completing this project—despite hearing the phrase "I'm *almost* done the book!" for more than a couple of years.

My research—particularly the fieldwork component—was made possible by funding from the Social Sciences and Humanities Research Council of Canada, the Cambridge Commonwealth Trust, the UAC of Nigeria Travel Fund, the Cambridge Political Economy Society Trust, and Gonville & Caius College. A special thanks also goes out to The Royal Commonwealth Society for supporting me during the first year of my PhD, including facilitating an initial fieldwork trip and allowing me the opportunity to publish preliminary findings. During my time at Huron my research has been supported by a multitude of funding bodies, including research supports from Huron itself as well as the Association for the Study of the Middle East and Africa.

An enormous thanks also goes out to Dan Fahey, who went above and beyond in ensuring that my manuscript was a more accurate, nuanced, and in-depth one. Chapters five and six, in particular, are substantially improved (I hope!) because of his feedback. A huge thanks for sharing his wealth of knowledge on this subject matter. Any errors are mine, and mine alone.

Finally, I would like to acknowledge Steve, my parents Val and Dan Scorgie, and my son Jake. Steve's humor, assistance, and encouragement were critical in helping me cross the finish line with this project. Writing is definitely easier with him by my side. Over the course of my education and career my parents have provided me with motivation and encouragement beyond measure. They amaze me with their generosity, and to put it simply, their support through the thick and thin of this endeavor was everything. Jake joined me for the last three years of this work. While he had more than a small effect on my productivity levels, he undoubtedly gave me the motivation to finally get this done and move on to projects with more family friendly fieldwork sites. This work is dedicated to them.

List of Abbreviations

ADF: Allied Democratic Forces
ADM: Allied Democratic Movement
AFDL: Alliance of Democratic Forces for the Liberation of Congo-Zaire
ALiR: Alliance for the Liberation of Rwanda
AMISOM: African Union Mission in Somalia
APC: Armée Populaire Congolaise
AQIM: Al Qaeda in the Islamic Maghreb
BLHRA: Bakonjo Life History Research Association
CAR: Central African Republic
CNDP: Congrès National pour la Défense du Peuple
COW: Correlates of War
CRC: Centre Résolution Conflits
CRG: Congo Research Group
DDRRR: Disarmament, Demobilization, Repatriation, Reintegration, and Resettlement
DFID: Department for International Development
DGM: Direction Générale de Migration
DRC: Democratic Republic of the Congo
FAO: Food and Agriculture Organization
FARDC: Forces Armées de la République Démocratique du Congo
FAZ: Forces Armées Zaïroises
FDLR: Forces Démocratiques de Libération du Rwanda
FEDEMU: Federal Democratic Movement
FIB: Force Intervention Brigade
GoU: Government of Uganda
GoZ: Government of Zaire
HRW: Human Rights Watch

IDP: Internally Displaced Person
IED: Improvised Explosive Device
IOM: International Organization of Migration
ISCAP: Central Africa Province of the Caliphate
ISIS/L: Islamic State of Iraq and the Levant
IWDP: Integrated Women Development Program
JATT: Joint Anti-Terrorism Taskforce
KST: Kivu Security Tracker
LDU: Local Defense Unit
LRA/M: Lord's Resistance Army (sometimes referred to as Lord's Resistance Movement)
M23: Mouvement du 23 Mars
MONUSCO: Mission de l'Organization des Nations Unies en République Démocratique du Congo
MP: Member of Parliament
MTM: Medina wa Tawhid wal Muwahdeen
NALU: National Army for the Liberation of Uganda
NAYODE: National Youth Organization for Development
NGO: Non-Governmental Organization
NRA: National Resistance Army
OCHA: Office for the Coordination of Humanitarian Affairs
PARECO: Patriotes Résistants Congolais
RCD/K-ML: Rassemblement Congolais pour la Démocratie-Kisangani/ Mouvement de Libération
RCF: Regional Conflict Formations
RDC: Resident District Commissioner
RFM: Rwenzururu Freedom Movement
RM: Rwenzururu Movement
RPF: Rwandan Patriotic Front
UCDP: Uppsala Conflict Data Program
UFM: Uganda Freedom Movement
UK: United Kingdom
UMSC: Uganda Muslim Supreme Council
UN: United Nations
UNDP: United Nations Development Program
UNHCR: United Nations High Commissioner for Refugees
UNICEF: United Nations Children's Fund
UNLA: Uganda National Liberation Army
UNRF: Uganda National Rescue Front
UPDF: Uganda People's Defense Force
US: United States
USD: United States Dollar

WFP: World Food Program
WNBF: West Nile Bank Front

Chapter 1

An Introduction to One of the World's Most Mysterious Rebel Groups

Since November 1996, a rebel group known as the Allied Democratic Forces (ADF) have operated in the Rwenzori borderland of western Uganda and eastern Congo.[1] Perhaps because they have often lived an existence akin to an insular 'state within a state,' they have never received the kind of attention from outsiders that other violent actors in the area have garnered. The ADF currently roam a country home to well over 120 rebel groups. And while they are one of the larger and certainly among the better equipped and militarily threatening groups, they are both severely misunderstood and understudied. In fact, this is a group that have remained shrouded in mystery. Not prone to propaganda, exceptionally skilled at blending into their surrounding population, with bases located high in the Rwenzori massif or deep in the Congolese jungle, and with few members having ever succeeded in escaping the force, the ADF have stayed out of the public eye and confounded outsiders. Their multifaceted composition has eluded and confused observers even further: many of the ADF's members are Ugandan or Congolese, however a great deal more nationalities are represented as well; they have a strong Islamic dimension, yet Islam has been inconsistently adhered to and practiced; they are regularly described as 'foreign,' but factions of the group have ancestors that have lived in the Rwenzori borderland for generations.

While accordingly being written-off as mysterious, secretive, or elusive, the ADF have by no means been a dormant, inactive, or even 'quiet,' group. They terrorized the population of western Uganda for the first several years of their existence, committing numerous mass atrocities, and causing significant displacement. While often coexisting with the eastern Congolese of the Beni region over the past couple of decades, they have been brutal and unforgiving to anyone and everyone suspected of cooperating with their enemies. They have furthermore fought the Ugandan army (the Uganda People's Defense Force—or UPDF), the Congolese army (the Forces Armées de la République Démocratique du Congo—or FARDC), and the United Nations' (UN) peacekeeping force (Mission de l'Organization des Nations Unies en République Démocratique du Congo—or MONUSCO) with vigor, ruthlessness, and skill. Indeed, despite having to contend with a multitude of antagonistic forces—including not only the above actors but a variety of hostile local insurgencies—the ADF have proven themselves to be an extremely determined and resilient rebel group.

Before delving into a more thorough breakdown of the ADF's various phases of their violent existence, it is worth describing the environment in which the group have subsisted. Chapter Three will discuss the origins, development, and territory of what is meant by the 'Rwenzori borderland.' In general, however, the Rwenzori borderland consists of those areas of western Uganda and eastern Congo in and around the Rwenzori Mountain range (also commonly referred to as the Mountains of the Moon). It is a landscape of stunning beauty and astounding natural diversity. It incorporates snow-capped mountains, lush valleys, dense forest canopy, and alpine meadows—and the ADF have lived, operated amongst, and taken advantage of, all of these features and more. The mountain range is approximately 70 miles long, and just over 30 miles wide, mostly consisting of densely forested terrain. While the mountains form what could be considered the 'heart' of this cross-border micro-region, the borderland extends to the plains surrounding them. Thus, on the western Ugandan side of the borderland, towns such as Kasese and Bundibugyo are within the borderland heartland, while Fort Portal—still influenced by the border, but more integrated into the Ugandan polity—falls within the realm of the 'outer borderland.' Likewise on the eastern Congolese side of the borderland: Kasindi and the city of Beni comprise part of the borderland heartland, while Butembo—at a slightly further distance from the border, yet still quite distanced from the 'mainstream' Congolese polity—falls under the intermediate borderland.

As will become apparent in the following chapters, the ADF have maneuvered throughout the above locales in varying ways over the course of their existence. For purposes of clarity, it makes sense to analyze the ADF according to three (approximate) time periods: 1996 to 2003, 2004 to 2013, and 2014 to 2021. Important continuities obviously exist between these three stages. Nevertheless, there were significant enough changes either in terms of the ADF's behavior or with regards to *perceptions* of the ADF by outsiders, as to warrant independent analyses of these time spans.

From their founding in 1996 until 2003, the ADF were principally active in western Uganda and had rear bases (including training camps and headquarters) across the border in eastern Congo. Any international attention on

Uganda at the time was focused on the Lord's Resistance Army (LRA) in the north of the country, or the state's unlawful occupation of parts of eastern Congo. Meanwhile, a highly violent rebellion was unfolding in western Uganda. The ADF inflicted attacks on Kasese, Bundibugyo, and Kabarole districts of western Uganda, leading to the displacement of hundreds of thousands of people. Between 1997 and 2000, 85 percent of the population in Bundibugyo district were displaced (Carr Center for Human Rights 2007).[2] The towns of Kasese and Bundibugyo were particularly hard hit, but the surrounding rural areas were as well. Not only were the majority of people forced into one of 84 internally displaced person's (IDP) camps, but agricultural productivity came to a standstill, the local economy collapsed, and tax revenues in Kasese District dropped by 75 percent (Carr Center for Human Rights 2007). The ADF also conducted a series of grenade attacks in Kampala in the late 1990s, which killed 88 people and injured 268 (De Temmerman 2007a). The rebels' rhetoric projected the image of a group fighting on behalf of Uganda's aggrieved Muslim population, and proclaimed to want to bring down the Museveni government in Kampala. In reality, the force was comprised of a multitude of different groups—a Muslim faction being only one of many—and consequently the ADF harbored a *variety* of grievances, agendas, and aims. Arguably the most influential faction in the ADF was actually the National Army for the Liberation of Uganda (NALU), a group composed principally of the Konjo tribe of western Uganda, and derived from the remnants of locally-rooted rebellions.[3]

Although initially slow to respond, military operations in the borderland by the UPDF against the ADF managed to partially quell the rebellion. As a result, their numbers dropped from 4,000–5,000 combatants in 1996, to an estimated several hundred by early 2003, and the rebels were forced to withdraw from western Uganda. Nevertheless, and contrary to what Ugandan officials led the public to believe, they were by no means fully eradicated. As employees from the western Uganda amnesty office explained, "The ADF were only partially defeated. This is important. The leadership were not killed—they were still in the Congo" (Interview Twenty-Six). The rebels were able to retreat to the relative safety of eastern Congo, and work at rebuilding their force.

During the second time phase examined in this book, from 2004 to 2013, the rebels' main theatre of action was eastern Congo. However, just as previously they had taken advantage of, and maneuvered throughout, the *whole* of the Rwenzori borderland (as in using both western Uganda and eastern Congo, albeit increasingly residing in the Congo from 1999 onwards), they did so during this phase as well. Military operations were principally in eastern Congo, specifically the Grand Nord area of the province of North Kivu, but western Uganda continued to play a pivotal role in their recruitment of personnel, acquisition of material resources, and so on.[4]

A significant development from 2004 onwards concerned the ADF's behavior towards civilians. During the previous phase, while the UPDF had technically been the ADF's enemy, it was nevertheless civilians who had borne the brunt of the conflict. As a result, the public had generally been hesitant to collaborate with the rebels, and the ADF experienced minimal popular support. Between 2004–2013, while violence, threats, and fear continued to underpin the ADF-civilian relationship, there was a noticeable improvement. The ADF's interests overwhelmingly became about maintaining their place in this micro-region. They had always been embedded into the political, social, and economic fabric of the Rwenzori borderland, however this enmeshment was taken to a new level between 2004–2013. They had a degree of political influence in the area, had intermarried and socially integrated into the larger Grand Nord society, and had highly lucrative business interests inextricably tied to the border and the transnational trade networks. They were able to establish schools, (very) rudimentary medical clinics, a court system and prisons, and operated a series of interconnected camps (which were essentially akin to villages). Their enemies were thus any actors that threatened their position and interests in this space, which still included the UPDF, but increasingly so MONUSCO, FARDC (at times), as well as rebel groups such as the Congrès National pour la Défense du Peuple (CNDP). Indeed, during this time period the ADF experienced significant threats to their interests and overall survival. In 2005 and 2010, in particular, the ADF faced the very real possibility of annihilation. And yet, they not only fully recovered from these events, but significantly built back their strength.

In many ways, from 2014 onwards the ADF displayed some changed patterns of behavior. Perhaps most significantly they went from largely laying low, living amongst their fellow borderlanders, and generally leaving civilians alone, to a far more aggressive and violently active force. They played a critical role in a series of horrifically brutal massacres in the Beni area (which are still ongoing today), and responded to the more assertive stance of FARDC and MONUSCO with a vigor previously unseen from the force. Arguably, however, the ADF were overwhelmingly still the same force as during prior time periods—a group entrenched in their local environment and concerned with maintaining that embeddedness. What *had* changed were perceptions of the rebels. Claims of ADF association with international Jihadist groups increased markedly. In fact, the vast majority of analyses began to ignore their borderland ties altogether, instead primarily portraying them as struggling Al Qaeda or ISIS affiliates. The local and micro-political elements of the ADF were wiped away; they were simply another node in the radical global Islamist terrorist movement. And yet, while the narrative surrounding the ADF was more detached than ever from their borderland existence, the rebels were arguably further enmeshed in this cross-border micro-region than at any previous point in their existence—and arguably 'thriving.'

In such a hostile military environment—one where rebel movements typically last only a few years before being either expelled from their territory, forced to disband, or made to reform to such an extent that the original movement is for all extensive purposes eclipsed—the ADF not only survived, but learned to thrive. The question this begs, and indeed the query this book seeks to answer, is the following: why have the ADF proven so resilient?

EXPLANATIONS OF ADF RESILIENCY

Since the beginning of their rebellion in 1996, the media, conflict management actors, donors, and academics have overwhelmingly understood the ADF's staying power through three (somewhat interconnected) prisms: (1) proxy warfare, (2) spill-over violence from the Congo, and (3) most profoundly, Islamist terrorism. And it is important to note that many of the assumptions from all of the above actors were not only often based on second- and third-hand sources of information, but also derived from those collecting their data far from the epicenter of ADF action (i.e. Beni and surrounding locales).

The first is the idea that that the ADF served as a proxy force for Sudan—a pawn in the hostilities between Kampala and Khartoum. Because they represented an opportunity to counter Uganda's support for the Sudan People's Liberation Army (SPLA), Sudan was willing to shore-up the ADF, not only financially, but also in terms of recruitment, training, material supplies, and so on. Scholars such as Gérard Prunier and William Reno are among those who have attributed Sudan with an extensive degree of influence in the actual formation, as well as subsequent development, of the ADF.

The second prism is an understanding that particularly in their formative stages, the ADF were significantly influenced by the violence in the Congo. Beginning in 1996, the Congo was engulfed in conflict, and served as the epicenter for battles between the militaries of nine African countries, numerous Congolese and foreign rebel movements, and countless militias.[5] What has been described as one of the post–Cold War era's most complex conficts and often referred to as 'Africa's World War' resulted in the deaths of millions, the displacement of tens of thousands, and regional instability. While the fighting was officially declared over in 2003, peace proved elusive in the core of the conflict, namely the Kivu provinces of eastern Congo. Some analysts understood the instability and violence in the Congo as having had a 'contagious' element, and having had 'spilled-over' into western Uganda. For example, in a 1996 *Africa Confidential* piece it was reported that "The chaos in Zaire was bound to spill across Uganda's dangerous western border and reignite some old rebellions" (Staff Writers 1996). The ADF's transnational activity was perceived as having been incited and stimulated by conflict spreading from Congo to Uganda.

Finally, the third and by far most commonly employed prism through which to understand the ADF's resiliency has been Islamist extremism. The force has been seen as a radical Muslim group intent on terrorizing the Museveni regime. One of the original founding factions of the ADF was a disaffected Ugandan Muslim group, the Tabliqs. They were responsible for operationalizing various lucrative transnational networks for the ADF, such as funding from foreign Islamic charities and countries. The understanding that the Tabliqs were representative of the ADF involved three important assumptions. First, the ADF were perceived as a Ugandan group, despite the fact that over half of the membership was Congolese and the vast majority of their existence has been spent in the Congo. Second, the ADF have been considered a Ugandan Muslim group in exile, using the Congo for safe haven and sanctuary purposes. Their connection with the Congo has been understood to be merely territorial, and as such, they have been classified by most conflict management actors, including the UN, as a 'foreign armed group' ('negative force') in the Congo. Third, the ADF's operations from nearly the beginning of their existence, have been interpreted as lacking any political purpose. They consistently tend to be written-off as 'rebels without a cause.' An account of their motivations from a Ugandan newspaper, *The New Vision*, is typical in this respect: "The ADF rebels have been using the same terror tactics as the LRA in northern Uganda. They murder randomly, rob everywhere and kidnap indiscriminately. They are not pursuing the classic guerrilla strategy of 'winning hearts and minds.' They are solely interested in sowing mayhem and causing disaffection in Uganda" (Staff Writers 1997).

REGIONALIZED CONFLICT

The explanations described above all rely on a particular framework for understanding the ADF's resiliency. While proffering quite different explanations, the three prisms nevertheless are all of the opinion that the group's *transnational* nature is important to their staying power. More specifically, they conceptualize the rebel group through the lens of what this book collectively calls the 'regionalized conflict literature.'

In 2001, then UN Secretary-General Kofi Annan noted, "no war leaves the neighboring countries untouched [. . .] What often begins as an internal dispute over power and resources can quickly engulf an entire region" (United Nations Meetings Coverage and Press Releases 2001). Indeed, in light of the apparent contagious nature of many post-Cold War conflicts, academics and practitioners in the 1990s and early 2000s began to explain the spread of wars such as those in West and Central Africa as still largely intrastate—yet with a tendency to produce one-off outpourings of arms, refugees, militants, and other conflict-promoting actors into bordering countries (Murdoch and Sandler 2002; Shaw 2003). Conflict theorists argued that civil wars could not be considered *purely* domestic phenomena; too often there were negative externalities from a neighboring conflict that resulted in cross-border contagion.[6]

This approach was important in moving the discussion away from a 'closed polity' perspective, namely, treating civil wars as confined to internal state borders and each state as an isolated unit. Instead, it drew attention to the conflict participants and processes that could move across borders. However, many analysts and observers became dissatisfied with this 'spillover' explanation, and rather concerned with stressing the significant regional character of so many contemporary conflicts. For example, a paper by the Crisis States Research Center criticized the way in which the regional conflict in north-central Africa, involving Sudan, Chad, and the Central African Republic (CAR), was originally analyzed: "Initially in 2005, when violence erupted in Chad and later in CAR, the media, human rights advocates and some analysts described these conflicts as a simple 'spill-over' from the war in Darfur, or the 'Darfurization' of the region. In this logic, the causes and symptoms of the Darfur conflict [. . .] had merely been transplanted from Darfur into neighboring cross-border areas" (Giroux, Lanz, and Sguaitamatti 2009, 1). Rather than a Darfurization occurring, however, the paper argued that a *system* of conflict was operating across areas of the three countries. A similar critique was offered by James L. Hentz, although his was applied to west Africa: "[Paul] Collier and [Anke] Hoeffler's work on civil war, for instance, treats the Liberian and Sierra Leone civil wars as separate conflicts. Given that the state is the unit of analysis, this is only natural [. . .] The two are listed separately only because the state is the analytical prism" (Hentz 2009, 8). Toni Weis presented an interesting critique of the spill-over approach, criticizing its passivist approach. Rather than looking to the decisions and acts of "men and governments," "forces of nature or 'conflict' itself" tends to be the culprit (Weis 2009, 61). He goes on to note, "the concept of 'spillover' not only misinterprets the dynamics behind regional conflict complexes and underestimates the importance of intention and agency; it also fails to identify those who are responsible for the spreading of conflict" (Weis 2009, 61).

Pointing to the lack of conformity to any traditional notion of civil or intrastate war, some authors prefer the term 'transnational' to describe conflicts such as the above, which so blatantly transcend state boundaries and thrive off of regional ties and activities (Rubin, Armstrong, and Ntegeye 2001; Studdard 2004; Taylor 2003). More specifically, the spread of conflict from Liberia to Sierra Leone to Côte d'Ivoire, for example, or the violent instability in the Balkans and Central Asia, has been termed 'Regional Conflict Formations' (RCF) (Rubin, Armstrong, and Ntegeye 2001).[7] Perpetuated and sustained by phenomena such as cross-border population movements and natural resource trafficking, an RCF is defined as "sets of violent conflicts [. . .] that form mutually reinforcing linkages with each other throughout a broader region, making for more protracted and obdurate conflicts" (Rubin, Armstrong, and Ntegeye 2001, 2). The means through which various violent linkages eventually become a regional conflict complex, is via overlapping social, economic, and military transnational networks (Carayannis 2003). In fact, 'network war' has been interchangeably used with RCF to describe such conflicts. It speaks to the multitude of parties enveloped in webs of violent interactions, and highlights the wide array of issues encompassed in the conflict arena. Networks provide a more useful conceptual tool for studying regionalized violence, argue RCF and network war theorists, than an analysis focused on isolated actors and issues (Carayannis 2003; Taylor 2003).

Specifically in terms of rebel group resiliency, RCF analyses are overwhelmingly interested in the support rebellions receive from outside states. In other words, they tend to see the sustainability of rebel groups as usually dependent on dynamics played-out by regional state actors. The use of rebel groups as proxies in inter-state rivalries allows insurgent groups to receive much needed material—most notably financial—support. An additional common explanation for a rebellion's success (or lack thereof) with regards to resiliency is the role played by neighboring states in terms of offering sanctuary or safe haven. Despite many rebel organizations being vastly weaker than their government opponents, they can manage to evade state repression for decades (Salehyan 2007).

ARGUMENT

While the RCF and network war approaches have their attributes—notably having helped to shift conflict analysis away from a focus on contagious intrastate wars, and towards a transnational, network-oriented explanation of regional instability—there are nonetheless important deficiencies. Perhaps most basically, they still conceptualize transnational conflict as being about *internal civil wars*, but with a regional or international angle. "Regional conditions are important for understanding how civil wars unfold," as Idean Salehyan says (Salehyan 2007, 241). Yet many rebellions with a transnational dimension are about more than simply a rebel group taking advantage of a neighboring state's territorial sovereignty, or a rebel group being used as a pawn in a proxy war. More specifically, the literature fails to unpack and scrutinize the developments and political processes that lead to the regional interconnectivity. As Reinoud Leenders explains, "the RCF model appears obsessed with identifying static manifestations of cross-border linkages without offering an exhaustive theory of the dynamics and processes through which they are formed, and through which they cause, fuel or prolong conflicts" (Leenders 2007, 968).

The issue at the heart of this problem is the employment of a state-centric framework, which manifests itself in a variety of ways. For example, most RCF and network war analyses are what could be called top heavy: emphasis is placed upon the agendas of *national* actors, and macro parameters in general. Hence, attention tends to largely be fixed on the activities of intervening *states*, their co-optation of local players, and *their* position in directing conflict-promoting activities such as war economies. While these factors undoubtedly influence the regional violence in important ways, any perspective that dismisses the influential role played by translocal sources of agency and activity, for instance, can distort and simplify.[8] Indeed, the operation of violent regional linkages has been considered in statist terms which gloss-over, obscure, and even hide, various other important dynamics. There is an evident poor fit between the neat dividing lines of the traditional levels of analysis used by RCF theory, versus the fluidity and complexity of regional conflict networks, with their meshing of state/non-state, domestic/international, informal/formal, and illicit/licit boundaries.

This is actually part of a deeper issue, namely an inability to capture the intricate, multidimensional, and multidirectional nature of cross-border processes and interactions, due to the political (both academic and policy oriented) mental architecture being transfixed on the territorial state (Soguk 2008; Jarvis and Camilleri 1995; Carla 2005). It stems from what has been coined by Liisa Malkki as 'the national order of things,' namely, "the degree to which the mental geography of international relations begins and ends with notions of states (and unitary national territories) as the natural categories between which, through which, and upon which all actions should be conceived" (Malkki quoted in Jackson 2006, 443). As Roland Bleiker (2000, 273) notes in a similar vein, "A long tradition of conceptualizing global politics in state-centric ways has entrenched spatial and mental boundaries between domestic and international spheres such that various forms of agency have become virtually unrecognized, or at least untheorized." This habitual adherence to Cartesian-defined space has resulted in restrictions to outdated modes of conflict analysis, and preclusions from coming to grips with the political processes taking place in transnational conflict arenas.

Existing analyses of the ADF rebellion have overwhelmingly applied traditional (state-centric) transnational concepts of cross-border conflict—such as proxy war, spill-over and contagion, foreign sponsorship, and so on—however have been unable to account for the ADF's staying power. Most of these explanations are pertinent to the ADF for only a limited period of their existence, concern only certain factions of the group and not the rebellion as a whole, and discount the local environment in which the ADF operates. The Nairobi Agreement signed between Kampala and Khartoum in 1999 signalled a move towards normalization between the two countries, and thus the ADF's importance for Sudan in the wider proxy war was greatly diminished thereafter. Support for the ADF from what was once their principal sponsor was even further reduced after the 2005 Comprehensive Peace Agreement between Khartoum and the SPLA. Yet importantly, when Sudanese support dried-up, the ADF were able to continue acquiring material resources and support themselves financially. Moreover, understanding the violence in the Congo as spilling-over or spreading to western Uganda, and being an influential stimulating factor behind the ADF's initial creation and then continuation, is to apply a very ahistorical and context-blind analysis to the rebel group. It ignores the profoundly integrated nature of the western Uganda-eastern Congo micro-region, the tradition of interaction between the populations on either side of the border, and indeed the deep history of conflict on *both* sides of the border. Finally, seeing the ADF through the prism of Islamic terrorism proved to have serious flaws as well. As will be discussed in much greater depth in Chapters Four, Five, and Six, the authenticity of the religious dimension was questionable at times, and ADF camps greatly differed in how 'Islamicized' they were. While many Ugandan and Congolese Muslims indeed joined the ADF through Islamic networks, there were also practical motivating factors of poverty, unemployment, frustration with the government, or false promises of future opportunities. There were also a multitude of recruits who joined for reasons connected in no shape or form to Islamic networks. Explanations such as the Islamic terrorism dimension furthermore fundamentally ignore pivotal sources of support for the ADF such as those derived from the businesses they were able to establish or become a part of (for example cross-border trade, agriculture, and the taxing of timber forests). They not only ignore these activities, but they are unable to explain how the ADF were able to practice, and become successful at, these ventures in the first place.

Applying a cross-border framework is undoubtedly pertinent for a group that operates so profoundly transnationally. Nevertheless, employing traditional (read state-centric) transnational approaches is misleading, and leaves a great deal to be understood about the ADF's cross-border character and activities. This book accordingly explores how the ADF's transnational dimension was more than a case of proxy warfare, cross-border spill-over, or foreign sponsorship. It moves away from framing their transnational dimension as one in which the rebels were merely a pawn in wider regional political issues, or the result of negative externalities from the Congo, or propped-up by foreign Islamic funding sources. Instead, it proposes that transnational processes and dynamics such as the following were influential in underpinning the movement for all of those years: the political, social, and economic history of the Rwenzori region; the previous rebellions that took place in this space; the multitude of different factions that helped constitute the ADF (not only the Tabliqs); and their political and socio-economic integration with neighboring communities.

If one takes more than a cursory look at the force's origins, it is immediately obvious that the ADF have been highly influenced by their place in, and interaction with, the surrounding cross-border environment. My research accordingly places the ADF within a *borderland* analytic framework, as opposed to traditional state-centric lens. As will be discussed in-depth in Chapter Two, borderlands (specifically conflict-affected borderlands, which are the type of borderlands that this book is concerned with) constitute their own political and socio-economic complex, and tend to exhibit the following dynamics: politically, a tradition of resistance against central authority; socially, the predominance of a border identity; and economically, a system built around independent cross-border trade. Together, what stands out most from these practices, are their anti-state character and liminal nature. As a result of the above, borderlands experience specific types of conflict, which are different from the violence and warfare found in other spaces.

Yet, conflict theorists (with some exceptions) have generally been uninterested in borderlands, viewing them as passive and reactive hinterlands, or marginal and peripheral areas with little state presence and thus of modest strategic importance. Following from this, borders themselves have tended to be thought of in strictly statist terms, as barriers of penetration, lines of separation, and the legal limits of a state's sovereignty (Van Schendel 2005; Baud and Van Schendel 1997; Donnan and Haller 2000). Assuming borders and the spaces around them to be unchanging and non-dynamic sites has serious implications for conflict analysis. It leads to the cross-border violence being understood through the concepts mentioned previously, such as proxy warfare, contagion, knock-on effect, spill-over, and so on. The embedded statism within these notions misses the profound cross-border interconnection found in many situations of transnational violence—the interlinking of neighboring peripheries to such a degree that to talk of distinct states obscures key conflict dynamics. Consequently, denying borderlands the recognition of being complex zones or entities in their own right, can also deny conflict explanations the ability to move beyond superficial paradigms of cross-border violence.

Taking a borderland perspective does not mean in any way that the state is discounted as an unimportant or irrelevant actor. In fact, a borderland perspective is very conscious of the vital role played by states in transnational dynamics (the importance of the state border being the most obvious example of this). Applying a borderland perspective rather entails a recognition that the state is relevant in ways often not fully grasped.

This book argues that the Rwenzori borderland of western Uganda and eastern Congo is profoundly anti-state in character and networked/liminal in nature. It is historically a space of conflict, the latest case being the ADF rebellion. My research discovered that not only were the ADF pivotally shaped by their critical interaction with the surrounding borderland, but that they used their embedded position to strategically take advantage of the resources 'on offer' from the borderland. From an exploration into the group's origins, development, and practices until 2021, my research found that the ADF used the political, social, and economic networks within the borderland to pursue their conflict agenda. This translated into a greater ability to attract recruits, generate material resources, and practice effective military strategies. NALU—one of the factions composing the overall ADF movement—was pivotal in providing the force with the ability to gain an initial foothold in the borderland. Despite hurdles from time to time, their enmeshment into the cross-border space increased over the decades. As such, today the ADF indeed have a solid place in the Rwenzori borderland.

To re-cap, then, this book argues that the ADF's interaction with, and enmeshment in, the Rwenzori borderland facilitated the movement's recruitment, retention, and organization practices; acquisition of material resources; and effective execution of violence. The ADF's resiliency and stamina in maintaining their position in the Uganda-Congo cross-border arena between 1996 and 2021 cannot be sufficiently analyzed without consideration of this borderland relationship.

MICRO-POLITICAL PERSPECTIVES ON REBEL CONFLICT

Wolfgang Zeller (2010, 116) describes his approach to the study of the border triangle of Sudan, Uganda, and Congo in the following way: "It [his study] does not [. . .] simply suggest a 'regional' or 'transnational' approach, as if widening the scope of the investigation was merely a question of 'zooming out' to a different geographical scale. A simultaneous 'zooming in' on the specific aspects of everyday life in the borderlands zones that result from, and further perpetuate, protracted violent conflict is necessary as well." My book applies a similar approach. It recognizes that phenomena not only at the macro level are pertinent to activities in the borderland, but dynamics transpiring at the micro—or translocal—level are important as well. Perhaps more importantly though, it accords special attention to the fluidity of borderland zones, recognizing that static distinctions between supra-national/sub-national, state/non-state, legal/illegal will fail to capture the inner coherence that so profoundly binds both sides of a borderland together. By not only 'zooming out,' but also crucially 'zooming in' on the inner workings of the Rwenzori borderland, this book employs the insights of a relatively new approach to the understanding of conflict, generally referred to as 'the micro-politics of civil war.'

Although this literature concerns itself officially with 'civil wars,' many of its insights pertain to other modes of conflict as well. And hence, due to its wider relevance, I have found it extremely useful for application to conflict in borderlands. A large part of this micro-political turn in the study of conflict stems from the increasingly obvious limitations of quantitative approaches. While of course having certain advantages over the case study method, larger civil war studies are nevertheless often unable to dig deeper and ask certain questions (for example, sub-national queries—not to mention transnational ones as well) about conflict. This is largely due to their being stifled by a strict adherence to the state as the unit of analysis, and the national, regional, or international as the levels of analysis. This national order of things is especially problematic during a time when warfare has only become more decentralized, varied, and locality-specific. Furthermore, research on conflict and political violence has to date largely tended to adhere to certain misinforming modes of acquiring and analyzing data—practices which Stathis Kalyvas has collectively termed 'urban bias.'[9]

Perspectives gleaned from authors such as Kalyvas, Jeremy Weinstein, and Séverine Autesserre help to shed light on the conflict dynamics and intricacies that take place 'below the surface.'[10] Thus, while recognizing that such authors take a number of different perspectives and use various methodologies, my book fits within this wider collection of literatures that seek to understand local dynamics of conflict.

After an attack in Kabul, Afghanistan in 2002, which resulted in the deaths of fifteen people, two main arguments were put forward as to the identity of the attackers: one viewpoint said they were Taliban, while the other maintained they were thieves prowling the area for revenue. As Kalyvas points out, the production of these two narratives of the event actually tells us quite a lot about current frameworks for violence: "it hints at a perception informed by rigid, binary categories linked to mutually exclusive motivations: that the attackers could have been either Taliban or thieves, and that their motivations could have been either 'political' (if they were Taliban) or 'private' (if they were thieves)" (Kalyvas 2003, 475). Fundamentally missing is any entertainment of the idea that the attackers could have held both positions, namely identities as thieves and Taliban, or that their actions could have been motivated by both political *and* private agendas (Kalyvas 2003).

As the Afghan incident indicates, there are "problems with our current understanding of civil wars, particularly our interpretation of identities and actions of the actors, along with their allegiances and motivations, and our take on the war's violence" (Kalyvas 2003, 475). Further, as the case of the Rwenzori borderland region illustrates, geographical location can also pose a problem to adequate understanding of conflicts. The ADF have been mischaracterized in many databases as a group specifically engaged in a civil war in Uganda, which for most of their existence is patently incorrect and completely ignores the nuances and complexities of the group and borderland region. Thus, a large part of this approach involves getting beyond macro level frameworks of conflict through problematizing the static labels we have thus far been so accustomed to using (King 2004). The emphasis on recognizing the constantly shifting nature of labels should not be interpreted, though, as rejecting analytical categories of this sort altogether; rather, it is a call for greater questioning of them (King 2004).

An important aspect of this, and one which is employed throughout this book, is moving beyond top-down, elite-driven rationales of conflict, and instead giving more attention to phenomena generated from the bottom-up, particularly with regards to the association between combatant and community (Mkandawire 2002). As James D. Long (2005, 3) notes, "the relationship between insurgent groups and the societies from whence they arise and for whom they struggle has not been systematically studied." A central facet of this is the idea that many of those labelled as 'rebels' can in fact have dual, if not multiple, identities. "We were peasants by day and guerrillas by night," one Filipino fighter explains (Kalyvas 2006, 415). Perhaps the first aspect of being able to understand the relationship between rebels and society involves recognizing that rebels do not appear out of nowhere (Long 2005). Grievances will usually have been voiced among the populace long before any rebellion transpires. Of course, over time the original political goals of a movement can often become superseded by other interests, particularly short-term economic ones. Nevertheless, even when this occurs, it does not transpire into a situation where connections with local society are non-existent. In essence, a great deal more than simple rebel coercion is involved here, as will be explained below.

In Elisabeth Wood's study of the El Salvadoran civil war, she notes that macro level interpretations of the conflict tend to explain it as one concerning a struggle of classes. Yet, Wood found explanations of the conflict derived from this framework to be largely unsatisfactory, particularly in terms of accounting for the quite extraordinary levels of civilian participation in the insurgency. Through micro-political analysis, Wood realized that in contrast to the above, "an emergent insurgent political culture was key to generating and sustaining the insurgency despite its high costs" (Wood 2003, 225). Indeed, Wood's work importantly draws attention to a critical aspect of rebel groups and the population, namely that of civilian collaboration. Derek Peterson denotes three gradations of this: at the elementary level, there is unarmed and unorganized opposition; next is more sustained and direct participation in a local armed group; and finally, there is membership in an armed organization (Peterson quoted in Wood 2003). Due to a traditional misreading—or more commonly, no reading at all—of agendas on the ground, it has often been assumed that if a rebel group is violent towards the citizenry in its midst, popular support of any sort will thence be minimal, at best. Yet, as Wood's work demonstrates, insurgent collective action can arise in a variety of contexts. And it can be motivated by a myriad of circumstances, including such seemingly inconsequential factors as 'rural norms of solidarity and honor,' which all tend to in some way or another have arisen from hidden transcripts of discontent (Wood 2003; Kalyvas 2006).

In fact, among the incentives for collaboration, Wood found moral and emotional commitments, and in particular, the act of participation itself, to carry the most weight (Wood 2003).[11] It was not simply the *outcome* of the rebellion that was deemed to be important, but the means, and *processes*, as well. Undoubtedly, insurgents represent a great deal more than simply political and military rebellion against the government. They can offer protection to a vulnerable population, or provide services that are usually the remit of the central government (Long 2005). Especially if the insurgents are strategic in their methods of control, locals may be kept unaware of 'competing sovereignty claims,' thereby making them potentially more willing to collaborate.[12] Of course, and as will be frequently discussed throughout this book, it is important to not discount the role of terror in influencing civilian involvement. Collaboration can arise because of the simple fact that it is a question of life or death; to not acquiesce could mean severe consequences for oneself, one's family, or even one's entire local community.

Just as there are numerous reasons behind *support* for insurgency, there is also a wide variety of *forms* of association. Wood recounts that one elderly local El Salvadoran explained to her that "the principal contribution of the residents of the case-study areas was 'silence,' the refusal to inform on the guerrillas: 'We used to help them by telling the military, "No, haven't seen anyone"'" (Wood 2003, 126). Indeed, in addition to overt insurgency support, civilians can find numerous other means of serving the movement, often in somewhat anonymous or buried, yet creative, ways. And many of these forms, especially those to do with acquiring information ('intelligence') can be overlooked if using macro level perspectives. To add to the complexity of this, not only do forms of participation vary and change, but degrees of it do as well. Those partaking in the action (explicitly or implicitly) tend to continually move in and out of participation, for various political or personal reasons (Wood 2003).

Related to the issue of dynamics behind collaboration or mode of association, is the question of why some people decide to fully join a rebel movement. Employing a micro-political perspective means looking beyond broad rationales for joining such as ethnicity or ideology, and considering the role of social network ties such as family, kinship, friendship, and so on. While many in the aftermath of a conflict tend to argue that coercion or abduction accounts for their involvement in conflict, this can often be a self-serving claim (Kalyvas 2006). Possible other motivations can include everything from the appeal of adventure or the lure of danger, to stark fear or revenge (Kalyvas 2006). Not only are there a range of motivations, but recruits can harbor several simultaneously; they can be more likely to join, for example, because of their membership in a specific ethnic group, but could also be spurred to action over an unresolved dispute with a neighbour. This relates to Kalyvas' observation that "civil wars are 'welters of complex struggles' rather than simple binary conflicts neatly arrayed along a single-issue dimension. In this sense, civil wars can be understood as processes that provide a medium for a variety of grievances to be realized within the space of the greater conflict, particularly through violence" (Kalyvas 2003, 479). Likewise, Abraham Lincoln remarked that the American Civil war represented a situation where "murders for old grudges, and murders for pelf, proceed under any cloak that will best cover for the occasion" (Lincoln quoted in Kalyvas 2003, 476).

Often, especially in marginalized areas, joining a rebel group is a means of expressing dissatisfaction with one's plight, where there is perhaps no other method of doing so. With reference to Alice Lakwena, the original leader of the LRA in northern Uganda, Ugandan historian Amii Omara-Otunnu argues, "Lakwena was merely a vehicle through which social discontent in the north of Uganda found expression. She was able to gain tenacious followers who were prepared to risk their lives against all odds because a cross-section of marginalized inhabitants recognized her as a symbol of both their plight and their aspirations" (Omara-Otunnu quoted in Finnström 2008, 78).

Recognizing the liminal nature of conflict also helps to move us away from, as Kalyvas states, the "dichotomous world populated only by victims and perpetrators, combined with the flawed perception that victimhood and guilt are mutually exclusive categories—hence victims cannot be guilty" (Kalyvas 2006, 21). Appreciation of the overlap between perpetrator and victim has several interesting aspects to it. One concerns the recognition that people can move from being victim one day to perpetrator the next, and vice-versa. Another is with regards to those traditionally considered victims (women and children, for instance) in actuality being frequent participants in insurgency. Finally, it includes what Kalyvas calls the 'grey zone,' referring to the large number of those who are involved in the *process* of violence (in all manner of ways), without actually being a direct part of its *outcome* (Kalyvas 2006).

Not only, then, does employing a 'zooming in' approach give civilians and victims more agency, but it also thereby helps to shed light on how so many rebel groups are able to sustain themselves amongst such seemingly hostile surroundings. As Autesserre (2010) describes in her work on the presence of Rwandan Hutu militias in eastern Congo, their continued existence is usually explained with reference to dynamics at national or regional levels. However, Autesserre found their success to actually be a result of the Rwandan Hutu militias enmeshing themselves in *local* dynamics. "Grassroots alliances were key to perpetuating the Rwandan Hutus' presence on Congolese territory and the violence associated with it," she argues (Autesserre 2010, 158).

Furthermore, looking through the lens of a micro-perspective moves us away from conceptions of rebel actors as static black boxes, instead encouraging us to recognize their frequent integration with different segments of society, incorporation of individuals with varying motives and identities, and so on.[13] Appreciating the internal diversity of movements helps us to understand what can often appear as counterproductive acts of violence by rebel groups. Thandika Mkandawire explains the importance of looking beyond the supposed irrationality and randomness of so many rebellions, or relying on only "economistic, culturalistic and militaristic interpretations of the conflicts": "fatally flawed and morally reprehensible though these movements may be, one needs to take their political roots and ideological cognitive components seriously, even as their banditry confounds their political agenda" (Mkandawire 2002, 182).[14] Perhaps one of the most bewildering violent practices committed by many rebel groups is the killing of civilians. But often such actions are strategic calculations performed to affect military performance. The killing of civilians can represent a strategy of pressuring the government into submission, or it can serve as a warning to civilians of the dangers of collaborating with the enemy (Hultman 2007; Kalyvas 2006). The micro-political method also places emphasis on looking to the internal structure and organization of the rebel group itself. Jeremy Weinstein contends that rebellions reliant on economic endowments tend to practice much higher levels of indiscriminate violence than those dependent on social endowments, for example (Weinstein 2007).

Applying ideas and insights from the micro-political approach to the study of conflict helps to get at the dynamics and phenomena occurring in the borderland that otherwise can be glossed-over. This does not mean that this book adopts a bottom-up approach instead of a top-down one, but merely that both the macro and micro levels are employed in order to understand the intricacies and complexities of the ADF conflict in the Rwenzori borderland.

METHODOLOGY

The ADF have attracted very little scholarship over the course of their existence. Even at the height of their campaign, there was a lack of serious or sustained attention accorded to them by the media, conflict management actors, donors, and academics (Hovil and Werker 2005). The lack of previous work done on the ADF, together with the contemporary nature of the subject, meant that it was vital extensive fieldwork be conducted to obtain as much primary material as possible. This particularly applied to the origins and early development stages of the ADF, on which there was an overwhelming paucity of information. As such, the bulk of my interviews were directed at gaining a better understanding of the historical origins and formative years of the group. Over the course of approximately two and a half years, between 2009 and 2012, I made five trips to western Uganda and/or eastern Congo expressly for this purpose, totalling approximately fourteen months in the field. Thereafter I continued to visit the Great Lakes region on a yearly (sometimes more frequent) basis. The intermittent yet sustained nature of the fieldwork has enabled me to observe the ADF during some of their most interesting and dynamic time periods and changes in behavior.

Fieldwork was mainly conducted in three locales: Kampala, western Uganda, and eastern Congo. In western Uganda principal fieldwork sites were the towns of Kasese, Bundibugyo, Fort Portal, Mpondwe, Bwera, and numerous small villages in the plains and mountains of the Rwenzories. In eastern Congo the majority of time was spent in the cities of Butembo, Beni, and Goma. Over the course of the fieldwork I conducted a total of approximately 125 interviews (many of these being focus group discussions with half a dozen or more individuals).[15] Not all of these interviews are cited in this book (and hence not all are listed in the references), however they still informed my understanding of the subject. Interviewees included, among others—and the following refer to *both* Uganda and Congo—foreign employees of international organizations, foreign aid and development workers, national and local government officials, Rwenzururu Kingdom officials, tribal chiefs, local staff of conflict and/or post-conflict NGOs, local conflict negotiators/mediators, grassroots community groups, agricultural co-operatives (in the Rwenzories), former ADF members, civilians from ADF-affected areas, academics, and journalists. The interviews varied not only in length (ranging in duration from half an hour, to nearly a full day as was the case with some ex-combatants), but also in terms of structure, with the majority being semi-structured discussions. Given the sensitivity of the subject, many interviewees preferred not to be named, and thus all are referred to within the book only by generic descriptions of their community or employment positions.

My time in Uganda and Congo informed my research in a variety of informal ways as well. In Uganda I was affiliated with the Center for Basic Research in Kampala. Especially in the initial stages of fieldwork, the discussions with academics based at the Center provided me with the introductions and connections so vital for doing research in the field. The Center also housed an excellent newspaper archive, which not only enabled me to access press articles and unpublished papers on the ADF unavailable elsewhere, but also allowed me to reach a better understanding of the group in those preliminary stages of my study. The everyday activities of simply living in the fieldwork locales were important as well. Discussions with taxi drivers, hotel staff, shopkeepers—even a two-day Rwenzori Mountain hike in former ADF-occupied territory—were all experiences which inform this book.

In Dan Fahey's (2010, 1) 'Researcher's Guide to Bunia, Beni, and Butembo (DR Congo),' the following is noted:

> Travel in northeastern Democratic Republic of Congo is not easy, and is not always safe. There are many physical and emotional challenges facing outsiders who voyage into Congo's North Kivu province and Ituri district. These include rough roads that can turn a short trip into a multi-day excursion; occasional rebel activity and banditry; widespread official corruption; language barriers; and cultural differences.

Throughout my time in the Congo I faced all of these situational challenges and more.[16] The ADF were an extremely sensitive topic in the areas I travelled to, and in Beni, especially (a city thoroughly infiltrated by the ADF, and only a few miles from ADF-controlled territory), it was pivotal to pay close attention to who I interacted with and how much information I exposed about my subject of study. Indeed, the proximity of Beni and Butembo to the ADF and other rebels had made the cities 'no-go' areas for most outsiders, and thus it was difficult to attempt any degree of conspicuousness.[17] Travel outside of the cities was perhaps the most dangerous aspect of my research, however. The Beni-Butembo road, for example, was one frequently affected by banditry, and any rural travelling had to be pursued with caution.

However, many of the challenges I faced in the Congo were simply of a logistical nature. While I was fortunate enough to be allowed to travel on MONUSCO flights between the cities, these were difficult to depend on, and often involved significant delays. Research in Uganda was needless to say much easier, and I encountered almost none of the difficulties described above. Not only was this because Uganda is a significantly more developed and politically stable country, but also because it had not experienced any recent ADF attacks. The ADF still used the western Ugandan space for a variety of crucial activities, but they were no longer waging assaults there. Eastern Congo, on the other hand, was an active conflict zone.

There were also challenges of a more academic nature. Researching the ADF meant attempting to make sense of narratives from disparate and even contradictory sources, as well as pushing past hollow explanations or characterizations of the conflict often espoused by national and local government officials (among others). Indeed, I heard very different accounts of the ADF conflict depending on who my interviewee was: whether they were Ugandan or Congolese, whether they were in the private or public sector, whether they were a borderland resident, and so on. In addressing this challenge I tried to corroborate the information that I received from as many different individuals and groups as possible, as well as from as wide an array of sources as was practically feasible. Interviews of course were pivotal in this respect, but this book is informed by a *breadth* of material collected in Uganda and Congo. Documents by local development organizations, reports by human rights groups,[18] PhD and masters theses from Ugandan and Congolese students, declassified Ugandan intelligence material, MONUSCO data, transcripts of Ugandan parliament discussions, radio reports, and print media sources,[19] were all crucially informative.

An additional challenge had to do with the borderland aspect of my study. Writing on the Congo-Rwanda border, Gillian Mathys (2009, 3) notes, "in order to do right to a border region *both* sides of a border need to be covered; in a way, all research has to be done twice." Similarly, Hastings Donnan and Dieter Haller state, "research on state borders requires a doubling of effort from the anthropologist, who may have to master at least two languages and deal with two national traditions of anthropological literature. Finance too may be a problem, since it can be difficult to find sponsors to underwrite multi-sited research" (Donnan and Haller 2000, 9). Indeed, these were all issues that I had to contend with to some degree throughout my research. Studying both sides of a border is undoubtedly more time-consuming, even if one merely considers the logistical issues involved: attaining visas for two countries, research permits for two countries, and so on.[20]

Finally, a note about secondary (principally borderland) sources: while this book draws heavily from the African-oriented borderlands literature, it also uses insights gained from scholars who have worked on borderlands in other areas of the world. In terms of disciplines, although my study of the ADF rebel group contributes to the political science subfield of conflict studies, it nevertheless employs the insights of borderland-focused anthropologists, sociologists, and geographers. Some of the anthropology, sociology, and geography borderland research has looked at these spaces specifically in terms of conflict, but most has not. Instead, they have been concerned with issues such as borderland identities, borderland social practices, or borderland economic systems—all crucial areas of attention if one is to have an in-depth understanding of the borderland space. Ultimately, consulting such a wide array of borderland perspectives was pivotal for, firstly, developing a thorough understanding of the anti-state and liminal/networked character of borderland dynamics, and secondly, application of this theoretical framework to the ADF conflict in western Uganda and eastern Congo.

BOOK OUTLINE

This book is based upon my PhD dissertation conducted at the University of Cambridge and submitted in 2013. Since that time not only have the ADF themselves of course changed in many respects, but interpretations of the group have as well, as previously mentioned. Needless to say, then, this book both extends and revises in significant ways the original dissertation. Similarly, I have published articles on the ADF over the past decade, including in *The Round Table* (Scorgie 2011), *Journal of Critical African Studies* (Scorgie 2013), *The Journal of the Middle East and Africa* (Scorgie 2015a), *Journal of Modern African Studies* (Scorgie 2015b), as well as a book chapter in *Introduction to Border Studies* (Scorgie 2015c). Parts of these works are incorporated into this book, especially into Chapter Two and sections of Chapters Four and Five.[21] However, these articles (and book chapter) tended to of course be much more restricted in their focus on the ADF, in terms of either the timeframe used, and/or thematic focus. This book again both extends and revises this previously published material. In other words, *Conflict at the Edge of the African State* is very much a culmination of researching, writing, and thinking about the ADF for well over a decade.

Chapter Two outlines the conceptual framework of this dissertation through a discussion of borderlands. It focuses especially on three dimensions of conflict-affected borderlands in Africa, namely: politically, a tradition of resistance against central authority; socially, the predominance of a border identity; and economically, a system built around independent cross-border trade. It explores how these features can be manipulated by those in pursuit of violent agendas, and how the border and borderland can be turned into conflict resources.

The conceptual framework from Chapter Two is first applied to Chapter Three, in order to understand how the Rwenzori area became a fully-fledged borderland. Chapter Three is divided into two main parts: the first considers the Ugandan side of the borderland, starting with its experience of colonial marginalization, then moving on to its continued peripherality in the post-colonial era, and finally looking at the resultant conflictual nature of the space and further consolidation of its borderland character. The time period under review here is from the colonial era, to the early 1990s—just prior to the formation of the ADF. The second section examines the same dynamics, but in relation to the Congolese side of the borderland. Western Uganda and eastern Congo of course each have their own historical trajectory, but as Chapter Three discusses, a pivotal dimension of each side's development was bounded and conditioned by its interaction with the other. As a lens through which to view the development and dynamics of the borderland, the trajectory of the main populations in each of these areas—the Konjo in western Uganda and the Nande in eastern Congo—are explored. Nevertheless, it is only a loose trajectory of these groups that are presented, as ultimately the main aim of Chapter Three is to consider the overall borderland *space* from which the ADF arose.

The framework from Chapter Two is then applied to Chapters Four, Five, and Six in order to understand the actions (and ultimately resiliency) of the ADF—namely, how the rebels manipulated and extrapolated borderland resources from the Rwenzori border zone to advance their conflict agenda. Chapter Four looks at the ADF conflict between 1996 and 2003; Chapter Five considers the conflict between 2004 and 2013; Chapter Six examines the time period of 2014 to 2021. I selected 1996 as the starting date of analysis in light of the group's first attack in November of that year. While the conflict is still occurring, and the ADF are as active as ever, 2021 is the cut-off date of this book simply for publication reasons. In examining the ADF during these time periods, three dimensions of rebel group behavior and activity in particular are considered: recruitment, retention, and organization; material resources; and the execution of violence.

The conclusion—Chapter Seven—briefly considers the policy implications of this book's findings for international conflict management. It looks at the responses that have been applied by MONUSCO to the ADF conflict, considers why they have failed to curb the rebellion, and offers some potential means to mitigate for these failures.

NOTES

1. For purposes of consistency and simplicity, the country currently known as the Democratic Republic of the Congo (and previously as Zaire) will be referred to as simply *Congo* throughout this book (this is obviously not to be confused with Congo-Brazzaville).

2. While these were the official districts in existence at that time, Ugandan districts have gone through numerous reconfigurations and name changes. It should be

noted, for example, that in 2017 Bunyangabu district was created out of a section of Kabarole district.

3. Technically the Konjo should be referred to as '*Ba*konjo,' as the 'Ba' signifies the plural form and thus refers to the tribe as a whole. However, this is rarely done in English, and thus throughout this book the tribe will simply be referred to as 'Konjo.' This is likewise for the Nande tribe (technically *Ba*nande), which this book will frequently be discussing as well.

4. As explained by Steven Spittaels and Filip Hilgert, "When people write or talk about North Kivu they often refer to the southern part of the province as the 'Petit Nord' and to the northern part as the 'Grand Nord.' Although legally the two regions are not distinctive administrative units, in practice there is a clear distinction between them because of historical and ethnic reasons. The 'Grand Nord' comprises the territories of Lubero and Beni and two 'villes': Beni and Butembo. The large majority of the population belongs to the Nande ethnicity, the same group that lives across the Ugandan border. Whereas Beni is the administrative capital of the area, Butembo is the commercial heart" (Spittaels and Hilgert 2008, 20).

5. The First Congo War (1996–1997) was to a large extent the result of a spillover from the 1990–1994 Rwandan Civil War and 1994 genocide, when around 1.5 million refugees—including exiled *Interahamwe* and members of the Rwandan Armed Forces—fled and set up de-facto army bases in the refugee camps of eastern Congo, forming the Army for the Liberation of Rwanda (ALiR). This rebel group terrorized the local population until the eastern Congolese Banyamulenge (Tutsi) led an uprising force to drive Rwandans out of Congo. In response, the national armies of Rwanda and Uganda formed the Alliance of Democratic Forces for the Liberation of Congo-Zaire (ADFL), invaded Congo, overthrew long-time dictator Mobutu Sese Seko in May 1997, and installed Laurent-Désiré Kabila to power. The Second Congo War (1998–2003), also often referred to as the Great African War, resulted from Kabila turning on Rwanda and Uganda as his previous backers, and forcing all Rwandan and Ugandan military forces out of the country. Another Banyamulenge rebellion erupted with Rwandan assistance, forming the Rally for Congolese Democracy (RCD), which was backed by Rwanda and Uganda. Meanwhile, the governments of Namibia, Zimbabwe, and Angola joined the conflict in support of the Kabila government, followed by Chad, Libya, and Sudan. Kabila was assassinated in January 2001, and his son Joseph Kabila took power. In 2002, he negotiated various peace deals with Rwanda and Uganda (which saw their withdrawal from the region), in addition to the various rebel groups, based on the promise of power-sharing. A transitional constitution was signed in April 2003, effectively putting a formal end to the war.

6. Kristian Skrede Gleditsch distinguishes between direct contagion ('non-actor-specific spillover effects') and indirect contagion ('actor-specific mechanisms') (Gleditsch 2007).

7. There have been a variety of terms proposed by different scholars—all essentially discussing similar phenomena. Damien Deltenre and Michel Liégeois (2016), for example, refer to 'regional war complexes,' Nadine Ansorg (2014) refers to 'regional conflict systems,' and so on (see Deltenre and Liégeois for an interesting discussion on this literature).

8. This book uses 'translocal' in the same manner as John Heathershaw and Daniel Lambach, namely: "local spaces can take subnational or transnational forms. Such 'translocal' spaces can take the form of [for example] cross-border networks of seasonal labor migrants or long-term relations between diaspora and the homeland" (Heathershaw and Lambach 2008, 282). Thus, translocal helps to draw attention to the transnational nature of local forces in borderlands, and their lack of operational confinement to state boundaries.

9. According to Kalyvas, urban bias manifests itself in six methodologically flawed practices: "it privileges (1) written sources over oral sources; (2) 'top-down' perspectives stressing high politics and elite interactions over 'bottom-up,' local, and grassroots interactions; (3) the ideological motivations of participants over their non-ideological motivations; (4) fixed and unchanging identities and choices over fluid ones; (5) clear demarcations between victimizers and victims over blurred lines between combatants and non-combatants; and (6) a culturalistic interpretation of rural violence over strategic and instrumental interpretations" (Kalyvas 2004, 8–9).

10. It is recognized that these authors all use very different perspectives and approaches to their research; however, they all employ a micro-political perspective to do so.

11. Thus, in this sense it may not be agreement with the political or military goals of the insurgents that is the determining factor behind civilian support, but rather an overriding dissatisfaction with the authorities: "some activists who had suffered at the hands of the authorities were driven by feelings of moral outrage" (Tarrow 2007, 593). In a similar vein, Wood notes, "most civilian insurgents appeared to support the guerrilla forces not out of an illusory desire for protection but out of their deepening conviction that the government no longer merited their loyalty or acquiescence" (Wood 2003, 120).

12. As Kalyvas (2006, 122) notes, "Political actors are obviously well aware that control spawns collaboration." For more information on strategies of civilian control, and its various effects on a rebel group's relationship with the population, see Kalyvas (2006) and Weinstein (2007).

13. This is certainly the case with the Rwandan Hutu militias, for included under that term one can actually find, among others, the former Rwandan Armed Forces, the Alliance for the Liberation of Rwanda, the Rally for the Democratic Forces for the Liberation of Rwanda, the Rastas, and the Rally for Unity and Democracy. As Autesserre explains, "Contrary to one of the central assumptions of the dominant narrative, groups such as the Mai Mai, the Congolese with Rwandan ancestry, or the Rwandan Hutu militias were not unitary actors." She goes on to note that the Mai Mai, for instance, were never united under one command structure. The so-called 'movement,' in fact, was just a "loose network of very different fragmented, micro-level armed groups following various—and often competing—leaders" (Autesserre 2010, 177).

14. Post-Cold War conflict analyses, especially with regards to African conflicts, have often applied a perspective that Paul Richards has termed 'New Barbarism': the assumption that rebel groups practice little more than "wanton and mindless violence" (Richards 1996, xiii-xx).

15. Interviewees were chosen largely through two methods. The first was via a series of 'pilot interviews' that I conducted on a short preliminary visit to the field in Uganda. During this trip I met with as many potentially relevant people as possible, in order to get a sense of which locations would be best to conduct my later fieldwork from, and what kinds of organizations and individuals I should pursue for interviews in those locales. This trip was pivotal in leading me to choose Beni and Butembo as the cities to base my fieldwork out of in the Congo, for example, and was important in providing me with a substantial list of initial contacts to pursue. The other method of choosing interviewees was the snowball technique. At the end of every interview I asked my interviewee(s) if they had advice on who else I should be talking to on this subject, and they nearly always did. I was aware that this could lead to potential biases—namely, a danger of pursuing one line of thought via talking with only like-minded groups and individuals. To prevent this from happening, I made sure to consult with people from as wide an array of backgrounds as possible.

16. The majority of the challenges I faced were what Raymond M. Lee terms 'situational dangers'—dangers that result out of the nature of my study—as opposed to 'ambient dangers,' which are those that affect the researchers and researched alike (for example, malaria) (Lee 1995).

17. Goma was quite a contrast in terms of fieldwork: the extraordinary number of international community representatives, foreign NGOs, researchers, as well as the substantially safer environment there, all facilitated a much easier stay and research experience.

18. While human rights groups' reports can be helpful in providing detailed information about attacks or the nature of the violence that has taken place, I tried not to rely on such documents for any kind of contextual analysis. Kalyvas explains the potential pitfalls of such reports: "A great deal of information, especially as far as human rights NGOs are concerned, comes exclusively from the victims of violence. Such evidence can be problematic insofar as victimization does not imply full or accurate knowledge of the actions that produced it; in fact, victims' testimonies are not sacred just because they come from victims. Like everyone else, victims forget, ignore, or misrepresent crucial aspects of the exact sequence of the actions and events that produced their victimization" (Kalyvas 2006, 50).

19. While both Ugandan and Congolese print media sources were consulted, it was difficult to find information about the ADF in Congolese print media—and of those sources, to find ones of sufficient quality to actually use was even more challenging.

20. The issue of languages posed some challenges as well. In Uganda the official language is English, however some of my interviewees in western Uganda spoke their native languages—which were usually either one of Lukonjo, Lutoro, or Kwamba—necessitating that I often bring along a translator to interviews. In Congo, particularly in Beni and Butembo, I also used a translator, as again, some of my interviewees spoke their native language, Kinande, or Swahili. In Goma my only interviews were with international personnel—for example aid workers, non-governmental (NGO) employees, and so on—and thus it was fine to rely on English and French. In Kampala all of my interviewees spoke English. There are of course challenges that come with using translators. They interrupt the flow of conversation with the interviewees, and

certain nuances are bound to be 'lost in translation.' Nevertheless, my translators were professionals (they all had previous experience working as translators for researchers), and they came recommended from reputable sources.

21. More specifically, these five pieces are incorporated into the book in the following ways: Chapter Two integrates material from all five articles/book chapter. Chapters Four and Five both include very minimally Scorgie 2011, and more substantially portions of Scorgie 2013, Scorgie 2015a, and Scorgie 2015b. Finally, nominal parts of this chapter incorporate material from Scorgie 2013. All previously published material is included here with permission.

Chapter 2

A Borderlands Conceptual Framework

PERCEPTIONS AND DEFINITIONS

Frontier,[1] boundary, march, no-man's land, buffer zone, borderland: there are numerous terms to describe that area which marks the end of one state, and the beginning of a next.[2] For purposes of consistency, however, this book uses the term 'borderland.' Constantly being renegotiated, especially during times of upheaval such as conflict, a borderland is a fluctuating geographic area straddling both sides of a state border. It is indeed important to emphasize the dynamic and oscillating character of borderlands: they are perpetually changing, expanding, or shrinking in accordance with both local and non-local forces (Morehouse 2004; Jackson 2009; Wastl-Walter 2011; Meehan and Plonski 2017). While by no means hermetically sealed units, borderlands nevertheless sit apart from interior zones due to the border-generated forces and processes that constitute them. Thus, while they are fluid spaces, they are nevertheless distinct spatial units (Piliavsky 2013). In essence, a borderland can be defined as a realm comprising the following three defining characteristics, as explained by William I. Zartman (2010, 6): "a population on the margins of power centers, traversed by a formal political boundary, living dynamic relations internally and externally (with the power center)." It is important to note as well that borderlands are not a phenomenon solely generated from the forces of modern-day states; they have been constitutive factors of empires, city-states, pre-Westphalian polities, and so on (Zartman 2010).

In terms of size, a borderland's reach inland depends on the strength of its networks, or more generally, on the potency of the border's influence (Baud and Van Schendel 1997; Morehouse 2004). Thus, a borderland can extend on both sides of a border, or simply one, and likewise can stretch for a significant distance from the border, or retain a quite shallow depth (Newman 2011). The territorial size of the borderland then, essentially depends on the degree to which the political, socio-cultural, and economic life of the space is fundamentally influenced and affected by the state border (Zeller 2010; Newman 2011; Meehan and Plonski 2017). To more precisely determine the strength of the borderland, including more specifically defining that point at which the power of the border is overtaken by the sway of the central state, borderland scholars classify the border region according to three geographic zones. Most significantly, there is the 'borderland heartland,' the area straddling the border and completely dominated by its existence; it has also been called the 'border landscape' and 'le voisinage' (Baud and Van Schendel 1997). Next is the 'intermediate borderland,' where the border's effects are felt, but only moderately so. And lastly, there is the 'outer borderland,' which experiences the border's influence just occasionally, usually during periods of intense political activity such as war.[3]

The character of borderland transactions is furthermore influenced by the borderland's position on the spectrum from alienation (a fortress border with zero contact between the citizenry on either side), to integration (total merging of the populations to the point where the border's influence is barely felt), as well as the degree of permeability or hardness of the border (Martinez 1994; Piliavsky 2013; Van Schendel and De Maaker 2014). Indeed political borders can take a variety of different forms—both material and non-material, securitized and non-securitized—which in turn affect how residents of the surrounding area perceive and experience their freedom of movement in the borderland (Wastl-Walter 2011; Paasi 2011; Brunet-Jailly 2011).

It is not only the influence of strictly the border that helps to produce such a dynamic zone. Also important to its character is the constant exposure to a range of external effects, including influences from adjacent areas of neighboring states, wider regional actors, and even international forces like global commodity and trade flows (Anderson and O'Dowd 1999; Meehan and Plonski 2017). What is perhaps the most interesting aspect to these 'frontier forces,' is the resulting myriad activities and actors operating conterminously in one area. Indeed, the non-conventional nature of borderland activity makes it often impossible to identify whether such forces are singularly local, national, or international, and so standard levels of analysis are often unhelpful (Kassimir and Latham 2001). In fact, sources of authority, power, and legitimacy in the borderland are often difficult to decipher or recognize from the outside, due to their hybrid and non-traditional nature (Conciliation

Resources 2017). This is not to argue that all borderlands experience the same kind of dynamics. Nevertheless, due to certain fundamental qualities of borderlands—such as being situated at the edges of states, being subject to foreign influences, and of course being traversed by a border—all borderlands and their residents critically share 'the border experience' (Martinez 1994).

THE MYTH OF BORDERLAND MARGINALITY

This book fundamentally challenges three common assumptions of African, conflict-affected borderlands. Before continuing, it is important to clarify that many of the dynamics discussed below draw on insights from work that has been done on borderlands around the world. However, the main focus in this book is on *African* borderlands. Furthermore, it is *conflict-affected* borderlands that this work is principally interested in. In other words, the discussions throughout this chapter will not necessarily apply to all borderlands throughout Africa, but rather to those that have experienced significant levels of conflict.

The first assumption to be addressed—and countered—is one that considers borderlands to be marginal or peripheral areas. While geographically they may be located far from the state center or metropole, they are not blank slates void of politics. They do not constitute a no-man's land, open space, or territory free to be occupied or conquered (Das and Poole 2004). Yet, this has conventionally been the opinion of political scientists. Traditionally, the study of borders and the wider area around them has been concerned with straightforward legal, geographical, or geopolitical questions (Baud and Van Schendel 1997). The borderland was understood to be peripheral to state dynamics, and the border was generally perceived in terms of constraints. Timothy Raeymaekers, et al (2010, 2) explain the source of this mindset about borderlands: "Conventional wisdom has it that states are built from the political center, and then gradually expand their power and knowledge over the periphery. The borderland is consequently treated as a margin, rather than an analytical unit that can be studied in its own right [. . .] This has contributed to a deep misunderstanding of borderlands as marginal spaces, fraught with avoidance, savagery and rebellion."

There is increasing recognition among political scientists, however, that borderlands constitute zones of highly dynamic interactions, and borders represent socio-political constructs and productive sites, rather than mere state boundaries. These ideas have contributed to a burgeoning understanding that these spaces constitute distinct entities in their own right. The move away from archaic conceptions of the state and borderlands has been especially pronounced in the study of African borderlands (Coplan 2009).[4] In the 1990s, spurred on by the multitude of perceived failing states across the African continent, political scientists started to take a closer look at border zones and the contributing role they could be playing in the volatility of areas such as the Ilemi Triangle of South Sudan, Kenya, and Ethiopia, or the Sudan-Chad-Central African Republic (CAR) corridor. Work in the field of African borderlands has now matured to such an extent that today it can arguably be considered an independent sub-field of the wider domain of borderland studies. Today its practitioners include not only political scientists and geographers, but also, among others, sociologists and anthropologists (Medard 2009; Dobler and Zeller 2009; Asiwaju 1996; Newman and Paasi 1998).[5]

Thus, from viewing the viability and workings of borderlands as dependent on the metropole—something espoused by scholars such as Igor Kopytoff—today scholars are increasingly recognizing the agency of borderlands (Hüsken 2009). Indeed, borderlanders, especially powerful borderland actors such as smuggling rings or rebel movements, use the border and the area around it in dynamic ways that not only transform the borderland, but can indeed influence the metropole. Yet still too often, missing from many political and historical accounts of center-periphery relations, are analyses of how borderlands have been able to reshape state authority, or at the least have represented spaces of creativity and inventiveness of alternative political, social, and economic systems (Das and Poole 2004; Vlassenroot, Perrot, and Cuvelier 2012). This book thus proceeds from a borderland perspective, which means taking the borderland as an analytical concept, and recognizing the agency, dynamics, and transformative power that it instigates.

EXPECTATIONS ABOUT BORDERLAND CONFLICT

Part of taking a borderland perspective involves recognizing that borderlands experience *specific types of conflict*. However, a large part of the scholarship on borderlands and conflict has tended to be of an entirely different nature to that which will be discussed in this book. It concerns a widespread, and often-times misleading, assumption of specifically African borders, and one which can cloud awareness of the workings of violence and warfare in African borderlands. Namely, it is often assumed that the artificiality, unjustness, and imposed nature of Africa's political boundaries is overwhelmingly behind the conflict experienced around many African borders.

As Paul Nugent (1996, 35) explains, "African boundaries have suffered a consistently poor reputation. As 'arbitrary' and 'artificial' colonial constructs, conventional wisdom has it that they were imposed upon unwilling Africans who, according to two recurrent images, have either suffered dearly from their consequences or merrily continued with life as if they did not exist." Many scholars argue that the Berlin Conference of 1884–1885—where the colonial powers portioned the continent into states—fatally spliced apart ethnic and social groups, disrupted regionally-integrated economic systems, and even destroyed natural ecosystems. But perhaps their most influential argument has been with regards to border artificiality and conflict.[6] It is purported that the cumulative results of Berlin were an effective Balkanization of the continent: a division of Africa into politically, socially, and economically non-viable micro-states, where wars were later (and continue to be) fought over the inexact character of the borders (Mbembe 2000). Speaking with regards to the Horn of Africa, for instance, Dereje Feyissa and Markus Virgil Hoehne (2010, 2) note, "Many local people as well as external observers perceive the arbitrary colonial borders as one of the causes for these conflicts Matthies observed that Africa is the continent of border wars 'par excellence,' due to its artificial borders that served colonial interests and disregarded local ethnic and economic conditions." Some adherents to this body of thought, such as [Wole] Soyinka and [Ali] Mazrui, have gone so far as to call for a re-drawing of African state borders as a conflict prevention measure (Nugent and Asiwaju 1996a).

There is no denying that European colonialism, and in particular the Berlin Conference, had an enormous impact on the cartography of Africa. While recognizing this, it is nevertheless important to move beyond such a conceptualization of borders and their legacy (Nugent and Asiwaju 1996a; Miles 2015). For one thing, "most African wars do not have their immediate point of origin in border disputes resulting from colonial divisions," as Achille Mbembe (2000, 271) points out. Many wars in Africa have indeed had a border dimension to them (to do with various consequences of the border), however these have not usually been with regards to the actual location of the boundary (Mbembe 2000). Furthermore, to say that they are arbitrary is somewhat of a moot point (Coplan 2011). There is no such thing as a natural border anywhere: all are subjective, contested, contrived, political constructs to some degree (Agnew 2008; Diener and Hagen 2010a; Diener and Hagen 2010b). As Nugent and Anthony I. Asiwaju (1996b, 10) point out, "However artificial they might once have been, there is a sense in which many African boundaries do now demarcate mental space." In a similar vein, Christopher Clapham (1999, 62) notes, "the demarcations between peoples left in the wake of colonialism are no longer altogether artificial. Ghanaians and Ivorians are distinguished not simply by the side of a colonially created dividing line on which they happen to find themselves, but by differences of historical experience and personal identity which may well deepen as they are transmitted to subsequent generations."

In fact, in the post-colonial period such boundaries have largely been accepted by the populace, not to mention upheld at significant cost on occasion.[7] The durability of African colonial boundaries has indeed been quite remarkable (Nugent and Asiwaju 1996). Borderlanders across the continent on a daily basis reinforce, manipulate, and vibrantly exploit their borders.[8] Even more noteworthy, perhaps, is that numerous guerrilla movements—Angola's UNITA, Mozambique's RENAMO, and Liberia's NPFL, for example—have demonstrated little interest in altering state boundaries, and instead have fought for control of the state within its prevailing borders (Nugent and Asiwaju 1996a, 267). It frequently gets forgotten in the debate that the borders are often viewed in a positive light by those living in their midst. Borderlanders frequently value the new trade and other economic opportunities which arise from their proximity to the state boundary (and thus separatist and secessionist movements often have limited appeal) (Grant 2008; Mattheis, Raineri, and Russo 2019).

Perhaps most problematic with the assumption outlined above is that it fails to grant borderlands and borderlanders the requisite degree of agency. If a borderland perspective or lens is applied, on the other hand, it becomes evident that the unique characteristics of borderlands—not merely the border line itself—can contribute to generating specific types of conflict. As Decha Tangseefa (2003, 6) states, "Border zones thus not only symbolize nation-states' powers and their limits, but also engender conflicts and accommodation." Many border zones around the world have of course been historically peaceful. However, as Jonathan Goodhand (2018, 3) reminds us, despite quite commendable reductions in armed conflict globally, "success at the national level masks sub-national 'black spots' of protracted conflict and extreme poverty. Borderland regions are frequently such black spots." Indeed, even countries officially considered to be in a state of peace may contain borderlands with astoundingly high levels of violence.[9]

An additional problematic trend that hinders adequate understanding of conflict in borderlands is the use of quantitative analyses based on country-level datasets. Used by many political scientists and economists when studying conflicts, these ultimately tend to theorize about conflict in a manner that is tied to the state, thereby ignoring the liminal quality of borderland conflict contexts. For example, the Correlates of War (COW) data project specifically defines and categorizes armed conflicts based on the experience of *states* (i.e., inter-state, intra-state, extra-state, and non-state conflicts). This can erase the importance of borderlands, as the nature of many conflicts that occur in these peripheral spaces fail to adhere to such rigid categories. Jonathan Goodhand (2018, 5) provides an accurate illustration of the problematic relationship between borderlands, conflict, and quantitative datasets: "This borderland blindness is compounded by the absence of robust, and reliable data on borderlands. Data sets and strategies of social inquiry are bound to the nation state. Statistics are largely based on national, aggregated data sets. Subnational and transnational data on conflict for example is extremely rare."

To re-cap then, not only is the conflict in borderlands in many cases not about the border line itself, but borderland conflict is different to the violence and warfare that takes place in other locales. As Tobias Hagmann and Benedikt Korf (2009, 3) explain, "the frontier is a political space with specific characteristics of disorder and violence [. . .] Particular configurations of order and disorder, often of a violent nature, are encountered in the frontier." Or as Oscar J. Martinez (1994, 13) states, "Borderlands strife is different from friction in other parts of nations because of the peculiar conditions in peripheries—they are vulnerable to international disputes and to crises produced by boundary instability." Thus, and in line with a borderland perspective, this book proceeds from a recognition that borderlands generate and experience specific types of conflict.

APPRECIATING THE ANTI-STATE AND LIMINAL QUALITY OF BORDERLAND CONFLICT

Finally, the third area that this book seeks to probe concerns the often volatile nature of the borderland-state association. This is a relationship that analysts far too often understand in simplistic state-centric terms, thereby leading to an under-appreciation of the degree to which conflict in borderlands is commonly influenced and shaped by the liminal nature and anti-state character of borderlands. While a great deal of the research done on borderlands certainly hints at the anti-state and liminal character of these zones, there has been a lack of direct investigation into these phenomena and their ensuing implications—such as how they shape the nature of conflict, how they influence the actors that evolve, and how they facilitate the development of borderlanders' grievances.

Reflecting on the association between borderlands and warfare, Judith Vorrath (2007, 13) asks whether borderlands are entry points or actual sources of conflict, alleging, "Most authors obviously do not ascribe the origin of violent conflict to borderlands." She (2007, 12) comes to the conclusion that they are merely "entry points for potentially destabilizing factors," as "there is little evidence or likelihood of irredentist sentiment in borderlands."[10] Because she underappreciates the agency and transformative dynamics of borderlands, she supports a simplistic understanding of conflict in borderlands. This has indeed been a common approach amongst conflict analysts in political science. In Goodhand's (2005b, 193) research on conflict in Afghanistan, he describes how despite the key role that borderlands have played in the workings of the opium trade and war-making, "the perspectives and practices of borderland societies are usually missing from this story. This is unsurprising, since we know much more about how states deal with borderlands than how borderlands deal with states." To accordingly rectify the situation, Goodhand (2005b, 193) suggests "reading against the grain," and venturing into the unwritten and untold history of the state. Doing so reveals more about the borderland-generated forces that can shape the conflict that takes place there.

Taking a borderland perspective helps to expose that a common trait of conflict-affected borderlands is a political, social, and economic climate of anti-stateness: namely, an 'anti-state' attitude amongst the populace, and the practice of a lifestyle distinct from, or in direct opposition to, the center. As Michiel Baud and Willem Van Schendel (1997, 215) note, "The confrontation between 'state' and 'people' was especially clear in marginal areas such as borderlands." The degree to which borderlanders harbor anti-state attitudes and practice anti-state lifestyles varies. Some contradict mainstream state policies and culture simply by virtue of their geographical and political distance from the core. Others exert more of an explicit political stance against the state through engaging in cross-border smuggling, for example. And finally there are those who actively work to undermine the state, more often than not through aggressive means. This class of borderlanders often encompasses the warlords, militias, and rebel groups that frequent Africa's borderlands.[11] Of course, it is worth re-emphasizing that many borderlands throughout Africa exist in harmony with the central state, and many borderland populations struggle for increased inclusion into the national framework. However, those that have experienced significant conflict in Africa are often (though by no means always) characterized to one degree or another by anti-stateness.

The second commonality of these zones is their liminal, or networked, nature. While the border itself is a fixed, unchanging entity, the area surrounding it represents a transitory zone of greyness and flexibility, dominated by cross-border (as opposed to national or state-defined) political, social, and economic networks. By virtue of being on the edges of two legally distinct states, a borderland is in essence a space of transition. The reach of the state is usually limited, and thus authority is often not a clear-cut concept, but rather fuzzy, hybrid in nature, and multifaceted (Newman 2009). This twilight zone character of borderlands hints at one of their central paradoxes, described here by Baud and Van Schendel (1997, 216): "Borders create political, social and cultural distinctions, but simultaneously imply the existence of (new) networks and systems of interaction across them." In a similar vein, Sven Tägil, et al state, "Boundaries separate people (or groups of people) and the separating qualities of boundaries influence interaction between them" (quoted in Baud and Van Schendel 1997, 216). This fluid and flexible nature of the borderland also extends to the category of 'borderlander': a highly liminal group, and one that can engage with state power in varying ways.

BORDERLAND POLITICS

The rest of this chapter will look more closely at the internal workings of borderlands by considering their political, social, and economic dimensions. Before delving into the politics that tend to characterize borderlands, however, it is worth briefly discussing the nature of the state in these African cross-border micro-regions. To do so, one needs to refer to the Berlin Conference of 1884–1885. Perhaps the event's most lasting impact with regards to borderlands lies with the metropole-periphery relationship that it helped to instigate. Hentz (2009, 15) expands upon this in the following quotation:

> It [the Berlin Conference] certified a state system where the political authority situated in the capital had legal suzerainty over a geographically defined space, but lacked political authority over all the people that lived within that space, particularly the farther you travelled from the capital [. . .] The more important legacy of Berlin for the trajectory of the post-colonial state is that the African colonial state consisted of either a small trading outpost and/or of a capital. There was little effort to project authority into the hinterland. Colonial powers were more interested in connecting their colonies to the metropole than in connecting them to their hinterlands.

Yet, there were few attempts by post-colonial African states to rectify these practices of extraversion. Indeed, as the work of Jeffrey Herbst (2000) has influentially demonstrated, African governments have struggled over how (and whether) to project power over the 'margins'—spaces which have frequently been lightly populated, often featuring inhospitable terrain (Lind 2018). Peripheries were commonly therefore left to their own devices, in minimal contact with the center, and overwhelmingly oriented towards those across the border (it was in the peripheries, after all, where those most affected by colonialism's partitioning practices resided) (Onah 2015). This has contributed to the national state consistently regarding these spaces as marginal, and the urban bias has thus continued to be ever-present. The capital tends to look down upon such zones as the following: poor, weak, dependent, backwards, provincial, deprived, even pre-modern, but above all else, inferior (Pollard 1997; Donnan and Haller 2000; Horstmann and Wadley 2006).[12] Often borderland spaces will be conceptualized in a problematic pragmatic lens as being underutilized, empty, and essentially awaiting state development and civilization (Michaud 2010). As Benedikt Korf, Tobias Hagmann, and Rony Emmenegger (2015, 884) describe with regards to the Ethiopian state and its dryland peripheries, "successive rulers from the Imperial to the current period have portrayed pastoralism as the 'other' side of modernity, civilization and development—an 'other' waiting to be included in the political space of modern Ethiopian statehood." And yet this is not only an African phenomenon. Ellen Bal and Timour Claquin Chambugong (2014) describe how the Garos, a group residing in the India-Bangladesh borderland, are severely looked down upon by other residents of their respective countries and considered primitive and 'jungly' tribals. This is similarly by no means a modern phenomenon. Sidney Pollard (1997, 10) explains that going back as far as the Middle Ages in Europe, one can find evidence of this attitude: "Anglo-Normans and Germans saw the men in marginal areas known to them, like the Welsh, the Scots, the Irish, the Scandinavians, or the Hungarians, not only as poor in an economic sense but also as barbarous and lacking the civilizing influence of effective government." It is important to emphasize here that a state's perception of borderlands as marginal goes well beyond consideration of the locational dimension. It includes a societal element (communities on the periphery of society) and crucially, a political element (peripheral areas that passively acquiesce to the power and influence of the center).[13]

However, central governments often do more than simply harbor a negative attitude towards their so-called peripheries: they practice one as well. Perhaps at the most rudimentary level, this is seen in the performance of central nation-building, where inclusion of the borderlands is at best a secondary concern. This is evident in the simplest of practices, such as the delivery of state services. In the Lebanese borderlands, for example, the border zone communities receive a vastly reduced proportion of electricity as compared to the residents of Beirut (Volk 2009). A large part of this has to do with the wider issue of the design of government in many (though of course not all) borderlands; namely, a lack of symmetry between the needs of borderland residents, and the state services provided. Indeed, local government structures in borderlands tend to be based on the political wants of the center, and thus designed according to national templates (Ngwato and Akech 2009). Such a situation characterizes the plight of Ugandan 'fisherfolk' working in various shoreline peripheries of the country. They are more prone to the water-borne disease schistosomiasis than nearly any other population, and yet their peripheral status means that they are the least likely to receive necessary social services for their care (Parker, Allen, Pearson, Peach, Flynn, and Rees 2012). This stems from the government's "tendency to treat them as 'feckless' and 'ungovernable'" owing to "the fact that so many fisherfolk live and work in places located at the country's international borders" and the "view expressed by many officials that border people are mostly migrants and that many are not proper citizens at all," as Melissa Parker, et al argue (Parker et al 2012, 98–100).

This lack of congruence between state services and a periphery's needs is made even more acute by the unique circumstances of borderland communities, such as those described above. Their orientation towards the other side of the border, as opposed to the metropole, means that education, trade-related, and police services—in some particularly integrated borderlands—should perhaps be designed in consultation with those working in municipalities across the state line. However, as Tara Polzer Ngwato and Jacob Akech (2009, 14) found on the South Africa-Mozambique border, "Local government officials were clearly oriented towards their respective capital cities, even when there is more commonality and everyday interaction across the border than with the capital." Besides the obvious inefficiency issues, this situation tends to breed corruption and embezzlement by the local government ministers due to the lack of accountability towards the locals (Ngwato and Akech 2009). Such problematic scenarios can be compounded by the disdain government officials often feel towards being posted in such remote locales. While conducting ethnographic fieldwork in the remote Himalayan town of Gopeshwar, on India's border with the Tibetan region of China, for example, Nayanika Mathur (2013, 89–90) noticed a common sentiment amongst official circles: "only one of 'the three Ps' can bring you [a government official] here: promotion, probation, or punishment [. . .] The most junior of the ones in 'need of being fixed or punished' were posted as far as possible from the action in Dehradun [the state capital]." It was believed that no one would ever *want* to reside and work in such a 'remote,' 'underdeveloped,' and 'backward' locale—and 'escaping' from this metaphorical prison to an urban center in the plains was always the goal (Mathur 2013).

The different quality of state services in borderlands points to the importance of 'geographically specific distinctions' when looking at more serious issues, such as state violence (Ron 2003). Sometimes, as Hagmann and Korf (2009, 3) note, "What is often perceived as an 'unruly' behavior by frontier inhabitants, is often tolerated, if not initiated, by metropoles who tolerate different political norms and levels of violence in their frontier areas as compared to the political center." In his exploration of the state margins of Serbia and Israel, James Ron found that despotic practices there by military forces and their unofficial military allies, were far more prevalent than in the center. Due to a combination of loose integration into the core, weak institutionalized setting, and hostile political attitudes amongst the populace, the state can operate differently there—the normal rules, so to speak, do not apply (Ron 2003). Such disparities between center and margin are, of course, more pronounced in weak states than strong ones. And while a state such as

Lebanon is perhaps not classically considered weak, it nevertheless certainly has more of a presence in some locales than in others (Volk 2009). Sometimes in especially restive borderlands, state activities like those mentioned above can be motivated by what James C. Scott (1998, 2) describes as an "attempt to make a society legible, to arrange the population in ways that simplified the classic state functions of taxation, conscription, and prevention of rebellion." Scott (1998) refers to this as the 'last great enclosure,' and it is essentially an attempt to politically and administratively pacify such zones. Given borderlanders' tendency to consider central authority as oppressive (a theme which will be discussed in the section on border society), not to mention the larger issue of their not being fully incorporated into the nation, borderlands can indeed be scenes of exceptional illegibility.

In those places where it is especially difficult for the state to maneuver and practice traditional statecraft, it can often appear as though the state is absent.[14] At many African borders, for example, an official state presence, both in an administrative, but also in a visible sense, is patchy, at best.[15] Hence the frequency with which borderlands are referred to as 'non-state,' 'ungoverned,' or 'no-go' spaces (Menkhaus 2007). Yet, areas where there are truly no governing authorities are extremely rare, and thus not only is a description of the borderland as ungoverned an exaggeration, but it is also a fundamentally state-skewed perspective.[16] As Hagmann and Korf (2009, 3) importantly point out, while "the political center of the nation state clearly fails to live up to the proclaimed image of the state as the guarantor of welfare and political stability in the frontier," nevertheless, "interpretations that stress the absence or weakness of the state in the frontier are misleading. Through population movements, public policies, property rights regimes, and variegated center-periphery relations—often of a patrimonial character—the metropoles govern the frontier from afar." Taking a borderland perspective allows one to recognize unusual and unconventional governance practices of the state in these spaces. It also helps to give due attention to the multitude of competing authorities operating in the borderland. Seeing the borderland through the lens of the periphery opens the way for consideration of new terms such as Forest's 'zones of competing governance' or Scott's 'places of low-stateness,' and allows for alternative conceptions of these spaces too.

With respect to the internal political workings of the borderland, this book builds upon Scott's work on perceived marginalized populations in Asia—or rather in 'Zomia,' as he terms the mountainous area of politically, socially, and economically connected hill peoples, living on the edges of ten states in the south-eastern corner of the continent. Instead of being 'left-behind' segments of the mainstream citizenry, Scott (2009, ix) argues that members of Zomia have throughout history *chosen* to distance themselves from state power. They have been defectors, so to speak, of the state: "runaway, fugitive, maroon communities [. . .] fleeing the oppressions of state-making projects in the valleys," and have voluntarily imposed self-marginalization or self-barbarianization onto themselves.[17] Such an argument goes directly against other accounts of state development, consolidation, and rule. These are not the primitive, 'living ancestors' of mainstream society, but a group of people attracted to out-of-the-way places for the distinct purpose of thwarting "incorporation into nearby states and to minimize the likelihood that statelike concentrations of power will arise among them" (Scott 2009, 8). These spaces where state-rejecting run-aways congregate, termed 'shatter-zones' by Scott (2009), have a few key components. The first concerns their status as a place of refuge and state avoidance.[18] They tend to take form in areas where large numbers have fled from either expanding states (for example, states attempting to consolidate their power up to the national boundaries), complex emergencies, and in the past, growing empires, or activities such as slave-raiding.

Perhaps not surprisingly then, shatter-zones tend to be found in hard-to-reach, lightly populated places such as inaccessible mountains, dense forests, marshes, and steppes, to name a few. Translated into cartographic geography, classic shatter-zone locations thus include edges of states (so as to be in reach of the refuge provided by the other side of a border, for example) in large tracts of Amazonia, the Balkans, the Caucasus, and areas of highland Africa, among others.[19] Applying this analogy to Afghanistan, Goodhand (2009a, 10) notes, "Even today, Pashtun tribes in the hills and deserts draw a sharp distinction between themselves as people who do not pay taxes (*nang*) and those Pashtuns who live under state control (*qalang*). As well as a means of escaping taxation, the hills constitute a place of refuge from political or religious persecution." Those shatter-zones situated on a border, as the majority tend to be, are effectively borderlands *par excellence.*

Borderlands (or shatter-zones) exist not only to hide from the state, though, but also because an anti-state lifestyle is much easier to pursue from such spaces (Scott 2009). This has been the case for groups resisting the pre-colonial, colonial, and post-colonial state. While it can sometimes appear as though shatter-zone occupants are simply a marginalized ethnic, religious, or other kind of group, Ernest Gellner makes the important distinction that in fact the marginality has most likely been cultivated as a political stance against statehood. Gellner uses the example of the Berber peoples of the Maghreb: the common understanding of their position vis-à-vis the Arabs is one of ethnicity (namely, the Berbers as a tribal people, and the Arabs as post-tribal). However, a more accurate reading of the situation, he argues, would involve recognizing the self-conscious tribalization practices of the Berbers, done with the intention of making their rejection and withdrawal from political authority more feasible (Scott 2009).[20] As Scott (2009, 30) remarks, "what becomes intriguing is that a distinction in political status is ethnically coded as if it were a fundamental difference in kinds of people and not a political choice." It is easy to see why the 'political choice' narrative has for so long been buried, for it exposes borderlands as polities which fundamentally threaten the state. They represent, to use Scott's (2009, 30) words, "an ever-present temptation to those who might wish to evade the state."

According to Victor Azarya and Naomi Chazan (1987), there are various modes of state disengagement—different ways of leaving statehood and entering the borderlands.[21] The first and mildest is what they call 'suffer-manage.' Under suffer-manage conditions, people may be highly dissatisfied with state conditions, but their reaction generally refrains from going beyond an aloofness from the state. At the opposite end of the disengagement spectrum is 'escape,' which signifies a clear-cut removal from any sort of dependency on, or usage of, state channels. In between is 'parallel systems,' which consists of networks developed to deliver services left non-rendered by the state. This mode does not necessarily have to involve antagonism or competition with the state—although frequently it does. Typical examples of parallel systems include black market activities, smuggling, and alternative forms of justice. Also in between is 'self-enclosure,' which like parallel systems involves a drastic reduction of reliance on official channels, but unlike it, does not include deviance from the state. Instead, it tends to represent a withdrawal into more local forms of subsistence: an adherence, for example, to a more rural lifestyle, a professed allegiance to narrower foundations of solidarity such as ethnicity or religion, and even a switch from export to subsistence crops. All four of these types of disengagement are common to borderlands. In fact, a borderland would arguably not be one if at least one of the four was not in operation. But most importantly, such practices are much easier to pursue from or within a borderland because of the presence of the state line and distance from central authority. Many aspects of parallel systems, for example, are only possible if there is a border available to take advantage of—and even more so, a border featuring infrastructure, trade routes, and so on, across the state line. Ultimately, the distinctions above are important because they help to define the character of a borderland, and what activities are likely to be taking place there. Suffer-manage techniques are common traits of a quiet borderland, for instance, whereas parallel systems or escape practices tend to signify an unruly, even rebellious, one.

As should have become apparent by now, the state is rarely, if ever, completely absent from these zones. Rather, its presence varies in quality and quantity, depending on the power of the capital versus the strength of the border networks. In fact, even in historically unruly borderlands, the state is often present in specific sites—what Nicholas Farrelly (2013) has termed 'nodes of control'—thanks to various forms of modern state-making technology. Indeed, many Zomian spaces have struggled in recent decades to retain independence from their respective states in the face of such technologies. However, even in areas where India, Myanmar, Thailand, Laos, Nepal, and Bangladesh have had success in encroaching upon the lives of the borderlanders, their state presence is usually restricted to towns deemed important by the capital. These include transport or commercial hubs, key population centers, or important sites along the border, and they often have to be strongly fortified by the state. Areas deemed less 'strategic' will—at least for the foreseeable future—likely be allowed to maintain a Zomian state of existence (Farrelly 2013). And of course it is not guaranteed that even the nodes of control will continue to exist as such; as Farrelly (2013, 209) notes, "in areas where there is a lingering perception that local people detest the government, there is a possibility that without these muscular impositions [the nodes of control] the ambitions of the central state systems would collapse." In the end, the importance that borderlanders attach to state weakness, the fluid nature of sovereignty in these spaces, the width and depth of disjunction between the center and so-called periphery, are all part of the overall anti-state and liminal character of these distinct spaces.

BORDERLAND SOCIETIES

Borderlands are also characterized by dynamic cross-border social networks. While traditionally borderlands have been viewed as arenas that passively absorb national culture and identity, a borderland perspective demonstrates that this is often far from the case.[22] First, a border not only represents partition, but also opportunity for different social forces to come into contact and interact with each other (Brambilla 2007; Chan and Womack 2016). As Donnan and Haller (2000, 13) describe, "borders have an ambivalent character: they represent dividing lines as well as thresholds of passage, they have a 'hinge function,' simultaneously bounding and excluding." Borderlands are thus areas where social identities can converge, coexist, or conflict (Newman 2011; Horstmann and Wadley 2006). While the conflicting aspect will be discussed later in this chapter, it is important here to recognize the converging and coexisting practices of the populations on either side of the border. There are numerous documented cases of borderland populations coming together and developing a creole or syncretic culture (Baud and Van Schendel 1997). Writing about the American-Mexican borderland, a news periodical described this situation well: "In truth [the border] is a world apart—a third very unsovereign nation, not wholly American and not quite Mexican either, with its own customs, mores, values, and even its own language, Spanglish" (Martinez 1994, 20). Yet the opposite can be the case as well: a pre-existing (in relation to the border) ethnic or other socio-identity group can straddle the state line, simultaneously existing as a cohesive entity, yet split between two differing political regimes. Often the border itself can help to maintain such a population's cross-border ties. As these groups are commonly engaged in cross-border trade or smuggling, for instance, business partnerships can ensure unity and even strengthen existing bonds.

Borderlands thus vary in terms of how integrated, co-dependent, and networked the populations on either side of the border become, with many of course not progressing as far as the amalgamated 'Spanglish' border culture (Stea, Zech, and Gray 2010).[23] Regardless of the shape or form that the cross-border relationship takes on, however, there are features simply common to all individuals whose lives are overwhelmingly defined by the borderland. As Zartman (2010, 8) describes, "one characteristic overshadows and contains all of the models—the fact that borderlanders constitute an identifiable unit unto themselves, distinct from the populations further back from the line by their experiences and their identity." Zartman's 'distinct population' concept arises firstly from various practices and relationships that borderlanders tend to acquiesce. Being in a space marked by fluctuation, flexibility, and often contestation, a certain frontier mentality usually takes root (Jackson 2009). Heavily influenced by the liminal nature of the borderland existence, it is one often marked by, first and foremost, cultural diversity. Other traits tend to include versatility, open-mindedness, and as many have noted, exceptional cosmopolitanism (Martinez 1994).[24] They furthermore "are often skillful at appropriating and posing canny challenges to state authorities and policies," as Yuk Wah Chan and Brantly Womack (2016, 96) observe.

Indeed, borderlanders' dexterity at traversing what can often be quite complicated and constantly changing surroundings is something Janet Sturgeon (2005) has termed 'landscape plasticity.' Although she coined the phrase specifically with reference to the Akha people of Southeast Asia, and their "ability to adjust complicated land uses over time in response to local needs, state plans, and border possibilities," it is an expression that nicely characterizes the juggling and manipulation skills of border peoples in many locales (Sturgeon 2005, 9). Another pertinent example, for instance, are the Thangmi—an ethnic group of roughly 40,000 spread over the highland region of central-eastern Nepal, north-eastern India, and the Tibetan region of China. While they have historically attempted to remain an 'ungoverned' group, more recently some Thangmi have sought a degree of incorporation into their respective states. Nevertheless, there remains an overwhelming 'non-state' identity amongst them, and an interesting array of practices to enable this (Shneiderman 2010). They will often attempt to deny the existence of a Thangmi culture to outsiders, for example, in an effort to keep the group relatively unidentifiable. As Sara Shneiderman (2010, 309), who experienced this first-hand while conducting ethnographic fieldwork in the Thangmi's borderland, describes their rationale, "Why point yourself out to the state if it only extracts resources from you rather than offering them?" And in fact the Thangmi have a very rich and complex cultural life, one "shaped by motifs of religious syncretism, linguistic creolization, and racial hybridity" (Shneiderman 2010, 310). Ultimately, the Thangmi have proven successful at 'cultural strategizing' and strategically deploying their 'multiple positionalities' to remain a non-state people.[25]

Until relatively recently, the myth of border artificiality skewed perceptions of border culture. It was assumed that due to the apparent arbitrary nature of the borders, identities would be predominantly characterized by ambiguity and confusion, even when on either side of the border there existed individuals of the same identity group. However, as researchers like Donna K. Flynn have discovered, for some borderlands it is precisely the opposite that has transpired. In her research on the Shabe residents of the Benin-Nigeria border, Flynn (1997, 319) found that a powerful 'border identity' had taken hold. She explains this in the following way: "The 'border' is not merely an arbitrary line dividing two nations; it is a social grouping based on historical, residential claims to the Okpara region." The Shabe identity had developed not only out of a long history with this transnational space, but also from an attitude that professed it was the Shabe's right to be the main participants in, and profiteers from, the borderland's cross-border trade. The Shabe in fact proclaim, 'we are the border,' denoting the degree to which a so-called arbitrary border can become embedded and entrenched into the very psyche of a group (Flynn 1997). To quote Flynn (1997, 312), "in the case of the Shabe, it is a local sense of *deep placement* instead of displacement, *deep territorialization* instead of deterritorialization, which forges strong feelings of rootedness in the borderland itself and creates a border identity."

Of course, it is significant as to whether the cross-border population existed as one community prior to the imposition of the border. For those groups where such a situation is the case, their border identity tends to be much stronger owing to its historical embeddedness. The following comment from Gérard Prunier (2004, 383) very much applies in this scenario: "we must remember that borders mean very little in such a situation. Not only are they often porous (the case of Zaire/Congo being extreme), but ethnic solidarities existing across them are much more powerful than the formal citizenships people happen to carry. A Ngbaka is a Ngbaka before being either 'Congolese' or 'Centrafrican,' a Kakwa is a Kakwa before being 'Sudanese,' 'Ugandan' or 'Congolese.'"

However, as hinted at in the previous section, the relationship between alleged center and periphery is one of "paired symbiosis and opposition," as Scott (2009, 29) says. In other words, it is impossible to fully understand borderland society without considering its relationship to that of the national state(s), as both are socially constructed positionalities (against each other).[26] Perhaps the most interesting implication of this distinct border identity is the ensuing relationship between borderlanders and heartlanders. For example, a 'sense of being different' from their fellow citizens frequently leads to interests and visions fundamentally at odds with those of the rest of the nation (Acuto 2008). As Goodhand (2009b, 233) argues, "The political loyalty of borderland populations cannot be guaranteed." Indeed, borderlanders' allegiance to the state is frequently questioned due to their national identity oftentimes being perceived as diluted (Evans 2013). This is for a number of reasons, the most influential being physical remoteness from the seat of power; a perceived sense of political isolation, marginality, or subordination; and constant exposure to, and interaction with, another nationality across the border (McKinnon and Michaud 2000).

Due to these factors, cross-border relationships often come to trump those of national ones. In the Ilemi Triangle, for instance, neglect on the part of national authorities towards borderland development, has translated into increased dependency among the borderlanders on their kin across the border (Simala and Amutabi 2005). Likewise for the borders between South Africa, Mozambique, and Swaziland, where the transnational relationships have become cohesive and dominant to a degree that many borderland residents define identity in terms of length of residency in the border area, as opposed to national origin. It is even the case that traditional South African authorities will recognize Mozambican and Swazi nationals as members of their borderland village, when national law has not confirmed their legal right to reside in the country (Ngwato and Akech 2009). A similar scenario can be found in the West Kalimantan borderland—an area of Indonesia that borders the Malaysian state of Sarawak—where the Indonesian residents use the Malaysian ringgit as their main currency, and children are enrolled in schools across the border (Eilenberg 2011; Eilenberg 2012; Eilenberg 2016). Perhaps not surprisingly, the borderlanders' flexible sense of national identity and strong feelings of cross-border solidarity has attracted the attention and suspicion of national authorities. The head of the provincial border development agency stated, for example, "The border area has not yet been properly socialized into the nation. The dominant merchant trading is carried in foreign currency and moreover, our citizens at the border are more familiar with the leaders of our neighbors compared to those of their own country" (Eilenberg 2016, 1339).

These kinds of affinities and cultural values can certainly have very tangible implications: it often leads to independent and self-reliant economic practices (as will be discussed in the next section), attitudes of resistance and self-assertiveness towards norms and laws imposed by the center, and in more extreme cases, subversive interests or even secessionist sentiments (Martinez

1994).[27] However, these factors should not be interpreted in a negative light. On the contrary, tending to perceive state authority as a largely oppressive force, many borderlanders *value* the distance from the core, and the societal (as well as political and economic) independence and freedom that comes with that. In fact, many of their cultural attributes—remarkable linguistic diversity, for example—can be partly read as purposeful attempts to keep their society out of bounds and illegible to the state (Scott 1998).

It must also be remembered that despite the deep rootedness in the border, not all other sources of identity necessarily become extinguished. William F. S. Miles (2005) found that on the Niger-Nigerian border, for example, Hausa and Muslim identities were still alive and well, despite an entrenched sense of 'shared borderlandness.' In other words, identity in the borderland does not have to be a zero-sum game. In the end, however, there is no denying the powerful 'joint community' mentality—and often a heavily tinged anti-state one at that. Although at times being described as 'political amphibians,' borderland societies are more likely to act as a social unit unto themselves, not willing to be co-opted into 'the national scheme of things' (Miles 2005, 20).

BORDERLAND ECONOMIES

The anti-state and liminal character of borderlands is arguably most noticeable in the economic realm. However, the practice of economic 'escape structures,' and the nuanced means through which this thwarting of capture and appropriation is achieved, have on the whole been insufficiently analyzed or appreciated.[28] This is no surprise, as a state-centric framework is fundamentally ill-equipped to examine transnational practices of this sort. Where borderlanders look at the border and see opportunity, the state sees barrier, boundary, or protector of national economy. Borderland economies have rarely been studied as economic systems in their own right, but rather have tended to be seen from a state perspective as arenas that attract and encourage smuggling, banditry, gun-running, livestock raiding, and the like. While of course these activities do take place, they are part of a wider historical system with its own dynamics, trajectory, and narrative.

Taking a perspective from the frontier, then, means beginning from borderlanders' economic understandings of their space. Above all else, they often see it as one economically marginalized by central authority. Flynn's (1997, 318) description of the Shabe's attitude towards the Beninois and Nigerian governments is typical of borderland sentiments: "From the point of view of border residents, the government has imposed only economic hardship on them and has done nothing to help them develop, while customs guards, as arms of the government, are only out to rob them." It is not only distrust and suspicion of government border officials (and the policies behind them) that characterizes the borderlanders' attitude, but it is often conceived around a sense of injustice.

This attitude translates into interesting practices. As described in the previous section, perceived inequality has led borderlanders in places like the Beninois-Nigerian border to actively strengthen border solidarity and interdependence, in order to appropriate what they see as their natural rights to the lucrative transborder trade. If they perceive their economic autonomy as being compromised, they often have no hesitation in responding with evasion or resistance. For some, however, it is simply a matter of survival: amongst Tunisian communities along their state's border with Libya, for example, due to government neglect of the periphery and failure to incorporate the space into the broader national economy, they often have no choice but to orient their livelihoods around the only resource available, namely, the border (Baky 2018; Lamloum 2016). In fact, although acceptance of the border amongst the borderland population is widely lacking, it is noteworthy that they nevertheless have significantly incorporated it into their everyday lives (Baky 2018). This is part of a wider phenomenon, namely the economic independence and self-assertiveness which tends to arise out of these spaces. For one thing, this tends to result in economic activity being directed outwards and over the border. It is common amongst African borderlands, for example, that economic and business cohesion is far greater and stronger amongst and between their border spaces, than between borderlands and their respective interiors (Migdal 2004). In fact, what are often referred to as 'twin towns'—namely, urban areas in close proximity to each other on either side of a border—tend to be far more economically integrated with each other, than with other nearby towns on the same side of the border (Migdal 2004).

The economic independence and self-assertiveness also tends to embolden an attitude of ambivalence with regards to cooperating with national customs and trade regulations.[29] According to Martinez (1994, 23), "borderlanders find it morally and culturally acceptable to breach trade and immigration regulations that interfere with the 'natural order' of cross-border interaction." Thus, when state practices in the borderland become too parasitic and a nuisance for the inhabitants, or more seriously, when they start to restrict their abilities to make an economic living, the residents can often have no qualms about circumventing the state (or bribing state officials in order to have their way). In the impoverished and neglected Tunisian cities of Ben Guerdane and Dhehiba along the border with Libya, for instance, residents rarely see themselves as practicing illicit activities, despite smuggling being extremely common. So long as the smuggling benefits this neglected and underdeveloped region, it is viewed as legitimate by the citizens (Lamloum 2016).

The government's economic disregard of the borderlands can also be a significant advantage for residents, however. As Lee Cassanelli (2010, 146) states with reference to the Horn of Africa, "By essentially neglecting the frontier districts, colonial bureaucrats and their African successors in both Kenya and Somalia afforded borderlanders the economic space to develop more extensive supply and market networks." Their remoteness in this case meant that despite "administrative maps and official ordinances [suggesting] that the states exercised sovereignty along the frontiers," they were simply too far removed from the political and economic center to be subjected to thorough enforcement (Cassanelli 2010, 146). Indeed, for many borderlanders, it is not only about having access to transnational practices in ways they perceive as acceptable, but it is also about being able to truly take advantage of the myriad economic opportunities which arise from having a border in the midst. Their everyday activities often revolve around continually crossing the border for low-level economic pursuits. While the majority of this transnationalism may be 'innocent,' there is nevertheless, as Ieuan Griffiths (1996, 75) points out, "a fine dividing line between casual, small-scale movement across a border and systematic illegal trafficking or smuggling." Crossing the border for alleged reasons of local petty trade or family visits, for example, can be used as smokescreens to engage in more substantial transnational activities such as 'illegal' long-distance trade (Flynn 1997). Borderlanders are not only uniquely positioned to take advantage of such nuances, but they are also highly experienced in the exploitation of different states' border regulatory regimes (Van Schendel 2005).[30] "Borderland communities learn to reconcile arbitrary state policy with economic rationality," Goodhand (2009b, 235) explains.

Indeed, borderlanders in numerous regions have long been practicing activities such as smuggling.[31] As Vorrath (2007, 7) explains, "Smuggling is completely dependent on the existence of the border since differences in prices, monetary currencies and the general 'atmosphere commerciale' between neighbor countries are naturally the incentives and driving forces of these activities." Or as described by Cassanelli (2010, 144), "borders afford opportunities for traders and herders who straddle them precisely because the 'national' markets on each side of the border are subject to their own demographic and regulatory trends." It is at borders where the value of an item increases or decreases, and hence they can be dynamic, active sites of economic exchange (Goodhand 2009b). And it is borderlanders, especially those part of a socio-identity group straddled across a border, that arguably understand more than anyone else how best to work this 'potential difference' and its attendant opportunities (Jackson 2009). In fact, their skill in this arena goes back centuries in some places. Discussing borderland traders in eastern Africa, Cassanelli (2010, 146) explains,

After the establishment of colonial rule, these experienced traders were well-positioned to circumvent colonial attempts to restrict or divert their commerce within the new, artificially constructed boundaries [. . .] the borderland traders relied on cross-territorial mobility to evade government taxation, registration and quarantines, and to move their animals and other assets to the most advantageous markets on either side of the border.

Historically, borderlands tend to have been crucial intersections in trading routes, with a corresponding history of licit and/or illicit cross-border commercial ties amongst their inhabitants, based on kinship, friendship, religion, profession, and so on (Baud and Van Schendel 1997; Jackson 2006). 'Illicit,' of course, is a label imposed on a practice that has been operating for a great period of time in many cases. Indeed in many ways, systems today simply represent a continuation of previous ones, supported by a local population that has retained a wealth of translocal knowledge on this front (for example, in details of old trade routes), and who ultimately remain connected to traditional economic practices (Van Schendel 2005). Oftentimes flourishing and vibrant borderland economies are perceived as modern phenomena. While it is assumed they are driven by new technology such as cell phones, robust vehicles, and so on, in actuality cross-border trade and smuggling practices tend to overwhelmingly be reliant on the bonds, alliances, and partnerships built up over numerous decades, if not centuries.

Importantly, while the state's presence (physically, politically, or administratively) at the border may be minimal, it still is usually the biggest determining factor behind the size and kinds of goods permitted in cross-border trade (Vorrath 2010). State borders are essentially filters, or nets, with varying and fluctuating gradations of porosity (Anderson and O'Dowd 1999). This means that depending on the character of the state line, for some goods the border may be highly porous, while for others comparatively impermeable (Van Schendel and De Maaker 2014). The type of good moving across the border helps to determine the type of borderland network that is activated to facilitate the move. Janet MacGaffey and Remy Bazenguissa-Ganga (1999, 187) explain this process, noting that at one end of the economic network continuum are the "highly structured networks organizing trade flows of particular commodities on a permanent basis," while at the other end are "the instrumentally activated personal networks [. . .] which] appear to be the most widespread for organizing the cross-border trade that takes place all over the [African] continent." It is interesting to think that while national efforts at achieving regional economic integration in Africa have on the whole been quite dismal, illicit and unrecorded trade practiced by borderlanders has helped to achieve quite remarkable levels of unofficial integration in many borderland spaces (and beyond) (MacGaffey and Bazenguissa-Ganga 1999).

Ultimately, borderlanders may harbor a significant anti-state stance in both economic attitude and practice, but the majority recognize the benefits that accrue from their uniquely liminal and interstitial position.[32]

THE BORDERLAND AS A CONTESTED POLITICAL SPACE

The remaining sections of this chapter will explore how these insights are important in shaping the kind of conflict that arises in violent African borderlands. More specifically, they will consider the influence of the following factors that have just been discussed: politically, the tradition of resistance against central authority; socially, the predominance of a border identity; and economically, a system built around independent cross-border trade. They will explore how those who pursue their agendas violently are keenly aware of the anti-state and liminal quality of borderlands, and how these spaces can be transformed into lucrative conflict environments. The resources 'on offer' from borderlands and their borders are extensive and wide-ranging, however they are not ready-made. They require skilled experience, insider-knowledge, effort, and manipulation. Yet, as Feyissa and Hoehne (2010, 12) argue, "there is a research gap—particularly in the Africanist literature—in the understanding of how people adapt to state borders and make use of them." Thus, whereas the predominant narrative of borderlands perceives them as constraints and their inhabitants as victims at the mercy of states, the following will focus on the agency of borderlanders and their skill in extracting and utilizing borderland resources for their own endeavors. It will take a similar approach to Feyissa and Hoehne (2010, 1–2), namely of engaging "with borders as institutions that can be made use of, and borderlands as fields of opportunity for the people inhabiting them"—and being aware of "the multiple possibilities engendered by marginal spaces and being marginal." It is important to point out that the following is by no means an exhaustive list of the conflict resources engendered or shaped by the anti-state and liminal quality of borderlands.

A common theme running through many descriptions of conflict in borderland regions is the important role of ideational dimensions. There are often references to discourses of marginalization, hidden transcripts of discontent, and unresolved political issues (Mosley and Watson 2016). In discussing the conflict in Northern Uganda, Terhi Lehtinen (2008, 2) notes, "There are several layers of grievances, symbolic representations and multiple co-existing conflicts which all converge in the narratives about Northern Uganda." Borderlanders complain of a range of infringements and injustices inflicted upon them by the capital, ranging from objections of too much state (hence the frequency of refusals to pay taxes), to protests of too little state (for example, claims to suffer from inferior quality schools, health services, and so on). Sometimes such grievances can formatively contribute to the development of a rebel group in a relatively straightforward way. As Jozef Merkx (2002, 115) explains, "Borderlands are actually dynamic areas with an interplay between restrictions and opportunities. Frequently, they are the setting of conflicts within a country, whereby a group (or groups) from the periphery considers itself marginalized by the center and starts a rebel movement."

More commonly, however, the process of transformation from perceived marginality to rebellion is a significantly more complex one. It is thus often necessary to look beyond the role of material factors, and also consider specific meta-narratives built around the aforementioned themes of marginalization and discrimination. These meta-narratives, under the right circumstances (including at times their being distorted), can powerfully help 'sing' rebel movements into existence.[33] Morten Bøås and Kathleen M. Jennings (2008, 154) explain: "micro-regions of conflict are set in motion by the elaboration, contestation and manipulation of meta-narratives of identity, power and betrayal, and their spread across borders is facilitated by the particular pathologies and failings that may grow out of the neo-patrimonial state."

Meta-narratives reflecting the unique lived experiences of borderlanders are not the only conflict-related political dynamics to arise out of this arena, however. The varying quality and quantity of state control also means that borderlands are simply more conducive spaces from which 'men of prowess' or 'men of violence' can find openings to operate. Thus, in addition to legal state authorities, there are often a multitude of actors attempting to exercise power in the borderland—what Raeymaekers (2009a) terms 'actual authorities'—and these can include armed bandits, rural militias, transnational companies, and even NGOs. It is important to recognize, however, that this distinction between state and non-state actors in the borderland is somewhat of an artificial and ideal one, as can be seen from the frequency of 'sobels,' state officials acting as smugglers on the side, and so on. The liminal quality of these spaces can clearly provide great advantages for those involved in conflict, as they are able to use this highly versatile environment to strategically enmesh themselves into the conflict zone.

The particular political climate of borderlands also generates lucrative conflict opportunities of a much more practical nature for non-state actors. According to Halvard Buhaug and Jan Ketil Rod (2006, 316), for example, "Insurgency, defined as guerrilla warfare, is favored by the presence of sparsely populated hinterlands, support of the local population, underdeveloped infrastructure, cross-border sanctuaries, valuable contrabands, and considerable rough terrain"—all traditional features of borderlands.[34] Lack of road infrastructure, for example, means that these spaces are often difficult for government forces to traverse, if not being completely out of their reach. Combined with the military's unfamiliarity with the local conditions of the area, and commonly a lack of support from the populace towards the state, rebels (would-be or actual) can find themselves with ample space from which to mobilize, organize, gain bargaining power, and implement their agendas (Buhaug and Rod 2006). All of the above-mentioned features, but particularly the remoteness, can also benefit such actors in helping to disguise, mask, or even make 'invisible' in a sense, their acts of violence. The following from Louisa Lombard (2012, 267), while specifically referring to the Central African Republic, can be said to describe a great number of African borderlands: "A key feature of violence and the exercise of sovereign capabilities in the buffer zones is that the remoteness and inaccessibility make it much easier to hide what happens here than in more-populated parts of the globe. With rare exceptions, the bush will swallow it. This has profound effects on both the ways that particular people and groups exercise authorities and the configurations of political power that emerge." Unfortunately the resulting environment of impunity can also mean that the violence practiced in borderlands can take quite extreme forms. Researchers have recently drawn attention to the influence of a lack of media scrutiny, for example, in encouraging (or at least not dissuading) actors to pursue quite disproportionate and indiscriminate modes of violence (Conciliation Resources 2017).

A common consequence of the above—namely, this opaque quality of borderlands—is that understandings and explanations of local dynamics of violence can be misunderstood or misconstrued, as well as even hijacked by others for political purposes. An ongoing example of this concerns interpretations of the violence committed by various Islamist groups throughout Africa. It is easy to interpret the work of organizations such as Al Shabab, Al Qaeda in the Islamic Maghreb (AQIM), and Boko Haram through the lens of de-territorialized, transnational Jihadism.[35] Analysts and politicians commonly highlight their cross-border movement and activities, and look to their burgeoning or potential alliances with other groups, as activities fitting into supposed wider trends in global terrorism (Lind 2015). Yet this is a simplistic reading of such groups, and one which conceals deeper narratives of grievances at play. As Jeremy Lind (2015, 2) explains, "On closer inspection a series of discrete insurgencies steeped in long-existing divisions between the center and societies at the margins, alongside sub-national rivalries and inequalities entwining with these macro cleavages is revealed." In other words, violence that might appear as part of the more recent wave of global Islamist terrorism actually has historical roots that reflect very local issues (Bøås 2012). The Islamist identity has indeed been made a salient one for conflict in the current era, however it often is masking older, more complex conflict motives in many cases.

All three groups mentioned above are skilled at exploiting the grievances of those in the peripheries, and thus use borderland injustices and center-margin contestations to further their causes. In the case of Al Shabab, for example, the group have preyed upon neighboring Kenya's disenfranchised and underdeveloped north-eastern and coastal regions (Lind 2015). AQIM have proven adept at taking advantage of the significant divide between the Malian 'center' and the north (Dowd and Raleigh 2013; Whitehouse 2018). With regards to Boko Haram, although they operate in a cross-border locale often described as lawless and ungoverned, the dynamics behind their existence in this space are about far more than the lack of effective governance. Boko Haram principally maneuver within the three northeastern Nigerian provinces of Yobe, Borno, and Adamawa, but have also been active (to a much lesser extent) in border areas of neighboring countries, such as Niger's Diffa region, the southwest of Chad, and especially Cameroon's 'Far North' region. These are marginalized spaces of their respective countries, with Nigeria's northeast, for example, being the most underdeveloped area of the state. This borderland zone of northeast Nigeria, southeast Niger, southwest Chad, and northern Cameroon shares ethnic and cultural affinities—in addition to porous borders—which together facilitate a more conducive environment for Boko Haram to conduct illicit economic practices, acquire weapons and other materials, have greater ease of mobility, maintain rear bases and safe havens, and recruit (Bearzotti, Geranio, Keresztes, and Müllerova 2015). Thus, while there is certainly a transnational dimension to Boko Haram's identity and activities, it is not the *global* transnationalism depicted in most analyses. Ultimately, as Lind (2015) argues, "The greatest threat from militant organizations in all three countries lies in how they exploit widely-held feelings of disaffection at the margins."

Of course, Al Shabab and AQIM do have formal affiliations with Al-Qaeda, Boko Haram have pledged their allegiance to the Islamic State, and all three groups certainly espouse Islamist goals and rhetoric. Nevertheless, they also have important grassroots dimensions: they not only derive from, but also operate within, localized cross-border spaces. As existing analyses rarely look into their interaction with these marginalized areas, these groups nearly always become understood through the misleading and decontextualized lens of global terrorism (Dowd and Raleigh 2013). And state leaders looking to deflect criticism of their responses (or rather lack thereof) to such violence, as well as seeking to appear as committed allies in the global fight against terrorism—encouraged by significant funding opportunities often available from the United States in particular—eagerly buy into, and promote, the totalizing Islamic terrorism narrative (Dowd and Raleigh 2013). In May 2014, for example, in reference to the Boko Haram conflict, then Nigerian President Goodluck Jonathan stated, "what started as a local insurgency in North

Eastern Nigeria has now evolved into the new frontier of the global war of terrorism against our civilization, our way of life, and against the many prospects of stability in our region" (Dowd 2018, 119). As Catriona Dowd and Clionadh Raleigh (2013, 501) explain, "regimes that witness the emergence of violent Islamist activity within their territory are well positioned to present themselves as bulwarks against a globally significant movement with transnational linkages and security implications, rather than localized movements emerging in response to specific conditions."

It is not just violent non-state actors who find borderlands to be political arenas of easy operability. As borderlands are often strategically situated within wider spheres of regional political and military state dynamics, they can provide opportunities for neighboring states to further certain political agendas. At times this can be for relatively simple security reasons, perhaps most commonly when a neighboring state crosses the border for purposes of restoring order. Mauritania, together with France, for example, launched raids in 2010 aimed at reducing the strength of AQIM in northern Mali (Walther and Miles 2018). Often governments will act according to different standards and practices in neighboring borderlands than their own. Indeed, the borderland represents a space where outside states can fund, strategically support, or even create, non-state proxies to act on their behalf, carrying-out activities which would be deemed unpalatable and unacceptable by their own population or wider international community. As Ron (2003, 16) explains, "Core agents may be involved in frontier politics, but their involvement is often indirect. Under these conditions, the rules states make for themselves, and that international actors make for states, do not fully apply, granting frontier agents substantial autonomy."

Often borderlands are subject to outside violent forces through much less clandestine means, however. These spaces can act as sanctuaries, shelters, and protection from an intrusive government, merely by virtue of their having a national border running through them (Van Schendel and De Maaker). Groups fighting next door can also use this space to rest, regroup, treat the wounded, recruit, and so on. Colombian guerrillas, paramilitary groups, criminal gangs, and other violent non-state actors use neighboring border zones with Venezuela and Ecuador, for example, to retreat and strategize (Idler 2016). Another recent example of this concerns the Syrian conflict, where opposition groups used the Syrian-Turkey borderland, and others such as the Free Syrian Army retained rear bases across the border in Jordan (Vignal 2017). The Syrian conflict also highlights how dramatically borderlands can be transformed from violence, with cross-border activity often intensifying (especially if the state itself is forced to retreat from these spaces) (Vignal 2017). Relatedly, conflicts originally confined to neighboring countries can extend into borderlands. This can occur, for example, when militarized refugees decide to make their temporary home in these zones, thereby subjecting borderlands to new and potentially volatile political dynamics.[36] Borderlands are often not isolated peripheries at all, but rather part of highly interconnected political systems.

THE BORDERLAND AS A CONTESTED SOCIAL SPACE

"Nationalism and interethnic hatreds often run so deep that borderlands sizzle with agitation and violence" (Martinez 1994, 16). This quotation from Martinez sheds light on the potential volatility of social dynamics in borderlands. The cultural heterogeneity of these micro-regions, the constant flux of groups migrating in and out of them, and the often tense ethnic environment, can all abet violence under the right conditions.[37] Particularly common flashpoints include tensions between the professed autochthonous population and liminal transborder minority groups such as nomads, economic migrants, religious minorities, refugees, or simply ethnic groups whose identity differs from the 'core' (Onah 2015).

Some authors have argued that the social atmosphere of borderlands engenders a certain martial quality amongst the populace. Pollard (1997, 91) explains this reputation: "The hardihood and toughness of men living in marginal lands were frequently associated with martial skill, courage, and military prowess." In the Roman Empire, for example, 'barbarians' (borderlanders on the fringe of the Empire) were highly sought-after soldier recruits. However, describing the social dynamics of borderlands as the result of particular cultural attributes of the inhabitants is extremely problematic. Rather, a more convincing argument is that borderlands have historically tended to attract certain groups of people (and tended to encourage particular types of responses to the state). Criminals seeking refuge are one such type, for example; others commonly noted are bandits, persecuted religious or political individuals, 'the pretenders who have often threatened kingdoms,' and the list goes on (Pollard 1997; Scott 1998).

Borderlands also tend to draw ex-militants, both those that have been demobilized and those that have not. A common occurrence amongst these former combatants is a social identity (as well as livelihood) dependent on their status as fighters. In essence, their loyalties are fluid and liminal, and as such, they represent an easy and cheap mobilization force for rebel groups (Kantor and Persson 2011). This is even more so the case because of their long-standing horizontal ties with 'fellow men in arms' (Debos 2008). Marielle Debos (2008, 233) argues that these pools of fighters have to be understood in light of situations of 'no war, no peace': "Between two wars, combatants may transform into road bandits or, more often, live as farmers or cattle herders with relatives or kinsmen—especially if they belong to an ethnic group which straddles the border." But when the continuum shifts more towards the violent end of the spectrum in the borderland, they can be relatively easily lured into rebellion. Such transnational fighters have been a common phenomenon in many of Africa's most violent and ungoverned borderlands, and as such have had a significant impact on the connected conflicts in Sierra Leone-Liberia-Guinea-Côte d'Ivoire, as well as those in Sudan-Chad-CAR.

Sometimes it is simply the case, however, that the state's abdication of responsibility in the borderland has included a reluctance to provide security to citizens in times of need, and thus violent non-state groups are formed for defense purposes. During the early phase of the LRA conflict in northern Uganda, for example, when state security forces were notably absent, it was necessary for borderland residents to find a means to protect themselves. Local vigilante groups known as the 'arrow boys' therefore developed to defend citizens from the LRA (Branch and Mosley 2014).[38] The state's inability or refusal to provide state services also often translates into violent non-state groups having much more civilian support than would otherwise be the case. Social services such as health care, transport infrastructure, and even local conflict resolution mechanisms, are provided by rebel groups such as the FARC and ELN in Colombia's borderlands, for example (Idler 2016). And while these are undoubtedly highly violent actors, as Annette Idler (2016, 2) notes, "In many marginalized areas without state control, communities are grateful to have some source of order to regularize everyday life. [. . .] People make pragmatic decisions to support FARC or ELN. This is often a question of survival, rather than an ideological choice." At times civilians do not even have to choose between these groups, however, as it is not unusual to find violent non-state actors having entered into transactional relationships and alliances with each other (Idler and Forest 2015). A phenomenon that Idler terms 'complementary governance,' can not only in some cases provide citizens of the area with more services and security than the state in question would provide, but it can also bring various strategic and tactical benefits to the conflict actors as well (Idler and Forest 2015; Idler 2018).

Instead of there being a 'martial quality' to borderlands, then, it is more often the case that borderland societies have to take matters into their own hands. And often this includes the law, owing to the lack of state judicial services and absence of official routes through which to pursue justice. Crimes of revenge in South Africa, for example, are disproportionately found in the country's margins, where effective state justice channels are lacking (Kramer 2006). In the West Kalimantan borderland mentioned previously, there is a long tradition of 'people's justice' owing to not only a lack of state judicial services, but also a high level of distrust of legal authorities (Eilenberg 2011).

Such distrust and suspicion means that local disputes are usually taken up outside of official realms. In fact, as Michael Eilenberg (2011, 241) states, "State law is only recognized to the extent that it is considered to fit local norms of fairness and justice." Yet in various other borderlands one can find a situation where different forms of justice are actually sanctioned by the state. Pakistan, for example, applies one particular legal system to the borderland zone known as the 'tribal areas,' and uses a different set of laws for the rest of the nation. While this arrangement has contributed to condemning the Pakistan-Afghan borderland to exceptionally high rates of poverty and human rights abuses, it is also sometimes praised for keeping the high levels of violence in the tribal areas contained to the borderland, and—pivotally from the point of view of the capital—away from Pakistan's major cities (Kalir, Sur, and Van Schendel 2012).

Building from the discussion earlier in the chapter on borderlanders' 'landscape plasticity,' it is important to note that borderland residents tend to develop particular sets of flexible social relations that prove easy for conflict entrepreneurs to take advantage of and manipulate. One concerns what Scott has termed their practice of 'jellyfish' social organization. Borderland societies, he argues, are often *plural* in nature. Importantly though, "Such populations do not so much change identities as emphasize one aspect of a cultural and linguistic portfolio that encompasses several potential identities" (Scott 2009, 211). According to Scott (2009, 211), such polymorphous, shape-shifting, and acephalous peoples—with their fungible and vague social units—end up having "certain political advantages; they represent a repertoire of engagement and disengagement with states and with other peoples." Practically therefore, in terms of conflict, this means they are relatively ungraspable and unconquerable to outside actors such as the state. To those pursuing violent agendas, skilful exploitation and co-optation of borderlanders who are able to "deploy a wider range of languages and cultural practices that allow them to adapt quickly to a broad range of situations," can prove valuable for strategic and tactical practices such as blending into populations, gathering information, planning assaults, and so on (Scott 2009, 211; Chan and Womack). Indeed, this ability to accommodate a variety of cognitive maps, and be comfortable interacting within a myriad of contexts (the national context being simply one of many) is a valuable intelligence resource (Van Schendel 2005). A large element of this, on the part of conflict entrepreneurs, is what Charles Tilly has called 'boundary activation': knowing which identities or grievances to call upon and activate, at the right time (Goodhand 2009b). This is made significantly easier if an ethnic or other kind of socio-identity group straddles the border and is hence accessible to differing legal, economic, even political, opportunity structures.

In the end, the specific social characteristics of borderlands—the often-times volatile interethnic relationships, malleable identities, residents capable of strategically adjusting their personas to different political and economic contexts—helps to shape the nature of conflict in these zones (Merkx 2002).

THE BORDERLAND AS A CONTESTED ECONOMIC SPACE

In describing popular perceptions of borderlands, Stephen Jackson (2006, 426) argues that they "have a reputation as either an anachronistic backwater or an anarchic hinterland compared to the metropole. Both views write off borderlands as marginal, with anything of political or economic significance unfolding in the capital. However, the postcolonial reality of Africa and elsewhere has consistently demonstrated that borderlands are, in fact, precisely 'where the action is.'" A large part of that action stems from the specific economic practices that take place in these arenas. Not only can borderlands be sites of interesting political and cultural conflict dynamics, but they can also serve as the space in which transborder trading practices become oriented towards the war economies that sustain insurgencies (Jackson 2006). Indeed, the powder keg tendency of some borderlands has a strong economic dimension, and it could perhaps be said that this starts with the distinctive profit opportunities available to borderlanders.

As briefly discussed earlier, due to issues of proximity to the border and connections to those on the other side, borderlanders tend to have a closer relationship with transnational commerce than heartlanders. The Mandingo community of West Africa, for example, is an example of a group that fundamentally revolves around participation in regional, if not international, trade (Jackson 2006). Their position is greatly aided by the trump card held in local knowledge of the area in and around the state line, allowing them to economically navigate the cross-border micro-region to a degree unmatched by others. This strong investment in the economic life of the borderland makes any state endeavors at interference—such as attempts at clamping-down on border crossings, monitoring border markets and their customers, or even pursuing transnational crime lords—that much more impracticable. As Gregor Dobler and Zeller (2009, 5) note, "state interventions in borderlands are often not very successful. Smugglers look for different routes; traders integrate customs' officials into their patronage networks; activities are relocated." A large part of the impenetrability of the borderland economy relates to issues of social justice, and the fact that an intrusion into this economic system can represent far more than merely a disruption of business activity, but an interference into the borderlanders' way of life (Van Schendel 2005).

This element of social justice is important. Because the frame of reference is the cross-border micro-region as opposed to the national unit, and because of harboring a lack of respect for the state, borderlanders can have no qualms in carrying-out types of transnational economic activity that others would be hesitant in performing.

This attitude consequently facilitates risky and daring economic ventures. Parallel to how the specific social environment of borderlands can be luring for violent-prone actors, the economic environment can be attractive to commercial actors who prefer relatively ungoverned and lawless operating environments (Martinez 1994). Yet this somewhat unruly economic atmosphere is not all down to those it attracts. As Bennet Bronson (1998, 200) explains, "True, most of the barbarians of history have been not only outsiders but poor and aggressive as well, but this is a logical consequence of their outside status rather than a part of the definition."[39] In any case, the important point is that the economic behavior unique to borderlands is a large part of what makes these spaces so appealing to conflict entrepreneurs.

One part of their enticing nature is what Jackson calls 'edge effects,' namely "the radical contrasts and discontinuities experienced by citizens on either side of a border" (Jackson 2006, 434). Common (and very lucrative) examples include official development assistance (when aid is delivered to only one side of the border), legal frameworks (differing licenses between the two states of the borderland, pertaining to commerce, for example), and international intervention (variations in demobilization payments, creating incentives for soldiers to disband on whichever side of the border is more profitable) (Jackson 2006). Conflict entrepreneurs in borderlands are skilled at spotting such edge effects and adjusting their activities so as to best extrapolate the benefits (Jackson 2006).

But most importantly, borderlands can be ideal spaces for war economies to flourish. The militarization of their cross-border trade systems can provide the funding and sustenance for military activities. The slide from peaceful transnational financial practices, to full-fledged war economy, is quite a slippery one in borderlands. It is easy for these economies to become involved in organized crime, terrorist systems, and of course rebel activities (Goodhand 2009b). A large part of the reason for this is the degree to which civilian economies can become fundamentally intertwined with war economies in a borderland, as explained by Zeller (2010, 124): "In a zone of protracted conflict like Sugango [the borderland of Sudan, Uganda, and Congo], this war economy is not insulated or separate from the wider 'civilian' economy. Resources not only move among an inner core of active members of armed groups, but also along transnational networks of trade and trafficking that reach around the globe." When this happens, the border can come to represent a strategic resource in itself, where conflict entrepreneurs vie with others to have a stake in the opportunities it offers. Diana Klein (2011, 78) explains this development in the following:

> Cross-border licit or illicit trade can resource warring parties, in particular if one party controls parts of it. If the border crossing generates a separate income and the 'border' element of the trade becomes an economic activity in itself, whether smuggling, customs levied by armed border guards, employing additional security, drivers, or porters; this can feed into a cycle of usually low level, but persistent violence: enough to maintain the conflict status quo and the nature of border crossing, but not to disrupt the trade.

Among the violent actors vying for economic access to the borderland can also be the state. An interesting example of this can be found in the volatile borderland region of Shan State within Myanmar. An area historically resistant to centralized control, Shan State is home to a thriving opium/heroin cross-border trade which the Myanmar government has been eager to assert its authority over. The government's aggressive military-led counterinsurgency campaigns, however, have only further fuelled the grievances of Shan State residents. The process of consolidating state power in the borderland therefore is one very much intertwined with illicit borderland economies and ultimately conflict (Meeham 2015).

As emphasized previously, the border and borderland do not signify ready-made resources; rather, they require skilled manipulation. In terms of smuggling, for instance, individual borders represent distinct challenges, and it requires expertise to navigate them. Borderlanders are often those most skilled at manipulating the particular differences of borders (Clapham 2010). It is important to recognize that the type of economic activity—informal, hidden, parallel, underground, and so on—that can transpire in such environments is not necessarily done clandestinely, but rather usually in connivance with particular state agents in the borderland (Raeymaekers 2009a). It is often local borderlanders who are vital to conflict entrepreneurs in this respect: they can provide them with the 'overworld' contacts that are necessary to gain access to operating in the transnational economic 'underworld' (Goodhand 2009a). Understanding the economic dynamics of borderlands undoubtedly can tell us a great deal about how conflicts in these zones are sustained.

While borderlands may be peripheral if understood in a state-centric spatial sense, they are by no means marginal zones in terms of consisting of powerful and influential political, social, and economic networks. Through applying a borderland perspective as opposed to state-tinted lens, this chapter explored how conflictual borderlands in Africa experience a specific type of conflict that tends to be influenced by two features of borderlands: first, the presence of a strong anti-state atmosphere, and second, a liminal/networked character. It was demonstrated that such borderlands tend to be characterized politically by a tradition of resistance against central authority, socially by the predominance of a border identity, and economically by a system built around independent cross-border trade. It was then shown how such features can be transposed into conflict resources when strategically manipulated and taken advantage of. The framework from this chapter will be applied to, first, Chapter Three in order to delineate how the Rwenzori area became a fully-fledged borderland. It will then be applied to Chapters Four, Five, and Six, which will help to explain the actions, and ultimately resiliency, of the ADF—namely, how the rebels manipulated and extrapolated borderland resources from the Rwenzori border zone to further their conflict agendas.

NOTES

1. This chapter includes material previously published in "Prominent Peripheries: The Role of Borderlands in Central Africa's Regionalized Conflict," Lindsay Scorgie, *Journal of Critical African Studies*, copyright © 2013 Centre of African Studies, University of Edinburgh, reprinted by permission of Informa UK Limited, trading as Taylor & Francis Group, on behalf of Centre of African Studies, University of Edinburg.

2. Many of these terms have elicited extensive literatures; this is arguably especially the case for 'frontier.' See Korf, Hagmann, and Emmenegger (2015) for example, for a discussion of the frontier and in particular the 'pastoral frontier.'

3. Indeed, conflict can dramatically transform borderlands, often extending them (Vignal 2017).

4. Of course, not surprisingly, the study of North American and European borders and borderlands still attracts far more attention and scholarship.

5. Perhaps what can be considered as one of the 'classics' in African borderland studies, and indeed was critical in moving the field forward, is Kopytoff's (1987) *The African Frontier: The Reproduction of Traditional African Societies*.

6. See, for example, Chabal and Daloz (1999).

7. Compared with other areas of the world such as Europe, there have been very few secessionist attempts in Africa. Some successful cases include Eritrea and South Sudan; the most notable unsuccessful examples include Congo's Katanga, Nigeria's Biafra, Senegal's Casamance, and Somalia's Somaliland (which interestingly represents an attempt to *return* to colonial boundaries). In fact, rather than a change of boundary due to a dispute over the line, Malcolm Anderson (1996, 86) notes, "Disintegration of states in Africa, since independence, seemed a more likely cause of frontier revision."

8. Nugent (2002, 7) argues that practices on the Ghana-Togo border confirm "that border peoples were not just victims of arbitrary European decisions, but were significant contributors to these arrangements in their own right."

9. Tatiana Zhurzhenko (2011) terms borderlands 'victim intensive' places due to their historical experience with violence.

10. Albeit, Vorrath does recognize in Vorrath (2010) that this is a subject warranting further investigation.

11. Indeed, included under the category of 'borderlander' can be violent actors such as militias and rebels.

12. It is important to note that the international community supported this trend and development, through its recognition of (and provision of legitimacy to) what were in essence quasi-states. See Jackson and Rosberg (1982) for a discussion on quasi-statehood.

13. For a variety of perspectives on both what makes a community supposedly 'marginal,' as well as the assumed stereotypical traits of marginal people, see, for example, Pollard (1997), Volk (2009), or McKinnon and Michaud (2000). For a discussion on the suspiciousness which often accompanies attitudes towards alleged marginal or liminal populations, see Anderson (1996).

14. If this is combined with a non-existent delivery of services, the apparent absence can seem even more acute (Bellagamba and Klute 2008).

15. Of course this is not the case for all African state borders, as some make attempts to noticeably and physically project claims to 'statishness.' Furthermore, Alice Bellagamba and Georg Klute's (2008, 8) description of the borderland town of Kidal in Mali, reminds us that the state's presence can vary in form: "In Kidal the state may be weak or even absent insofar as guaranteeing services and economic rights to its citizens is concerned, but it is dramatically present with its military and coercive apparatus, made of soldiers, trucks and weapons." And lastly, it is worth remembering that even if the state is absent in all of the above-mentioned fields, it may still attempt to give the appearance of being present. "At borders, states take great trouble to highlight their territorial sovereignty. Demarcation by means of highly visible symbols such as pillars, flags, fences, and signboards is commonplace," Van Schendel (2005, 40–41) explains.

16. According to James Forest (2011, 3), truly ungoverned spaces include "the most remote parts of African jungles and deserts, distant ocean passages, and huge tracts of frozen land in northern Canada, Greenland, northern Russia and Antarctica."

17. For an interesting discussion on the challenges that Zomia studies confront in the state-centric world of area studies and political science, see Farrelly (2013). Similarly, see Michaud (2010) for a discussion on the related challenges of studying transborder societies. And for a look at studying the Zomian space through a network lens, see Giersch (2010).

18. While this framework applies to many of the communities living in such borderlands, it does not account for, or apply to, indigenous populations living in these spaces.

19. For a fascinating discussion of the Caucasus shatter-zone—and one which avoids the geographical determinism that tends to be quite common with regards to this region—see Radvanyi and Muduyev (2007), and particularly their discussion of the 'Confederation of the Mountain People of the Caucasus' project.

20. In a similar vein, Lucassen, Willems, and Cottaar (1998) argue that Gypsies originated from people practicing and cultivating an anti-state lifestyle (for example, nomadism), rather than being a group derived from a common ethnicity.

21. See pages 116–131 of Azarya and Chazan (1987) for more of the discussion on disengagement.

22. It is outside the realm of this book to discuss the historic lack of academic focus on border cultures. For more on this subject see Wilson and Donnan (1998).

23. It should also be noted that central governments often resent deeply creolized border cultures (Baud and Van Schendel 1997).

24. An example of an astoundingly diverse (ethnically and linguistically) borderland is provided in Brown (2004), in a discussion of the 'right-bank' Ukraine area.

25. For fascinating discussions of cultural strategizing amongst borderlanders, see for example Debojyoti Das' (2014) work on the Naga people of northeastern India, Bal and Chambugong's (2014) analysis of the Garos people in the India-Bangladesh borderland, and Alexander Horstmann's (2014) work on the Karen of Thailand and Burma.

26. Scott (2009, 27) describes this positionality well: "It would be like writing a history of antebellum slavery in the United States while leaving out the freedmen and the lure of freedom in Canada. In each case, an external frontier conditioned, bounded, and in many respects constituted what was possible at the center. Accounts of lowland states that miss this dimension do not merely 'leave out' the hills; they ignore a set of boundary conditions and exchanges that make the center what it is." For more on the socially constructed nature of border identity see Romo and Marquez (2010).

27. Of course not all borderlanders living within the same border realm will necessarily harbor identical sentiments towards the capital. There are often differences in this respect between 'core' and 'peripheral' borderlanders, for example. For more on this subject see Martinez (1994).

28. I borrow the term 'escape structure' from Scott, who uses it in reference to strategies pursued by inhabitants of Zomia. See, for example, Chapter Six of Scott (2009) for a more in-depth discussion on this concept.

29. David Coplan (2009) notes that there is more trade done between African borderlands and North America, Europe, and the Middle East, than with their national state(s).

30. Goodhand (2009b, 234) refers to this as a "comparative advantage in illegality."

31. In the absence of a viable alternative, I use the term 'illicit'; however, I recognize its value-laden and problematic nature.

32. This is exactly why suggestions to alter so-called 'arbitrary' or 'artificial' state boundary lines in Africa are rarely met with enthusiasm by borderlanders themselves.

33. For a more in-depth look specifically at meta-narratives, see for example, Bøås and Jennings (2008), or Bøås (2004).

34. It is important to point out that, as Kalyvas (2006, 132–133) describes, "Rough terrain is not synonymous with mountains; plains can sometimes offer an environment favorable to guerrilla war." Thus, while borderlands often feature rough terrain, this does not necessarily equate to a mountainous environment.

35. For an interesting discussion on current (and misleading) trends in understanding Islamist groups as de-territorialized in character, see Pinos (2018).

36. Michele Acuto (2008, 7) importantly clarifies the role of refugees in this respect when she says, "refugees are neither a source of contagion, nor fighters, but rather, facilitators. They do not carry conflict with themselves as if it was an illness, but instead are used as a medium to augment grievances, and are exploited to foster further hostilities."

37. Especially in Africa, these situations tend to be exacerbated by the lack of security measures and personnel at borders. There is often a severe weakness—if not absence—of policing on many African state boundaries, thereby at times, for example, allowing for a sudden and uncontrolled movement of volatile populations across borders. As Anderson (1996, 83–85) says, "African states lack the trained personnel, the technology and the financial resources to prevent the unauthorized movement of persons and goods across their frontiers. Movements from one state to another of starving people, ethnic groups threatened with massacre, migrant workers, guerrilla fighters, diamond smugglers, drugs and weapons dealers can threaten the interests of a neighboring state. International tension results if the conviction grows that more could be done by the 'exporting' state to control the problem, and that this neglect is willful."

38. For an interesting discussion of vigilantism in the African context more broadly, see Kantor and Persson (2011), and Persson (2012).

39. 'Barbarian,' according to Bronson (1998, 200), simply refers to "a member of a political unit that is in direct contact with a state but that is not itself a state [. . .] He is a barbarian not because he is uncultured but because he is on the outside looking in." For an interesting discussion of the various causal roles barbarians can play in the downfall of states, see more of Bronson (1998).

Chapter 3

A Burgeoning Borderland in the Rwenzories

THE CASE OF UGANDA

"The origins of boundary difficulties are curiously varied," noted the famed British geographer Arthur R. Hinks (1921, 417) in the early 20th century. The Alaska border, for example, is a result of "inexact definition," the Chile-Argentine boundary a "contradictory definition," and the Peru-Bolivia line plagued with "unascertainable previous jurisdiction" (Hinks 1921, 417). With regards to the Uganda-Congo boundary, Hinks (1921, 417) described it as suffering from "unsuitable definition." While there is some merit to his description, as will be discussed below, this alleged border defect has encouraged the Rwenzori zone of the Uganda-Congo border to develop into an anti-state, liminal, and networked borderland, one from which various rebel groups have operated out of over the past several decades. Detailed analysis of this cross-border micro-region can facilitate a better understanding of the violence and destructive rebellions that have taken place there, most notably the ADF conflict. Indeed, in light of how pivotal the ADF's interaction with their wider environment has been, it is accordingly necessary to understand exactly what *constitutes* this space.

Chapter Three will hence explore how the Rwenzori zone of the Uganda-Congo border was consolidated as a borderland, with the first half of the chapter focusing on the Ugandan side and the second half the Congolese. Both sections will start with the experience of colonial marginalization, then move on to the area's continued peripheral status in the post-colonial era, and finally look at the resultant conflictual nature of the space and solidification of its borderland nature, including its political, social, and economic cross-border networks. The time period under review here is from the colonial era, to the early 1990s—just prior to the formation of the ADF. Although the actual borderland of course constitutes both sides, it is useful to explore the development of each separately, considering, for example, the relationships with respective capitals, responses to marginalized statuses, and so on. Western Uganda and eastern Congo have their own historical trajectories, but as this chapter will demonstrate, a pivotal dimension of each side's development was bounded and conditioned by its interaction with the other.

While looking at the historical formation of the Rwenzori borderland, the influence of the three component-parts of Zartman's (2010, 6) definition of a borderland will be considered: "a population on the margins of power centers, traversed by a formal political boundary, living dynamic relations internally and externally (with the power center)." Or, in other words, the effects of the following will be probed: distance from central authority; proximity to the state border; and interaction with the national government, most notably in the form of marginalization by the state, and self-induced marginalization by various ethno-religious borderland populations. Furthermore, the development of the borderland's anti-state and liminal qualities will be considered, and how these shaped the overall character of the space. Geography is also a significant factor in understanding the dynamics and development of the borderland, and will be taken into account. The Rwenzori borderland region features the massive Rwenzori mountains with steep, rugged terrain and dense alpine forests, in addition to being flanked by the Congo rainforest to the west. More specifically, the borderland characteristics discussed in Chapter Two will be explored, namely: politically, the tradition of resistance against central authority in the Rwenzori space; socially, the predominance of a border identity; and economically, a system built around independent cross-border trade.

As a lens through which to view the development and dynamics of the borderland, the trajectory of the main populations in each of these areas, that is to say, the Konjo people in western Uganda and the Nande in eastern Congo, will be explored. While of course other groups lived in the western Ugandan and eastern Congolese spaces, the Konjo and Nande were those who most profoundly shaped the borderland nature and networks of this micro-region. Furthermore, it was the Konjo and Nande who were closest to the Uganda-Congo border, and whose lives intimately revolved around the border and surrounding borderland. The western Ugandan districts of (what are today called) Kasese, Bunyangabu, Kabarole, and Bundibugyo, for example, were home to other ethnic groups; however, these were never marginalized by the central state like the Konjo were, and nor did they form a borderland identity as did the Konjo. This was likewise the situation with the Nande in eastern Congo—although the Congolese side of the Rwenzori borderland was a much more homogeneous place, and the Nande overwhelmingly formed the majority ethnic group. In any case, it is only a *loose* trajectory of these groups that will be presented, as ultimately the main aim of this chapter is to consider the overall borderland *space* from which the ADF arose.

Before moving on to the Ugandan arena of the Rwenzori borderland, however, it is useful to briefly consider the origins of the actual Uganda-Congo boundary. Following the Berlin Conference of 1884–1885, a rough approximation of a border was established through the western Rift Valley, separating what was then the British East Africa Company (and shortly thereafter the Uganda Protectorate) from the Congo Free State. As was the case with so many African boundary demarcations, this one had a strong arbitrary quality to it, even cutting through physical landmarks such as the Rwenzori massif and Lakes Albert and Edward. The unfamiliarity of the Europeans with the Rwenzori area at the time was quite considerable. As Edward I. Steinhart (1999, 28) writes of the Ugandan side of the borderland, "The first element of the interaction that must be emphasized is the remoteness and inaccessibility of the western region to the outside world, which held European penetration to a minimum until the scramble was well underway."[1]

The lack of knowledge concerning this area on the part of the European authorities created various contestations over land, leading to a series of border treaties starting in 1907, and finishing with the Uganda-Congo boundary settlement in 1918. The complexity surrounding this space during that time period hints at the first fledgling signs of a borderland coming into being. Importantly, even before the advent of colonialism, this was a highly dynamic micro-region owing to among other factors, conflicts and frequent migrations (Pennacini 2008). Describing the treaty negotiations and their impact on the area's residents, Governor of the Uganda Protectorate (1905–1909), Sir Hesketh Bell, remarked, "The combined boundary commissions were working in territory claimed by both sides. The natives, not knowing to which side they might belong, and probably fearing that they might be backing the 'wrong horse,' were afraid to show much sympathy for either one party or the other" (Sadler et al 1909, 153–54). While the boundary eventually became more settled, confusion surrounding the space nevertheless lingered, as communities found themselves split between two colonizing powers. Bell (Sadler et al 1909, 154) describes the impact this had on the ground: "if the territory of a native king be arbitrarily divided between two different European powers, the unfortunate potentate in question is obliged to opt for either one side or the other, and will in most cases have to lose all that portion of his territory which does not fall within the sphere to which he has elected to belong."

The population most affected by this sequence of events were the Yira, for whom the border split their community almost in half. The border represented not only division, but also subjection to differing colonization processes. Of course, living under these distinct colonial systems meant that the Konjo (the Yira who found themselves in Uganda), and the Nande (the Yira who ended-up in Congo), developed varying modes of political organization, socio-economic systems, and of course different official languages. These disparities undoubtedly in many ways served to separate the two populations. And yet, "they thought of themselves as one," a Ugandan civil society expert on the region explained (Interview One). The two groups continued to use the same (unofficial) language, have similar social and familial organization, and ultimately practice lifestyles that revolved around the Rwenzori micro-region (Facci 2009; Mbalibulha 2008a). Of course, not all traditions remained the same. Polygamy, for instance—once a common practice amongst the Yira—only survived within the Konjo community.[2] Nevertheless, as Serena Facci (2009, 353) notes, "The Bakonjo say that merely by crossing the border, they become Banande, and vice versa." In fact, some go so far as to claim that "The borderline between Uganda and the Democratic Republic of Congo is just an imaginary line that does not hamper the intercourse between the people in that area" (Ruhunda, et al, 3–4). However, the border has clearly greatly influenced the respective communities, and thus it in fact *does* represent more than an imaginary line.

COLONIAL MARGINALIZATION IN WESTERN UGANDA

"There's many different narratives, and *a lot* of history to this area," was a Ugandan development worker's response to the question of why the ADF first arose in the Ugandan Rwenzori area (Interview Eleven). The historical embeddedness of rebellion and violence in the country's western sub-region is profound. Although the ADF were not formed until the mid-1990s, dynamics that influenced their formation stretch back over a century, and are very tied-up with the development of the borderland itself. The rest of this first half of the chapter will thus explore some of these influential dynamics, looking in particular at how various political, social, and economic conditions in western Uganda were instrumental in solidifying the area's status as an integral component of the Rwenzori borderland. It will first consider the colonial state's marginalization of Kasese, Bunyangabu, Kabarole, and Bundibugyo districts, and the sentiments this aroused amongst the population during the colonial era. Next it will reflect on the continued post-colonial marginalization of these areas and the decision taken by locals to respond with violence.

And lastly, it will look at the implications of their decision to resort to violent rebellion, but most of all will consider the consolidation of this space as a critical part of a borderland, including the continued development of political, social, and economic cross-border networks.

The western Ugandan Rwenzori area has long been a liminal zone: a place of flux and fluidity. Even in pre-colonial times, one can find evidence of its inherently oscillating character, largely derived from its geographical positioning between the interlacustrian culture system based around the Great Lakes, and the communities situated in the Congo Basin forests (Pennacini 2008).[3] Its location on the edges of these different systems did not make it a peripheral zone, but rather a *transitional* one. It was a space where various groups met, mixed, and created 'specific cultural formations' (Pennacini 2008). Not surprisingly, then, it has historically been an area comprising a significant number and variety of communities, home to not only both agriculturalists and pastoralists, but also to numerous ethnic groups such as the Toro, Banyabindi, Amba, and Konjo, among others. As Gianluca Forno (2008, 309) states, "The area of Rwenzori and the district of Bundibugyo in particular, which has always been on the limits of the frontier, is a place where a great flow of different people have left their mark on a system of coexistence, including a legacy of colonial exploitation."

Before discussing the colonial era, however, it is important to point out that various push factors throughout the early and mid-19th century—including disease, warfare, and the expanding Nyoro and Toro Kingdoms—led those who would later come to be called the Konjo, move their settlements further into the Rwenzori Mountains. Surveyor and explorer Richard George Tyndall Bright, who travelled the area during this time, described their environment in detail. "The mountains are, considering their impassable character, fairly closely inhabited. The Bakonjo live in neatly kept small villages in the secluded valleys, and up to a height of 7000 or 8000 feet"; he also noted their ability "to ascend the Ruwenzori mountains to heights to which no other natives can attain" (Bright 1909, 136 and 146). Indeed, while managing to largely retain the societal traits shared with their co-ethnics (namely, those who would later come to be known as the Nande), they adopted a unique mountain lifestyle.[4] According to Syahuka-Muhindo, this was highly significant in terms of the direction Konjo cultural development (and to a lesser extent that of their neighbors, the Amba) would take. He argues (2008, 19–20) that it sealed "their fate as marginal tribes in Toro Kingdom. These people not only preserved historical traditions elsewhere obscured by the creation of the colonial Toro Kingdom and the British colonial state, but retained linguistic forms—Lukonjo and Kwamba—that sharply distinguished them."[5]

With the advent of colonialism, and the British practice of 'divide and rule,' the Toro were chosen as the regionally dominant power. Accordingly, the British fully subsumed the Konjo and Amba under the Toro Kingdom, and thereby also under the Ugandan colonial state. A treaty officially declaring Busongora and Bwamba, the territories of the Konjo and Amba respectively, to be subsumed under the Toro Kingdom was signed by the British Administrator, Lord Frederick D. Lugard, and the King of Toro, Daudi Kasagama, on 14 August 1891. Unsurprisingly, the Konjo and Amba were not signatories to this treaty, nor to several other similar agreements (Rubongoya 1995).[6] The Konjo went from being an autonomous and sovereign group, to essentially being relegated to second-class subjects (Rubongoya 1995).

Nevertheless, this Konjo position of inferiority vis-à-vis the Toro was a relationship that predated colonialism. For example, the Konjo used to suffer from a lack of food at certain times during the year, and thus would come down from the mountains to serve as laborers for the Toro. One interviewee recounted a prevalent anecdote that the Toro would refuse to permit the Konjo to eat off of plates, and rather would force them to use yam leaves (Interview Eleven). While the attitude of superiority towards the Konjo had thus existed in the pre-colonial era, it was nevertheless dramatically heightened with colonialism. In fact, above everything else, it was the Toro's opinion of the Konjo as primitive and unworthy of holding or sharing political power that was most troublesome to the Konjo (Kasfir 1976). In any case, the Toro had difficulty in managing their newfound subjects.[7] The Konjo rejected as much as possible their minority position, the increasingly solidified divide between oppressor and oppressed, and their subjection to what was in essence 'double colonialism' (Magezi 2004).[8]

A pivotal outcome of the above dynamics was the Konjo's perception of the state's political system. Seeing it as fundamentally unfair and based on structural inequalities, they gradually decided to pursue its exit. For some, state disengagement meant joining their kinsmen in the Congo. In fact, Pennacini (2008) notes that in Swahili 'Banande' means 'those who go,' and that the Nande continue to recognize their Ugandan origins. Or as Francesco Remotti (2008, 169) says, "the Banande are nevertheless aware that their origins are 'elsewhere.'" Two factors in particular made joining the Nande in eastern Congo feasible. First, the Konjo identity encompassed the Nande and vice versa, and thus it was socially very easy for Konjo to settle across the border. Second, the Yira in general, similar to many borderland populations, displayed tendencies towards polymorphous or jellyfish social organization. Namely, they exhibited a strong element of flexibility in their identity. Thus, for example, they could emphasize one aspect of their cultural portfolio over others, depending on the situation, thereby making it relatively simple to socially adjust to different situations.

Another direction taken by the Konjo was practicing what could be called self-induced exile, by increasingly isolating their communities at ever higher altitudes in the Rwenzori massif—one of the most peripheral and inaccessible areas of the Ugandan state. Syahuka-Muhindo (2008, 49) contends that this resulted in their being "Deprived of interaction with the population in the lowlands," and thus being forced into "a secluded life. Cultural isolation and stagnation occurred among the mountain people in a particular historical and environmental context." The very high Rwenzori mountains run in a north-south orientation, right along the eastern Congo and western Ugandan boundary line, creating a vast wall of steep and rugged mountains that serves in a sense to underscore the political border. The mountains feature a large alpine area, with 70 percent of the region at an altitude above 8000 feet, large swathes of dense and even impenetrable montane forests, steep-sided alpine lakes, marshy deltas, and peat bogs—making the region almost unreachable to outsiders. However, seeing the Konjo's shatter-zone existence on the edges of the Ugandan state as one simply of seclusion and isolation is misleading. Absent from Syahuka-Muhindo's analysis is consideration of specifically *who* they were secluded and isolated from (and who they were not), as well as any agency on the part of the Konjo. Similar to Scott's borderland populations in Zomia, the Konjo on the whole *chose* to react to their marginality by practicing this state-evading, state-escaping lifestyle. Second, while they may have been cut-off from the Toro Kingdom and the rest of the colonial state in many respects, they remained highly connected to the Nande across the border.

Yet a further course of action pursued by the Konjo was to express rejection of Toro rule through refusing (oftentimes violently) to pay taxes such as hut and poll fees.[9] Similar to many borderland populations, the Konjo responded with evasion or resistance to their economic plight. In addition to the aforementioned taxes, as Stacey (2003, 45) describes in his personal account of interacting with the Konjo community, "there was also levied *busulu*, the peasant's tribute for his right to hoe, six shillings a year, going to the Batoro lords of the land. The language of administration, the language of authority, the language of any chance of advancement, was Rutoro." As the education system began to develop, the Konjo found themselves excluded from scholastic opportunities. Perhaps most severe in this sense was their inability to participate in the school system after the fourth grade, owing to the language of instruction being in Lutoro. Similarly off-limits for them was joining the elite in any shape or form, such as working in administrative or governmental affairs. In fact, it was not until 1961 that the Konjo or Amba were at all involved in district government, having gone over half a century with no county chiefs, high-level local administrators, or cabinet representation.

This was similar to their economic position: toiling the soils of the Rwenzori hills and plains were the Konjo and Amba, who produced 54 percent of the tax revenue grossed by the Toro Kingdom, while administering the colonial economy were the Toro, overseen by the British (Peterson 2009). The astoundingly unequal nature of the system was exemplified by the credit arrangement: the Uganda Credit and Savings Bank awarded 120 loans to the Toro, and a mere seven loans to the Konjo and Amba (Rubongoya 1995). Thus, returning to the issue of taxes, in light of the lack of socio-economic opportunities extended towards the Konjo, it is possible to see why taxation policies were perceived as unfair. By the 1950s, taxation without representation and other practices such as forced labor, had instigated a great deal of frustration amongst the Konjo.

It is worth clarifying the nature of their grievances, however. Various sources have written-off the turmoil in western Uganda as simply ethnic or tribal strife. Jackie Sharon Bamuturaki and Christopher Busiinge (2004, 10) state, for example, "Bundibugyo is a district with a diverse number of ethnic groups, each with its own unique cultures and norms. Unfortunately, this diversity has borne another type of conflict in the district: tribal conflict." While negative sentiments and attitudes did of course exist between various groups in the area, it was the nature of the center-periphery relationship that had ultimately initiated such discord.[10] There were profound meta-narratives of marginalization and discrimination at play, and dissatisfaction with their plight led the Konjo towards an anti-state stance, and a search for a new source of empowerment and identity (Kambale 2007).

POST-COLONIAL PERIPHERALITY IN WESTERN UGANDA

Instrumental to furthering this discord was the means through which the Konjo population reacted to their marginalized status, namely via pursuing a lifestyle increasingly oriented westwards to the Nande in the Congo, and an anti-state modus operandi devoted to achieving some form of political, social, and economic autonomy.[11] A likely contributing factor to this was the lack of a sense of 'Ugandan' nationality in various areas of the country, including the Rwenzori region of western Uganda. Yet, Peterson (2009, 176) argues that the structural inequalities and corresponding grievances "were not in themselves enough to mobilize Bakonjo and Bamba people against Toro overlordship. It took intellectual and political work to create a radical state of mind among mountain dwellers." Building and consolidating this kind of lifestyle was perhaps a more difficult task than would appear at first glance, as shatter-zones by their very nature—namely, being state-evading spaces—are not usually conducive to unified administration. In describing the Konjo mountain culture, Stacey (2003, 30) provides a flavor of the kind of perplexity involved: "mountain societies do not readily make for the collective figurehead.

Steep-sided valleys divide communities, centralized authority eludes them [. . .] A sense of *operative* unity among those living fifty or a hundred spurs distant was not easy to envisage." Nevertheless, through the efforts of what became known as the Rwenzururu Movement (RM), this was eventually achieved. Pennacini (2008, 85) notes in the following quotation the awareness amongst the Konjo elite of the need to turn a shatter-zone population into an organized community: "Realizing that under British indirect rule the a-cephalous groups fall under the control of more centralized and structured societies like the Batoro, the Bakonjo undertook a process of centralization which aspired to transform their scattered political organization based on local chiefs [. . .] into the kingship (*obusinga*)."

In 1954 the Bakonjo Life History Research Association (BLHRA), a Konjo initiative led by school teacher Isaya Mukirane, was begun. It was tasked with revitalizing their traditions and customs, and conducting an exploration into the history and cultural traditions of the Konjo. Within an atmosphere of societal repression, it was an important vehicle for generating a greater sense of collective identity and confidence amongst the Konjo community. Yet, BLHRA's agenda was not only about creating a societal historiography. It also quickly developed into a deeply political organization. When Uganda started its decolonization process, with no signs to come of better socio-economic opportunities for the Konjo, the BLHRA sought to dramatically distance the Konjo community from the national framework. On 15 August 1962, just two months before independence, BLHRA wrote to the Ugandan Prime Minister, Milton Obote, requesting greater rights for their people through independence from the Toro Kingdom and the creation of their own district, 'Rwenzururu.'

When the request was turned down, the mood in the area changed: a great deal more focus began to be directed towards politically defining Rwenzururu (Peterson 2009). As one Rwenzururu veteran explained, "If we have no forum in which to be heard, then we better stand on our own" (Albere 2007, 63–64). A move to use Lukonjo as the *lingua franca* within Konjo territory was put in place, along with an anthem, flag, and other nationalistic symbols. Their own schools were set-up, in addition to fourteen different ministries and an independent police and army force (Alnaes 1969; Magezi 2004). Peterson (2009, 173) contends that "Their bureaucratic and historical work lifted Rwenzururu out of Uganda itself, making it possible for international brokers to recognize an independent nation." Yet, he also points out that there was a divergence of opinion running through the post-independence Konjo community, over whether Rwenzururu should constitute a distinct district but within a wider state, or whether Rwenzururu should constitute an independent state altogether (Peterson 2009).

The lack of headway with the moderate agenda appeared to give more credence to the hardline and militant path. Mukirane declared himself *Obusinga*

(King) of the Rwenzururu Kingdom state, leader of the Rwenzururu Secessionist Movement, and informed President Obote in writing that the Rwenzori Mountains were now independent from Uganda. Addressing the subject of why the Konjo decided on the creation of a *kingdom*, Peterson (2009, 172) explains, "Separatists were often royalists because they needed to distinguish their polities from the flattened-out citizenries that national governments sought to create." While there was a group of anti-*Obusinga* amongst the Konjo, the overwhelming majority of the community was in favor of the institution.[12] Chiefs were appointed, and a governmental bureaucracy set-up to administer the Kingdom, as well as to collect taxes from the populace. An article in *The Economist* at the time remarked, "what may well have irked Uganda's prime minister most about the Rwenzururu secessionist movement was the way its ex-schoolteacher leader, Mr. Isaiah Mukirane, styled himself 'King of the Mountains of the Moon'" (Correspondent in East Africa 1963).

By February 1963 a state of emergency had been declared throughout the mountainous area, and the Uganda Rifles were called in to subdue the populace. It marked the start of a brutally violent and grisly revolt, and one that would last for over twenty years. It was a rebellion fought by a people using spears, bows, and arrows, versus a national army equipped with heavy weaponry. But the Rwenzururu fighters had the 'local' factor on their side. Popular support from the peasantry and an intimate familiarity with a terrain non-traversable to outsiders, meant that it was extremely difficult for the Uganda Rifles to penetrate Rwenzururu territory. Except for a rather complicated and intricate series of steep footpaths throughout the area, there existed no roads in the mountains at the time, making them nearly inaccessible (Doornbos 1970). Together these dynamics helped to make Konjo space 'illegible' to government forces, and thereby relatively unconquerable and ungraspable. The way the steep, rugged terrain and dense alpine vegetation of the Rwenzoris worked in favor of the Rwenzururu, offering them a space that essentially guaranteed their continued existence, further highlights the significance of geography as a factor in understanding the borderland dynamics. Further disadvantaging the Ugandan forces was the fact that terminating the movement through heavy military action would probably have only brought their enemies closer together and solidified their support (Doornbos 1979).

It is interesting to note that when Mukirane was first informed of the government's unwillingness to grant them an autonomous district and/or recognize their Kingdom, he responded with the following: "we are prepared to join the province of Kivu in the Congo where we have the backing of twelve members of our tribes in the Congo National Assembly" (Rubongoya 1995, 86–87). Indeed, going back to the BLHRA, a significant part of the Rwenzururu identity and ideology involved the idea of being integrated, or at the least extremely interconnected, with the Nande. That helps to explain why, for instance, the mandate of the BLHRA was confined not just to working in, and studying about, the Konjo in Uganda, but also to extending the focus to deep inside Nande territory. And this philosophy was one their kinsmen across the border shared. Both Nande chiefs and peasants were enthusiastic towards the Rwenzururu leaders and their ideas of unification. In fact, not only did the BLHRA have branches in the Congo, but the Rwenzururu Kingdom was divided into six *sazas* (counties), with Kiatenga Saza located on the Congolese side of the Rwenzoris, and the actual headquarters of the Kingdom positioned inside the vast Congolese forest (Magezi 2004; Mamdani 1996).

Nevertheless, the goal of political reunification with the Nande was quite a distant one, as many Konjo recognized. But over the next couple of decades as the Rwenzururu struggle continued, the interaction between the Konjo and Nande would prove critical for the Movement, in many ways allowing it to continue for so long. Accounts of this time are replete with stories of Rwenzururu fighters escaping to Nande territory while being pursued by the Ugandan army, for example, and Mukirane taking shelter amongst the Nande for long stretches of time when the Ugandan Rwenzoris were too dangerous. Indeed, any account of the RM would be incomplete without consideration of the pivotal role played by the Nande and eastern Congo.

Yet, it is significant to point out that this was not a one-way relationship, for when the Nande required assistance, they too were able to cross the border and find safe haven amongst their kinspeople in Uganda. In the early to mid-1960s, for example, when the Kivus were undergoing a period of tumult and turmoil, Nande refugees were able to enter Konjo territory and temporarily settle in the lowland areas of the mountains (Syahuka-Muhindo 1991). A Congolese Reverend recounted his experience in 1963–1964 during the Mulele Rebellion, when his family had to flee Oicha in North Kivu province, and settle for a period of time in the Ugandan Rwenzoris: "We have relatives on this side and the other, so we ran to where we knew people" (Interview Seven).

While the Amba also took part in the struggle, by far the secessionist rebellion's most pronounced following came from the Konjo. For them, the Rwenzururu Kingdom represented a means of securing a political voice that had thus far been silenced. It also symbolized the struggle to overcome a marginalized status and attain the political and socio-economic opportunities that had for so long been denied to them. It symbolized their freedom from second-class status, and a recognition of their identity (Nkuutu 2003).

Of course, it is important to acknowledge that one dimension of their marginal status was simply to do with physical remoteness. Not only was the capital Kampala a significant distance away, but there was a lack of road infrastructure connecting the area to the rest of western Uganda, resulting in a significant disconnect from both Ugandan society and the capital's influence. Bundibugyo ('an appendix on Uganda' as some have referred to it), only about 2.5 miles from the Congo, was most affected in this sense. It suffered from extreme isolation, with only one road (of very poor quality until relatively recently) linking it to the rest of Uganda (Alnaes 2009).

While the geographical element of western Uganda's marginality was important, the political dimension was undoubtedly more so. The center-periphery divide in Uganda goes back to colonial times, when social services such as education and hospitals were concentrated in the capital and surrounding areas (Finnström 2008). Throughout the decades following independence, sentiments of structural oppression and resentment towards the capital for alleged political neglect were only reinforced and heightened due to the lack of government resources directed towards the area. "There are times when a part of a country seems to be 'forgotten' by its government. Bundibugyo is one of these," Kirsten Alnaes (2009, 98) maintains. It was the last region in the country to receive electricity or a decent road network, for example. There was no secondary school between the town of Fort Portal and the Congolese border until 1972, and even after that, education, health, and communication services continued to remain comparatively substandard (McGregor 2007; Ntambirweki 2001; Interview Seventy-Seven). In fact, not only was it one of the poorest Ugandan districts, but it also had one of the highest infant mortality rates in the country, and an over-population problem exacerbated by little access to land (Alnaes 2009). Residents of the area frequently complained about their 'abandoned status' from the government, and their being left to fend for themselves in terms of security, health care, and education. In Ugandan Parliament on 15 July 1999, in fact, the Kasese Representative powerfully described her area's historic neglect: "The first time that a Mukonjo and a Mwamba living in those mountains ever knew that there was Central Government Administration was when the NRA [National Resistance Army] soldiers went into the mountains during the 1986 war. That was the first time the Bakonjo of those mountains felt the presence of Central Government. They were lacking education, they were lacking transport, they were lacking economic support" (Uganda. Parliament July 15, 1999). Similarly, as a Konjo tour guide from the area explained, "The government didn't know how we were living. They never came up the mountains" (Interview Forty-Two). Even NGOs had a history of staying away, tending to take their services to more accessible locales (Bamuturaki and Busiinge 2004). The meta-narratives of marginalization and discrimination amongst the populace, and overall anti-state sentiment, only grew stronger.[13]

The rebellion made a concerted effort to address the area's deficiencies, and education in particular was a great focus of Mukirane's. In terms of genuine accomplishments, the RM instituted a system of appointing village chiefs independently of the state (Titeca and Vlassenroot 2012). Various other advances by the RM were also achieved, notably during Idi Amin's reign when they were granted autonomy in the form of a new district, Rwenzori (now Kasese), to consist of a majority Konjo population. Nevertheless the movement lost substantial steam over the years, and among ordinary peasants came to lack any momentum. Only hardliners with the most extreme vision of autonomy remained interested in pursuing the cause militarily. The substantive aspects of the struggle were unrealized by the time it came to an anti-climactic political and military end in 1982. After twenty years of armed resistance, the leadership agreed to peace with the Milton Obote II government. They were granted amnesty, and willing Rwenzururu soldiers were amalgamated into the Uganda National Liberation Army (UNLA). The Rwenzururu King, Charles Wesley Mumbere (who had taken on the position after the death of his father, Mukirane, in 1966), came down from the mountains and resumed Ugandan citizenship. Instrumental in bringing about the armistice between the Rwenzururu leadership and the Obote II government was Amon Bazira, who later went on to lead NALU (and was killed in Nairobi in 1992, most likely by agents of the Ugandan government) (Prunier 2004). While the conflict may have come to an end on paper, however, the political and socio-economic undertones that had propelled it for so long were as ubiquitous as ever.

A CONSOLIDATED BORDERLAND IN WESTERN UGANDA

In some respects, the independent Rwenzururu Kingdom nation was a figment of the Konjo imagination. But at the same time, as Peterson (2009, 184) reminds us, "it was also real: it limited citizens' movements, redirected their tax revenues, reoriented their tongues, and reshaped their religion." Perhaps the most 'real' consequence to have resulted from this imagined community was the role it played in helping to eventually solidify the Ugandan Rwenzori space as a deeply anti-state, networked, and liminal borderland. Indeed, post-1982 the issues and grievances behind the RM (although it had officially ended) were by no means resolved. For one thing, the population's aspiration to have the Rwenzururu Kingdom recognized had never been achieved, and they were consequently left dissatisfied that yet again their institutions were unacknowledged. What proved to be even more ominous, however, was the substantial number of Rwenzururu fighters who felt cheated of a military victory, and were of the opinion that an agreement with the Ugandan government should never have been made. Compounding this tumultuous environment was the fact that the hard-core Rwenzururu militants were never disarmed or demobilized, thereby contributing to the overall militarized nature of the area. Unsurprisingly, many of them decided to return to the mountains. They shortly thereafter formed the Rwenzururu Freedom Movement (RFM) under the leadership of Richard Kinyamusitu, former Chief of Staff for the RM, who had chosen life in the Rwenzoris over agreement to ending the rebellion (Mbalibulha 2008a).

It was not long before western Uganda was enveloped in violence once again, when an insurgency by the name of NALU arose in 1988. Having a nucleus formed of battle-hardened ex-Rwenzururu militants—principally those from the RFM, such as Kinyamusitu—the rebellion mobilized support by reigniting former animosities, foremost among them the long-standing meta-narratives of marginalization and discrimination, and the sentiments of local autonomy. In fact, Prunier (1997, 19) describes the group as having simply been "the latest modern incarnation of the old Rwenzururu Movement." It also drew upon other non-demobilized units in the area, including disenfranchised NRA soldiers, and former Idi Amin fighters who were living at the time in the Congolese town of Beni (Interview Seven). Borderlands are often catchment areas for the 'remnants' or 'castaways' of various movements, and the Rwenzori zone was no different in this sense. NALU were successful in reawakening the area's unaddressed grievances and attracting a significant number of Konjo youth. The collective imaginings for an independent state among the more ideologically hard-core portion of the population, and a desire for a representative political voice by nearly the whole community, were issues that NALU propagated in their agenda. Of course, the Konjo Kingdom in particular, was a subject the Rwenzori population felt extremely passionate about, and one that many were willing to take up arms for. According to one Ugandan development worker, NALU were strategic in "riding on the back of the Bakonjo issue" (Interview Eleven). The head of a Kasese-based civil society group explained that so long as the Kingdom issue remained unresolved, "there would always be the potential for conflict. Any rebel group could pray on that psychology, knowing people would fight seriously for that issue" (Interview Sixty). The generally disgruntled nature of the area at the time, and the wide rift between the population and national government, thus proved to be conducive for mobilizing rebellion.

It is interesting in this respect to consider some of the reasons provided by former NALU combatants for why they joined the rebels. One former fighter explained that he "joined the tribal conflict between Fort Portal and Kasese" because he was "unhappy with the government" (Interview Seventy-Four). His response demonstrates his belief that NALU were a continuation of the Konjo fight for independence from the Toro, hence his reference to the towns of Fort Portal (headquarters of the Toro Kingdom), and Kasese (center of the Konjo community). Another described himself and fellow fighters as "wanting our freedom for the [Rwenzururu] Kingdom," and generally being unhappy with political conditions in their area of western Uganda (Interview Seventy-Four). Despite such rationales appearing to mesh with the original agenda of the RM, the fact that a great deal of the NALU force were actually abducted, signals a grave difference between the two groups. While the RM was perceived to have genuinely been fighting for the Konjo people, even despite having had an extremely violent nature at times, the same could not be said of NALU, some of whose members appeared to be in the business of rebellion for financial and material gain. Inflicting great insecurity on western Ugandan districts such as Kasese, many local inhabitants came to oppose the violence practiced by the group. Not surprisingly, then, NALU proved unable to make much headway with their espoused political agenda, while militarily they were far from winning on the battlefield. Of course, that did not mean that they lacked a destructive capacity. As a European development worker described western Uganda between 1991 and 1994, "Kasese was a no-go place, and Fort Portal was accessible really only with UNHCR [United Nations High Commissioner for Refugees]" (Interview Twenty).

An interesting dimension of the conflict was the lack of information and consequent confusion surrounding it. A great deal of this perplexity seems to have essentially been due to where the rebellion was taking place: namely, in a liminal space characterized by a highly fluid institutional landscape, with ambiguous relationships between state and non-state, legal and illegal, and so on. It was furthermore a micro-region with a tradition of resistance against the state, and thereby had a comparatively large proportion of the population that had at one time or another taken up arms, and more often than not, had never been disarmed after conflict. Also, its proximity to the border and easy accessibility to the people and places on the other side meant constant movement between and across the boundary zone. The following press articles from the time illustrate how the above factors contributed to this atmosphere of confusion and perplexity, and also just how fertile this space had become for rebellion.

- *The Independent Observer*, 24 August 1989: "According to the residents in the area where rebels attacked, the attackers were not Rwenzururu rebels, but those based in Zaire which include former Uganda Army, UNLA, UFM [Uganda Freedom Movement] and FEDEMU [Federal Democratic Movement] plus NRA deserters" (Staff Writers 1989). This clip exemplifies just how many non-disarmed groups there existed in the area at this time, and the connections between Ugandan groups and the Congo.

- *The New Vision*, 24 September 1992: "The question whether the Rwenzururu Freedom Movement and the National Army for the Liberation of Uganda are friends and are working together to perpetuate insecurity in Kasese District lingers on the minds of many Ugandans" (Nzinjah 1992). Here the confusion with regards to the collaboration of groups is very apparent.
- *The New Vision*, 19 October 1994: "A combined force of National Army for the Liberation of Uganda rebel remnants and the deposed Rwanda government militias (*Interahamwe*) is reportedly preparing to attack Uganda from Zaire"; "According to the reports, the *Interahamwe* had contacted the NALU rebel remnants asking them [NALU] to combine efforts with them to attack Uganda from Zaire crossing the common border in Kasese district"; "Reports from Kasese say there have been at least three meetings between NALU and *Interahamwe*. Zairian troops were also reportedly teaming in areas of Kudi, Igabiro and Lhukuka, a few kilometers from the common border" (Nzinjah and Mugisha 1994). This article helps to demonstrate the nature of collaboration between Ugandan and Congolese (and purportedly even Rwandan) rebels and the fluidity across the border.
- *The New Vision*, 17 March 1995: "Twenty more rebels who had infiltrated Ntoroko county, Bundibugyo district while fleeing an NRA offensive on their camps in Hoima, were killed in a battle with the NRA and LDU [Local Defense Unit] forces in the area, on Monday"; "The military source described the remnant rebels as a disorganized group which was ill-equipped and lacked a central command. 'They even don't know for sure what they are fighting for,' a senior security officer who declined to be named told *The New Vision* yesterday"; "Forty-three of them were reported to have crossed into Zaire via Lake Albert in Bundibugyo district" (Sserwanga 1995). These clips clearly illustrate the aura of mystery surrounding the rebels, and the significant lack of information on their origins and modus operandi. And again, they demonstrate the ease with which rebels could move back and forth between the two countries.
- *The Monitor*, 29 March 1995: "The presence of rebels in Bundibugyo district has caused a lot of concern and panic among the local folk, with everybody expecting another rebel attack any minute"; "Talk doing the rounds in Bundibugyo is that the rebels are operating from Zaire, just some miles from River Semuliki, separating Uganda from Zaire"; "It is believed that the rebels are organizing themselves in Zaire" (Jamboree 1995). These passages reveal just how profoundly interconnected the

two sides of the border were in terms of conflict, with the rebels training and basically residing in Congo, but attacking in Uganda.

- *The New Vision*, 13 July 1995: "According to sources in Bwera, Muzimye died of severe injuries sustained in a clash between the remnants of Rwenzururu rebels and those of the National Army for the Liberation of Uganda" (Nzinjah 1995). As the Rwenzururu rebels were actually incorporated into NALU, this excerpt—which is claiming they were fighting each other—demonstrates an absence of basic knowledge amongst the community as to who the conflict parties were.

While the lack of clarity with regards to the conflict was undoubtedly difficult for civilians, it was arguably an asset for NALU. In fact, a variety of factors to do with the nature of the space, helped to ensure that NALU's lifespan was significantly longer than could have originally been expected. First, while the population may not have been wholly behind NALU, it was nevertheless not in support of the government, especially when Kampala proved rather inept and disinterested in bringing peace to the area. As Stacey (2003, 376) describes, "The Bakonjo as a whole had not identified with NALU [. . .] Yet in Amon Bazira [NALU's leader] they felt they had lost a hero who for awhile had played the national stage and latterly—if ineffectually—the international stage; and they remained unreconciled to [President] Museveni's 'National Resistance Movement' government." The general anti-state character of the area, greatly exacerbated by the unresolved status of the Rwenzururu Kingdom issue, meant that NALU could count on a populous full of resentment and antipathy for the central government. They could thereby count on recruits (albeit not always enough). A great deal would have also been swayed to join out of their experience with profound levels of poverty, unemployment, and lack of education.

Second, and similar to the RM, the ethnic continuum between the Konjo and Nande was critically important. As living in western Uganda was generally out of the question for NALU, they found sanctuary within Nande territory in the Congo. One former NALU member argued that because of the same language, similar appearance, common culture, and so on, it was easy for NALU to disguise themselves as Nande civilians (Interview Seventy-Five). Their existence amongst the Nande community was not always done secretively, for other accounts have described a more open atmosphere—including intermarrying, and starting various businesses (trade in timber and minerals) with the locals (Interview Twenty-One). This integration and cohabitation with the Nande on the other side of the border allowed them to set-up bases in and around Congolese towns such as Beni, and to essentially conduct their conflict *from* the Congo.

Third, and related to the above, they clearly benefited from the close proximity of the border—and an extremely porous, unmonitored one at that. The advantages of the border went well beyond being able to escape one state's jurisdiction and enter another's. It also gave them access to a whole range of other local armed forces with whom they could forge alliances. As the above newspaper articles demonstrate, NALU had a wide variety of potential allies to choose from in the Congo.

Lastly, NALU's strategic location between two rivalling states, not to mention being in the center of the wider tumultuous Great Lakes zone, meant that they could take advantage of various conflicts between the regional powers. For example, Kinshasa and Kampala's poor relationship led President Mobutu Sese Seko to lend support to NALU, in the hopes that they would be a destabilizing force for Uganda. Ultimately, NALU's place in the borderland proved pivotal in terms of them having the necessary adaptability and resiliency to withstand an otherwise harsh operating environment.

By the early 1990s, then, the Ugandan dimension of the Rwenzori zone displayed all of the classic features of a borderland: it was distanced (both geographically and politically) from the central government, it was strongly influenced by its proximity to the state border, and there existed an exceedingly conflictual and dynamic relationship with the center. It exemplified a highly anti-state, liminal, and networked borderland, and displayed a great many of the borderland characteristics described in Chapter Two. Politically, for example, it was inhabited by a population that practiced self-distancing activities from the state. According to Azarya and Chazan's rubric of state disengagement, the Ugandan Rwenzori space demonstrated signs of both 'escape' and 'parallel' systems. This disengagement was fuelled by meta-narratives of marginalization and discrimination from the center, as well as hidden transcripts of discontent—sentiments that became less hidden with the outbreak of rebellions such as the RM and NALU. Socially, the Konjo exhibited a strong frontier mentality, and closely identified with their place on and around the border. Their sense of border identity encompassed their Nande co-ethnics, and they were overwhelmingly culturally oriented towards and across the border. Interestingly, their societal organization in many respects (acephalous and polymorphous, situated in remote areas, and so on) helped to keep the state at bay. In other words, they were relatively illegible to the center, and demonstrated great flexibility and skill in taking advantage of the area's liminality. And finally, in terms of the economy, the Konjo used economic practices that are classic of borderlands: they felt fiscally unjustly treated by central authority, they were assertive in terms of their economic escape practices, and as to be discussed more with the Nande, were deeply involved in (usually illicit) transborder commerce.

Pivotal to the political, social, and economic trajectory of the Konjo over this time period was their interaction with, and influence from, the Nande—and more generally, eastern Congo. While the focus here has been largely on the Konjo population group, this was done for the purpose of being a lens through which to understand how the western Ugandan *space* became part of a borderland. Indeed, the trajectory of the Konjo people tells a significant part of the story of how this micro-region became part of a wider Rwenzori borderland. The next half of the chapter will discuss the development and trajectory of the remaining half of the Rwenzori borderland—eastern Congo—through focusing on the Nande.

THE CASE OF THE CONGO

"Border regions which are situated far from the national market could find themselves marginalized by national politics of development. It happens then that populations living in the borderland, and abandoned by the national state, create local dynamics based on proximity with their neighbors. Informal exchange networks then tend to develop" (Kabamba 2008, 148). This quotation by Kabamba describes what occurred to the Nande in eastern Congo. As will be discussed, they faced a similar situation of marginalization by their central government as had the Konjo. However, while the Konjo's reaction to their peripheral status took the form of a quest for autonomy (whether via advocating for a separate district, independent state, or most fervently, a kingdom), the Nande's response to marginalization by Kinshasa took a quite different route. Theirs revolved around a dynamic transborder trading system, operated largely independently from and outside of official state structures, based on networks of trust, and highly reliant upon the Ugandan border and Konjo territory. Indeed, the development of this trading system and sense of Nande identity surrounding it, was very much bounded and conditioned by the interaction with western Uganda.

Once again, the first section here will consider the early development of this system during colonialism. It will be followed by a discussion of the post-colonial Congolese state and its influence on the eastern Congolese area in question. And finally to be looked at, will be the continuation and expansion of the trade system, and most significantly, the consolidation of this space as a pivotal part of the Rwenzori borderland.

COLONIAL MARGINALIZATION IN EASTERN CONGO

In order to consider how the Nande's particular lifestyle originated, it is necessary to start with a brief consideration of the troubled North Kivu colonial milieu. The first open sentiments of agitation expressed by the Nande occurred when the Belgian colonial powers interrupted their tributary system of production (MacGaffey 1987). Amongst the volcanic hills, lush and fertile plains, and rich arable soil, the colonizers initiated a mercantile economic arrangement based on plantations and cash crops of coffee, tea, wheat, and vegetables, as well as gold and tin mining. These were brutally sustained through a large working class and forced labor. The introduction of wage labor, taxation, and commerce in general, meant profound changes for the Nande's traditional mode of economics (MacGaffey 1987).

In addition to the fiscal dimension, there were also changes made to customary Nande political practices. Tribal authorities were replaced or challenged by new political and judicial ones, which served to largely abolish the cohesive small-scale political units that had existed previously (Raeymaekers 2009a). Transnational mining and agricultural companies constituted new, disruptive forces in the area, and in effect represented government proxies in their imposition of a new economic regime (Raeymaekers 2009a). Indeed, the state was far from being the only authoritative actor in the area. In fact, authors such as Raeymaekers have argued that the Nande came to be ruled by a 'trinity' of actors: the international companies, the colonial administration, and the local Catholic and Protestant missions (Raeymaekers 2009a).

However, the Nande by no means passively accepted the imposition of these colonial authorities and practices, and in a fashion similar to their co-ethnics across the border, they openly and actively resisted them. Also like the Konjo, their attitude towards official governance brought them into disrepute with their overlords, resulting in their being relegated to a lowly, marginal status within the colonial state. Not surprisingly, then, North Kivu was passed-over in allocations of state resources. Socio-economic development of the sub-region accordingly progressed at a rate comparatively slower than other areas of the country. In terms of education, for example, it was almost wholly reliant on missionaries—the Assumptionist Fathers, to be exact, whose teachings were to a lower standard than those of the Jesuits or Marist Brothers of other locales (MacGaffey 1987). While Nande territory was largely pacified by 1925, resentment towards the state continued, and hostility was again openly expressed during World War Two (MacGaffey 1987). Rejection to colonial rule instigated the development of a strong meta-narrative of marginalization and discrimination that became an important part of the Nande identity. It was reinforced by other dynamics occurring in the area at the same time. In the 1920s and 1930s, for instance, when Rwandan immigrants were brought over, the Nande opposed any kind of integration or affiliation with them. A sense of 'Nandeness' took form, which was very much based on an attitude of self-containment from the colonizers, Rwandan settlers, and other neighboring communities (Jobbins 2008).

Out of this combination of marginalization by the state and subsequent decision to maintain a distance from both central authority and adjacent populations, the Nande interestingly turned to transborder trade conducted largely outside of state structures. For a marginalized people, this was a way to forge their own socio-political path (Kabamba 2008). Their ability to do this was aided by the presence of a border in their midst, as well as the lack of significant state presence. Even more important, however, was the territory's history dating back to pre-colonial times, of having been a space strategically tapped into regional trade (Raeymaekers and Jourdan 2009). Eastern Congo in general, had a tradition of having been a transit-zone for various regional trading routes, with the main ones including the following: north-eastern Congo to Uganda via Beni and Butembo; Bukavu to Kampala via Goma and Rutshuru; Uvira to Bujumbura; Uvira and Kalemie to Zambia or Tanzania via Kigoma.

North Kivu had historically served as a stop-over for Arab traders who were part of a commercial network stretching from Lake Tanganyika to the interior of Congo (Pennacini 2008). This was not the only pre-colonial economic system that helped to solidify the practice of long-distance trade in the area, however. Perhaps even more significant was the presence of a dynamic and expansive salt trade, the routes for which ran right through the heart of Nande territory. An item in high demand in the area due to its use not only in cooking, but in preserving meat and fish as well, for centuries the salt deposits in Lake Katwe had provided salt for the peoples of the Great Lakes region, including for those in the present-day countries of Congo, Uganda, Rwanda, and Burundi (Muranga 2008). While the commercial exchange of salt dated back to the 17th century, it was during colonialism that the Nande began to 'reclaim' their history and take the trade to a more organized and networked level.

Pivotal to the trade's development and intensification was the Nande-Konjo relationship. The following account from a Nande trader provides a fascinating insight into the nature and importance of this connection (and thus is worth quoting at length):

> During the colonial period some young people from my village went to Uganda to search for salt. Once they were settled there, they called others to join them for business. Thus, some six years before independence I was going to Uganda to sell my coffee. We were travelling on foot in a group of four or six carrying our 25 kg of merchandise on our heads. We travelled during the night, on foot,

through what is known today as the Virunga Valley. We avoided the Park guards. In our group we always had a former 'Park guard' who knew the road very well. In the morning we arrived at Mpondwe, a town on the border of Uganda. We were welcomed by people from our own village. They gave us accommodations and facilitated our contacts with potential buyers, usually the Hindi (Indo-Pakistanis) in the neighboring commercial center of Bwera. Contacts with the Hindi were made through their *Kapita* (headman) who was usually a Konjo (Kabamba 2008, 156).

A few aspects in particular stand out from this trader's story, the most obvious being the advantages that flowed from the ethnic interconnections across the border. Having this built-in and highly integrated relationship helped to facilitate the trade in numerous ways.[14] Albeit the border was a porous and nominally administered one, the Nande-Konjo ties were crucial in providing the connections and local knowledge necessary to traverse the boundary zone. These ties were dense, often even impenetrable, and in some areas like Lake Edward—which the Konjo and Nande regularly traversed—were unpoliceable by authorities (Stacey 2003). Second, the trader's story points to the historic origins of many of the region's current economic hubs, such as Mpondwe and Bwera. In fact, many of today's key Nande trading nodes had their beginnings with the salt trade. For example, the socio-economic center of Nande life, Butembo, originally developed as a stop-over village called Lusambo, for salt traders passing through with their caravans. The city grew substantially from 1928 onwards, when it became the administrative center for the *Minière des Grands Lacs*—a company with the mineral concession rights to that area of North Kivu. The historicity of these economic hubs again highlights the role of geography in the dynamics of the borderland: their strategically advantageous placement south of the Rwenzori mountains, providing an easy access point for people to cross the border for trading purposes, contributed to the development of Mpondwe and Bwera as lively economic centers.

Perhaps what most interestingly stands out, though, is the informal nature of much of the practice. The trader's description of having to use local guides to traverse the boundary at night, for example, is exemplary of this. It relates to what Raeymaekers has termed the 'contested' nature of borders. While this trade had been going on for centuries, the imposition of a border suddenly made it highly taxable, very profitable, and usually illegal (Raeymaekers 2009b). But despite the dangers of the business—including the boundary zone being rife with adventurers, entrepreneurs, criminals, and combatants of some form or another—it became a prestigious one. Travelling in caravans of fifty to sixty people, having to traverse an official border, and crossing the hazardous Semliki plain, often resulted in a trader acquiring a higher social and economic status, and perhaps even a bride (Kabamba 2008).

The confluence of the above dynamics ultimately resulted in this networked economy becoming a defining feature of Nande life. For one thing, it provided livelihoods for a significant proportion of the population. Bright's (1909, 146–49) description of the Uganda-Congo border area in the early 1900s helps to shed some light on this:

> The inhabitants have no means of livelihood except by trading. Salt is carried in canoes from Katwe, and sold to the natives at marketing prices on the lake-shores. The salt belongs to the main-land people, but the islanders act as merchants, and charge commission, which is paid in food [. . .] Commerce in hides is carried on, the skins of cattle and goats being obtained from natives by purchase or barter and conveyed to Buganda for sale. A considerable carrying trade occupies a proportion of the natives of Toro. Ivory and rubber from the Congo, small quantities of the same from British territory, are constantly being conveyed to Buganda for shipment by the lake steamers to the Uganda railway.

Yet, perhaps more significantly, it strengthened the Nande identity (the sense of 'Nandeness'). Excluded from state development initiatives and exploited by the colonial economic system and a predatory state, networked transborder trade was a means through which they could assertively express their anti-stateness, and acquire a space outside of state structures. In a sense it represented a co-opting of their marginal status, and a forging of their space into one that was not peripheral, but rather *purposely* in opposition to, and distinct from, the state.

POST-COLONIAL PERIPHERALITY IN EASTERN CONGO

The signs of a burgeoning borderland character were thus apparent by the time of Congolese independence in 1960. There was not only a strong anti-state mentality defining the micro-region, but an overall existence directed eastwards towards the Konjo and western Uganda, and outwards towards the wider Great Lakes region and beyond. Furthermore, there was a modus operandi oriented around a networked trading economy external to state structures. In the post-colonial era the nascent borderland character of this space grew stronger and more pronounced.

Understanding its progression and development, however, first requires a comprehension of the nature of the post-independence Congolese state. Jason Stearns (2011, 126) captures the essence of the state in the following:

It is this legacy of institutional weakness that for many Congolese is almost as depressing as their physical suffering. Since the 1970s until today, the Congolese state has not had an effective army, administration, or judiciary, nor have its leaders been interested in creating strong institutions. Instead, they have seen the state apparatus as a threat, to be kept weak so as to better manipulate it. This has left a bitter Congolese paradox: a state that is everywhere and oppressive but that is defunct and dysfunctional.

The country's post-1960 civil history is indeed one of extreme political mismanagement. Both Presidents Joseph Mobutu and Joseph Kabila were more concerned with creating a system of patronage and maintaining power, than building a functioning state (Stearns 2011). Strong public institutions—a capable army, an independent judiciary, and a functioning parliament—were viewed as threats and kept down at all costs. In fact, what is striking is the degree to which post-independence Congolese political systems and practices continued—and even mirrored—those of the pre-independence era: the purpose of political rule was in effect to funnel wealth to the rulers, at the expense of civilians, whilst simultaneously failing to protect or represent them. While a comprehensive look into the post-independence politics in the Congo falls outside of the relevant scope here, for the purposes of this chapter, what is worth noting is the *complexity* of state weakness in the Congo. Not only did it geographically vary greatly across the country, with the most notable difference being between peripheral border zones and the Kinshasa region, as will be discussed below, but extreme state weakness did not necessarily translate into total state collapse or a complete absence of the state. Indeed, to claim state failure would be akin to (wrongly) saying that at one point in time the state was actually a fully functional one. In this respect, state weakness and the preclusion of societal governance do not necessarily have to go hand-in-hand, and in many places there is a mediated zone where processes of adaptation and accommodation come to the fore. In these situations, new kinds of authority and domination may arise, and 'mediated governance' and 'a new sense of order' can evolve in the midst of otherwise anarchy and chaos (Raeymaekers 2007).[15] Where this dynamic arose most prominently in the Congo, was the Nande-dominated portion of (what is today known as) North Kivu.[16]

Like western Uganda, North Kivu's marginality had a significant geographic dimension. The province is physically one of the furthest away areas of Congo from the capital. Indeed, not only is the east linguistically and economically distinct from Kinshasa, but there is more than 600 miles between them (Garrett and Seay 2011). With air travel the only feasible option for visiting the capital, the vast majority of eastern Congolese never step foot in Kinshasa. Further contributing to the geographical dimension of North Kivu's marginalization is its physical position as flanked on either side by the dense Congolese rainforest to the west, and the steep, western side of the Rwenzori mountains to the east. Compounding this is its rugged terrain, making the region difficult to access from outside areas. It existed, in this sense, as a sort of island on the edge of the state; the same sort of socio-economic ties that would contribute to development in other areas of the country were unavailable to this space. But North Kivu was arguably also the most politically marginalized area by the center in the post-colonial period, and had traditionally the most tumultuous relationship with the capital (Hale 2010). Ever since independence and the beginning of various nationalism projects—which the east responded to with lackluster interest, to say the least—Mobutu held the Kivus in suspicion and distrust. In line with the east's rejection of central government during colonialism, there was a continuation of working and existing outside of state arrangements after independence.

The structure of this relationship was a mutually reinforcing one, as with greater disengagement from the state, came a correspondingly increased policy of marginalization from the center. For example, top political positions would be granted to the Banyarwanda Tutsi, and control of the economic sector would be strictly regulated via Mobutist elites. In other words, as the area found itself progressively excluded from the state's political scene, with few opportunities for participating in national decision-making, and the recipient of extremely low levels of investment due to the majority of funds being funnelled to Kinshasa, Lubumbashi, and Kisangani, at the same time it also became more independent and distanced from the state through its own self-governing societal structures (MacGaffey 1987).

Thus, while resentment towards Kinshasa grew, there nonetheless arose new opportunities for self-government, grassroots-propelled development initiatives, and most of all—and as the next section will discuss—expansion of their informal economic practices. The sense of detachment from, and disrespect for, the parasitic center encouraged the Nande to look inwards towards their own community, to distrust outsiders (most notably, the Rwandophone population also residing in North Kivu), and to ultimately build a self-sustaining community based on a sense of Nandeness. This included, of course, their Konjo co-ethnics across the border. The center of this community came to be the city of Butembo: a metropolis made up of over 90 percent Nande, and conveniently located just 85 miles or so from the Ugandan border. While the actual provincial capital and administrative center of North Kivu was Goma, this was a city considered too affiliated with Kinshasa and too remote from the Nande-Konjo sphere to be of great importance to them. Butembo thus became not only a thriving commercial and trading center, but also the arbiter of what would have traditionally been state functions (Interview Twenty-Four). It should be noted that Beni was another city important for Nande governance. Essentially, Butembo could be considered the commercial center, while Beni the more political hub.

The Nande essentially held the monopoly of violence in the region, and the Rwenzori area became a conducive one to the organization of rebellion (Jourdan 2008). For one thing, its continual lack of post-conflict disarmament translated into a perpetually armed and militarized space, where violent elements were usually available for mobilization. Indeed, Debos' concept of transnational combatants, with identities structured around their livelihood as fighters, was very much a feature of eastern Congo. In terms of the Nande in particular, the mobilization of violence to safeguard their community was a practice commonly resorted to. Similar to borderland groups in other locales, they preferred to take the law into their own hands, rather than rely on state avenues. For example, relations between the Nande and Tutsi, and between the Nande and Rwandans in general, have historically been a source of great political tension in North Kivu. And thus in 1993, Nande militia groups the Simba, Bahandule, and Kasindiens, were called upon by Nande chiefs to defend Nande land from Congolese Tutsi pastoralists moving into Lubero territory (Raeymaekers 2007; Kabamba 2008).

It was not only Nande leaders that became affiliated in one way or another with armed resistance movements, but other members of the Nande (and Konjo) community as well. In fact, as the economic trading system of the Nande became more established, they would make use of violent movements such as the Kasindiens to protect their cross-border illicit goods and activities (Raeymaekers 2007). Rwenzururu rebels were also attracted to this business of taxing and providing protection for smugglers. And of course, as discussed previously, this area of North Kivu was periodically the nerve center for leaders and fighters of the RM, and later served as the home base for NALU. Thus, while eastern Congo has often been likened to an anarchic, powerless vacuum, Raeymaekers and Luca Jourdan (2009, 319) importantly point out that, in actuality, "some new institutions have emerged among the frontier populations who live in this space, especially among the Banande and the Bakonjo. These new institutions have served both as a substitute for, and as a protective buffer against, dominant institutions that historically have tried to absorb them." The anti-state and liminal qualities of this space thus helped to inspire interesting developments.

A CONSOLIDATED BORDERLAND IN EASTERN CONGO

It was the Nande's unique economic practices that were most illustrious of their response to the Congolese state. Due to their lack of education or political clout during colonialism, upon independence they faced an inability to move into the bureaucracy or professional sphere, and an underrepresentation on the national political scene (MacGaffey 1987). But the Nande chose to make the most of their position in the post-colonial period, and continued to work on creating their own space beyond state structures. Thus, the indigenous mode of economic development that had taken off during colonialism was continued into the post-colonial era as a means through which to 'fend for themselves.' In essence, their experience of marginalization encouraged their involvement in the 'informal' economy (Kabamba 2008). Indeed, it inspired the trading networks to develop their own norms, values, and practices that took distinct advantage of the lack of formal rules (Jobbins 2008). It is important to note that this economic system in fact represented much more than a mere coping economy or means of survival. As will be discussed below, it became a way of acquiring (often great amounts of) wealth, bringing development to their micro-region, and ultimately asserting their own political and socio-economic complex.

Nande trading networks during colonialism had mainly been small-scale and subsistence in nature. They were carried-out largely between North Kivu's urban centers and the surrounding countryside, as well as across the border into Uganda. But with independence there was growing insecurity in the rural areas, withering state control, and an increasingly porous Uganda-Congo border. All of these dynamics presented the Nande with an augmented opportunity to take their colonial trading practices to heightened levels and new markets. First of all, in terms of the rural insecurity, Raeymaekers (2009a, 14) argues that it "produced a favorable climate for inland trading, albeit indirectly: due to repeated attacks by armed bandits and local militias in the countryside, the urban population in North Kivu rocketed, which resulted in growing levels of subsistence trade and the opening of several boutiques (*kabutike*) in the cities." The Mulele rebellion, for instance, led to the rural population being blocked from food and hence moving into urban centers, as well as many food staples becoming unaffordable. In terms of market opportunities, then, the towns became increasingly appealing for peasant traders.

Consequently, there developed a group of commercial middlemen who transported cash and food crops from the productive countryside, to Kivu's deprived urban centers of Beni and Butembo (Raeymaekers 2007). The Nande were soon extending their practices to Kisangani and Kinshasa as well. With this expansion they were able to import products not available in North Kivu, and export those they were comparatively well-endowed with such as beans, potatoes, onions, leeks, cabbages, and carrots (MacGaffey 1987). In fact, the Nande had the monopoly on both the transport of vegetables from the North Kivu area to Kisangani by 1979, as well as the shipping of beans to Kinshasa (MacGaffey 1987). The Lubero highland's *Légumes Sans*

Frontières company sent cabbages and onions weekly to Kinshasa, and by the 1980s vegetables were being dispatched on a bi-weekly basis to the capital via airplane (Raeymaekers 2007). With the extreme lack of infrastructure in the east, the traders often had to be creative and courageous in their trading ventures. The road from Beni to Kisangani, for example, was a mere bicycle path by the 1990s; large quantities of traded products were thus shuttled back and forth via *toleka* (bicycle travelers) (Raeymaekers 2007).

Much of their trade, though, was directed outwards to Uganda, and often on from Uganda to other east African markets. This eastern Congo-western Uganda route was very much at the heart of the Nande trade network. Indeed, Nande and Konjo territory together touted a political climate ripe for cross-border smuggling, hence the constant ferrying of agricultural and other products across the border to be sold in markets Uganda-side. It was given a strong stimulus in the early 1960s when some Baptists from the eastern Congolese city of Katwa were expelled to Uganda's Konjo territory. There they put their Nande adaptability and entrepreneurial ethic to work, enmeshing themselves in the trade industry, and acquiring expertise in the business of sending products back to North Kivu to be sold there. In 1966–1967 they returned home, and with their firmly established Konjo economic ties, became highly adept at setting-up successful cross-border trading businesses (MacGaffey 1987). The system was given increased impetus in the 1970s, when the turmoil of the Ugandan economy—a result of Idi Amin's reign—created a keen demand for North Kivu's agricultural products.

There were other reasons, though, for why this space represented such a favorable smuggling environment, with North Kivu arguably being Congo's *most* lucrative smuggling arena (Vwakyanakazi 1991). In addition to the proximity to the Uganda-Congo border, the short distances to the borders of Rwanda, Kenya, and Sudan were also important. Moreover, the isolation of the area and limited breadth of employment opportunities encouraged innovative developments in the informal economy (MacGaffey 1991). The towns of eastern Congo and western Uganda became increasingly oriented around the trade industry, as well as profoundly interconnected with each other. The Nande economic hub during colonial times, Butembo, retained its position in the post-colonial era as the key node connecting Ugandan markets with Congo's.[17] Indeed, it became a veritable merchandise warehouse and marketplace.[18] The Ugandan equivalent to Butembo (though on a smaller scale), and capital of the Konjo people, was Kasese. It developed into a significant commercial center as well, and according to Muranga (2008, 342), was "the most important connecting city between Congo and Uganda in particular and East Africa as a whole, as well as being a transit point for trade from Arabia, India and the rest of Asia. Many goods lorries and trucks loaded with containers destined for Congo enter Africa via the port of Mombasa in Kenya and pause at Kasese." Different from Butembo, though, was Kasese's multi-ethnic character. This was mainly due to its proximity to the Kilembe Copper Mines, which drew in people from across the country to work there.

With the expansion and routinization of trade, due to growing populations and heightened opportunities for profit, traders started to invest in the necessary infrastructure to support this growth, such as the building of roads and purchasing of transport equipment. Indeed, from the 1960s onwards, the migration of Nande from rural to urban areas was significant. Butembo's population went from 11,189 in 1958 to 22,236 only eight years later (Kabamba 2008). The investments encouraged local traders to expand to new routes, and gave impetus to the more experienced and wealthier Nande traders to solidify their monopolization of the northern trade routes (Hale 2010). Not only did this lead to greater control of trade throughout the North Kivu area, but it also instigated a move into more distant markets. This went well beyond the east African economic spheres of Kampala, Nairobi, and Dar es Salaam, but stretched to Asia (Hong Kong, Taiwan, Singapore, Thailand, and Indonesia) and the Middle East (Dubai). By the 1980s, the United States (US) dollar was even being used in the Kivus so as to facilitate this transnational trade expansion. Beginning in the mid-1980s, Nande traders decided to visit these foreign markets for themselves. When one set-up an exporting office in Hong Kong to better facilitate the importing of various household and business goods, others soon followed suit (Raeymaekers 2007).

While some of the Nande's transnational economic activities were legal, significant proportions were unrecorded, and this was especially the case with products such as coffee and gold. In 1985–1986, for example, the percentage of local coffee production being clandestinely smuggled out of the country was estimated to be as high as 60 percent (Vlassenroot and Romkema 2002). Uganda's more favorable export regime meant that if eastern Congolese coffee could be smuggled into Uganda and passed-off as Ugandan coffee, it could then be sold on international markets and command a much higher price. This scenario applied to a range of other eastern Congolese products as well, such as vanilla and cacao. According to one Congolese public official at the time, "almost everything produced or sold in North Kivu [was] smuggled into Rwanda and Uganda: coffee, vegetables, palm oil, gold, *papaine* (papaya latex), cattle and goat skins, and small merchandise of all kinds" (Callaghy 1984, 284). The Nande-Konjo relationship was pivotal to this smuggling industry, especially with regards to coffee. Authorities largely had their hands tied when it came to curbing the rampant coffee smuggling, as the product would be moved via non-traversable, unguarded mountain paths—areas of the Rwenzoris that essentially were only known and navigated by the Nande and Konjo (Syahuka-Muhindo 1991). Nevertheless, oftentimes unrecorded trade traversed identical routes to the recorded merchandise. It is interesting to note that just as an economic middle class was taking form amongst the Nande, the same was happening within the Konjo community. Many of them included former Rwenzururu Kingdom leaders who had taken up the coffee trade (Syahuka-Muhindo 1991).

However, it is important to distinguish what exactly is implied by the expressions illegal, informal, parallel, unrecorded, second economy, and so on. According to the Nande, their trading system did not necessarily fit any of those one-dimensional terms: their activities were a logical, if not essential, response to a predatory state. Kabamba explains this rationale as the following: "Nande traders never qualified their activity as being 'illegal.' They argue that 'legibility' and 'illegibility,' 'legality' or 'illegality' conjure the false impression of a state functioning 'normally.' The Zairian state failed its people, they reason, so the notion of 'illegality' no longer applied because there was and still is no working state" (Kabamba 2008). And for that reason, trade was often conducted in such a way as to evade taxation.

It is important to recognize that unlike the Konjo, the Nande did not seek full autonomy from the state. They needed the state in order for their trading system to thrive—they just needed it to be as weak and distant as possible. A dysfunctional and politically weak state was considered a favorable environment for the Nande's business activities (Vwakyanakazi 1991). There are several other facets of the trade that helped to transform it into such a dense economic network. One aspect concerned what various scholars on the subject have termed the 'Nande trust network.' MacGaffey and Bazenguissa-Ganga (1999, 180) make the important distinction between 'structured' and 'instrumental' networks: the former "are permanent" and "operate over time for the trade of specific commodities," while the later are "activated only sporadically to further the interests of individual traders from a latent set of relationships." Although structured long-distance trade networks are most common in West Africa, the Nande's trading system resembled this type. The Nande used tightknit family, friendship, and most of all kinship, networks of trust, to provide them with unique trading opportunities in a country where doing business was unreliable and unpredictable (MacGaffey 1987). In an atmosphere where business contracts were difficult to enforce, or were simply non-existent, these connections of trust were a means to ensure a deal. While the network was highly exclusive and restrictive, the Konjo were still an important part of it, and in fact considered to be integral to the system.

This cohesive sense of Nandeness not only helped to bind the traders together, including those outside of the eastern Congo-western Uganda arena, but it also helped to further generate a community mentality. And this was encouraged by the continued neglect from the central government, and widening disconnect between North Kivu and Kinshasa. This disconnect was not only in the political sphere, but had a cultural element as well, and in particular a religious dimension. The impact of the Roman Catholic Church in eastern Congo has been enormous, stretching back to the colonial era. The pioneering Catholic missionaries in eastern Congo—the 'White Fathers'—established outposts in the region spanning from Lake Tanganyika in the north to Lake Albert. This occurred some fifteen years before the Congo Free State did such activities in 1888, meaning that the Catholic Church was present in eastern Congo long before any real state influence. The close allegiance between the Catholic missions with King Leopold's Congo was consolidated in 1906 with a treaty between the Free State (and from 1908, its successor the Belgian Congo) and the Vatican, in which the colonial state agreed to promote the spread of Catholicism in the country. The Belgian colonial state then authorized and subsidized primarily Belgian Roman Catholic missions to establish schools, hospitals, and other infrastructure throughout the country. The colonial state viewed the Catholic Church's function as one which would accomplish the 'civilization' of the Belgian colony, whereas the Church viewed its function as primarily evangelization. The two goals were complementary; hence, the White Fathers were drawn into the colonial state's orbit and for over half a century until independence in 1960 the Church essentially fulfilled the functions of the state in the region.[19]

On 9 April 1934 the region of Butembo-Beni was made a mission *sui iuris*—a rare type of Catholic mission established in often isolated or remote areas with low numbers of Catholics. It was elevated to the status of Diocese of Beni in Congo on 10 November 1959 and renamed Diocese of Butembo-Beni on 7 February 1967. Since 1998 it has been under the spiritual authority of Bishop Melchisédec Sikuli Paluku. Post-independence, the exceptionally close affiliation between the Catholic Church and the state that had existed during the colonial period has largely been reversed, with the Church coming to represent one of the state's main critics. Interestingly, however, the decline of the Congo state since independence coupled with the remoteness of Butembo has caused the Church to maintain, and even increase, its profound importance in the region. As Bishop Melchisédec has been quoted saying with regard to Butembo, "The indifference of the state has led the Catholic Church to take on a special role [. . .] We are 1500 miles from the capital. As the government is doing nothing here, we must take care of ourselves. We do not receive any help" (Oliver 2021). Indeed, as Butembo is 90 percent populated by the Nande, the Catholic Church has clearly taken on a profound importance in their lives.[20]

Returning to the Kinshasa–North Kivu disconnect, the capital came to be increasingly perceived as a center of 'decadence and predation,' while Nande hubs like Butembo developed more of a 'globalized' culture due to the close interactions with both the translocal level and also global markets

(Raeymaekers 2007). In light of such an unwilling and incapable government, a sort of self-help and mutual assistance system developed. The border came to be regarded by the community as their most important 'resource,' and the key to their development. Compounded by the traders' close ties to the rest of the Nande community, a scenario evolved whereby the Nande economic elite took on many of the functions usually considered the preserve of the state. Although a great deal of their trading system was oriented eastwards and outwards, it was nevertheless more than just a productive economy, but a distributive one as well.

While some of the traders accumulated quite significant amounts of wealth, there was nevertheless the mentality that a great deal of this should be invested back into the community, especially in order to counteract the damage done by the Congolese state's patrimonial system (Raeymaekers 2007). Some of the functions they took on included repairing roads, instituting a modest banking system, and contributing towards health care and education. More generally, the trading system stimulated a modest industrialization process in the area. Their banking practices in particular highlighted the great extent to which the Nande were inventing their own political community outside of state structures. At the first level, Nande businessmen would provide interest-free loans to each other; if something more extensive was required, there were unofficial lending institutions to go to; in the case of the borrower defaulting on a loan, informal courts were in operation to deal with the dispute; and finally, if punishment needed to be exacted, there were a range of measures from which to implement (MacGaffey 1987). Ultimately, these developments led to the senior Nande traders acquiring the status of *personnes de références*————or 'village lords'—with responsibilities of providing advice, mediating business disputes, and essentially being power brokers (Raeymaekers 2007).

Perhaps the dimension of their trade that was most crucial to its successful development and consolidation, was the built-in Uganda connection. The entire enterprise in many respects was predicated on the dense interconnections with the Konjo across the border, and the fact that the Konjo were incorporated into the Nande identity. The cross-border connection facilitated the day-to-day running of the trade: once across the border, for example, the Konjo were there to advise Nande traders on security, where to store goods, arrange taxi services, provide contacts and accommodation, inform them on the latest merchandise trends and prices, and so on. But it was not only in the area immediately across the border where the Konjo proved vital. Konjo intermediaries in Kampala, where a great deal of manufactured products were purchased, and which in general served as the most important transit center in the Nande's regional and international trade system, were pivotal as well.

Thus, the Nande trading system represented much more than simply a successful business enterprise. It was the means through which the population could take their marginality, and contribute to the formation of a new political and socio-economic complex. In fact, it was the means through which the Congolese dimension of this Rwenzori zone consolidated its borderland character, including a networked political, social, and economic cross-border trading system. This space undoubtedly exhibited all of the traditional features of a borderland: distanced geographically and politically from the center, strongly characterized by its proximity to the state border, and part of a dynamic center-periphery relationship. Indeed, it exemplified a highly anti-state, liminal, and networked borderland area, and displayed a great many of the borderland characteristics described in Chapter Two. Politically, the Nande were resistant to central authority to such a degree that they had largely removed themselves from state structures. Socially, the Nande drew upon a strong frontier mentality: their identity was very much intertwined with the border, and they were far more culturally connected to the Konjo than to those westwards in the rest of Congo. And economically, of course, the Nande helped to shape that area of eastern Congo into a space defined by its intimate relationship with transnational commerce.

This chapter explored the historical paths and development of the Konjo in western Uganda and the Nande in eastern Congo, in order to show how the Rwenzori region over time—especially from the colonial period to the early 1990s—developed into a distinct political and socio-economic complex, and ultimately consolidated its status as a full-fledged borderland. Both sides of the border experienced profound marginalization by their national government(s), but they were by no means marginal spaces. Furthermore, although western Uganda and eastern Congo each experienced different trajectories, and responded in varying ways to their lived experiences with marginalization, they remained intimately connected to each other. In fact, each was bounded and conditioned by its experience of interacting with the other. Neither one's 'exit' from the state—which for the Konjo represented their quest for a Rwenzururu Kingdom, and for the Nande occurred via their development of a transnational trade system—would have been possible without the other, and without mobilization and utilization of the political, social, and economic cross-border networks that so densely traversed the micro-region. In essence then, by the time the ADF were established, the Rwenzori area of western Uganda and eastern Congo was profoundly integrated; but more importantly, it was a highly anti-state and liminal borderland. As Chapters Four, Five, and Six will discuss, not only are the undercurrents behind the ADF's formation closely tied-up with the development and subsequent dynamics of the borderland itself, but their resiliency very much relied upon their embeddedness into this borderland milieu, and ultimately their extrapolation and manipulation of this space's borderland resources.

NOTES

1. For more on the history of western Uganda during this time period, see Steinhart (1999) and Struck (1910).

2. For a fascinating discussion on the continued similarities between Konjo and Nande culture, specifically in music and dance, see Facci (2009).

3. Arthur Syahuka-Muhindo (2008, 48) argues that the Semliki Valley "was not only a corridor for both population movements and the spread of epidemic disease, but also a melting pot in which new societies were formed."

4. According to Cecilia Pennacini (2008, 68), in this region it was common for groups to keep their own cultural identity, but also to be exposed to other ethnicities: "The fluidity of the borders certainly allowed numerous cultural exchanges, but at the same time the groups living in the Semliki Valley and on the slopes of the surrounding mountains defended their specific ethnic identity against the expansion of the kingdoms."

5. The neighboring Amba did not settle as high into the Rwenzori Mountains as the Konjo, but rather occupied—as Bernhard Struck noted in 1910 (277)—"the land between the middle course of the Semliki and the northern and north-western slopes of Ruwenzori."

6. It is important to point out that the Toro leaders were very much under the power of the British colonialists; Toro was by no means an independent entity with sovereign rights of its own.

7. Perhaps this should not be surprising, considering Nelson Kasfir's (1976, 130) remark that "the mountains have never been brought under effective administrative control, and Bwamba county (home of the Bamba) was not opened up until a road was completed through the foothills in 1938."

8. What should also be mentioned here, given the amount of attention this topic receives in western Uganda itself, is the difference in appearance between the Konjo and Toro. As Tom Stacey (2003, 15) describes, "they [the Konjo] are, on average, stocky, notably sturdy, and significantly shorter than the plainland tribes on the east side of the mountains—Banyankole, Banyoro, Batoro—who are tall and elegant, especially among the lordly castes."

9. Pennacini (2008, 83) argues, "Their resistance towards the imposed system must be seen in relation to the introduction of a monetary economy—beginning to be spread also in relation to the taxes introduced by the British—which the Bakonjo were reluctant to enter."

10. For more on the relationship between the center and various peripheries in Uganda, see Southall (1996) and Van Acker (2000).

11. As Kamukama Dixon (2004, 39) explains, "No particular effort was made [during colonialism, and with the system of indirect rule] to create a spirit of nationalism

among Ugandans, but nonetheless a nation known as Uganda was strongly held together by colonialism."

12. Surveys as recent as 2000 have found that 85 percent of the Konjo supported the installation of the monarchy, 12 percent were opposed, and 3 percent were ambivalent. The Kingdom was not officially recognized by the Ugandan government until October 2009 (Albere 2007, 9; Bollingtoft 2006).

13. It is important to recognize that the center-periphery divide in Uganda has by no means simply remained static. Rather, there have been shifts over time, under different regimes. Under Museveni's rule, central south-west Uganda has seen more incorporation into the center, but the rest of the west has undoubtedly experienced a continuation of its historic neglect.

14. For an interesting discussion on the relationship between cross-border ethnic interconnections and trade (including pre-colonial trade patterns) in the Great Lakes area, see Titeca (2009a).

15. Raeymaekers (2009b, 59) explains the relevance of mediated governance for the Congo: "'Mediated' statehood probably best describes this current status of the Congolese political system, in which several governable spaces coexist in semi-autonomous fashion."

16. While at the time of independence the Kivu region was one administrative unit, it subsequently in the 1980s became decentralized into three provinces: North Kivu, South Kivu, and Maniema.

17. Butembo was by no means the sole city to have deep market connections in this sense; another pivotal urban hub was Bunia, located in today's Ituri province, to the west of Lake Albert. The Belgians' significant use of the lake to receive goods created an east-west cross-border trade corridor that continues to this day.

18. According to Patience Kabamba, 60 percent of North Kivu's traders are Nande, while 99.9 percent of Butembo's traders are Nande (Kabamba 2008).

19. See Northrup 1998 for more on this subject.

20. The economic success and social cohesion of the Nande in Butembo has been attributed by *some* scholars to the role of religion during the colonial period, in which the Nande were heavily influenced by their contact with western Catholic missionaries (both Belgian and British, from each side of the border) who nurtured a so-called 'Weberian Protestant Work Ethic' within the culture. Jack E. Nelson (1982), for example, has argued that the influence of the Catholic missions helped to instill within the Nande an 'entrepreneurial spirit' and ethic of hard work and self-reliance which was only strengthened with the relative decline of the state.

Chapter 4

Formations and Consolidations: The ADF 1996–2003

As Chapter Three discussed, by the time the ADF launched their first attack in the fall of 1996, the Rwenzori area was a profoundly anti-state and liminal borderland. This chapter will build upon the argument set forth in the introduction to show how the rebels used the borderland features of anti-stateness and liminality to their advantage. More specifically, it will look at those characteristics of conflict-affected borderlands discussed in Chapter Two—politically a tradition of resistance against central authority, socially the predominance of a border identity, and economically a system built around independent cross-border trade—and how the ADF manipulated and extrapolated from these. While the rebels faced serious challenges throughout this time period (especially in 2002 and early 2003), their embeddedness in the borderland provided them with unusual resiliency.

To examine the ADF and the conflict they waged between 1996–2003, Chapter Four will consider three dimensions of rebel group behavior and activity: recruitment, retention, and organization; material resources; and the execution of violence. The first enquires into policies and practices related to the acquisition and organization of human resources. The second considers the ADF's financial strategies, as well as methods of procuring and retaining weapons, equipment, foodstuffs, and importantly, territory/land. By 'territory/land,' this refers to the ADF's means of acquiring territory for living quarters and bases, but also for the pursuit of other land-related material resources, such as those concerning agriculture, trading, the taxing of civilians, and so on. And finally, the last major section of this chapter looks at the execution of violence by considering the various military strategies and tactics used by the ADF against their enemies, including methods of attack, civilian collaboration, and the functions of violence. At the beginning of each of these three sections will be a discussion of the most prominent explanations of that particular issue (what this book terms 'misguided explanations'). These discussions will look at why such explanations—which are overwhelmingly analyzed at the macro level and concerned with the national and regional levels of analysis—are insufficient, or fail to tell the whole story behind ADF resilience. The rest of each section will then apply a borderland perspective, and ultimately demonstrate why understanding the ADF's resiliency is only possible if explained as part of borderland phenomena.

PART I: RECRUITMENT, RETENTION, AND ORGANIZATION

MISGUIDED EXPLANATIONS OF THE ADF'S RECRUITMENT, RETENTION, AND ORGANIZATION

The Allied Democratic Forces were officially established after a September 1995 meeting between Ugandan extremist Muslim leaders and the heads of NALU in eastern Congo. During this meeting an alliance was concluded, and initial details such as the organization of training camps and military supply lines were established (Titeca and Vlassenroot 2012). They launched their first attack in November 1996, when they invaded western Uganda from eastern Congo. Ugandan newspapers immediately after this initial invasion reported, "Ugandan dissidents who invaded the country at Mpondwe border post in Kasese last week were to install Jamil Mukulu as President of the Islamic State after ousting the Museveni government" (Sserwanga and Nzinjah 1996b). Those associated with the Ugandan regime appeared especially keen to highlight the ADF's Islamic terrorist tendencies. A UPDF Brigade Commander at the time of the first attack declared, "The invaders were purely Tabliqs. They were fighting a Jihad" (Sserwanga and Nzinjah 1996b). "ADF rebels are collaborating with Sudan to make Uganda an Islamic state," said Uganda's Minister of Health, Dr. Crispus Kiyonga (Karugaba 1997). A former Security Adviser to President Museveni, Amama Mbabazi, claimed, "Khartoum's plan is to destabilize the region to prepare the ground for the spread of Islamic fundamentalism and Arabism" (Prunier 2004, 379). And a local government official in western Uganda used the terms "fundamentalists" and "Jihadists" to describe the group, while an official working for the Kampala amnesty office explained their goal as "fighting to take-over the government through Jihad, and then rule by a code of Islam" (Interview Thirteen; Interview Thirty-One).

These interpretations of the ADF demonstrate a belief that the group was (1) composed principally of Islamic terrorists, (2) strongly backed by Sudan, and (3) had the sole objective of taking down the Museveni regime. This particular understanding of the ADF's 1996–2003 period was prevalent not only in the Ugandan press and government, but also popular within academia, NGOs, and some of those civilians affected by the violence. Andrew McGregor (2007, 1), for example, described the ADF as "a little known group of Islamist radicals," and Moshe Terdman (2006) argued, "The ADF has few links with western Uganda—its leaders come from areas in central Uganda with strong Islamic communities such as Iganga, Masaka and Kampala itself." Writing in 2001, African Rights (2001, 1) stated, "The ADF has at its core the followers of an Islamic sect, the Salaf Tabliq, who claim that Muslims are marginalized by the Ugandan government." Local NGOs that had operated in the ADF-affected areas of western Uganda understood the conflict in similar terms, namely as having to do with Islamic extremism. A community leader in Kabarole district and sub-dean of the local cathedral, who sheltered hundreds of internally displaced persons [IDPs] in the late 1990s, explained that although believing the ADF had support from foreign actors, "local people knew this group as a Ugandan terrorist force" (Interview Forty-One).

This chapter will demonstrate that the ADF and their operations between 1996–2003 cannot be explained with sole reference to explanations reliant on state-centric concepts of proxy war or the influence of transnational forces of Islamic terrorism. Nevertheless, it is of course necessary to recognize their role in the ADF's recruitment, retention, and organization practices. An important component of the original ADF was a group of disaffected Muslims from Kampala, and a significant recruitment network in the years to follow was one centered around Islamic connections throughout the region. The roots of this Islamic angle to the ADF conflict stemmed from a perception on the part of Uganda's Muslims that they had historically been socially and economically marginalized (Kananura 2005).[1] In the early 1980s this perception was translated into action when, partly inspired by militant Islam, the Tabliq Youth Movement was formed.[2] The Tabliqs became increasingly political throughout the 1980s, announcing their goal of transforming Uganda into an Islamic state after the Ugandan Supreme Court moved in favor of a rival and more mainstream Islamic faction (Nantulya 2001).[3]

With support from the Sudanese embassy in Kampala their numbers, militancy, and radicalism grew (Romkema 2007). In 1991 President Museveni imprisoned several members after a round of street clashes and violence in the capital.[4] Upon their release two years later, the Tabliqs fled and set-up camp in Buseruka in Hoima district, near Lake Albert. But for a variety of reasons—including a lack of support from the local populace, and a tradition in urban violence and thus unfamiliarity with rural terrain—Buseruka was not a strategic location to launch their struggle from (Interview Eleven). Their main military training camp there was overrun by the UPDF in 1995, and having still at that time been in training mode, they suffered extensive casualties. The survivors subsequently fled yet again, this time ending-up in Bunia, eastern Congo. There they came into contact with a variety of forces, including the Sudanese Army Security Services, who were using the Bunia airfield to ferry supplies to the Ugandan West Nile Bank Front (WNBF) rebel group and Rwandan *Interahamwe* (Prunier 2004). It should be noted that Kampala and Khartoum had long been fighting what some termed an 'undeclared war' against each other, and Sudan's support for anti-Museveni rebels can be seen as a balancing act to counter Uganda's backing of the Sudan People's Liberation Army.

The dominant understanding of the ADF, which sees the Islamic element as being representative of the group, ascribes the Sudanese angle a great deal of weight in terms of the ADF's origins. It credits Sudan with actually *creating* the ADF through strategically linking the Tabliqs to an "unlikely blend of former Hutu militiamen [. . .] and disaffected tribesmen," so as to provide them with tangible links to the Rwenzori terrain (Prunier 1997, 19). With regards to what he calls the "Khartoum-sponsored" origins of the ADF, Prunier (2009, 87) argues, "the key element in that union was that the Sudanese operators soon realized that without a good peasant grounding in local realities, the guerrillas [the Tabliqs] would be defeated again. This is why they worked at incorporating the guerrilla force into the remnants of NALU, the old Bakonjo Rwenzururu movement of the Ruwenzori Mountains."

There is no doubt that Sudan provided important support in the formative stages of the ADF, elevating the status of the Tabliq faction within the group, and thereby also the religious dimension. Numerous testimonies from former ADF combatants (both willing and forced recruits) described, for example, the religious indoctrination that took place in some of the camps during this time, and the forced conversion of those members who were not originally Muslim. One former ADF captive recounted, "They later took us to Congo for training. In Congo, they picked eight of us and we boarded a plane to another place. There we found many Moslems who taught us how to operate landmines and heavy guns" (Kabarole Research and Resource Centre 2002/2003). Another ex-combatant, who had been recruited into the ADF with his brother, described how his sibling was killed when he refused to convert to Islam (Interview Seventy-Four). However, the influence of the religious dimension of the ADF during this period has to be questioned. For one thing, camps could differ in how 'Islamicised' they were. When asked how many fighters within his camp were Christians, a former major with the group answered, "all, except two Ugandans who were Muslims" (MONUSCO Document Eleven). In assessing his file, MONUSCO's Disarmament, Demobilization, Repatriation, Reintegration, and Resettlement (DDRRR) Beni team wrote, "the fact they were not forced to be converted to Muslim shows that ADF is not more a religious movement but just a rebel group with economic and political goals" (MONUSCO Document Eleven). In other words, the Islamic angle was to a certain degree used as a strategic tool for recruitment or funding purposes. Lucy Hovil and Eric Werker (2005, 15) quote an ex-combatant as saying, "The religious aspect came later as a way to get support and recruits [. . .] the ADF adopted the grievances of Islam in order to appeal to these people [. . .] Islam was a ticket, so the leaders disguised their political motives in religion." Reducing the Islamic element of the ADF to being merely a 'ticket' or façade is going too far; but so too is understanding the entire human resource dimension of the ADF through this lens.

As will be discussed below, the various other actors that formed the ADF had nothing to do with fundamentalist Islam, were by no means Sudanese pawns, and nor were their goals strictly Ugandan-oriented ones. And yet, they would prove just as pivotal to the group as the Tabliqs (if not more so). And thus while a Ugandan Ministry of Defense official argued that the ADF's position in the Rwenzoris was simply an arbitrary result of geography, it will be demonstrated that their place there was in fact no mere coincidence. The borderland was central to the group's recruitment and organization of personnel: the force grew out of the borderland, they were overwhelmingly composed of borderland actors, and they pursued borderland-related goals (Interview Twenty-Eight). To properly understand the ADF's human resource component, then, it is clearly necessary to go beyond the religious or proxy-force interpretations of the ADF.

FORMATIVE PERIOD AND COMPOSITION

The Formation of the ADF

On 12 November 1996 the ADF brazenly conducted their first attack, through a brutal assault on the western Ugandan border towns of Mpondwe and Bwera.[5] An ADF soldier who took part in this battle described how it unfolded:

> We attacked that place [Bwera] using five sections of 300 fighters.[6] Our commanders' objectives were to capture one town after another systematically until we overran Kampala [. . .] The real battle continued for three consecutive days. During the first days we killed a number of UPDF soldiers. When the UPDF got a large number of reinforcements we went to Kasindi to get more briefings from our commanders. The meeting couldn't take place because the UPDF were shelling us with powerful guns. We withdrew back to our base in the Congo (African Rights 2001, 10).

Despite being initially repulsed, the ADF were soon launching regular attacks into Kasese, Bundibugyo, and Kabarole districts of western Uganda from their camps in eastern Congo and the bordering mountains of Uganda. Having taken the populace—not to mention Ugandan government—by surprise, it was difficult at first for outsiders to discern exactly who this force was.

This could be expected, considering the complexity of the ADF. It comprised a wide-ranging conglomeration of various borderland-based groups, foremost among these being NALU. In fact, after their defeat in Buseruka, the Tabliqs had chosen to relocate to the Rwenzoris precisely because of NALU's presence there (Jourdan 2008). The micro-region's long-standing tradition of rebel resistance against central authority, compounded by the proximity to the border, and the Congolese state's lack of effective authority over its territory, represented ideal rebel terrain. While it can be debated as to what degree Sudan and/or Mobutu engineered the initial merging of the Tabliqs and NALU, it is important to note that by no means were those the only two groups that come together to comprise the *Allied* Democratic Forces. Among those additionally a part of the force in the initial phase—as will be discussed throughout this section—included former Idi Amin loyalists, ex-Forces Armées Rwandaises soldiers, Rwandan *Interahamwe*, and remnants of various other Congolese rebel groups living in North Kivu.

Partly owing to this heterogeneity, the ADF's political objectives in this early stage came across as incoherent, leading to descriptions of the conflict as a "rebellion without a cause" (Hovil 2003, 5).[7] As Prunier (2004, 375) explains, "Since the Tabliq component of the ADF was at the same time preaching through its mosque circuit that it was fighting for an Islamic state with Jamil Mukulu as its president, while Bakonjo prisoners told UPDF interrogators that they were fighting because they had been promised that they would finally get their autonomous kingdom, there seemed to be a radical problem of political coherence." It appears that the ADF tried to compensate for this by creating (or at least attempting to give the appearance of) some synergy between the various factions' objectives. They thus issued statements and communiqués describing somewhat vague and lofty goals, such as "liberating Uganda," or aiming "to reintroduce multi-party politics in Uganda, stop [President] Museveni's nepotism giving all the juicy jobs to Westerners [. . .] and re-establish cordial relations with Uganda's neighbors" (Prunier 2004, 27; Interview Thirty-Two). A 19 June 1998 article in *The New Vision* described one of the ADF's attempts to be somewhat more specific:

> The ADF said in its manifesto that when it captures power, it would hold multiparty elections within 34 months and hand over leadership to an elected president and his party. The rebels said they intend to re-write the national Constitution by removing "articles unacceptable to Ugandans such as land

ownership, form of government, citizenship, human rights [. . .]" They charged that the existing Constitution was "fraudulently and treacherously made by Museveni's sycophants through bribery and exploitation" (Kakande 1998).

In the end though, when asked what they were fighting for, many former combatants could only mention such indefinite and imprecise ambitions as liberating Uganda from an oppressive regime, bringing economic prosperity to all citizens, implementing democracy, and combatting injustice (Interview Eighty).

The NALU Factor

However ill-defined the stated objectives of the ADF may have been, there is no denying that elements within the group had serious political and socio-economic grievances. Indeed, the various factions comprising the rebel force harbored individual and quite distinct agendas of their own—as can be blatantly seen with NALU. Before being incorporated into the ADF, NALU had been biding their time in the Beni district of eastern Congo. They had not been a strong enough force to act independently as a rebel group, however their members had no intention of disbanding and demobilizing. Through the support of the Congolese government and local political actors (most significantly the Nyamwisi family), in addition to the already-existing and embedded Konjo-Nande ties, NALU was not only able to maintain their bases there, but even integrate with surrounding society. They took part in coffee cultivation, engaged in agricultural smuggling to Uganda, shopped in the local markets, and through all of this steadily gained more Congolese members to their 'community.' One former combatant described NALU's pre-ADF period as living "disguised as civilians," but with the surrounding local population knowing their identity and being "fine with it" (Interview Seventy-Five).

Perhaps most importantly, though, NALU members continued to exude a deep sense of resentment and frustration over the unresolved status of their long-standing grievances. Foremost amongst these was of course the *Obusinga bwa Rwenzururu* issue discussed in Chapter Three (indeed, the military trajectories of many ADF ex-combatants stretched back to the RM) (Bollingtoft 2006; Interview Seventy-Five; Interview Seventy). Despite NALU essentially being leaderless after Bazira's death in 1993, a combination of factors had prevented them from ever leaving the bush. In addition to still being aggrieved over the Kingdom issue, these included never having been disarmed or demobilized, there being no amnesty program in place in Uganda at the time (and consequently an uncertainty as to how they would be handled by Ugandan authorities), leading relatively settled lives in Congo, and most importantly, harboring serious objections to central authority (Interview Forty-Five). Indeed, fear of prosecution upon return to Uganda was a common theme among ADF ex-combatants who had served in the RM and/or NALU (Interview Seventy). According to one former rebel, "When NALU joined the ADF, all of us members voluntarily accepted. No one went home after NALU disbanded. We stayed in the mountains and joined the ADF" (Interview Seventy-Five). Thus, incorporation into the ADF was perceived by many NALU followers as a positive and natural evolution for their force.

This points to the importance of looking beyond accounts of the ADF that focus on religion and proxy warfare, and considering instead the wider historical context in which this movement arose. While many analyses of the group paint a picture of an overwhelmingly Islamic-heavy force, it is worth bearing in mind that the ADF's military leader ('Chief Commander'), Yusuf Kabanda, was a Konjo from NALU. Kabanda originated from Kasese and had family that fought in the RM and NALU. Albeit, he did convert to Islam from Catholicism, and change his name from Bwambale to Yusuf; however, many argue that this was done for strategic reasons (for example to appeal to Arab donors) (African Rights 2001). Many other senior officials in the ADF were former Rwenzururu leaders too, such as Christopher Ngaimoko and Fenahasi Kisokeranio (Mbalibulha 2008b). According to African Rights (2001, 7), it is examples such as these that shed light on the "extent to which the history of strife in the Rwenzori region facilitated the formation of the ADF." It would be an exaggeration of course to perceive the ADF as a descendant of, or successor movement to, the RM or NALU. Nevertheless, "neither is it purely by chance that the ADF emerged in this particular area," as Bøås (2004, 291) observes. It is telling, for instance, that when local residents of Kasese, Bundibugyo, and Kabarole districts were asked to describe the causes of the ADF conflict, the vast majority started with the time period of the RM of the 1950s. Some have been harsher than others in their assessment of the lasting legacy of the RM: "There's been a group all along that has stirred trouble—always agitating for a Kingdom," remarked an employee of a conflict prevention and peacebuilding NGO (Interview Fifty-Two). In any case, as Prunier (2004, 383) succinctly states, "the ADF would not have got off the ground, had it not been for the festering sore of Bakonjo resentment since the 1950s."

Other ADF Components

It was not only the 'festering sore' of NALU that helped to solidify the ADF in their formative stage. A myriad of other parties—all sustaining their existence in the Rwenzori borderland at the time—were important in this regard as well, albeit their levels of integration into the ADF varied. One such faction was former Idi Amin loyalists. It is commonly noted in Uganda that the country's national army has in fact often not been *national*, but rather strongly allied to individual leaders. And thus, when a regime falls out of power, the army goes with it. This was certainly the case in Amin's defeat, with many of his soldiers later joining rebellions such as the WNBF or Uganda National Rescue Front (UNRF) I and II. Among those part of the original ADF, then, were former fighters from such groups, as well as other Amin loyalists led by Moses Ali (Romkema 2007; Muhangi 2004). Another constituency to become a part of the ADF were disgruntled UPDF soldiers (or simply soldiers looking for a supposedly more lucrative livelihood). In fact, the ADF Chief of Staff until 2000, 'Commander Benz,' had been a UPDF officer before joining the rebellion.

According to Prunier (1997, 18), next to the Tabliqs and NALU, one of the most significant groups in the ADF's formation was the "Rwandan Hutu radicals who were former members of the *Interahamwe* or FAR and had fled the attacks against the camps in the Goma area, moving northwards along the Rutshuru-Lubero-Butembo-Beni road." Media reports at the time of the ADF's first attack were replete with references to *Interahamwe* involvement: "the supposedly extinct NALU rebels, with the thinly disguised support of the *Interahamwe* exiles and Zairian troops invaded Uganda through corridors in the Rwenzori ranges," stated Benson Tusasirwe (1996), for example. Unlike the previously discussed ADF factions, the Rwandan parties were not completely encompassed into the ADF, but rather operated more in terms of an alliance system. African Rights (2001, 10) argues, "This connection emerged not only for practical reasons but also because the two groups share some ideological ground," namely a dislike for President Museveni. In the ex-FAR and *Interahamwe*'s case, this was due to him previously supporting the (Tutsi) Rwandan Patriotic Front (RPF).

Thus, the ADF's place within such a transnational context pivotally influenced their formation and composition. The group had essentially grown out of the borderland context, being composed of factions from the borderland, and also harboring borderland-defined grievances and goals. The ADF's constitution was neither Ugandan nor Congolese: members saw their identity as conditioned not by the national state, but by the borderland. While the ADF may have rhetorically preached *Ugandan*-related aims, elements such as NALU had much more pressing *borderland*-related goals. And the force as a whole, ultimately had as their principal goal maintaining their strategic space in the borderland (and everything that comes with that, such as practicing various economic ventures to be discussed later). The next section will demonstrate that the force's ability to continue with recruitment was similarly bounded by, and dependent on, the borderland.

CONTINUED RECRUITMENT STRATEGIES

Islamic Networks

The ADF's heterogeneous constitution, shaped by their place in the borderland, provided them with an advantageous choice of networks from which to draw on for continued recruitment. The two most obvious in this sense were those associated with Islam and the Rwenzururu Kingdom (or Konjo population in general). The ADF established links with extremist mosques in western Uganda; Bwera's mosque represented a focal meeting point for Muslims of the region, and recruitment pamphlets were regularly circulated there (as well as in Kasese mosques) (Nkuutu 2003; Titeca 2009b). Connections to mosques throughout the rest of the country were made as well, and recruits were drawn from Muslim-dominated pockets of Uganda such as Masaka, Mbarara, Iganga, and Kampala (Muhangi 2004; Namutebi 2000; Interview Twenty-Six). This contributed to the multi-ethnic nature of the group, as it brought in personnel from, among others, the Baganda, Banyankole, Basoga, and Batoro tribes (Mbalibulha 2008b).

Recruitment on a religious basis extended into the Congo as well, and was particularly focused on Eringeti, Beni, and the villages between those two towns (Titeca and Vlassenroot 2012). According to Titeca and Vlassenroot (2012, 163), "In Eringeti, the local mosque was frequently visited by rebel forces and, from this mosque, local businesses generated some resources for the movement." Nevertheless, this Islamic-centric network was only one of many recruitment avenues operationalized.

Konjo Networks

Throughout 1996–2003, great effort was expended at recruiting members of the Konjo tribe. Not only were they a strategic target considering NALU's role in the force, but they were also highly valued due to their intimate familiarity with the terrain. As the rebellion became increasingly violent (an issue to be discussed in the third part of this chapter), and voluntary recruitment drastically diminished, the ADF stepped-up their appeals to the Konjo. *The New Vision* reported, "The Bakonjo who formed the bulk of the Allied Democratic Forces were told that at the fall of Kasese town, a Mukonjo king would be installed" (Allio 1996). Former rank and file ADF combatants described the promises made by their leaders with regards to the Rwenzururu Kingdom being installed, specifically the return of their 'King,' Charles Mumbere, from exile overseas (Allio 1998a; Ruhunda, et al; Interview Seventy-One; Interview Seventy-Five).

Indeed, of all the 'promises' issued by the ADF during this time period to entice recruits, those surrounding the issue of the Rwenzururu King and Kingdom were the most persuasive (Interview Sixty-Five). The Konjo recruits' credulity was aided by an unclear stance towards the rebellion by Mumbere himself. Although later making his condemnation of the ADF clear, in the rebellion's first few years there was talk that Mumbere had at one point distantly supported NALU (Albere 2007; Interview Sixty). The evidence was dubious (mainly consisting of some pictures of the King in army fatigues), but nonetheless influential for a time (Interview Seventy-Six). Reflecting on this, members of a female development co-operative in Kasese district explained the symbolic importance of the Kingdom in the following: "The Rwenzururu Kingdom means culture, and culture means our identity" (Interview Sixty-Six). And while they were adamantly against the ADF conflict, they displayed an understanding for why people would take up arms if they believed they were fighting for the Rwenzururu Kingdom.

Further compounding the Konjo's susceptibility to recruitment was a lingering resentment towards the government over another issue. During Museveni's conquest for power, the Konjo community had helped the NRA when it pitched camp in the Rwenzori Mountains and occupied former RM bases.[8] Through aid to the NRA in the form of cover, food supply, and espionage, they greatly enabled the success of the NRA's operations. As a result, they expected favorable relations with Museveni upon his capture of power, and members of the rump RM sent a memorandum to the new government with a list of requests for their community. The requests included, for instance, the recognition of *Obusinga bwa Rwenzururu*, employment of Konjo in government structures, and medical care and other social services extending higher into the mountains. But the dismissal of these demands, and then marginalization of their area by President Museveni, left the Konjo feeling betrayed; it greatly contributed to the overall 'disgruntled' nature of the area (Interview Eleven). As one ex-combatant explained, "President Museveni forgot about the Rwenzururu and the promises he had made to them" (Interview Seventy-Three). The ADF undoubtedly used tactics of deceit—if not outright lies—to attract Konjo recruits. But it is worth bearing in mind some of the above factors when attempting to understand why such deception was oftentimes successful, and why to many in the region, the ADF appeared to represent an opportunity to rectify their marginalized plight (Interview Thirty-Eight).

Disenfranchised Borderlanders

In western Uganda recruitment was not only directed at the Konjo. The ADF also tailored their strategies to the disenfranchised and neglected borderland population in general. Kasese and Bundibugyo districts suffered from especially deplorable levels of representation in positions of political power, unemployment, and access to schooling, with Bundibugyo's education levels amongst the worst in Uganda (Kyambogo University 2002). Resultantly, of those who willingly joined the group, many reported being swayed by promises of lower tax rates, schooling opportunities, assistance in acquiring houses, or positions in local and national government structures once the ADF took power (Interview Sixty-Four; Interview Seventy-Two; Interview Sixty-Six). One Bukana Rural Development Association member explained, "Many of our children joined the ADF because of idleness or loss of hope in the government, and promises of jobs when Museveni fell" (Interview Sixty-Six). Women additionally described being promised capital to start small businesses after the conflict (Interview Seventy-Two). Prunier (2004, 371) interestingly observes that many UPDF officers seemed unable to comprehend this recruitment dynamic, asking, "we fought for an ideal; how can these people fight for money, especially so little money?" But although Uganda had experienced economic growth throughout the late 1980s and into the 1990s, the results of such growth were mostly felt in more 'central' areas of the country (Prunier 2004). He (2004, 371) goes on to note that, in terms of these officers, "It was hard to get them to admit that, if their 'ideal' had brought them a certain modicum of prosperity, they were now facing the very people whom the so-called 'Ugandan economic miracle' had passed by." Through exploiting the socio-economic hardships of neglected border communities, then, the ADF were able to mobilize those with few opportunities and choices—ultimately, those who felt they would have little to lose by participating in rebellion.

The ADF also took advantage of a different dimension of this phenomenon, namely the lack of peaceful avenues through which grievances could be addressed in the borderland, and the belief that "[President] Museveni only understands the language of the gun," a Kasese-based civil society worker stated (Interview Sixty). Indeed, even still to this day many local peacebuilding groups emphasize how prevalent the belief is throughout the region that grievances and disputes can only realistically be resolved through violence (Interview Forty-Five). One ex-commander's justification for why he joined the ADF is telling in this respect: "I was a student in Masaka. Unfortunately I saw no democracy so I was forced to join ADF" (Interview Eighty). A Human Rights Watch (HRW) report (1999, 127) argued that despite "important reservations about the purported political motivations of Ugandan rebel groups, it would be a mistake to suggest that rebel activity is completely unrelated to the suppression of political opposition activity in Uganda."[9] The report discusses this in relation to various national political issues, such as Bugandan federalists and multi-partyists "who turned to armed opposition [the ADF] after their proposals for a federal, multi-party system were rejected at the 1995 Constituent Assembly" (Human Rights Watch 1999, 128–129).[10]

Yet on a much more local level, in the borderland, this phenomenon had been at work as well. The relative absence of the state, and heightened 'lawless' character of the area, very much encouraged this. Numerous former ADF fighters recounted their decision to join the rebels due to what they had perceived as undue or excessive harassment by the UPDF, unfair treatment by local authorities, or simply revenge for individual grudges (Interview Seventy-One). One described joining the ADF out of anger after his land was stolen by fellow villagers and there were no official means of resolving the dispute, while another enlisted in order to exact revenge on the UPDF who had unlawfully ransacked his store (Interview Seventy-One).

Of course, while these scenarios refer to voluntary involvement, the ADF gained a significant proportion of their force—arguably at this point even the majority of their cohorts—through more coercive methods. At one end of the spectrum was abduction, usually done during violent raids on villages or IDP camps. Between 1996–2003 it is estimated that over 3,000 abductions took place in Kasese district alone (Interview Thirty-Six). Yet the ADF also employed more subtle and conniving strategies of forced recruitment, often involving the manipulation of transnational kinship or ethnic networks. One of the most common strategies was to have ADF fighters cross the border and infiltrate villages where their family members or co-ethnics were located and warn them of an impending attack. They would be ordered to advise their relatives and/or friends to join the rebellion in order to save themselves from being killed in an upcoming raid (Interview Seventy-Three). One former female ADF rebel from Kasese district, for example, joined when her husband, already in the ADF, convinced her that "it would be safer on the other side [of the border, in Congo]" (Interview Seventy-Three). Indeed, many ex-combatants described joining the force due to warnings from kin members.

Congolese Conflict Dynamics

Dynamics on the ground in Congo during this time period were quickly changing, and the country was engulfed in a brutal regionalized war. In terms of the borderland, it is important to note the effect that the UPDF's occupation of northeastern Congo (occupying many districts along the border in North Kivu and Orientale provinces) had upon the borderland. Indeed, a radical transformation of the borderland ensued whereby from the First Congo War to the end of the Second (roughly 1996/7–2003) the border was effectively erased. The UPDF's increased deployment at the beginning of the Second Congo War and expansion of occupation west to Equateur province saw their forces increase their area of control far beyond the immediate borderland, further rendering the border virtually non-existent. Although the UPDF's focus was not on the ADF at this time—which their expansion that far west indicates—this erasure of the border had a major effect on the ADF's strategies and activities.[11]

With the bulk of the fighting taking place in the east, the ADF were presented with two significant opportunities. First, there was an increase in the already considerable size of non-government-secured territory in North Kivu, and thereby an enlarged potential recruiting ground for the ADF. As Major Shaban Bantariza of the UPDF stated, "They [the rebels] have taken advantage of the non-existence of the state in much of eastern DRC to move around" (IRIN News 2004). The ADF's popularity was beginning to dwindle due to their attacking of civilians in western Uganda, and the more pronounced this was, the more their recruitment initiatives became Congo-focused. Congolese were recruited not only for military or military support functions, but also to be part of the group's work force involved in, among other pursuits, mining and timber (to be discussed in the second part of this chapter) (Interview Twenty-Two). Abductions were common, but so were attempts to exploit the marginalized status of the Congolese side of the Rwenzori borderland. The Konjo-Nande continuum was important in this respect, with many Nande joining due to the Konjo presence within the ADF (Interview Thirty-Seven; Interview Twenty-Three). Also because of the NALU faction, there was a second generation contingent of ADF members. As mentioned previously, after the RM was officially disbanded in the early 1980s, many of the hard-core militants had established themselves in eastern Congo. There they lived amongst the Nande, intermarrying, raising families, and some of them eventually becoming a part of NALU. Their children were thus born and raised in the camps, and by the late 1990s many were ready to actively be a part of the rebel force.

The second opportunity arising from the wider regional war was a multiplication of rebel groups and consequent proliferation of potential partners. One humanitarian official noted, "This [the ADF] rebellion was concretised by the war in Congo" (IRIN News 1999). The following quotations from Ugandan newspapers—although not always entirely accurate in their conceptualizations of the ADF's heterogeneity—provide a flavor of the kinds of networking the ADF were able to perform: "It is very clear that most of the attacks in the district [Bundibugyo] were carried out by a joint force of ADF, *Interahamwe* and Mai Mai"; "The Ugandan authorities claim the ADF rebels have teamed up with Congolese militias to beef up their capacity"; "the ADF was establishing fresh linkages with a Lendu militia gang in Ituri, to plan new attacks"; "The rebels [ADF] plan to fight alongside the Wangelima to defeat Zaire's Banyamulenge rebels"; "Ugandan troops have been deployed along the border [. . .] to fight the ADF rebels who are trying to join forces with remnants of the late Mobutu Sese Seko's defeated army" (Muhanga, 1999a; IRIN News 2000; Mugabi 2008; Sserwanga and Nzinjah 1997; Sserwanga 1997; Sserwanga 1998c). In an important sense the above claims can be seen as projections of the authors themselves. In other words, they arguably reveal more about the sources, than the ADF. And undoubtedly the borderland context played a major role in this: the liminal and opaque nature of this zone encouraged this kind of—often times wild—speculation. Not surprisingly, then, there were continually claims during this time period that the ADF had additionally joined forces with the Lord's Resistance Army (LRA). This was however never proven. They did share the same Sudanese training base in Juba, and there was almost certainly a degree of 'theoretical collaboration.' For example, the DDRRR testimony of one former ADF member discusses how he and his fellow combatants were told that in the case of a difficult battle against Ugandan forces, they would be reinforced by Dominique Ongwen from the LRA. Nevertheless, an actual alliance of forces was never an actuality (Ochieng 1998; MONUSCO Document Eleven).

Networking with a number of Mai Mai militias, from 1998 onwards, was especially common (Muhanga 1999a; Interview Seventy-Four). Collaboration, coordination, and even various degrees of integration with the Mai Mai, took place both for practical support reasons and ideological motivations. The Mai Mai were committed to expelling foreign troops (namely those from Uganda and Rwanda) from Congolese soil, and this obviously meshed well with the ADF's anti-UPDF and anti-RPF/Rwandan stances.[12] Ex-combatants described how they sang anti-Rwandan songs in the camps, and were taught, for example, that President Museveni was a Rwandan and thus had to be removed from power (Muhangi 2004; African Rights 2001). Even during attacks, this anti-Rwandan stance was evident. Describing an ADF assault on the town of Bundibugyo, *The Sunday Vision* wrote, "They [the ADF rebels] commandeered pick ups and lorries and started driving around, singing victory songs in Runyankole, Swahili, Lingala, and Luganda accusing [President] Museveni of being a Munyarwanda, and asking him where his strong army had gone. Using maps they came with, they located and broke into shops belonging to Banyarwanda" (Kalema 1997). Thus, when looking at the ADF's continued ability to acquire new members—their exploitation of various borderland dynamics and borderlanders' grievances and goals—it becomes even more clear how pivotal a role their transnational setting played.

INTERNAL STRUCTURE, GOVERNANCE, AND CONTROL OF INFORMATION

When it comes to discussing the organization of the ADF, as Titeca and Vlassenroot (2012, 154) state, "the word 'mystery' will feature prominently [. . .] Very little is known about its background, ideology, internal organization, military capacity, lines of supply and supporters." *The New Vision* in January 1998 alleged, "The most intricate and intriguing of Ugandan rebel groups is ADF rebels who have no pronounced leadership" (Allio 1998b). Similarly, *The Economist* wrote, "With just a few hundred people, no clear goal, confused leadership and in difficult terrain, these rebels are waging a small, but damaging war" (Staff Writers 1999).

While it is true that the ADF were a notoriously 'private' rebel group, it was not the case that they lacked leadership or were disorganized—in fact, quite the opposite. As one Ugandan development worker explained, "The ADF have been a more determined and focused force than the LRA. They had an urban wing, a website, strong international connections [. . .] They have had the capacity to use a double-pronged approach of guerrilla warfare and urban terrorism. They could generate resources internally and externally, and the military command structure was clear" (Interview Eleven).

The ADF adhered to a strict chain of command. Brigades were divided into four to six companies, and further subdivided into detachments. These reported to the general military headquarters, which was composed of a Chief of Military General Headquarters, a Chief of Military Operations and Logistics, and a Chief of Administration and Director of Military Intelligence. The military branch of the ADF, led by Yusuf Kabanda, reported to the political branch, known as the Allied Democratic Movement (ADM), headed by Jamil Mukulu (Mukulu is widely recognized as the leading figure of the ADF). The ADM constituted what could be thought of as the 'support structure,' feeding the group their intelligence, and having an extensive presence in terms of contacts, spies, and sleeper cells throughout the borderland and other areas of Uganda and Congo (Interview Sixty-Three).

Aliases were frequently used for leaders and chiefs, and in the case of some personnel, the real names have never been known—this being especially true for Field Commanders. The leadership of Mukulu was particularly shrouded in secrecy, as he was essentially only ever heard through cassette tapes distributed by the ADF (McGregor 2007). It is important to emphasize that the group maintained their anonymity as a matter of *strategy*. As Bøås (2004, 292) notes, "The obscurity of the leadership and membership helps to keep internal and external networks intact, relatively safe from state intelligence operatives." This anonymity was essential for a group whose theatre of action stretched across a border, entailing continuous movement between two states. Between 1996–2003, travel between camps was often a cross-border affair, as the ADF had provisional camps in western Uganda, and rear bases and headquarters Congo-side (the main training wing was at Buhira in North Kivu, and the command base nearby at Kirivata). Camps varied in size, with some as large as 800 (Interview Seventy-Three). However, from accounts of former members, it appears that 130–150 was average, with smaller stations throughout the borderland for monitoring purposes (Interview Ten).

The secrecy and clandestine nature of the group extended into camp life, where information was tightly controlled and discipline harshly enforced. Ex-combatants described having essentially no access to news from the outside world, unless they found a way to illicitly listen to a radio (Interview Seventy-Four). Leaders deemed this to be essential for keeping-up morale in the face of adverse military conditions. For example, many former rebels recalled how they were regularly shown pictures of western Ugandan towns or landmarks that had been 'taken over' by the ADF (Interview Seventy-Four). They described their belief at the time in the substantial progress being made by the ADF, and their confidence that the take-over of Kampala was on the horizon. They were furthermore kept motivated through a scheme that involved them filling-out forms stating their employment aspirations for when the ADF 'took over' government. According to many ex-combatants, they were continually assured such requests would be taken into account (Interview Seventy-Two).

The tight lid on information meant that members' movements were monitored closely. Those who grew too tired to continue on the frequent and long food-carrying trips were sometimes killed as they simply knew too much information about the group to be left behind (Interview Seventy-Five). Likewise, escapees were usually pursued (again in light of the information they held about the group) and subjected to harsh treatment if captured (Interview Forty-One). In fact, often an entire village would be punished if it was discovered that an escapee had returned and was living there. The control of information also meant, however, that escaping was extremely difficult in the first place. Most ADF camps were deep inside the Rwenzori Mountains or forests of North Kivu, and rebels were simply unaware of where they were living—even to the extent of them often not knowing whether they were in Uganda or Congo. This also resulted in many of the Ugandan rebels being completely unaware of Uganda's Amnesty Act, which was brought into effect in 2000 and provided a blanket amnesty to rebels. Many found out about the Act either after having left the ADF (often through, for example, capture by the UPDF), or via being informed by Congolese civilian neighbors in the bush (Interview Seventy-Two).

It is estimated that in 1996 the ADF had 4,000–5,000 well equipped and trained combatants. Of course, as they lost popular support and were the target of a UPDF military offensive, their numbers decreased, and by 2003 they had only several hundred rebels left. As their size was reduced, abductions became more common, as was discussed previously. Despite the ubiquitous comparisons between the ADF and LRA, the two groups were actually substantially dissimilar in organization, and nowhere was this more obvious than when it came to the practice of abductions. There were a few reports from western human rights groups accusing the ADF of substantial child abduction, akin to the kind practiced by the LRA.[13] However, the testimonies of former ADF members, and statistics from the amnesty commission do not support this in the least. For example, only 3 percent of ADF reporters (a term used for those who have gone through the amnesty process in Uganda) were under the age of 18; this stands in significant contrast to the LRA, with 27 percent. What was quite unusual for a rebel group, in fact, was that the bulk of the force's reporters were in the 31–45 age group category. Perhaps even more uncommon was the substantial number in the age 45 and above bracket. Indeed, when abductions were practiced, the intended targets were usually young adults so as to acquire able-bodied personnel with the requisite stamina to withstand operating in and across the Rwenzori Mountains. Being fit enough to traverse the Rwenzori Mountains was undeniably of great importance for many positions in the force. One ex-combatant described his role as an 'ambulance'; namely, carrying ADF casualties on his back from the scene of attacks in Uganda, to camps in the mountains (Interview Seventy-One). While not to as great a degree as between 2004–2013, the ADF's internal structure, governance, and control of information was clearly influenced by, and designed to take advantage of, the borderland space in which they were operating.

Despite most accounts of the ADF (in the Ugandan press, amongst NGO reports, and so on) understanding the group in state-centric terms—specifically with regards to the role of extremist Islam and Sudanese involvement—this section demonstrated that dynamics related to the borderland were pivotal to the force's human resource pursuits as well. Instead of viewing the rebellion solely through a macro-level lens, the above discussion used a borderland perspective, considered the micro-politics of this space, looked at translocal dynamics, and recognized the agency of borderland actors. Undoubtedly, Islamic networks played a role in the formation, and then continued recruitment strategies, of the ADF, as did Sudanese dynamics. But seeing the ADF as a group merely manipulated and supervised by forces at the national or regional levels, leaves out a large part of the story. The ADF's formation, composition, objectives, and organization were very much influenced and facilitated by political, social, and economic borderland undercurrents, and more generally the anti-state and liminal nature of this space.

There was a multitude of actors within the Rwenzori borderland who harbored anti-state sentiments and hostile attitudes towards central authority, NALU being foremost amongst these. Borderlands tend to be catchment areas for such actors, and the Rwenzori borderland was especially fertile in this sense, having attracted over time a multitude of non-demobilized groups and militarized communities. With minimal prodding, a number of these forces came together to form the ADF. The borderland environment not only facilitated the actual formation, and shaped the constitution, of the ADF, but it also significantly affected the group's ability to continue to recruit members. Meta-narratives of marginalization and discrimination amongst civilian borderlanders, for example, factored-in extensively: people on both sides of the border were motivated to join, or at least made more susceptible to recruitment, due to issues surrounding their historic maltreatment and disenfranchised status at the hands of their respective national state. Similarly, the relative absence of certain state services in the Rwenzori borderland (a common feature of borderlands, as discussed in Chapter Two), including lack of official routes through which to pursue justice and resolve problems, led many borderlanders to join the ADF.

On the surface it may appear that the ADF were driven by Islamic ideals and goals, were influenced by Sudanese scheming, or were solely interested in taking-over the capital. But unresolved political and socio-economic injustices amongst the people of the Rwenzoris were just as significant motivating sources, and maintaining their strategic place in the Rwenzori borderland was an overriding objective for the rebels. While the ADF appeared to have trouble articulating these grievances, let alone their general political agenda, this does not deny their importance. From the RM, to NALU in the 1980s and early 1990s, to the ADF, issues surrounding the status of western Uganda in the Ugandan polity, and eastern Congo in the Congolese polity, remained unresolved, and thus animosity towards central authority ever-present. Bøås and Jennings (2008, 158) argue, "Joseph Kony's LRA is a reflection and distortion of meta-narratives of betrayal deeply entrenched in Acholi identity"—the same could surely be said for Rwenzori borderlanders and the ADF. And yet there have been few attempts to dig deeper or look beyond the more prevalent understandings of this group, and explore the buried narratives of the borderland.

PART II: MATERIAL RESOURCES

MISGUIDED EXPLANATIONS OF THE ADF'S MATERIAL RESOURCES

In 1997 Uganda's Speaker of Parliament, James Wapakhabulo, claimed that the ADF were "groomed and sponsored by Sudan" (Sentongo 1997). *The New Vision* in October 1998 reported,

> Several factors have been identified to favor the ADF operations in the mountainous areas from where they descend [. . .] The main factor is the support from other countries. Sudan has been very instrumental to the ADF operations by providing equipment and training. Khartoum hopes by supporting ADF in Western Uganda and Lord's Resistance Army in the north of the country, will keep the UPDF constantly engaged and its strength over stretched so as to succeed in destabilizing Uganda (Matsiko 1998).

As these quotations help to elucidate, it is often believed that Sudan was the principal source and provider of material resources for the group. And there are two main views regarding this. The first sees Sudanese assistance in light of a *religious* agenda: "Guided by the subversive ideology of the academic Turabi and bankrolled by Iran, Bashir's Sudan sought to Islamicise all of sub-Saharan Christian or pagan Africa," writes Stacey (2003, 406) for instance. However, the more common thread is evident in those such as Prunier, who focus on the *political* dimension of Sudan's involvement, using the lens of a wider Khartoum-Kampala proxy war in which the ADF was a pawn. Prunier (2004, 359) explains,

> In many ways Sudan and Uganda have been running an undeclared war on their common border since 1986 [. . .] But what is often not noted is that this undeclared war has also been fought, largely through proxies, on the territory of the neighboring Republic of Zaire, later the Democratic Republic of Congo. This proxy war has centered on the creation of the Allied Democratic Forces, a coalition formed from a variety of anti-Museveni movements, aided and abetted by Sudan.

It should additionally be noted that Sudan was providing assistance to other Ugandan rebel groups at this time as well, including the LRA, WNBF, Former Ugandan National Army, and UNRF II.

There is no doubt that the ADF's significance extended beyond the immediate Rwenzori borderland. While their impact may have been localized, they were very much a part of wider regional geopolitical dynamics. Discussions between Ugandan Members of Parliament (MPs) at the time shed light on the important position of the ADF within the tense Khartoum-Kampala relationship: "the condition for normalization of relations between Uganda and Sudan is that Sudan must stop sponsoring terrorism in Uganda. They have sponsored terrorism, supported the ADF, supported the dropping of bombs in Kampala and supported the bandit group led by Kony in the North" (Uganda. Parliament September 20, 1999).

Sudan certainly provided valuable material support to the ADF, both directly and indirectly, in the group's first few years. In terms of direct assistance, former combatants described regular airdrops (often delivered via parachutes from helicopters) from Juba of military supplies, uniforms, and food into the area of Lume, eastern Congo (Nzinjah 1997b; Prunier 2009; MONUSCO Document Four). Military supplies included grenades, rockets, rocket-propelled grenades, machine guns, sub-machine guns, AK 47s, Dusker-12s, 82mm mortars, and accompanying ammunition for the weapons (MONUSCO Document Eleven). A Ugandan intelligence officer reported Sudan's use of the Congo as a 'reception center,' and its delivery of eight trailers of arms before the conflict commenced in November 1996 (Hovil and Werker 2005, 13). Weapons and other military ware were often stockpiled in caves in the Rwenzori Mountains—many of them the same caves as those previously used by NALU (Matsiko and Thawite 1998). Indirectly, Sudan supported the ADF through training, both on Congolese soil and, for some of the more senior members of the group, Sudanese soil (Muhanga 1999b; Etengu 1996). The Sudanese intelligence service ran a training camp in Juba, for example, which many high-ranking ADF militants attended (McGregor 2007).

Nevertheless, Sudanese backing of the ADF was drastically reduced following the signing of the Nairobi Agreement between Khartoum and Kampala in 1999 (it had already started to diminish in the years prior in fact). Shortly after this event, *The New Vision* wrote, "Ugandan rebels [the ADF] no longer enjoy external support and had no base after the [. . .] move to normalize relations with the Sudan" (Sserwanga and Nzinja 2000). Yet, when Sudanese support dried-up, the ADF were able to continue acquiring material resources. Thus, explaining the ADF's ability to materially survive as being conditional on Sudanese support is inaccurate. When considering the ADF's acquisition of material resources, both during Sudan's principle period of involvement, and then beyond to 2003, it is necessary to look at other sources.

Importantly, the ADF's extremely heterogeneous nature provided them with the opportunity to pursue a multifaceted approach to securing material resources. The various factions composing the ADF each brought their own assets and abilities with regards to this. It is the Tabliq faction that has received the most attention by the Ugandan government and in the press, though. Of course, they were crucial in terms of funding, owing to their connections with Islamic patrons—which extended well beyond Sudan. Prior to his career as leader of the ADF, Mukulu had studied in Saudi Arabia and established contacts with various Jihadist movements throughout the Middle East, Europe, and Africa. He subsequently used these connections extensively, both for obtaining "direct financial contributions for the ADF, but also to establish partnerships in income-generating business ventures," according to a UN Group of Experts report (Group of Experts on the Democratic Republic of the Congo December 2, 2011). Africa-wise, his strongest support cells were from Uganda, and specifically Kampala, as well as in Nairobi and the city of Tanga, Tanzania (Group of Experts on the Democratic Republic of the Congo December 2, 2011).

One of the Tabliq's more unusual connections was to that of Saddam Hussein's regime. Although the exact extent of Iraqi assistance to the ADF has never been verified, in 2003 concrete evidence of at least initial communications were discovered in the ruins of Iraq's intelligence headquarters in Baghdad. There a cache of documents was found, illustrating correspondence between the ADF's chief of diplomacy, Bekkah Abdul Nasser, and the Iraqi charge d'affaires in Nairobi, Fallah Hassan al-Rubdie. The papers suggested a degree of potential cooperation, with one document reading, "We in the ADF forces are ready to run the African mujahedeen headquarters. We have already started and we are on the ground, operational" (Smucker and Bowers 2003, 2; Terdman 2006, 2). Beginning soon after 9/11, the Ugandan government was extremely keen on calling attention to these kinds of connections. For example, Mbabazi declared, "Uganda's domestic terrorist groups have been subsidized and trained by al-Qaeda," while the country's Acting Chief of Military Intelligence, James Mugira, claimed, "We think [Mukulu] will become the next bin Laden of Africa" (McGregor 2007, 2–3). However, this interest on the part of Ugandan authorities should at least partly be interpreted in light of Uganda's lucrative beneficiary status of the United States' $100 million East Africa Counterterrorism Initiative.

Various sources claimed that the Tabliqs also had extensive diaspora networks—notably in Canada, Congo-Brazzaville, South Africa, the United Kingdom (UK), and the United States (US)—which were useful for generating revenue for the group (i.e., Interview Sixty-Three).[14] Material support was said to have not only transferred directly to the ADF by states such as Iran, Saudi Arabia, Sudan, and the United Arab Emirates, but frequently support (mainly in the form of funding) was channelled indirectly to them as well. This apparently usually transpired either through Pakistani or Bangladeshi intermediaries, or via Ugandan-based international Islamic NGOs, such as the Islamic African Relief Agency, Islamic Call Society, International

Islamic Relief Organization, and Africa Charitable Society for Mother and Child Care (McGregor 2007; Terdman 2006). The Tabliqs were undoubtedly important during the ADF's formative and early stages in generating external support, however their material contribution largely stopped at that. Thus, an explanation with regards to the ADF's ability to acquire and generate material resources that relies on them, leaves a great deal to be explained—such as how the ADF were able to maintain a relatively large and strategically important parcel of land, how they were able to set up local businesses, and so on. There were clearly other factors at play in terms of the ADF's ability to attract funds and supplies.

THE NALU CONTRIBUTION

Integration into Local Economic Activities

NALU is one segment of the ADF that has tended to be left out of the story with regards to material resource acquisition. As mentioned previously, by the time of the ADF's formation, NALU was a movement that due to their cross-border ethnic ties had become embedded in the local Congolese environment. For some members, cohabitation had been practiced as far back as the early 1980s. When NALU became a part of the ADF, their members continued this practice, which allowed for the other segments of the ADF to partake in this local integration as well. As a report by the Information Counselling and Referral Services (2008, 14) described, the "ADF as a rebel group is far more embedded within their community, and is a more community-oriented guerrilla-led insurgency. This is supported by contextual evidence that suggests that ADF personnel and their families are very mobile, often operating as a cohesive military-family unit." And this is corroborated by several interesting figures: for example, quite unusually for a rebel group, the proportion of ADF members with a combat function was only 19 percent, while those in a support function position was 81 percent (both the LRA and WNBF, for example, had ratios of 43 percent to 57 percent). In a similar vein, a mere 6 percent of ADF members possessed a weapon; an astounding 94 percent of the force were not armed (the LRA's weapon possession figure was 27 percent and the WNBF's 70 percent) (Information Counselling and Referral Services 2008).

Having this faction of the ADF essentially living amongst their own kin—sharing the same language, culture, family connections, and so on—brought advantages to the force of a very practical nature. A group of ex-combatants who were all Konjo and had originated from Kasese district in Uganda described how they "felt comfortable amongst the Banande community" and "were within our own people" (Interview Sixty-Two). Not only did they "make friendship with the Congolese," but "these people even gave us [the ADF] part of the mountain to live on" (Interview Sixty-Two). One former Konjo female member of the group, who had served as a 'wife' to two fighters, recounted the extremely rough conditions her camp had been living in during the time of her child's birth. However, local Nande villagers came to her aid during the delivery, helping care for her newborn, and sharing food with her family (Interview Forty-Three).

In essence, NALU brought to the ADF the 'local factor.' Practices that had been common to NALU pre-ADF, such as intermarrying, doing business with native inhabitants, and recruitment of local Congolese, were continued post-1996. These helped to provide the ADF with access to (extremely arable) land and freedom of movement; it allowed them to engage in profit-making economic practices; and it made possible their acquisition of resources such as food and other items of a practical nature essential for survival. They were even able to obtain medical treatment from supporters in local health centers, and Congolese chiefs assisted them in the levying of taxes on traders. The large percentage of the movement dedicated to support functions meant that the ADF could engage in agricultural activities such as the harvesting of coffee, timber, and a local source of marijuana known as *chanvre*. The coffee and timber tended to be exported illicitly to Uganda via the local trading networks, while the *chanvre* was usually sold in the Watalinga market. Such practices only increased in importance with time, as external sources of funding diminished from around 1999 onwards.

Monopoly of the Border

The Nande-Konjo ethnic continuum across the Uganda–Congo state line—what could essentially be thought of as their 'monopoly' over the border—was pivotal to these economic activities. Prior to the ADF's formation, attempts had been made to monitor border activities in light of the pivotal role they were playing in the area's upheaval. A 1992 article from *The New Vision*, covering the reaction to a NALU attack, was demonstrative of this: "The RC [Resident Coordinator] III Chairmen of Karambi and Kitolhu are reported to have ordered the closure of foot-paths leading from Uganda into Zaire. The two officials have also stopped Zairians from coming to Ugandan border markets" (Vision Reporter 1992). With regards to the ADF, attempts were initially made by the UPDF to control the border, and thereby sever some of the group's supply lines. Eventually, however, this practice was largely abandoned. There was simply too much civilian cross-border traffic to permit any effective targeting of cross-border activities.

Within the Rwenzori borderland, the two most relevant border crossings for the ADF were those at Bwera-Kasindi and Bundibugyo-Kamango. Each location was a commercially vibrant space, boasting thriving formal and informal economies, and centrally tapped-in to the historic regional networks discussed in Chapter Three (Titeca 2009b). Both were important nodes in the wider trading transit routes connected to east Africa. According to Titeca (2009b, 302), "Together with Aru, Kasindi is the main border market on the Ugandan-Congolese border, and historically has been an important trading post for the distribution of goods into eastern Congo." Titeca (2009b, 302–3) illustrates the pivotal economic role of such border towns:

> These goods [those going into eastern Congo] originate from places such as Dubai, Hong Kong or China and arrive in the port of Mombasa, from where they are transported to the Kenyan-Ugandan border town of Busia, pass through Uganda, and finally arrive in Kasindi. From Kasindi onwards, goods are not only distributed into eastern Congo, but also smuggled back into Uganda, and more specifically to Bwera. This allows traders to dodge Ugandan taxes, as goods on transit to the DRC (Kasindi) are exempt from Ugandan taxes. From Bwera, goods are distributed back into south-western and central Uganda [. . .] Bwera town has therefore grown in parallel to the border market of Kasindi: it is the last Ugandan stop before Kasindi, and the main distribution point for goods smuggled from Kasindi. Bwera's economy is therefore closely connected to that of Kasindi. Most of the population of Bwera is involved in cross-border trade, and many farmers also sell their goods in Kasindi.

The markets of Bwera-Kasindi and Bundibugyo-Kamango were situated on both sides of the border, less than one mile from the state line. During market days people streamed continuously in large numbers back and forth across the border. For those living in relative proximity on either side, almost all household and business products were bought from such markets in light of the considerable (and in the Congolese case somewhat impossible) distance from the major cities in the interior (Interview Sixty-Two). Indeed, those Congolese not in the cities of Beni or Butembo were especially lacking in basic supplies such as salt, soap, and school materials, thus being even more dependent on the markets (Interview Eighteen; Interview Forty-Two; Interview Twenty-Four). The markets were thus part of a local economy that was not only significantly controlled by the Nande, but profoundly transnational, with each side fundamentally oriented towards the other. The volume of market-goers was so profound, and the border so fluid, that formal immigration controls at Bundibugyo, for example, were at times simply non-existent. Especially during the height of the Congolese conflict in the late 1990s and early 2000s, when cross-border traffic increased and markets grew substantially in size, there were interesting implications in terms of refugees.

As Emmanuel Bagenda (2004, 2) noted, "there [were] no means of establishing the precise numbers of incoming, settling or repatriating refugees." Other intriguing practices developed as well. Residents crossed the border not only to visit relatives and friends, access health and education services, and take their cattle to graze on the other side, but it was also the case that during national immunization campaigns in Uganda, those in the North Kivu borderland were encouraged by Ugandan authorities to partake, since the interaction between the cross-border populations was so intense (Interview Eighteen; Interview Thirty-Nine). The profound fluidity of the border is captured in a statement from a leader of the Kabarole Research and Resource Centre in Fort Portal: "We [borderlanders] will always move—the boundaries mean nothing to us" (Interview Thirty-Nine).

Territorial Accessibility

What this all speaks to is the profoundly liminal nature of the Rwenzori border and wider borderland, and the strategic benefits this offered rebel groups interested in, and capable of, undertaking certain economic activities. As Raeymaekers (2009b, 61) explains, "Border towns like Kasindi, Beni and Butembo are widely renowned for the fluidity with which [their] inhabitants shift roles from government worker to smuggler, and even armed rebel." And indeed, the ADF were able to 'blend' into this environment: members merged with an already existent and extensive informal trading tradition through building-off of previous NALU economic networks, or taking advantage of kinship relationships with Nande traders. They were likewise able to integrate into the local economy in Butembo and Beni, where they had businesses and stores. And on a micro-level, the ADF were able to cross the border relatively easily and purchase supplies or visit markets to buy foodstuffs. It was not only the border locales mentioned above that were used by the ADF, but other locations as well, including at Katuna, Kyanika, Ishasha (to Rutshuru), and Bunagana.

But the benefits of local embeddedness extended beyond these economic aspects; they also simply facilitated easier operating conditions for the ADF. *The New Vision* in 1998 commented that the group had "enlisted the help of former Rwenzururu combatants to guide them to areas where they can take shelter from extreme conditions" (Matsiko 1998). Indeed, much of the territory traversed by the ADF included difficult mountainous terrain. For those unfamiliar with such an environment, it would have essentially been non-traversable. Not surprisingly then, as *The Monitor* noted in 1999, the ADF had employed "some local people to help them, especially the Bakonjo people with their extensive knowledge of the mountains" (Anonymous 1999).

Various Konjo ex-combatants explained that specific roles were usually reserved for *them* in particular (or Nande members), such as positions that involved acquiring local intelligence, and "knowing the mountains well, the caves, and other secret hide-outs" (Interview Seventy-Two). A former (Konjo) member who had held the post of 'Communications Agent' at one time in the late 1990s, for instance, described his role as one of "carrying communications back and forth between Fort Portal and Bundibugyo" because of his "information of all the roads and paths between the towns" (Interview Seventy-Four). Konjo and Nande personnel were usually those selected to play the more 'visible' roles of the rebel group, such as Yalala, a Konjo woman and ADF operative, who was tasked with managing a 'coordination point' in Butembo between ADF in the bush and contacts from the external wing (MONUSCO Document Four). Clearly, the NALU constituent was palpably pivotal in terms of access to material resources.

MATERIAL RESOURCES AND THE STATE

The Mobutu Regime

There were a variety of other actors of significance in terms of material resources. It is also important to consider the role of the state, for instance. The Mobutu regime allowed NALU to operate from Congolese territory. As Romkema (2007, 68) explains, "The rebel movement was given access to Mumbiri (Beni region) in eastern Zaire, from where it was allowed to run a destabilization campaign against the GoU [Government of Uganda] in western Uganda." He (2007, 68) goes on to note, "The GoZ [Government of Zaire] also supplied arms and ammunition, while the FAZ [Forces Armées Zaïroises] provided intelligence and logistics support for the military operations of NALU. These contacts between the NALU leadership and President Mobutu were facilitated by Enoch Nyamwisi, a former minister and powerful local politician in the Beni region who was killed in Butembo in January 1993."

Pivotally, the Mobutu regime maintained this same stance when NALU was incorporated into the ADF. The ADF were able to have freedom of movement within a significant parcel of land—territory very loosely controlled by the Mobutu regime. It appears that the intermediary this time was Enoch's younger brother, Mbusa Nyamwisi, who later became leader of the rebel movement controlling the Beni and Lubero territories of North Kivu during the Congo wars, the *Rassemblement Congolais pour la Démocratie-Mouvement de Libération*. Lyavala Ali, an original leading member of the ADF, said that "under the direct authority of President Mobutu" camps were opened in Bunia, Buhira, and Beni (Titeca and Vlassenroot 2012, 166). Ali also maintained that "during [President] Mobutu's regime, it [was] Zairian troops that were providing us with security and they were the ones coordinating our operations. They were the ones escorting our commanders to Kinshasa for meetings with [President] Mobutu and Sudanese government officials" (Titeca and Vlassenroot 2012, 166). It is likely the Congolese leader imagined the ADF as a potential counterweight to invading forces (de Waal 2004).

Evidence abounds that President Mobutu not only helped the ADF in terms of access to North Kivutien territory, but that the Congolese national army contributed military equipment, intelligence, food, and frequented the ADF's Beni headquarters (Mulenga 1996). Captured ADF combatants in late November 1996, immediately after the force's first assault on Kasese, stated that Kinshasa had been providing them with training, arms, and cash for the past year (Karugaba 1996). Former ADF Chief of Staff, Commander Benz, shed more light on the relationship with the President when he surrendered in 2000: "At first during [President] Mobutu's regime, some of the supplies came through Kinshasa by air. Others by road. Others from Sudan were landed at Beni airport where we had some of our offices at Henera" (Thawite 2000). When asked by a journalist how these supplies were transported to the bush, Benz replied, "We used [President] Mobutu's army base at Henera, assisted by Lt. Col. Mayere who was the commander of [President] Mobutu's personal army. The supplies included sub-machine guns, their bullets, machine guns, mortars and RPGs [rocket-propelled grenades], medical drugs, uniforms and money" (Thawite 2000). Benz later revealed that the leader had furthermore given them mineral fields in Mugwato, Mombasa, Ibale, and Nyangoli, where they were able to mine gold, diamonds, and coltan (Karugaba 2001).

The Kabila Regime

Much more debated, but less documented, was the Kabila government's relationship with the ADF, specifically as to whether it officially provided assistance, or merely failed to ensure security along its eastern border. Kampala in fact re-invaded Congo in August 1998 using the argument that it was acting in self-defence against the continued ADF attacks on its western districts, which Kinshasa was doing nothing to stop. For a number of reasons this argument is implausible (as will be discussed in the next chapter), and indeed the International Court of Justice (December 19, 2005, 5) reached the same conclusion in 2005: "No satisfactory proof of involvement of Government of the DRC in alleged ADF attacks on Uganda."[15]

While the Ugandan government's description of the situation may have been misleading or exaggerated, Kinshasa nevertheless indirectly supported the ADF during this time period. One such example was its lack of ability (and/or interest) in governing the borderland, which the ADF were able to strategically take advantage of. As an International Crisis Group (August 14, 1998, 7) report explained, "Exploiting the incapacity of the Congolese Armed Forces the ADF has managed to control areas of North Kivu neighboring Uganda. Congolese military units are limited to urban areas like Goma, Walikali, Butembo, and Beni, thus giving the ADF rebels enough room to establish training bases, hospitals and operational centers." Or as an employee of the Voice of Tooro radio station in Fort Portal, remarked, "It's [eastern Congo] ideal for rebels. Civilization only exists in townships; then there is just forest and rural existence. The central government is too far away, and they don't have eastern Congo among their priorities" (Interview Six).

Yet it was not only territorial control that was enabled by this lack of governance, but also access to weapons, as arms networks essentially had free rein. Congo became "a conduit for supply of ammunition to the rebels," as one senior Ugandan government official noted (Sserwanga 1998a). Arms networks tended to follow the trade networks: those traders involved in the importing and exporting of materials to Congo, often added the sale and trade of arms and ammunition to their business portfolio. This was greatly facilitated by not only the exceptionally fluid nature of border crossings, but also the fact that the rest of Congo's borders were "almost completely open to arms supply networks using land routes" (All Party Parliamentary Group on the Great Lakes Region December 2004, 26).

Civilian Borderlander Networks

Another source of material resources for the ADF came from borderland civilians, mainly in Congo around the group's principal camps, but in western Uganda to some extent as well. Two dimensions of civilian assistance were evident: voluntary and forced. Before delving into these two forms, however, it should be noted that even with regards to so-called 'voluntary' civilian assistance, this largely still operated within an environment of pervasive fear. In other words, many of the civilians who chose to 'help' the ADF, did so because they feared dire consequences otherwise. In the ADF's formative stages, they were relatively easily able to attract collaborators. A former combatant who spent nine years with the force described how "We bought food and supplies from the locals. We had a very good relationship with the locals" (Interview Eighty). Following the first attack on Kasese, for example, a press report stated, "An old woman told *The Monitor* at Kinyamaseke that some of the Lukonjo speaking rebels bought sweet bananas from her and paid in

Makutha (Zaire currency)" (Mbabazi 1996). Another former rebel who held the rank of Political Commissar explained, "People in the villages were good because ADF could sleep in the village amongst them and go back with food and intelligence" (Interview Eighty). Hovil and Werker (2005, 16) attribute such actions to "the low economic development of the area." However, as will be discussed later, there were much more complex dynamics surrounding collaboration.

With regards to material resources, civilians often provided foodstuffs, cooked meals, or even shopped in the markets for the rebels when the security situation was deemed precarious (Interview Sixty-One; Interview Forty). One former rebel explained how his commanding officer would acquire resupplies: "Food is bought by General Sasungweso from local markets. He is using pretty ladies for buying things. Then, porters from Kanyarugambe village bring the items to our location accompanied by himself" (MONUSCO Document Eleven). Ex-combatants described how other forms of 'shopping' would work: the civilian would be given money to purchase goods and would then leave the items in his or her house. The ADF would later 'break in' and 'steal' the supplies, so as to not implicate the collaborator (Interview Seventy; Interview Seventy-Four). Often this was done on a village-wide scale: villagers would descend to the border markets to buy items such as fish, oil, and rice in bulk, the foodstuffs would be left in pre-arranged locations throughout the village, and the village would subsequently be 'raided' and the products taken (Interview Seventy; Interview Seventy-Four).

However, as the conflict continued and the force increased their practice of violence against civilians, assistance was more difficult to come by. Thus, whereas previously the ADF would pay people for their help, they instead began to use coercive methods. "Women would be forced to steal food from gardens, and then carry everything back like goats, escorted by gunmen," employees from the Kasese amnesty office described (Interview Twenty-Six). The ADF resorted to raiding gardens, looting stores, stealing from civilians, and attacking camps for supplies (Interview Ten). Nevertheless, throughout this period there still remained those who would assist the group, supplying them with World Food Program (WFP) aid meant for the IDP camps, for example, or reserving parts of their gardens for the rebels (Belz 1999).

Most analyses of the ADF have interpreted their ability to acquire material resources as down to Sudanese support, or to the Islamic links the Tabliq faction was able to activate and use. However, resources derived from national and regional actors only tells part of the story; using a macro level lens fails to explain how the ADF were able to tap into local economic businesses, partake in translocal trade, or access Rwenzori territory. Applying a borderland perspective, on the other hand, sheds light on such dynamics, and helps to reveal how the ADF were able to capitalize on the borderland's anti-state and liminal characteristics. Indeed, through endowing the ADF with agency of their own, a borderland perspective importantly moves the ADF away from being interpreted as a reactive and manipulated force in a marginalized area of the state(s).

The border, in particular, was critical to the group's access to material resources, and to economic practices in general. Largely through NALU's connections, the ADF were able to extensively manipulate and extrapolate from the border. The Rwenzori borderland's historic place as a regional trading hub meant that there were a multitude of embedded transnational economic networks, including smuggling systems, which the rebels could lucratively access. Indeed, the nature of the Rwenzori space was a fundamentally transnational one, with the bulk of economic activity oriented outwards and across the border, as opposed to inwards towards the capital(s). As was discussed in Chapter Two, borderlanders tend to exert an attitude of economic independence and self-assertiveness, and are more willing than heartlanders to engage in what would technically be considered 'illegal' economic activities. The result of the above dynamics, was that the ADF were presented with a relatively welcoming and accessible atmosphere for pursuing various income-generating endeavors.

Compounding this was of course the political environment, namely the end of Mobutu's long reign and beginning of an extended period of instability in eastern Congo. The increasingly weak state, together with foreign occupation of the area, was critical to accentuating the borderland context. Indeed, the outbreak of the Congolese wars, and the increasing transformation of the area's transfrontier trading practices into a war economy, made the ADF's own financial efforts and weapons/supplies acquisition that much more practicable. Also important was the exceptionally weak nature of the Congolese state in the borderland (as well as the Ugandan state, although to a lesser degree), which not only facilitated the group's access to strategic territory, but also enabled an easier flow of military hardware and supplies into the area. Thus, while there were important sources of support for the ADF from Sudan and Islamic groups, it is impossible to understand the rebels' ability to materially survive—to maintain land, and to engage in mining, timber, and taxation—without considering their place in the borderland and integration into borderland networks.

PART III: EXECUTION OF VIOLENCE

MISGUIDED EXPLANATIONS OF THE ADF'S EXECUTION OF VIOLENCE

"They attack indiscriminately, just to kill," said Bundibugyo's assistant Resident District Commissioner (RDC) (Anonymous 1999). "They are just a gang of thugs in disarray terrorizing the people," claimed Brigadier James Kazini (Baguma 2000). And according to President Museveni, "These bandits have no worthy cause, they are simply bandits who enjoy the mayhem and suffering they inflict on innocent people" (Mugisa 1999a). In President Museveni's 1999 State of the Nation address, his portrayal of the ADF as bandits was abundantly clear: "since 1996, the following areas were added to the list of banditry infested areas. These are Kasese, parts of Kabarole and Bundibugyo. These areas have, of course, been endemically affected by banditry since 1962, in the form of Rwenzururu" (Uganda. Parliament, June 2, 1999). As these quotations by Ugandan officials demonstrate, the ADF's operations between 1996–2003 were interpreted as lacking any political purpose.

But it was not only members of the Ugandan government or military that shared this perception of meaningless conflict. It was also found amongst academics, the local press, and many civil society actors and civilians of the affected areas. Prunier (2009, 322), for example, classifies the ADF as belonging to a group of rebels that "are actually, for all practical purposes, bandits." Alnaes (2009, 98 and 116) describes them as "killers, embodying death and unleashing their frenzy on an innocent population," where "The cruelties and stark brutality of these 'democratic' rebels are beyond any imagination." And even more dramatically, she (2009, 119) argues that the ADF were creating "their own death-world mythology where human beings are only 'bare life' that can be killed—worth less than a goat." A report by the Carr Center for Human Rights (2007, 18) argues that the ADF's "method of operation was based on calculated random terror," and that "While raiding, the ADF seemed to go out of their way to ensure maximum terror." In the media, comparisons with the LRA were abundant: "The ADF rebels have been using the same terror tactics as the LRA in northern Uganda. They murder randomly, rob everywhere and kidnap indiscriminately. They are not pursuing the classic guerrilla strategy of 'winning hearts and minds.' They are solely interested in sowing mayhem and causing disaffection in Uganda" (Staff Writers 1997).

The above depictions and understandings of ADF violence mesh with the wider view of the ADF discussed in the previous two chapters. The violence was interpreted through the lens of terrorism, and hence was seen as stemming from the group's extremist Islamic ideology, proxy relationship to Sudan, and goal of terrorizing Kampala to bring down the Museveni government. A piece from *The New Vision* emulated this well: "It is not surprising that the ADF and LRA are using the same terrorist methods because they are both sponsored by the Sudan. These are their orders" (Staff Writers 1997). And according to *The Monitor*, "President Yoweri Museveni has said that rebels of the LRA and ADF under Joseph Kony and Jamil Mukulu respectively are fighting a proxy war for other people" (Mugisa 1999a). Another article in *The Monitor* asked, "What, besides murder and terrorism, is the agenda of the so-called Allied Democratic Forces?" (Mulera 1998). Finally, the RDC of Kabarole district, Charles Chemaswet, stated, "Their prime motive is to instill terror and they have done it. There is confusion, a lot of terror, rumors and fear" (Wamboka 1998).

The violence was also understood as being a symptom of the conflict raging in the Congo—a 'spill-over' of 'chaos' from next door. A discussion on the ADF in the Ugandan Parliament on 22 July 1999 was illustrative of this: "So, when we are debating these things, we must be careful; because we are surrounded by, I do not like to call it a fictitious state, but a state lacking many attributes of a state, and its problems flow into Uganda [. . .] What is happening is that we are having institutional fluidity of a neighboring country flowing into our country; and we are using many methods, including hot pursuit to address these matters," explained Professor Apolo Nsibambi (Uganda. Parliament July 22, 1999). In fact, the Ugandan Minister of State for Foreign Affairs in Charge of International Cooperation, Dr. Martin Aliker, in reaction to the ADF's initial November 1996 attacks, remarked, "I think it is the general lawlessness caused by the crisis in eastern Zaire" (Sserwanga, Nzinjah, and Wasike 1996). Likewise, *Africa Confidential* explained the situation as simply down to the following: "The chaos in Zaire was bound to spill across Uganda's western border and reignite some old rebellions" (Staff Writers 1996, 2). And the local media in October 1997 described the ADF as "taking advantage of the still anarchic situation in eastern Congo to continuously infiltrate back into Uganda" (Staff Writers 1997).

Both of these interpretations have elements of truth to them. For example, the relative lawlessness in the Congo *did* facilitate certain dimensions of the rebellion. There is also no doubt that at times the ADF practiced a very brutal form of rebellion. Not only were killings of civilians common, but their rape, maiming, and mutilation were as well (Human Rights Watch 1999; Kabarole Research and Resource Centre 2004). The following is a typical description of an ADF attack, for example: "Twelve people were burnt alive and at least ten others slaughtered by the ADF rebels in Bugombwa village west of Bundibugyo town, witnesses said yesterday" (Tumwine and Muhanga 1997). There were reports of the cutting off of victims' ears, the removal of tracheas, decapitations, and on more than one occasion cannibalism. An article in *The New Vision* in 1998 stated, "The ADF rebels have eaten an unspecified number of the abducted people and one of their sick commanders, Lt. Col. Francis Okello, commanding officer of the 53rd battalion has said" (Sserwanga 1998b).

The violence came across as even more horrific due to the focus on soft targets, such as non-combatants, women, children, and the elderly (Interview Forty-One; Interview Two). As one IDP in Hakitengya Camp recounted, "Mostly at dusk a group of 5 to 10 fighters used to come down the mountains to carry out 'hit and run' attacks. During those they used to kill, mutilate and abduct so many people, often selected on a basis of vulnerability" (Kabarole Research and Resource Centre 2002/2003, 13). Even less dramatic encounters with the group tended to still be terrifying. The operator of a local tour company in Fort Portal described being stopped by the ADF on a road outside of town: "They stripped us of all our clothes, took everything we had, and gave us a lecture about how the government was bad. They wore soldier uniforms with wild grass hats. They were very frightening" (Interview Fifty-Seven). They also tended to attack institutions such as hospitals, local health care facilities, and even the major prison in Fort Portal. The most notorious ADF assault during this time period was the raid on Kichwamba Technical College in Kabarole district, on 8 June 1998. Although the circumstances surrounding the event are still somewhat murky, it seems the ADF set numerous buildings on the premises on fire, resulting in the deaths of over 80 students (the majority in their teenage years). The traumatic event was compounded by the fact that many students were forced to kill their own classmates, and approximately 200 students were abducted (Interview Two).

However, there is a serious danger in concentrating on explanations of the ADF's use of violence that focus merely on the pageantry aspect. Andrew M. Mwenda (1999) commented in 1999, "For a long time [President] Museveni and his spin doctors have presented the ADF as a marauding Islamic fundamentalist group that targets civilians instead of the military. They have also presented the ADF as a small footloose army of fanatics whose complete elimination has been made difficult by the terrain of the Rwenzori Mountains rather than the group's survival tactics." This portrayal of the ADF painted the force as an irrational, even 'insane,' actor, similar to the LRA (depictions of which also overwhelmingly focused on graphic violence and 'nonsensical' goals such as founding a government on the Ten Commandments). Seeing the ADF in this light took the pressure off of the Ugandan government to try to address their grievances or attempt negotiations. But the narrative also focused on *descriptions* to a much greater extent than *explanations* of the violence. This thereby prevented deep or sustained analysis of, among other things: the functions of the ADF's operations and perpetrated violence; the reasons behind the Ugandan government's oftentimes ineffective response; the dynamics around civilian collaboration; and ultimately, the political, social, and economic context in which the ADF was carrying-out these attacks.

STRATEGIC USE OF INTERNAL ADF FACTIONS

The Nature and Logic of Violence

Faced with taking on one of the most powerful armies in Africa, the ADF had to employ unique strategies against the UPDF. Many of these revolved around using the group's multifaceted composition to the best of their advantage, as well as exploiting the area's poor relationship with central authority, and its networked/liminal character. First of all, it is important to recognize that the ADF were a militarily very capable force, known for their courage, zealousness, and acumen (De Waal 2004). Their status as a relatively proficient group military-wise was largely due to the training provided by the ex–Idi Amin element. Many of these had formerly been either part of Amin's security forces or commanders in his army, and had been professionally trained in places such as Israel (Interview Sixty-Three). Their presence in the force was an important factor behind why training was accorded high priority within the ADF. The following, taken from a DDRRR file of one ADF combatant, tells of a typical scenario: "He was trained for three months non-stop, and then he was sent on different missions for five months to ensure he had become a real combatant. After, he underwent another six months non-stop training" (MONUSCO Document Sixteen). And as an employee of the Center for Basic Research in Kampala explained, "Unlike Kony, they actually captured land. They were good fighters, well-trained, knew what they were doing" (Interview Fifty-Nine). "They were clever, very clever. Once they had attacked a place, they left it, and only would come back once the people there had forgotten about it," explained members of the Integrated Women Development Program (IWDP) (Interview Seventy-Six). Every time that it appeared as though the UPDF had gained the upper hand and forced the ADF to splinter into smaller units, the ADF would strike back in a larger formation—and often once UPDF operations had become relaxed or were focusing efforts elsewhere. The rebels were particularly adept at taking advantage of, and assaulting, neglected and unguarded areas. According to the Carr Center for Human Rights (2007, 20–22), their operations across

Kasese and Bundibugyo districts demonstrated that "the ADF had the capacity to communicate, to coordinate their attacks for maximum publicity value and to strike back directly at government forces [. . .] The effort required from government forces was enormous in comparison with the damage the ADF were able to inflict with a comparatively tiny force."

The various groups within the ADF, as well as those they came to be allied with, were by no means militarily swallowed into one homogeneous entity. Rather, the different elements were in many ways able to retain their independent identities. Training, planning, and attacks were usually coordinated, but the style or method of violence used, for example, differed. According to the Kasese-based civil society worker, "You could tell who conducted which attacks from the way they behaved" (Interview Sixty). He maintains that the Tabliqs, for example, "followed terrorism; they would kill, but would not steal" (Interview Sixty). NALU, on the other hand, brought to the force the brutal fighting techniques of the RM, and the Mai Mai introduced practices such as rape. This helps to account for ex-combatants' drastically differing interpretations of practices and policies of violence against civilians. Many recounted the punishments issued by superiors on those who behaved improperly towards the public. An internal ADF memo from 1999 even shows ADF leaders debating over whether to discipline one of their members in front of civilians for stealing a villager's t-shirt (Interview Eighty-One). Two former ADF members described what was entailed in their positions as 'political commissioners': "to give moral teachings and lessons [to ADF fighters] about how to handle yourself properly with civilians" (Interview Seventy-Five). And during a December 1999 attack on Nyahuka trading center, locals recalled hearing an ADF commander constantly ordering, "Don't harm civilians" (Justus 1999). Indeed, a great deal of former combatants maintained that it was strictly UPDF who were targeted in attacks, and that any civilian casualties were solely the result of their being caught in the cross-fire (Interview Eighty). Of course, actual events throughout the conflict belie such beliefs: houses were torched, villages destroyed, and civilians killed. Yet some factions within the ADF appeared to have condemned such policies, and the Kichwamba incident, for instance, provoked serious internal disagreement.

Furthermore, it is worth pointing out that however horrific some of the violence was, it was by no means as random or as meaningless as was depicted in many analyses. A zooming in on the acts of violence reveals that they served particular purposes. These included sending a message to the public, punishing perceived collaborators, acquiring manpower (as in Kichwamba), or simply looking for food and supplies. Indeed, life in the camps was often quite difficult. Living conditions appeared to deteriorate drastically whenever the group was in 'escape mode' and forced to become more mobile.

During these periods very primitive structures would constitute as shelters, food was scarce, and there was a marked increase in mortality rates of their non-combatant personnel (particularly infants and the elderly). This is when a noticeable rise in looting would occur—either to acquire food, medical items, or other supplies—and the ADF would not hesitate in punishing those who were unwilling to co-operate. A piece from *The New Vision* in September 1998 was telling in this respect: "Military sources said the rebels approached the town [Kasese] on two fronts. The sources said that after the rebels failed to break into the hospital and the army detach, they turned onto the market, looting it before setting it ablaze. A senior military said the rebels wanted supplies. He said after the dislodgement from their strongholds in the Rwenzori Mountains, the rebels are hard-pressed for food and medicine" (Nzinjah and Thawite 1998).

Indeed, contrary to the depictions of random and meaningless terror, there clearly were functions—no matter how controversial or deplorable—behind the violence.[16] Describing a raid on Bundibugyo town, for example, Mbabazi stated, "The ADF staged a desperate raid on the town in search of drugs, food and other essentials which they desperately lacked in their hideouts in the Rwenzori Mountains" (Kakande 1997). Moreover, simply the nature of the conflict—namely, guerrilla warfare, blurred distinctions between civilian and combatant, and an absence of clear battle lines—made civilian casualties more likely (Weinstein 2007).

The Significance of NALU

The knowledge and skills that NALU brought to the wider force were especially significant for the borderland battlezone. NALU, of course, had been very much shaped by the military experience of, and knowledge passed down from, the RM. Thus, not only were their fighters battle-hardened and experienced, but they were familiar with the terrain and skilled in traversing the border. More specifically, the NALU faction's ability to blend into the transnational Konjo-Nande community gave the ADF significant advantages in cross-border realms such as transportation of personnel and supplies, communication, and the utilization of attack and retreat tactics. It enabled them to cross the border undetected, blend into target populations, and scout future attack sites. Although a great proportion of the force were abductees, this translocal dimension was still invaluable. One interesting element of this concerned the infiltration of villages and towns before an attack. The first major offensive on Kasese, which saw the assault of so many key locations (the attack and torching of the Shell Station, for instance), was largely down to the ADF's penetration of the town beforehand. Employees of the Agape Foundation in Kasese explained that prior to the offensive, the Konjo/Nande members had come into the town disguised as hawkers, studied the area, learned the different entry and exit routes, and gained a thorough understanding of its geography (Interview Forty-Six; Interview Twelve). Similarly, in order to ensure 'safe passage' when moving through potentially unfriendly or unfamiliar territory, Konjo or Nande members of the force would be put at the front, so as to encourage trust from the locals (Interview Sixty-One). This ability to integrate into the local setting was also relevant once an attack had occurred. As Alnaes (2009, 98) recalls of her time in Bundibugyo following its first major assault on 16 June 1997, "While I was still there, I was told by an old friend, now a local government official, that 'according to our intelligence, there are rebels here but we don't see them because they look like anyone else.'"

It is undoubtedly the case that the terrain of the Rwenzori borderland greatly favored the ADF in this respect. And this is something the UPDF were well aware of: "The terrain remains the biggest problem. 'We have to cut their supply lines or they may never be finished,' one official said" (Anonymous 1999). First of all, a significant proportion of the ADF were intimately familiar with this type of landscape having been born and raised there. Furthermore, of that segment of the group, many were "the indigenous rebels"—those acquainted with the terrain in a *military* sense, due to participation in the area's previous conflicts (Interview Seventy-Three). It was a terrain of valleys and hills, dense forest and thick vegetation in some areas, and even in the more penetrable locales a very undulating landscape. Crucially, much of this was traversable only by foot and was difficult for outsiders to 'know.' It was thus highly unbefitting for large troop convoys, armored vehicles, or aerial bombing, let alone aerial surveillance. Combined with the endless hiding possibilities and presence of the border, it was an environment instead greatly favorable to hit-and-run style attacks. Describing a June 1997 assault, for example, *The New Vision* stated, "Rebel Allied Democratic Forces last week invaded Bundibugyo district from their hideouts in Lume [Congo] on the western slopes of the Rwenzori. The ragged terrain with deep valleys, snow-capped hills and thick forests helped conceal their hideouts" (Allio 1997). And even where roads did exist, such as between Fort Portal and Bundibugyo, the historic underdevelopment of the region meant that they were in notoriously poor, at times almost unusable, condition. An employee of the WFP recounted that his travels on the Fort Portal-Bundibugyo road, only a distance of 47 miles, would take the better part of a day during the conflict (Interview Three). The ADF would often use alternative local routes, or travel via rivers such as the Muzizi and Semliki.

This also speaks to the isolation of many of these places, again an asset for the ADF. The strategic town of Bundibugyo, for example, had only one entry and exit point.[17] So long as the ADF could control this, which they often did or attempted to do via roadblocks, they could control the town (Angurin 1997; Mbabazi and Karugaba 1997; Kyankya 1997). They thereby would have easy access to the vast Ituri forest in the Congo, which Bundibugyo was connected to. Even more remote, however, were the mountains. Settlements in the Rwenzoris were not clustered into villages, but rather quite evenly spaced throughout, with farming plots all the way from the lowest to highest points of the mountains. Connecting the settlements were a labyrinthine network of footpaths, that would only make sense, let alone even be visible, to inhabitants. The challenges this presented to a traditional military force unfamiliar with the terrain were immense. The area was essentially unmapped, and thus attempting to traverse the mountains through the multitude of valleys and hills would be extremely time-consuming, not to mention enormously strenuous. Indeed, as *The New Vision* reported, "UPDF field commanders say it takes almost a day in some sections of the mountain for the troops to move a kilometer uphill because of the soggy grounds and forests" (Matsiko 1998).

The ADF thus essentially had an advantage (and one that they skillfully exploited) in that they could attack the western Ugandan towns of Kasese, Bundibugyo, Fort Portal, and Mpondwe, quickly retreat, and then disappear into their camps in the mountains, or to their bases in the forests of eastern Congo. Describing the first assault on Kasese, press reports stated, "Fleeing civilians told *The Monitor* that the fresh rebel influx had been through the mountains overlooking Kisinga and Kinyamaseka sub-counties both in Bakonjo county" (Mbabazi 1996). In the first few years of the conflict, mainly between 1996 and 1998, the ADF attacked in large numbers: "An estimated 500 rebels attacked Bundibugyo after crossing from eastern areas of the Democratic Republic of the Congo, overrunning both the police and army units in the border town" (Kyankya 1997). However, as the UPDF gradually became more adept at pursuing the rebels, the ADF changed tactics and began to operate in smaller groups, crossing the border and attacking in bands of five to ten. They also tended to keep camps, many of which in fact dated back to the RM, situated very close to the border so as to facilitate quick escape across the state line (Sswerwanga 1999a).

While at times the heterogeneity of the group appeared to cause discord—such as disagreement over conduct with civilians—this arrangement nevertheless enabled the ADF to take advantage of the different groups' particular strengths. Their unique composition even enabled the ADF to in a sense have multiple frontlines simultaneously. There was of course the Bundibugyo-Kasese arena, but Kampala constituted a theatre of operation for the ADF as well. The Tabliqs' style of fighting had previously been in urban violence, and consequently this was put to use for the Kampala bombing campaigns. Whereas the dominant understanding of ADF military behavior frames the ADF during this time period as moving from rural conflict to urban terrorism, it was much more a case of the group having the capacity to maintain a double-pronged approach. Nevertheless, the principal frontline was undoubtedly in the borderland, and their main objective was about maintaining this transnational space.

STRATEGIC USE OF BORDERLAND GRIEVANCES

Kampala's Response to the Conflict

The ADF also strategically manipulated another resource for military advantage, namely, the borderland public's poor relationship with central authority. In the ADF's main theatre of operation during this time period, western Uganda, this was especially critical, as the area's historic distrust (if not outright hostility) towards Kampala meant potential collaboration opportunities for the force. First, the Museveni regime's historic treatment of western Uganda as a peripheral area of the country led it to underplay the severity of attacks in the initial phases. As an employee of the UK's Department for International Development (DFID) in Kampala observed, "If this had been happening closer to the capital, it would have been a much different story"[18] (Interview Forty-Eight). According to African Rights (2001, 25), "There is a perception among some victims of the conflict in the west that much more could and should have been done to bring the rebellion to an end. They argue that initially the government did not give sufficient attention to the ADF conflict, concentrating instead on the greater threat posed by the LRA in the north." Not until Kazini was appointed in 1998 to lead a UPDF Alpine Brigade, was serious attention or resources directed towards combating the ADF.

In fact, the government continually portrayed the conflict as being close to over and the rebels having been crushed, when neither was the case. In the initial weeks of the violence, Uganda's Internal Security Organization refused to admit the group even existed. When the rebellion was finally acknowledged, President Museveni accused the local press of exaggerating the scale of attacks (Muhangi 1996). And in mid-December 1996, a Ugandan military source claimed, "What we know for sure is that the ADF rebels are a spent force" (Sserwanga and Nzinjah 1996a). Such statements by the government continued: in February 1997 it was asserted that the UPDF had taken full control of the ADF's strategic positions in the Rwenzori Mountains; in December 1998, that they had been dislodged from all major camps and merely "roamed the ridges" of the mountains; in July 1999, that the UPDF had killed over 1,500 combatants, and only 500 were left; and in February 2000, President Museveni referred to the ADF rebellion as "a small problem" (Nzinjah 1997a;

Nzinjah 1998; Mugisa 1999b; Sserwanga and Nzinjah 2000). But various declarations issued in Parliament were even more profoundly inaccurate: "We have decisively defeated ADF completely in the west and arrested all the urban terrorists," President Museveni affirmed in his 2001 State of the Nation Address (Uganda. Parliament July 27, 2001). Such statements continued until 2003, when the ADF were truly forced to retreat from Uganda and to their rear bases in Congo.

All of this is not to say that the ADF did not experience blowback from the UPDF—and at times, quite devastating blowback. June and July 1998, for example, saw numerous ADF camps overrun and militants killed, with subsequent starvation and a dwindling of supplies. Nevertheless, they clearly survived such ordeals. And so as one former Ugandan politician noted, "The government should carefully calculate the words used in making announcements about rebels. Comments like: 'We have finished them; they have been crushed; they are thieves, etc.' are not of great help. If anything, they're a catalyst to violence" (African Rights 2001, 34). Indeed, various remarks by the ADF showed that at times the rebels were at least partially spurred to action by this attitude from the government. After a significant attack on Bundibugyo in June 1997, for example, the Secretary General of the ADF, Ssentamu Kayira, signed a release that read, "The attack we carried out on Bundibugyo, Ntoroko, Ntandi, etc., was intended to disprove government's false and wishful allegations that it had stamped us out of the fighting industry" (Kyankya 1997).

For residents of the borderland, however, what perhaps appeared even more confusing than the government's *statements*, were its *actions*. Arguing that President Kabila was failing to provide security along the eastern border with Uganda and thereby enabling ADF infiltration, the Museveni regime entered the Congo in supposed hot pursuit of the rebels. However, when the UPDF effectively went past the borderland and into the interior, concentrating its efforts around the city of Kisangani in Orientale Province, it became apparent that targeting the ADF was not at the top of the agenda (African Rights 2001; Otunnu 2004). As Prunier notes, "the fact that the UPDF is deployed 'more than 1,000 kilometers from [the Uganda–Congo] frontier' is prima facie evidence that [President] Museveni and his government have other goals" (Clark 2004, 149). The International Court of Justice (December 19, 2005), in its investigation of the situation, also found that Uganda's 'self-defense' argument was wanting, to say the least. The issue was debated regularly in Parliament, with many parliamentarians expressing confusion over the matter. Member of Parliament John Ken Luyamuzi stated in July 1999, "we want to know why we have gone so far [into the Congo] and yet people come in and kill people in Bundibugyo, in Kasese. How do we reconcile the two?" (Uganda. Parliament July 14, 1999). Likewise, the

Worker's Representative, Bakkabulindi Charles, commented in Parliament in July 2000, "he [President Museveni] is talking of having modern soldiers, well equipped with high skills. Then we are talking about ADF as being these small indisciplined boys. The question comes to my mind, 'If our soldiers are well equipped with modern machines and skills from abroad, what has been stopping us eliminating all these people who are just disturbing us all these months?'" (Uganda. Parliament July 13, 2000).

As attacks continued, western Ugandan residents grew restless. Oftentimes the UPDF seemed completely caught off-guard, failed to act promptly, or their military presence was suspiciously negligible, as was the case in the Kichwamba incident (Interview Thirty-Two). Employees at Kichwamba, who had been present during the attack, described how the UPDF had previously been warned of possible impending assaults on the school, but failed to take any action. They were then slow and ineffective in responding when the attack eventually transpired (Interview Seventy-Eight). Furthermore, it became apparent that the UPDF was facing quite serious internal discipline and morale problems, with cases of 'ghost soldiers,' desertion, and even collaboration with the rebels. The phenomenon of ghost soldiers refers to the deaths of army personnel not being reported, in order for their salaries to be collected by other soldiers (often commanders). As a result of this practice, the UPDF was often involved in battles with substantially less than the required or recommended number of men. Kazini ended-up admitting that he had 6,000 soldiers in Congo to fight the ADF, as opposed to the 10,000 officially in his books. With regards to UPDF collaboration, at times it appeared that the ADF proclaimed this was taking place simply as part of their disinformation campaign. The following incident, reported by *The Monitor*, would seem to be one such case: "Kabanda who cocked his gun and later fired some bullets to prove a point that he was at his command post in the bush, said his rebels get supplies from inside Uganda most especially 'from UPDF'" (Okee 1999). However, the number and range of sources that reported the existence of UPDF collaboration makes it highly unlikely that such a practice was *only* ADF propaganda.

Ultimately, after a December 1999 prison raid in Fort Portal (the prison was adjacent to a major military barracks) Mwenda (1999) asked the question that was on many people's minds: "How can Ugandan troops who have been deep inside Congo for a whole three years on grounds of eliminating ADF's supply bases still be facing military assaults from the rebels deep inside Uganda?" Indeed, there was a significant rumor mill in existence as to the intentions—or lack thereof—of the Museveni government with regards to the ADF conflict. The following statement from an employee of a Kasese peacebuilding NGO, reflected a widespread sentiment amongst locals: "I think the Ugandan government invented the ADF, and then let the war persist, to subdue a traditionally dissident area of the country" (Interview Forty-Five).

Actions from Kampala seemed to continuously demonstrate a lack of commitment to ensuring peace in western Uganda, including lacklustre support for the amnesty process. There was a common perception that President Museveni himself was not sincere about promoting the amnesty act, and there were numerous cases of former ADF members applying for amnesty only to be imprisoned (Hovil and Lomo 2005). Ex-combatants frequently complained of their promised amnesty packages never materializing, thereby being "back in the same conditions that forced us into the bush"—a condition the ADF exploited for recruitment purposes (Interview Eighty). Compounding this were the attitudes of several top UPDF soldiers. As *The Sunday Monitor* reported in January 2000, "Army Chief of Staff Brigadier James Kazini has dismissed the effectiveness of the Amnesty Bill that grants pardon to rebels who surrender [. . .] 'ADF rebels do not understand the word amnesty,' said the Brigadier who is operations commander for the western Axis covering Kasese, Kabarole, parts of DRC and Bundibugyo" (Baguma 2000). This was related to a lack of interest on the part of the government towards pursuing any kind of discussions or negotiations with the rebels. The issue was brought up quite regularly in the press and Parliament, with politician Ken Lukyamuzi inquiring in July 1999, "Do you not think it is necessary—on top of amnesty—for the President to accept to talk to the rebels outside Uganda for the good of ensuring that all can be listened to whether enemies or not?" (Uganda. Parliament July 14, 1999).

But perhaps it was the government's response to the IDP camps that the ADF was able to capitalize on the most. The massive displacement of civilians in western Uganda undoubtedly carried with it various costs for the ADF, including no longer being able to hide amongst, or obtain resources from, civilians, and of course the alienation of future supporters (Hovil and Werker 2005). However, the rebels nevertheless experienced significant gains through the mass movement of locals into what the government euphemistically called 'protected villages.' They were able to make use of abandoned land and supplies, for example, but most importantly, a general impression was created of a national government incapable of and/or unwilling of protecting its citizens. The ADF launched numerous raids on the camps, to which the UPDF often failed to respond to, or did so in a less than adequate manner (Kabarole Research and Resource Centre 2004). The IDPs were furious about this, considering that many had not even wanted to leave their homes in the first place. They had essentially been forced into the camps, as the alternative was to be labelled a collaborator by the UPDF—a label that could entail great punishment. Furthermore, the conditions of the camps were deplorable, and the few international aid agencies operating in the area complained about the government's irresponsive attitude towards providing the requisite funding, supplies, and most of all, attention, to the matter (Ahimbisibwe 2004).[19] The Uganda Human Rights 2000–2001 Report in fact stated the following: "In spite of this responsibility [to protect and promote IDPs' rights], and in spite of the fact that IDPs have been a common feature for a considerable time now, government response to their problems has at best been ad hoc. There is no known policy and programs for dealing with the problems of IDPs. Responses to situations of IDPs have often been intermittent, unplanned and inadequate" (Uganda. Human Rights Commission 2001).

In 1998, during a supposed lull in the fighting, the government convinced IDPs to leave the camps and return home. This was ill-informed advice, as the situation was by no means secure, and many people were killed as a result (Uganda. Human Rights Commission 2005). In light of all of the above, the ADF were provided with a great deal of fodder for their anti-government campaign, and issued messages to IDPs such as the following:

> In Bundibugyo District, documents in the chief administrators office indicate a constant loss of public funds in terms of developing targets, health targets, and universal primary education. These funds are raised from the collection of money from you the local people in different sources of income. This exercise has contributed nothing else other than cheating you the displaced people in the camps [. . .] Allow me to flash you briefly on the recurred problems you are facing while the government is seated comfortably watching you without steps taken to restore the situation [. . .] Hunger is in your neck whereas the district officers are feeding on your money collected as tax. Diseases such as cholera, typhoid, malaria, etc. are claiming lives daily due to absence of medical services and facilities in the district (Interview Eighty-One).

While the ADF's messages were clearly dramatic and exaggerated in tone, civilians were nevertheless frustrated with the peripheral treatment they were receiving from the government—first in the form of negligible military protection, and then the neglect of other concerns such as health care and food supplies. In a June 1998 article, *The Monitor* described the "growing restlessness among *wanachi* [civilians] who are fed up with rebel atrocities and unfulfilled 'security' guarantees from government. Their message is unequivocal: Either arm us to protect ourselves or talk peace with the rebels" (Wamboka 1998).

CIVILIAN COLLABORATION

"The problem of rebel collaborators is widespread and apart from the UPDF being thin on the ground, security sources said collaboration with the rebels had greatly hampered efforts to pacify the region [. . .] 'In the company of collaborators, the rebels have managed to beat our own intelligence system and the forces on the ground to exercise their killings,' says Muluuri Mukasa, Minister of Security" (Sserwanga 1999b). At first glance, these comments from the local press could appear confusing. Considering that the ADF did not exactly endear themselves to the local population, the practice of collaboration with rebels might perhaps seem irrational or nonsensical. Crucially, however, due to the dynamics discussed above, the ADF's failure in winning the 'hearts and minds' of the populace did not translate into support for the Ugandan government. Kampala's inability and/or disinterest in providing security during the rebellion, on top of all of the other historic center-periphery antagonistic dynamics (such as the overall underdevelopment of the borderland), induced a general attitude of distrust, if not outright animosity, towards the UPDF.

This dynamic has been difficult for outsiders to comprehend. As such, the possibility of any form of collaboration between civilians and the ADF during this time period has usually been dismissed in analyses. However, it is very similar to the situation described by Sverker Finnström in northern Uganda, another marginalized area. "In the 1996 and 2001 presidential elections, fewer than 10 percent of the voters in the north supported President Museveni and his no-party Movement system; in 2006 some 16 percent did so. The number of people who have welcomed the Movement government, then, is basically as small as the number who welcomed the LRA/M rebels," Finnström (2008) explains. The brutal violence committed by the LRA against civilians has tended to overshadow the fact that the population has traditionally been very unsatisfied with both their general relationship with the central government, and also Kampala's response to the conflict. Despite most understandings of the conflict emphasizing the willingness of civilians to join the government in their fight against the rebels, Finnström argues that the occurrence of this was actually quite rare. He (2008, 129) goes on to note,

> rather than being satisfied with the fact that cosmetic surgery can be done today in Gulu town, most of my young informants would vote for LRA/M's promise to provide "free basic primary health care for all." This is not to say that these informants actively support the LRA/M, or that the LRA/M is an organization that they think is able to realize its promises. But the experience, again as taken up by the LRA/M, that the "population at the grassroots are hardly feeling the economic achievements of the Museveni regime."

The conflict essentially only widened the gap between the population and government, with civilians feeling even more disconnected from the development taking place in the rest of Uganda.

Zooming-in on the ADF conflict, very similar sentiments and dynamics existed amongst the Rwenzori population. While support was not usually overtly displayed for the ADF, neither was it for the UPDF. Yet, if using a micro-political approach, various modes of more hidden forms of collaboration can be detected. Some western Ugandan residents chose to support the ADF in a very direct manner, such as through the provision of food and shelter (Ruhunda, et al). However, this form of collaboration became less frequent after the first year of the conflict. Instead what many civilians chose to practice was a more passive mode of collaboration. For example, when the UPDF would come to a village asking for news about where the ADF were, or if they had been spotted recently, civilians would withhold such information or provide inaccurate data.

Collaboration with the rebels, whether pro-active or passive, has not been extensively documented, and this is perhaps in large part due to the amnesty process and shame now associated with aiding rebels. Nevertheless, the practice of collaboration unquestionably had important implications. After all, according to the majority of ex-combatants whom I talked with, the primary reason behind the ADF's resiliency during this time period came down to "indigenous people collaborating with us [the rebels]" (Interview Seventy-Three). Or as a local market vendor in Kasese said during the time, "The ADF have many Bakonjo supporters amongst us. That's why the war has been on for the last five years" (African Rights 2001, 45). Of course, it should be noted that it was by no means only Konjo residents who were collaborators.

Eventually, the UPDF appeared to gain a better understanding of the ADF's modus operandi. After surprisingly successful ADF attacks in Hoima, Kibale, and Bushenyi in 2000, the army's 'Operation Mountain Sweep' campaign became more aggressive. Strategies and tactics were tailored to target the ADF's local supply lines, mountainous refuge areas, critical roads, and most importantly, the border. Furthermore, the UPDF made attempts to interact more responsibly with the population, and 'home guards' and 'LDUs' (vigilante groups) were initiated to work alongside the army (Kabarole Research and Resource Centre 2004, 12). Many locals in Kasese and Bundibugyo districts indeed attributed the change in UPDF strategic effectiveness as down to an improved relationship with the population. This included the UPDF appearing to finally be interested in providing security, as well as getting civilians 'onboard' through the home guards and LDUs (Interview Sixty-Four; Interview Sixty-Six). The ADF were greatly reduced in numbers, their Secretary General, Ali Bwambale Mulima, was captured along with several other leaders, and operational capacity was generally diminished. Nevertheless, the ADF managed to hold-out until 2003, when they were finally forced to abandon operations in Uganda. What is of course important to recognize, however, is that although the ADF were weakened in numbers and strength, they were not defeated or disbanded.

The above discussion has demonstrated that it is not sufficient to explain the ADF's military conduct and activities by looking through a macro level lens, and using state-centric explanations found at national or regional levels of analysis. The ADF were not solely interested in wreaking random terrorist havoc on Kampala, or indiscriminately killing civilians with no rationale: they were principally concerned with maintaining their place in the borderland, and their military activities largely reflected this. A borderland perspective revealed that a great deal of the ADF's strength and resiliency in the face of a hostile military environment came down to their ability to take advantage of their different internal factions, especially those already embedded or experienced with the translocal milieu, such as NALU. Being a force that in crucial ways had grown out of the borderland itself, the ADF had a distinct advantage over the UPDF in terms of ability to traverse the border, intimate familiarity of the terrain, and so on.

Yet, while the ADF's internal constitution was important, so too was the nature of the civilian borderland population. Borderlanders tend to practice polymorphous, shape-shifting, and acephalous lives, and as Scott (2009) has pointed out, this makes them relatively ungraspable and unconquerable to outside actors such as the state. They also tend to have a volatile relationship with central authority, preferring various forms of self-rule, or the rule of the socio-political community on the other side of the border, to central power. Combined with a powerful sense of border identity, behavior in opposition or defiance to the national state is often tolerated, if not outright encouraged and supported. All of the above were traits of the Rwenzori borderland population between 1996–2003. As such, it was a highly conducive environment for the ADF to reside in and conduct their military endeavors from. The ADF were able to blend into the population when needed, manipulate the civilian residents' distrust of, and animosity towards, the government(s), and even garner a degree of local collaboration. Despite the rebels practicing a significant amount of violence against civilians, the borderlanders' dislike for central authority (and consequently animosity towards the UPDF) proved paramount, and the ADF were able to extract the necessary support needed from locals.

Again, the national and regional levels of analysis can be useful to analyze the ADF's execution of violence—for example, the influence of global Islamic terrorism in the ADF's bombing campaigns. However, the ADF's military resiliency in their principal theatre of action, the western Ugandan–eastern Congolese transnational space, cannot be understood without consideration of the micro-politics of the borderland, the borderland's anti-state and liminal qualities, and ultimately its very *non*-peripheral significance.

Chapter Four has shown why a borderland perspective is necessary to understand the ADF conflict. Taking the borderland as a unit of analysis helped to shed light on the anti-state and liminal qualities of this space, and their potential consequences for this conflict. It was revealed that the ADF's ability to enmesh themselves within certain borderland networks was critical to their survival during this time period. Despite failing to establish a positive relationship with the western Ugandan population, the ADF proved skilled at manipulating the political tradition of resistance against central authority in the area, the social predominance of a borderland identity, and the economic system of independent cross-border trade. Through taking advantage of these characteristics, and building-upon historic relationships with the borderland, they were able to navigate a relatively hostile environment. Although they were forced to abandon operations in western Uganda in early 2003, the conflict was not over. As Chapter Five will elucidate, the rebels' proved skilled in rebounding from such setbacks, and throughout 2004–2013, they would continue to demonstrate quite remarkable resiliency.

NOTES

1. Muslims have traditionally represented approximately 15 percent of Uganda's population. With Idi Amin's coming to power, many within the Muslim community believed their historically marginalized position might be soon rectified. One of the Muslim President's primary points on his agenda was to redress the religious imbalances between Christians and Muslims sowed during the colonial period and maintained or deepened throughout successive independent Christian governments. One of the main actions he took in this regard, besides the creation of the umbrella organization the Uganda Muslim Supreme Council (UMSC), was to promote Islamic education for young Ugandans across the country. Amin cultivated ever-closer relations with Arab states, and most particularly the Kingdom of Saudi Arabia which welcomed young Ugandans to study at the Islamic University of Medina. Throughout the 1970s and 80s several hundred Ugandan Muslim students went to study at said University, and upon their return preached a stricter version of Islam—the Salafi doctrine—which had not previously been known in Uganda. For more on the history of the Muslim population more generally in Uganda, see Kanyeihamba (1998).

2. For more on the background of the Tabliqs, see de Waal (2004).

3. As previously mentioned, following Amin's rise to power he created the UMSC. This was housed within the old Kampala mosque, and all Muslims in the country were placed under its authority. However, after Amin was deposed in April 1979, the organization quickly began to unravel. After numerous court battles at the Ugandan

Supreme Court between various Muslim factions—each claiming to be the legitimate leaders of Ugandan Muslims—the court ruled against the Salafis on 19 March 1991. This ruling, it is argued (Nsobya 2015–2016; Chande 2000) was the spark that caused the young Ugandans who had studied abroad in Saudi Arabia (the first generation of reformist Salafis in Uganda) to become a full-fledged radical Islamist movement.

4. On 22 March 1991 around 1,000 Muslim youths attacked the UMSC headquarters and seized control. The government responded by sending in the military, and at the end of the confrontation some 400 Salafi activists—including Jamil Mukulu—were imprisoned and others had fled into exile (Nsobya 2015–2016).

5. This first ADF attack was backed by Mobutu's regime. As Rwanda's ally in the First Congo War, Uganda was seen as an enemy by Mobutu. Thus the anti-Ugandan ADF afforded him a useful and convenient vehicle to both punish Uganda, as well as attempt to keep their forces occupied with defending their own territory (rather than coming to Rwanda's aid). The ADF, in turn, had a key interest in defending Mobutu's rule, due to fear of what his deposition and loss of this support would mean for their rebellion.

6. Reported numbers of rebels in this assault vary, and this particular soldier's estimate may be slightly exaggerated. Most reports put the number closer to 800.

7. *The Monitor* printed an article on 10 December 1999, for example, titled "The ADF: Rebels without a cause" (Anonymous 1999). Hans Romkema's (2007, 63) description of the group during this time period is a typical analysis: "The ADF had no clear political objectives and failed to take political advantage of the conditions it had created."

8. Some (technically former) RM fighters actually joined the NRA as well; their numbers are estimated to have been between 100 and 400 (Titeca and Vlassenroot 2012).

9. During this time period, President Museveni's 'movement' system of government (one-party system) was in place, which by its very nature prevented organized political opposition from developing.

10. Indeed, there are many reports of Bugandans joining the ADF during the initial phases (Amooti 1999; Mulingwa 1998).

11. UPDF troops largely maintained a presence in a large swath of northeastern Congo parallel to the western Uganda border in pursuit of ADF rebels from both sides of the frontier. Thus, when fighting broke out between the RCD and Congo's armed forces on 2 August 1998—signaling the beginning of the Second Congo War—UPDF forces were already present in the country (Human Rights Watch 2001). However, the UPDF did not enter the Congo *in force* until later in the month of August 1998. They added to the number of troops already deployed, occupying about 600 miles of Congo territory inland to Equateur province from the eastern border, which they maintained until they pulled out in 2003 after the transitional government took power.

12. It is interesting to consider the possibility here that the Mai Mai did not extend the 'foreigner' label to the ADF.

13. See for example Carr Center for Human Rights (2007) and OHCHR (2010).

14. It is important to note that a lot of these claims are just that: unproven assertions, perhaps simply for propaganda purposes.

15. The UPDF had occupied a large swath of northeastern Congo parallel to its border since the First Congo War of 1996–1997. That occupation was simply reinforced when the Second Congo War broke out in August 1998, as Uganda declared war on Congolese President Laurent Kabila's government alongside Rwanda. The UPDF's area of occupation included the territories of Beni and Lubero in North Kivu province and the districts of Ituri and Kibali in Orientale province. Throughout the period of occupation, the UPDF played a decisive role in local affairs, exercising ultimate authority over all military and security matters in each district and even altering administrative boundaries and designating provincial officials. The UPDF as an occupying power claimed to be a 'peacemaker' in a region torn by ethnic strife, but in reality provoked political confusion, insecurity, and manipulated ethnic loyalties in the regions under its occupation. Although Uganda claimed its occupation of the northeastern region of Congo was important for securing its border, the area also offered abundant natural and commercial wealth, which the UPDF reaped.

16. For an interesting discussion on the functions of violence in the Congo (in general), see Beneduce, Jourdan, Raeymaekers, and Vlassenroot (2010), and Van Acker and Vlassenroot (2001).

17. Bundibugyo's relatively recent bout with the Ebola virus substantiates the area's extreme remoteness and underdevelopment.

18. Likewise if this had been happening in Museveni's home area, the southwest of the country, it also would have 'been a different story.' Essentially Museveni tended to neglect everywhere *other* than the capital and southwestern region.

19. Ugandan United Nations Children's Fund (UNICEF) employees recounted how many IPDs had found the conditions so intolerable that they would attempt to sneak into the UNHCR refugee camps instead (Interview Seventy-Nine).

Chapter 5

Setbacks and Recoveries: The ADF 2004–2013

Despite[1] suffering a significant loss in numbers and being forced to halt campaigns in western Uganda by early 2003, the ADF's enmeshment in the borderland fabric enabled them to survive. They had soon regrouped and rebuilt their strength in eastern Congo, and within several years had managed to increase their numbers to 1,500 combatants.[2]

The Rwenzori area in many ways was a changed environment between 2004 to 2013: western Uganda was now effectively in a state of negative peace, and eastern Congo had theoretically entered a 'post-conflict' phase. Nevertheless, both sides of the border remained characterized politically by a tradition of resistance against central authority, socially by the predominance of a borderland identity, and economically by a system built around independent cross-border trade.

In essence, the Rwenzori space was still profoundly anti-state and liminal, and the ADF proved capable of once again using these characteristics to their advantage. Through applying a borderland perspective, Chapter Five will discuss how the ADF responded and adapted to the changed environment in the borderland, and how they continued to take advantage of, and maneuver throughout, the whole of the Rwenzori cross-border space. It will consider how despite facing significant threats to their survival in both 2005 and 2010, the ADF rebounded each time, and ultimately demonstrated enormous resilience. Similar to Chapter Four, Chapter Five will explore these issues through consideration of three dimensions of rebel group behavior and activity: recruitment, retention, and organization; material resources; and the execution of violence.

PART I: RECRUITMENT, RETENTION, AND ORGANIZATION

MISGUIDED EXPLANATIONS OF THE ADF'S RECRUITMENT, RETENTION, AND ORGANIZATION

An online North Kivutien news source discussed the long-running issue of "Ugandan rebels" in Beni territory in a 19 July 2011 article (Bahati 2011). "The Ugandan army has deployed forces near the border of neighboring DRC following reports that Ugandan rebels had regrouped in nearby Congolese villages," reported IRIN News (2004). "The FARDC-Congolese 'governmental' forces are fighting the NALU-Ugandan rebel forces [. . .] The ADF-NALU is a phantom-like rebel group from Uganda. There are rumors about how well they're trained, and how dangerous they are, yet they're extremely hard to pin down," claimed Amy Ernst (2010–2012), an NGO worker blogging from Butembo. All of these comments have one significant aspect in common: they portray the ADF as a Ugandan rebel group.

As Chapter Four discussed, between 1996–2003 prevalent explanations of the ADF's recruitment, retention, and organization practices demonstrated a belief that the group was (1) composed principally of Islamic terrorists, (2) strongly backed by Sudan, and (3) had the sole aim of taking down the Museveni government. During the 2004–2013 time period this view persisted, although slight shifts could be detected. The focus on a Sudanese role received less attention in light of Sudan's diminished interest in Ugandan affairs. However, attention to Islamic terrorism increased, as did focus on the group's objective, which was supposedly overthrowing the Ugandan government. The ADF were overwhelmingly seen as a Ugandan force: while they may have received some help from outsiders, they were characterized as composed of Ugandan nationals, with Ugandan-oriented objectives. Of course, at this point their leadership was still predominantly Ugandan, but the group was overall a hybrid, with a steadily increasing Congolese component. Nevertheless, the ADF's connection with the Congo was perceived to be merely territorial: they were a group living and operating in exile in the Congo, taking advantage of the state's weakness there.

It is difficult to find any analyses of the ADF that do not describe the internal structure as Ugandan. The Museveni government was at the forefront of proclaiming the group's Ugandan status. It continually refuted the commonly cited statistic of the force being 60–80 percent Congolese (some sources say as high as 85 percent) and 20–40 percent Ugandan, instead usually claiming the reverse to be the case (Interview Fifteen). Indeed, it is interesting that despite estimates that the ADF were composed of more Congolese than Ugandans—or that they were quite close to equal proportions—the dominant perception of the group was still that they were overwhelmingly Ugandan (Interview Fifty-Six). But nearly just as steadfast in their belief of the ADF being Ugandan were international actors. The UN for instance, ever since the 1999 Lusaka Ceasefire Agreement, consistently classified the rebels as one of the many 'foreign armed groups'—or 'negative forces'—operating on Congolese soil. Other global bodies also followed this approach: "International partners agreed to support these national processes as well as put their weight behind attempts to extricate all foreign armed groups from the DRC," a World Bank (2009, 2) report stated with reference to the ADF (among others). Likewise, a foreign aid worker in Kampala explained, "We consider them [the ADF] a Ugandan group in exile, a bit like the LRA, I guess" (Interview Sixteen). And a DFID employee in Uganda asserted, "The LRA and ADF have exported Ugandan issues" (Interview Forty-Eight). Scholars have also largely characterized the ADF as being an external invading insurgency. One of the most thorough and in-depth reports on the ADF, by Romkema (2007, 16), is part of a study specifically devoted to "foreign AGs [armed groups] that operate in the North and South Kivu provinces of the DRC." The study classifies the ADF as a group "rooted politically and militarily in countries other than the DRC and that have a significant armed presence in the DRC" (Romkema 2007, 16). This misrepresentation of the nature of the ADF is also reproduced in the academic realm through many conflict databases. The Uppsala Conflict Data Program (UCDP), for example, has consistently portrayed the ADF as a Ugandan rebel group, based in western Uganda, fighting specifically in opposition to the Ugandan government. It has coded the ADF as engaged in intra-state conflict (within the *Ugandan* state), which of course ignores their significant presence not just in the Congo, but in the whole of the borderland region. UCDP's analyses have made some small nods to the links of the ADF rebellion's Congolese context. However, it has largely theorized the ADF presence there as a means to the rebels' supposed desired end of overthrowing the Ugandan government, thereby failing to acknowledge the significant activity of the rebels against Congolese civilians and military forces (among other actions and characteristics of the group).

An important source of recruits for the ADF throughout this time period undoubtedly did come from Islamic networks tapped into by the ADF—and specifically those involving disenfranchised and aggrieved Ugandan Muslims. For example, in a MONUSCO DDRRR debriefing note about Colonel Bwonadeke Winny, the ADF's former Director of Military Intelligence, it is noted that Winny explained the following: "The sheikh [in Ugandan mosques] will give a message and those that are interested will express interest and recruiters [from the ADF] will see if they are suitable. The message is that Shari'a is the supreme law and that in Uganda Muslims are not allowed to practice freely. They are told that if you fight and die you go to paradise and that if you fight and win other blessings will come to you" (MONUSCO Document Four).[3] From 2005 onwards, taped recordings of sermons delivered by Mukulu were played in mosques. "Muslims should kill non-Muslims, and kill also Muslims who are not fighting for Jihad," and "Let curses be to Bush, Blair, the president of France—and more curse goes to [President] Museveni and all those fighting Islam," he proclaimed in one of the recordings (Terdman 2006, 3). Various important mosques in Kampala, such as those led by Sheikh Sachimbi Abdoulhakim on William Street, and Sheikh Suleiman Kekedo on Market Street, were alleged to be in connivance with the ADF.[4]

An additional Islamic recruitment source was former ADF fighters of the Tabliq faction, who had gone through the amnesty process, but later opted to rejoin the rebels, with some even becoming double agents (Mwenda 2010a; Mwenda 2010b). According to intelligence reports from a body of Uganda's security apparatus, the Joint Anti-Terrorism Taskforce (JATT), many reporters were extremely unhappy with their treatment from the Ugandan government upon leaving the bush. At an October 2008 meeting in JATT's headquarters in Kololo, Kampala, leaders of the ADF reporter community conveyed messages of deep resentment over having been "forgotten, used, and dumped" by the government (The Independent Team 2010b). Minutes from the meeting noted accusations of "rampant arrest and prolonged detention without trial mainly targeting members of Muslim Salaf sect and other Muslim youths based on trivial information. They have [. . .] been subjected to physical and psychological torture [. . .] and use of dangerous objects to extract information. Many of such nature are languishing in government prisons with some having been deliberately denied amnesty" (The Independent Team 2010b). The minutes also made reference to more mundane complaints, including: "the resettlement package given to former ADF was too small to start up new meaningful life as most of them have no capacity to start an income generating activity. As a result, they now live below poverty line, hence making them idle and redundant. Most of the reporters are vulnerable and potential recruits who can easily be lured back into terrorist activities against the government" (The Independent Team 2010b).

While it was noted above that typical analyses of the group between 2004–2013 focused less on the ADF-as-proxy idea, this perception by no means disappeared entirely. In December 2001 the ADF had been added to the US 'Terrorist Exclusion List.' In order to reap the benefits that derive from being seen to be fighting terrorism, the Ugandan government was thereafter steadfast in its efforts to highlight the group's ties to Islamic networks. Mbabazi in the Ugandan Parliament in 2003, for example, had stated, "It should be noted that the ADF is a core group of terrorists composed of militant Islamic radical fundamentalists whose aim is to create an Islamic state in Uganda" (Uganda. Parliament April 29, 2003). While the ADF's previous relationships with regimes such as the Sudanese had drastically declined in importance, by 2008 there began to be reported incidences of communication and movement between the ADF and the Somali Islamic group Al Shabab, as well as suggestions that the ADF were partly acting as a proxy for the force. In December 2009 the African Union Mission in Somalia (AMISOM) noted a significant number of Ugandan Al Shabab fighters, and Major Ba-Hoku Barigye, the AMISOM spokesman, met with one who discussed his ADF membership (Bogere 2009). As the UPDF became more embroiled in Somalia through its participation in AMISOM, Al Shabab threatened the Museveni regime with bringing its war to Uganda (Interview Thirty-Four). Then on 7 July 2010 a series of bomb blasts went off in central Kampala, killing over eighty people and wounding dozens more. While Al Shabab claimed responsibility for the attacks, the Ugandan government argued that the ADF had a significant role to play as well, although this is unlikely. In an interview with a member of JATT, it was claimed that while the government knew who had physically carried-out the bombings, the bigger question of who had ordered them—Al Shabab or the ADF—was very much unknown (Interview Twenty-Nine). Various journalists jumped on the government narrative bandwagon. For example, in addition to one of the suicide bombers being identified as Ugandan, Mwenda (2010a) noted that further evidence of "The link between the two terrorist organizations is [. . .] the theory that ADF knows Kampala very well; Al Shabab, not so much [. . .] ADF has internal sources within Uganda's intelligence services especially JATT. For Al Shabab to succeed in its operations, it needed the ADF infrastructure."

Regardless, the significance of the ADF–Al Shabab relationship tends to be overstated. International conflict resolution experts in close contact with the ADF remain doubtful over how close the relationship between the two groups actually was. For one thing, the ADF's top leadership were divided over how far to pursue their association with them (Interview Four). The following analysis by Titeca and Vlassenroot (2012, 167) is therefore convincing:

> this Islamic linkage should be considered sporadic and not too strong [. . .] The relationship with Al-Shabaab—which was held responsible for the July 2010 bombings in Kampala—has to be seen in the same light. Even if our sources indicate that there has been some communication with Al-Shabaab representatives, the ADF has not taken up any concrete action in support of Al-Shabaab because it is not willing to do so. Several sources point at the division within the ADF leadership on this issue: while the current leadership does not want to

follow the path of further radicalization, some commanders feel "trapped" and argue that this radicalization is the only way out.

Most problematic with regards to the 'misguided' explanations of the ADF's recruitment, retention, and organization practices, however, is their interpretation of the ADF as being overwhelmingly Ugandan, and their goals as being solely concerned with the Ugandan polity. For one thing, Islamic recruitment networks were not only limited to Ugandan mosques. Enlistment increasingly took place in eastern Congolese mosques, and as many as over half of newly acquired Muslim recruits were Congolese. Neighboring states also played a role in this respect. For example, according to the UN Group of Experts, ADF Islamic recruitment efforts were confirmed in Burundi: "The Group interviewed a Burundian child soldier who had been recruited from Bujumbura by a Ugandan imam who had recently arrived to send Muslim young people to the Democratic Republic of the Congo to join the rebels" (Group of Experts on the Democratic Republic of the Congo December 2, 2011, 26).

Moreover, the actual Islamic ideology behind the recruitment of Muslims to the ADF was often questionable, to say the least. Government personnel were keen to talk of the rebels' drive for Jihad, obsession with infidels, and goal to Islamicise Uganda. However, looking at the wider context paints a more nuanced picture. For example, it is worth bearing in mind that the Muslim community in North Kivu is an extremely tolerant one, with little tendency towards extremist behavior. And while many Ugandan and Congolese Muslims indeed joined the ADF through Islamic networks, they were often spurred to enlist because of practical issues of poverty, unemployment, frustration with the government, or false promises of future opportunities (Interview Fifty-One). The following testimony offered by a Muslim recruit is typical: "My recruitment was by a Muslim fellow Mr. Ali Joseph who introduced himself as a new convert to Islam and wants to learn Qur'an from me on high payment in dollars in Saudi Arabia and promised to prepare passport and visa for me" (MONUSCO Document Eight). There were other small factors and developments that put into question the importance of extremist Islamic ideology as a recruiting force for the ADF. For example, there is evidence that over time the volume of recruitment targeted specifically towards Muslims significantly decreased. And interestingly, by 2011 it appeared that Christian recruits were no longer being forced to convert to Islam (Group of Experts on the Democratic Republic of the Congo 2011). Furthermore, even in areas heavily under the ADF's influence in Beni territory, Shari'a law was not enforced. Perhaps what is most telling, however, is that during the preliminary negotiation talks with the Ugandan and Congolese governments in 2008 (an event to be discussed in more depth later in this chapter), the ADF's initial list of demands contained no religious-related requests (Interview Twenty-Two).

Of course, it would be going too far to attribute the Islamic factor to representing nothing more than an instrumental ploy. It is undeniable that it continued to affect the recruitment, retention, and organization practices of the group throughout this time period. However, characterizing the ADF rebellion as one predominantly inspired by Islamic ideology, largely Ugandan in composition, and fighting solely out of Ugandan-related grievances, is not only misleading, but as the following section will demonstrate, inaccurate. The borderland was central to the ADF's recruitment, retention, and organization practices: the force continued to grow out of the borderland, remained overwhelmingly composed of borderland actors, and focused the majority of their efforts on pursuing borderland-oriented goals. To properly understand the ADF's human resource component, then, it is clearly necessary to go beyond the popular understandings of the ADF.

STRATEGIES FOR RECRUITMENT AND RETENTION OF PERSONNEL

The NALU Factor

As mentioned previously, the Rwenzori borderland between 2004–2013 was a different environment to that which existed between 1996–2003. While the Islamic dimension of the group certainly helped to ensure a continued supply of recruits in this changed context, other elements within the force—especially those strongly embedded in the borderland context—proved pivotal for recruitment efforts as well. This was so much so the case that by the end of the time period under consideration in this chapter, namely 2013, the ADF had a relatively consolidated human resource base. In fact, they had grown into a larger force than at any time in the previous ten years, going from only 200–300 fighters in 2006, to an estimated 1,500 in 2013.

One significant dimension was the influential role played by the NALU component of the group. At the most obvious level, there were still those attracted to the ADF due to the presence of various Rwenzururu Kingdom 'diehards' in the force, and their claims of fighting for the establishment of a Rwenzururu Kingdom. Interestingly, even after the Kingdom was actually granted in 2007, this dimension still pulled weight. In early 2011, for example, UN officials were presented with two former ADF officers who had deserted; they talked of the ADF "planning to establish the Rwenzururu Kingdom in the name of the Supreme Chief of both the Banande [. . .] and Bakonjo (Uganda), tribes" (Muhame 2012). Despite the majority of Konjo being happy with the official recognition of their Kingdom, there remained a hard-core element that vied for a more independent arrangement. Many also remained enthusiastic about the idea of being officially joined with the Nande, as Facci (2009, 353) describes: "The movement's representatives pursue the dream of reunification with the Banande people, at least as an ideal." Some Konjo hoped for an autonomous Rwenzururu state, and saw joining the ADF as a means of attaining this.

However, such sentiment was by no means exclusively limited to western Uganda, but could also be found amongst many Nande communities in North Kivu. While not uniformly throughout Nande society, there were sections that purported as high a degree of loyalty to the King (Mumbere) as western Uganda. From 2007 onwards, many traditional Nande chiefs paid allegiance to Mumbere, and according to Capson Sausi, the Master of Ceremonies at the King's coronation, multitudes of delegations and officials travelled from eastern Congo to attend the event in Kasese (Baguma and Thawite 2009; Interview Fifty-Two). It is important to clarify that by no means did the Rwenzururu Kingdom or its figureheads ever condone the ADF conflict, before or after the official establishment of the institution. Nevertheless, there were radical Kingdom supporters who did, and there existed a general perception that those in the Konjo-Nande population were more inclined to be sympathizers with the rebellion. Numerous non-Konjo residents of Kasese, for example, professed with certainty that they knew of local Konjo men who had joined the ADF (Interview Twenty-Eight). A missionary's account of his time in the Rwenzori region shed light on this: "We learned yesterday that since the latest spurt of attacks in the Kirindi area, Busaru leaders have held a series of meetings encouraging the Babwisi population to arm themselves against their Bakonjo neighbors. (The ADF rebel group includes many tribes, but people here perceive the minority Bakonjo as supporting them)" (Belz 1999, 4).

Perhaps the NALU faction's larger impact when it came to recruitment during this time period, however, was the sizeable number of ordinary Nande they helped to attract, albeit in an indirect manner. NALU's long-term establishment in eastern Congo and their integration into the population had engendered a certain degree of trust amongst the locals towards the ADF. Konjo-Nande cross-border ties were as strong and interconnected as ever, and they were both overwhelmingly more oriented towards each other than their respective national populations. When asked how they identified themselves, for example, their tribal affiliation was nearly always stated ahead of their nationality (Interview Sixty-Five). Since the Nande saw the ADF as being partly composed of their brethren the Konjo, they were that much more inclined to join. This helps to explain why the majority of the Congolese in the ADF were of Nande affiliation (Kavanagh 2010).

With the increase in Nande members, came changes in the rebellion's overall character and objectives. For one thing, the anti-Rwandan stance grew in significance. The Nande and Rwandophone populations in North Kivu have historically been hostile towards each other, but during the Congolese wars (between 1996–2003) the Nande's anti-Tutsi discourse, in particular, intensified. Thus when the Congrès National pour la Défense du Peuple (CNDP)—which was a traditionally Rwandan-backed, Congolese Tutsi rebel group—began to be enfolded into FARDC, the Nande turned even more against the national state and its army (Beni Lubero Online 2011). They perceived the ADF as a force that could help stave off this Rwandan 'infiltration' into North Kivu, but more specifically, could counter the 'Rwandan-tainted' military (Interview Fifty-Five). According to a conflict specialist at the NGO Search for Common Ground in Goma, ethnic sentiments were so strong with regards to the Rwandophone-Nande relationship, and the hatred towards FARDC so severe after the incorporation of the CNDP that Nande were joining the ADF "just to ensure that FARDC didn't succeed with Operation Rwenzori" (Interview Eight). Relatedly, many of the Nande who had once voluntarily joined the ADF, described having been motivated to do so for reasons of 'protecting' their local community—most often from FARDC, but also from other rebels (Interview Fifty). Like many other borderlands, there were few official avenues through which to pursue the resolution of grievances in eastern Congo, and thus support for rebellion appeared to be a logical solution in such an environment.

Disenfranchised Borderlanders:

Many Nande were motivated to join the ADF for far less political reasons, and rather out of concerns of a much more socio-economic nature. In North Kivu the Congolese wars had left a population of young men with little education and few employment prospects. Furthermore, an extremely high percentage of them had been members in various rebel factions, and post-conflict were often demobilized, but not reintegrated. Many returned home only to find the same conditions that had led them to fight in the first place, making successful 'reinsertion' effectively impossible and leading them to reconsider rebel life simply to meet basic needs (Thakur 2008). As the eastern Congolese borderland had been the heart of the violence during the Congo wars, the Grand Nord of North Kivu was inundated with militarized young men. Frequently compounding these issues were grievances on a local level concerning citizenship and land rights. Eastern Congo was an area very much marginalized by Kinshasa, where mistrust of central authority was rife, and "the linkages and fibers between the community and government were weak," as a civil society practitioner on reconciliation explained (Interview Forty-Five). As a result of all of these factors, North Kivu simmered with violence—and sometimes open conflict—post-2003, and in many respects remained the ideal recruiting ground for rebel groups.

Similar to before, the ADF moulded and tailored their strategies to appear as though responding to the disenfranchised and neglected state of the borderland population in general, and according to Ndungo, "used the socio-economic gaps in the community" (Interview Forty-Five). There were indications that—at least in the earlier years of this time period—they paid USD $100 a month to members (MONUSCO Document Nineteen; Interview Five). "This is huge money, relatively speaking," a MONUSCO DDRRR official in Beni explained, especially when considering that for most rebel groups in eastern Congo, payment was simply the provision of a weapon (Interview Sixty-Three).

Partly for this reason, the ADF during this time period saw higher rates of voluntary membership than most of the other rebel groups operating in the Congo (Interview Fifteen). UN officials estimated that the majority of Congolese in the ADF joined on their own free will. The force undoubtedly still extensively practiced forced recruitment, however this was less so than during 1996–2003. Furthermore, in the past the majority of these local Congolese recruits would have "known little of the tactical strategy of ADF High Command," instead "being used mostly to provide services and support for the camps" (MONUSCO Document Eighteen). However, the changing composition of the group helped to alter internal power structures, and Nande ADF consequently started to attain positions of higher authority—roles that in the past would have almost solely been filled by founding members of the group. "We can see a shift in the weight that the Congolese members now carry," Solidarités noted, principally due to sheer numbers, but also because of the important access to the local area that the Nande provided (Interview Fifty-Five). Recruitment of Nande was largely focused along the Beni-Eringeti axis, slightly further south in the Graben valley, as well as in the towns of Butembo and Bunia (Tusiime 2008; Mugisa 2008; Interview Fourteen). In ADF-controlled regions recruitment drives were carried-out quite openly, but in front-line propaganda areas—namely those where ADF presence was more precarious—it was done relatively quietly, for example through brochures and pamphlets; small church, mosque, and social gatherings; or private meetings. Indeed, it is necessary to point out that while the ethnic factor is important when considering recruitment, religious identity was critical as well. In other words, for many of the Nande (and more broadly Congolese in general) joining, being Muslim was pivotal. And this applied to both those who voluntarily joined, and those who were coerced.

It was by no means only the Congolese side of the borderland that was heavily targeted for recruitment. Initiatives to attract western Ugandans (and to a lesser extent Ugandans from other regions of the country) continued as well. While no longer waging direct attacks against western Uganda, the ADF still used the area for a multitude of purposes and had extensive networks throughout the territory. Interestingly, several factors directly related to western Uganda's 'post-conflict' status affected ADF recruitment attempts. For one thing, the conflict had contributed to higher levels of poverty, and in 2010 it was estimated that 56 percent of Bundibugyo residents lived below the poverty line, compared to the national average of 31 percent (Womakuyu 2010). The ADF consequently worked at exploiting the residents' dismal occupation and education opportunities. According to the Kasese amnesty office in 2010, there was no need for the ADF to appeal particularly to Muslim populations, as the area's exceptionally high rate of unemployment was providing a sufficient amount of recruits.[5] They stressed the idleness faced by a significant proportion of young men in the area, and their consequent susceptibility to promises of "high-paying jobs in factories," "job opportunities of gold and timber in DRC," "scholarship to Kenya, Tanzania, and Saudi Arabia," and so on (Interview Seventy-Five). Particularly vulnerable in this respect were those living in the more isolated parts of the western Ugandan borderland, where employment opportunities beyond subsistence farming were essentially non-existent due to the abject underdevelopment and neglect from the state.

Recruits from Uganda and elsewhere were usually brought to the western Ugandan border towns of Kasese, Bwera, and Mpondwe, where the ADF had extensive intelligence personnel who then transported them across the border to ADF training camps in the Congo. The transit of personnel to Congo was usually done on market days, when the traffic of locals across the border was so dense that monitoring by officials was impossible (MONUSCO Document Eight). The ADF were skilled at manipulating border dynamics and employed various strategies to move personnel. The following account of a recruit's initial journey to the Congo describes how this worked: "We took the bus from Kampala towards Mbarara and spent a night in a hotel. The following day we reached Mpondwe border. He [the recruiter] gave me new clothes and shoes. Then he told me to cross road blocks and camouflage as market attendant we shall meet at a place where lorries-transit goods are parked" (MONUSCO Document Eight). Various other pretexts were employed for this as well, such as disguising the recruits as businessmen selling fish in the Congo, or as fishermen traveling the Semliki River between the two countries (The Independent Team 2010c; Interview Forty-Five). In fact, in the summer of 2011 there were reports of fishermen on the Semliki River being abducted and forced to facilitate this mode of transport for the ADF (Muhame 2012).

It has become popular practice amongst NGOs, human rights groups, and other international actors to focus on the issue of recruitment of child soldiers amongst African rebel groups. The ADF has been no exception in this respect, with a Channel Four (2011) special on the group entitled 'The Children Who Came Back From the Dead,' noting, "there were lots of child soldiers in his [an ADF child soldier] rebel army's ranks, and many of them forcibly recruited." However, interviews with both former members of the group, as well as conflict experts familiar with the force, paint a different picture. Forced child recruitment does not appear to have been a widespread practice. When it did occur, it tended to be for quite specific reasons, and usually involved a parent handing their child over in the belief that they were ensuring a better future for them (MONUSCO Document Fifteen). Indeed, numerous MONUSCO DDRRR reports of former ADF child soldiers tell of children being given to the rebels by their parents, who believed their children would have better education opportunities, and a more sufficient intake of food, with the rebels (MONUSCO Document Fifteen). But most commonly in the ADF's case, many parents brought their youth with them when joining the ADF, or the children had simply been born into the force. As discussed in Chapter Four, the ADF were distinctive amongst rebel groups in that they lived, moved, and operated as a community, as opposed to a force composed simply of fighters. Thus, children were born and raised with the ADF, schooled in handling weapons and manning outlook posts from the age of ten, and taught to do menial tasks such as bringing foodstuffs from the fields to the camps (MONUSCO Document Twelve). They assumed more active roles in the force upon turning twelve years old, and there were reports of children in their early teens being used as spies (Romkema 2007; MONUSCO Document Twelve). But in the end, these children were part of the ADF community.

Alliances

When considering the ADF's recruitment and retention activities during this time period, it is also important to take into account their practice of instituting alliances with other groups. Chapter Four discussed how the outbreak of conflict in the Congo in 1996 had resulted in a multiplication of rebel groups and consequent proliferation of potential partners for the ADF to work with. While officially the Congo wars were now supposed to be over, this was far from the case in North Kivu. Borderlands are ideal places for rebel groups, both active and dormant, to eke out their existence, and hence North Kivu was a strategic place for the ADF to acquire some allies. In fact, between 2004–2013 the ADF were able to expand and strengthen their network of alliances—something that would have been more difficult had they been operating in a non-borderland zone.

The ADF's alliance network included Lendu militias in Ituri, and by the summer of 2011, the LRA (Mugabi 2008). An ADF-LRA collaboration had been speculated about for some time, but in July 2011, after a meeting between ADF, LRA, and ex-FARDC officials—allegedly in Eringeti—it appears that this finally materialized, if having not been implemented previously (Interview Sixty-Three). One of their main collaborators though, were the Mai Mai. Working with the Mai Mai provided the ADF with a variety of benefits, perhaps the most important being what Solidarités terms the "local rooting" (Interview Fifty-Five). While 'Mai Mai' has a somewhat slippery definition, encompassing everything from "nationalist resistance movement," or "locally oriented youth militia without any kind of political superstructure or motive," to "different local ethnic militias acting independently of one another," in general Mai Mai can be conceptualized as a "generic term for all militias in North Kivu with some form of relationship to autochthonous authority and tradition" (Bøås 2008, 60–61). As such, when operating in an area of North Kivu outside of the ADF-controlled territory, it was extremely beneficial for the ADF to have a favorable relationship with the local Mai Mai group. In the earlier stages of the alliance, the mantra of 'the enemy of my enemy is my friend' was the governing factor behind the two forces' association with each other. However, with time the relationship moved from being purely practical, to one shaped by shared narratives of resistance to central authority, marginalization, and importantly, an anti-foreigner stance. What is most interesting about this, is how the Mai Mai did not conceive of the ADF as being a part of this 'foreigner' category. Rather, they perceived the force as belonging in this space. On the other hand, groups like the CNDP were fervently hated due to their outsider status.

Some sources have inaccurately gone so far as to claim that certain Mai Mai factions, especially post-2007, actually joined the ADF as opposed to just allying with them. The more correct interpretation of the situation is that they continued to strengthen their collaboration practices: sharing intelligence, warning each other of impending dangers, and coordinating attacks so as to create a greater impact. In fact, as will be discussed later in the chapter, the ADF had several camps specifically designated for training purposes, and these were frequented by forces such as the Mai Mai.

INTERNAL STRUCTURE, GOVERNANCE, AND CONTROL OF INFORMATION

In many ways the ADF displayed continuity during the years 2004–2013 with their previous modes of internally structuring, governing themselves, and controlling information. However, there were some important changes and developments, and these were most often related to the force's further entrenched position in the borderland.

As mentioned previously, from their very earliest stages the ADF were known for their apparent mysterious and clandestine nature. It appears that this characteristic of the group only increased with time. The UN Group of Experts described the ADF in 2011 as "a highly secretive organization," and NGOs and conflict management actors on the ground continuously noted how elusive the rebels could be (Group of Experts on the Democratic Republic of the Congo December 2, 2011, 25). It was extremely difficult for outsiders to make any contact with them. According to a DDRRR MONUSCO official in Beni, MONUSCO's greatest challenge was "getting the chance to talk with the ADF physically, and actually know what they want" (Interview Sixty-Three). When meetings were established or plans for peace negotiations set in motion, imposters often presented themselves, thereby significantly confusing outsiders. Solidarités in Goma, for example, recounted their difficulties in getting in-touch with the group: whereas with FARDC, the FDLR, or the Mai Mai, all that was often needed to make contact was a small amount of money, the ADF proved far more elusive and much less receptive to material incentives. However, they did note that once contact was made, the ADF were fairly easy to work with. Centre Résolution Conflits (CRC) also mentioned that in approaching the ADF, enticing them with material incentives such as clothes—again, a common practice with other rebel groups—was futile, and instead offers of transportation or airtime had to be used (Interview Sixty-Eight). Regardless, what is clear is that with time the ADF grew more secretive and insular; they were more bent on retaining their place in the borderland and overall survival, and less interested in liaising of any sort with outsiders.

In fact, the Ugandan government did not even have a physical profile of Mukulu, as there were no known pictures of him for a significant period of time (Interview Twenty-Two; MONUSCO Document Eighteen). He had a multitude of passports, dozens of aliases, and was known to vary his look from clean-shaven and bald, to dreadlocks, to devout Muslim, to even disguising himself as a woman (The Independent Team 2010d). He apparently had homes in Burundi, Rwanda, Tanzania, and Kenya, and often travelled to the UK where his wife resided just outside of London (Group of Experts on the Democratic Republic of the Congo December 2, 2011).[6] Indeed, he moved with ease between a multitude of countries, and according to JATT, "continuously supported, directed and coordinated ADF operations uninterrupted from UK, Kenya, DRC and USA" (The Independent Team 2010e; Bagala 2011). More generally, the ADF was, as the MONUSCO DDRRR Beni official declared, "skilled at confusing people" (Interview Sixty-Three). If a leader was killed, for example, his/her name and identity would continue to be used (Interview Sixty-Three). It is interesting to consider an August 2008 JATT memo on ADF intelligence, which discussed the success the rebels had in evading Ugandan authorities and traversing the border. It noted, for instance, how "The ADF operatives have continuously acquired forged identification and travel documents [. . .] These documents simplify their mobility and makes it difficult for the unsuspecting public to identify them as wrong elements." 'Spies' often engaged in work as truck drivers, hawkers, and boda-boda/pikipiki riders, and in an interesting development, were increasingly female. Furthermore, they had infiltrated Ugandan security organizations, acquiring information, for example, on JATT's "internal structures, their operational plans, the names, home addresses and car number-plates of security operatives" (The Independent Team 2010e; Mwenda 2010a).

Again, the ADF's internal configuration was highly unusual. And despite its structure frequently being described as disorganized or even non-existent—as the following quote from a Ugandan peace and conflict graduate student argues: "The ADF are not an established movement"—it should more accurately be described as unconventional (Interview Fifty-Eight). As the UN Group of Experts noted, they are "without a traditional military ranking system" (Group of Experts on the Democratic Republic of the Congo December 2, 2011, 25). Nevertheless, during this period they could essentially be understood as having three main bodies. First (as of fall 2010), there was a hierarchy of leaders, with Mukulu at the top, followed by Chief Director Musa Baluku, Army Commander David Rukwango, Deputy Army Commander Amisi Kasada, and Chief of Operations Costa Kasada. Under them the force was divided according to the main camps: the Nadui headquarters (later replaced by the Chuchubo headquarters), the Bundiguya first battalion, the Mwalika second battalion, and the Makoyoba third battalion (MONUSCO Document Nineteen). It was estimated that each of these main camps had over 300 combatants, excluding dependents. Secondly, there was a 'Group of Directors,' and they covered the fields of finance, health, education, welfare, records, logistic support, and training and recruitment (MONUSCO Document Nineteen). And thirdly, there was an Army Council—composed of Brigade and Battalion Commanders, Intelligence Officers, and a miscellaneous of other Commanders—that reported to a National Community Council, that in turn answered to Mukulu (MONUSCO Document Nineteen).

Outside of these three main branches of the force, there were several other notable positions. These included the Coordinator of the London Bureau, Hamza Kigozi; the Coordinator of the Nairobi Bureau, Badru Magara; Martial Arts Instructor, Kassim Kyambalangu; and interestingly, Woman Coordinator (based in Goma), Yalala. During 1996–2003 most senior positions were reserved for Ugandans, however post-2003 Muslim Congolese members of the group increasingly acquired leadership roles. The ADF were not fixated on nationality; religion, background, experience, and skill were largely the determining factors when it came to decisions about positions.

Supporting this entire arrangement was the ADF extended community of combatants' wives, children, and so on. Video footage obtained by the UN of an ADF training camp showed women with AK-47s participating in training drills, and various FARDC units allegedly testified to having fought against a female brigade.[7] As a 2011 UN fieldwork document noted, "There are a lot of children and women present in their camps, and although the majority are dependents, however, obtained video clips, under possession of JIC-E reveal that these people do not only receive religious/modern education but are also seen carrying out combat training (musketry, karate and field craft)" (MONUSCO Document Seventeen). Indeed, female combatants were according to some sources capable of both independent attacks, as well as operating jointly with men (MONUSCO Document Seventeen). Nevertheless, there is no doubt that men carried-out most of the fighting, and women were used in more support function roles. Of course crucial to the ADF network was also the North Kivutien civilian support structure. As the same UN document describes, "There is a large group of Congolese citizens, not necessarily Muslims, amongst their midst, who work as informants or are employed for menial jobs such as farming in the fields and labor in mines controlled by ADF" (MONUSCO Document Seventeen).

It was ADF protocol to keep sensitive information amongst only the top echelons of the group. Those involved in MONUSCO's DDRRR of former ADF members remarked how the ex-combatants were unable to provide them with much data on the group, such as numbers of the force or camp locations (Interview Sixty-Three). This was because on the ground, information was kept extremely decentralized and dislocated. In the earlier years of this time period, the majority of regular combatants had never even seen Mukulu. The ADF were ruthless towards anyone that betrayed the movement, be they inside members, collaborators, or business partners. For example, in 2011 a Nande doctor was kidnaped in Oicha by the ADF and held for a USD $56,000 ransom. He had failed to honor a business transaction involving the sale of medical supplies, and was forced to treat sick and wounded ADF members until his release payment could be made (Group of Experts on the Democratic Republic of the Congo December 2, 2011; Bahati 2011; Interview Thirty-Seven). ADF members who were captured by enemy forces and later attempted to rejoin the force were subjected to rigorous interrogation. Colonel Winny, for example, was captured by the UPDF in 2001; when he eventually made his way back to the ADF in 2004, he was kept in an underground prison in Chuchubo camp for six months before he could resume work with the rebels (MONUSCO Document Four).

The tight control over information, including the radio, meant that knowledge of Uganda's amnesty program and Congo's DDRRR system could be restricted (Interview Twenty-Six). Unlike other rebels operating in eastern Congo, voluntary surrenders for amnesty or demobilization from the ADF during this post-2003 time period were sporadic (Interview Forty-Four). In 2005 Uganda even opened a branch of its amnesty commission in Beni, in the hope of better luring Ugandan members of the ADF out of the bush. This proved unsuccessful, as very few surrendered themselves, and most of those who did turned out to be of Congolese nationality. Yet the very structure of the group also served to hinder chances of initiatives such as DDRRR fully succeeding. Because they were so community-based (if any travelling had to be done, for instance, whole families would move) it was more unlikely that individual ADF personnel would come forward for demobilization. More importantly, they were fundamentally a transnational force, and thus 'returning home' to Uganda, for example, made little sense for many of the members. Despite most accounts of the ADF using the national or regional levels of analysis to understand the group, the first part of this chapter showed how dynamics related to the borderland were pivotal to the force's recruitment, retention, and organization of personnel as well. Islamic networks were used to attract members, but focusing on them alone leaves a large part of the story untold—such as the important role played by recruitment networks associated with the Konjo-Nande continuum, militarized ex-combatants, populations of disenfranchised and marginalized youth, and alliances with rebel factions eking out their existence in the borderland. A significant proportion of the recruits who joined during this time period did so because of their association with the above networks, and not out of any Ugandan Islamic connection.

Shifting analysis of the conflict from solely the macro level, to consideration of the micro-political level as well, revealed that the recruitment networks tapped into by the ADF were not nationally defined ones, but rather trans-local, borderland-constituted networks. Such networks were fundamentally cross-border, and largely generated from the borderland's anti-state and liminal nature. The ADF's internal character reflected these recruitment networks: the rebel force did not consider themselves to be a Ugandan movement. While Titeca and Vlassenroot come closest to moving beyond a purely Ugandan lens for understanding the ADF—focusing instead on their transnational orientation—they too ultimately use a state-centric framework. They (2012) conceptualize the ADF's heightened focus on the Congolese side of the borderland and the increase in number of Congolese recruits as representing a process of 'Congolization.' Yet, just as the ADF were not a Ugandan rebel group, neither were they a Congolese one. The majority of recruits were drawn to the group for issues and ideals distinctly to do with the borderland, and not their national state. Thus, the ADF were simply continuing their development as a borderland force—one not definable in terms of a state identity.[8]

ADF rhetoric in part promoted the image of a group concerned with the injustices of Ugandan Muslims, and former combatants have described how they were told they would one day militarily attack Kampala (MONUSCO Document Six). It is unsurprising that actual details on such an assault were never forthcoming; the ADF leaders knew that fighting their way into Kampala would "be suicide," as one expert explained (Interview Twenty-Two). Thus, in reality, the ADF's true intentions were a very different story to the ideals and agenda in their rhetoric. The various factions within the force harbored a variety of grievances, and hence pursued diverse goals. The NALU contingent, for example, were concerned with creating a Konjo-Nande kingdom, while the Nande were aggrieved over the presence of so-called outsiders in their territory. Essentially, the ADF during this time period were a group defined by their place in the borderland, and consequently their goals were associated with rectifying various borderland-related issues. But the ADF had also become an embedded community within this micro-region: they had intermarried and socially integrated into the larger Grand Nord society, they had business interests inextricably tied to the border, and they had a degree of political influence in the area. Overall, therefore, the rebellion's *raison d'être* had become one about maintaining their position in this valuable borderland space.

They pursued recruitment, retention, and organization strategies towards this objective. The rebels continued their practice of capitalizing on the disenfranchised status of the borderland, namely through tapping into the borderlanders' meta-narratives of marginalization and discrimination by the center. Both western Uganda and eastern Congo remained underdeveloped, conflict-ridden (or in a state of 'negative peace,' in western Uganda's case), and ignored spaces by their respective central governments. As such, the ADF found that promises of employment and education opportunities resonated with the borderlanders. In a region confronted with an abundance of somewhat demobilized but non-reintegrated combatants (from the Congo wars, but also from the multitude of smaller rebellions throughout the past decades in both eastern Congo and western Uganda), as well as a lack of formal work opportunities, the ADF's USD $100/month salary also proved enticing for many. The strong transnational bonds between the Konjo and Nande factored into the ADF's increased ability to voluntarily recruit during this time period as well. Seeing many of their brethren (Konjo) already in the force, members from Nande society were that much more willing to join. Ultimately, the misguided explanations fail in their treatment of the borderland as a peripheral and marginally important arena, and in their assumption of the ADF as a state-defined actor (and one with little agency at that). A borderland perspective, on the other hand, draws attention to the more hidden, but ultimately influential, dynamics behind the group's recruitment, retention, and organization strategies.

PART II: MATERIAL RESOURCES

MISGUIDED EXPLANATIONS OF THE ADF'S MATERIAL RESOURCES

Similar to the time period of 1996–2003, analyses of the ADF's acquisition of material resources throughout 2004–2013 continued to be predominantly concerned with outside Islamic funding sources. When it first started to become clear that the ADF were not a spent force despite their 2003 retreat from Uganda, the Ugandan government attributed the ADF's financial and material revival to various international Islamic actors. According to Lieutenant-Colonel James Mugira, Uganda's Acting Chief of Military Intelligence, the ADF were "receiving funding, operational training, and weapons such as Kalashnikov assault rifles, mortars and bomb-making equipment from Islamic fundamentalist groups in Muslim countries" (Sheikh 2005). In 2005 JATT's Operations Officer, Captain Joseph Kamusiime, claimed that countries such as Saudi Arabia, Pakistan, Afghanistan, but most importantly Sudan, which apparently wanted to encourage the 'Islamism' of neighbors such as Uganda, were providing considerable assistance to the group (McGregor 2007). Kamusiime furthermore asserted that the ADF were "motivated by Islamic fundamentalists—more in line with al-Qaeda ideology like other African terrorist organizations with global reach, such as the Armed Islamic Group of Algeria, Egypt's Muslim Brotherhood, and Somalia's Al-Ittihad al-Islamiya" (McGregor 2007, 3).

With time the narrative shifted slightly to more of an emphasis on the ADF's links with Al Shabab, emphasizing the importance of the funds, weapons, and training (most notably in bomb-making) received from the Somalis. If it was not this Islamic dimension being focused upon, then government officials stressed that the 'bandit' nature of the ADF was behind their material sustainability—a typical opinion of governments about actors in 'marginal' areas of the state. "They practice highway robbery," argued one JATT official (Interview Twenty-Nine). "A lot of the men do criminal activities on the side, and give the proceeds to the ADF," he further elucidated (Interview Twenty-Nine). But it was not only government personnel that characterized the ADF's material sustainability as due to nothing more than banditry and thievery. Press statements such as the following were also common: "Hungry rebels of the Allied Democratic Forces attacked border villagers in western Uganda as they foraged for food after government forces isolated their supply routes"; "The ADF and NALU are harassing civilians in areas of Eringeti and Alubani villages in eastern Congo. They are stealing food and abducting people" (Staff Writers 2010; Xinhua 2007).

There is no doubt that the ADF practiced various forms of robbery, including several times ambushing aid convoys and making off with supplies (Stearns 2010b). It is also unquestionable that the ADF received external support, guidance, and funding throughout 2004–2013, with funds largely channelled via Mukulu's financial networks (Stearns 2012). They had accounts at two banks in Butembo into which foreign deposits were regularly made (Interview Thirty-Four). And then according to an ADF assessment document written by MONUSCO, "It was reported that a man named Benjamin, the son of a former NALU leader Kiso Keranio, used to go to collect cash at Codefi Bank or Soficom in Butembo every month" (MONUSCO Document Eighteen). Furthermore, numerous sources, including UN officials and ADF defectors, reported regular visits to ADF training camps by 'Arabs'—mainly Sudanese, but also Somalis, Eritreans, Libyans, and South Asians. According to the UN Group of Experts, "local Congolese intelligence agents near Mutwanga reported to the Group [of Experts] that they had obtained information about foreigners near Nzelube who were accompanying an ADF unit. FARDC had also sighted foreign instructors in the general area of Kamango" (Group of Experts on the Democratic Republic of the Congo 2011, 27). UN personnel on the ground similarly described frequent helicopter visits to ADF-controlled areas, and the delivery of arms and support equipment (Interview Five). Indeed, it is clear from the accounts of former combatants that the ADF operated an extensive trans-local support network. An April 2009 article by *The Independent* (2009b), for example, described how several "arrested terrorists revealed their network in Sudan, Uganda, Kenya, Tanzania and other countries. Some of them have confessed to having done their underground training in terrorism methods including assembling and handling IED in Nairobi Kenya."[9]

It is difficult to determine to what degree the cumulative amount of assistance from outside sources during this time period was lower than during 1996–2003. Furthermore, the ADF's supposed 'bandit' nature was also far less of a factor in their attainment of material resources than during the previous era. In fact, by 2006, Sudanese support, previously the ADF's most significant source of foreign funding, was drastically reduced. The 2005 Comprehensive Peace Agreement between Khartoum and the Sudanese Peoples' Liberation Army had rendered groups like the ADF effectively useless for the Sudan government's cause (McGregor 2007). And yet despite this, many analyses of the group continued to attribute Sudan with an important role in terms of ADF material sustainability. In an article by *The Monitor* in March 2011, for example, it was asserted, "The ADF rebels are allegedly backed by the Khartoum government" (Okello 2011).

Although the ADF's contributions from outside sources were likely somewhat diminished, they remained a materially strong force throughout this time period. For one thing, they were well trained and well supplied. A UN fieldwork document described their capabilities as the following: they "retain the capability to execute conventional battle attacks at lower tactical level i.e., Section (11–15), Platoon (30–35) and Company (50+)"; "in the event of close combat, the combatants of ADF are trained in close hand-to-hand combat employing karate skills and typical bayonet drills"; "combatants are well trained in weapon skills and can fire effectively on different firing positions (lying, sitting, kneeling and standing)"; "combatants are physically fit and therefore capable of harassment operations in small teams (hit and run tactics) over long distances in jungle terrain" (MONUSCO Document Seventeen). The ADF also had significant arsenals of weapons—nearly all of which were eventually captured by FARDC—including rocket-propelled grenades, AK-47 assault rifles, and anti-aircraft weapons to counter helicopter attacks (Group of Experts on the Democratic Republic of the Congo December 2, 2011).

Thus, it is necessary to look beyond the 'misguided explanations' of the ADF, and consider how other facets of the group's composition equipped them with the ability to remain materially strong. In Chapter Four their enmeshment into local trading networks and other borderland economic activities was discussed. With the ADF's diminished sources of outside support during 2004–2013, such practices only increased. As mentioned previously, Titeca and Vlassenroot (2012, 164) conceptualize this as a process of 'Congolization.' Specifically in terms of material resources, they argue that it was "hastened by the fact that the group had lost most of its external support, which forced the movement into a struggle for its own survival and to start commercial activities in DRC, cultivate grounds." But this was not a new initiative, nor was it a case of a Ugandan group becoming Congolese. Rather, the ADF were further deepening and building upon their lucrative positions in the borderland.

Chapter 5

STRATEGIES FOR GENERATION OF INCOME, ACQUISITION OF SUPPLIES, AND MANAGEMENT OF TERRITORY

Business Practices

By the mid-2000s it was unrealistic for the ADF to substantially rely on external backing, and accordingly they focused more on independent income-generating endeavors. Two factors greatly enabled this: first, eastern Congo's economy was almost entirely an informal one between 1996 and 2003/4, controlled by armed groups and national armies. The ADF's integration into this was thus part of a broader phenomenon happening within the borderland. Second, their incorporation into the borderland's economic networks between 1996–2003 had provided the platform through which such activities could be expanded upon and strengthened. Of course, NALU were pivotal with regards to this. It was NALU that had originally enabled the ADF—through their provision of the 'local factor' and ethnic connections—to set up camp amongst the Nande in the North Kivu borderland. For the most part between 2004–2013 the relationship between the ADF and surrounding civilian environment was one of negative peace: there was certainly the use of terror and fear to encourage the cooperation and acquiescence of civilians, but there was relatively little outright violence. Because the ADF had become so established and invested in the borderland, and their overall objectives revolved around maintaining this position, there was a noticeable difference in their treatment of civilians. This was so much so the case that in 2011 FARDC officers estimated that the ADF "benefits from the popular support of nearly half of the population of Beni territory" (Group of Experts on the Democratic Republic of the Congo December 2, 2011, 30). Local authority leader Commissaire Kaniki, who presided over 1,400 families in ADF-controlled North Kivu villages, remarked, "We lived side-by-side with the Ugandans [the ADF] with no problem" (IRIN News 2006b). To characterize the connection between the ADF and civilians as one involving 'no problems' is arguably quite an exaggeration, as it has to be remembered that—akin to the working of a mafia—threats and terror underpinned the relationship. There were two major attacks on the ADF during this time period that disturbed the group and forced them to temporarily abandon their holding grounds. However, other than these disruptions, they were remarkably settled, generally refraining from overt violence and harassment, and maintaining a low profile.

This significant change in character (as compared to the previous time period of 1996–2003), in some ways speaks to Weinstein's thesis about rebel violence: namely, that without access to an environment rich in natural resources, or without external sources of material support, rebel groups will be forced to rely more on the population and thus commit less acts of violence against civilians (Weinstein 2007). The ADF indeed had previously demonstrated characteristics of an 'opportunistic rebellion,' in light of their support from Sudan and thus less of a perceived need to establish ties with the citizenry. However, as already discussed, between 1996 and 2003 the ADF were by no means completely detached from the surrounding area, and despite their mistreatment of civilians, they still managed to obtain a degree of collaboration. Furthermore, during the 2004–2013 time period the ADF not only continued to have access to natural resources, but even increased their pursuit of economic activities based on the borderland's natural resources. Thus, to wholeheartedly apply Weinstein's thesis to the ADF conflict would be simplifying a very complex situation and environment. In any case, there is no doubt that between 2004–2013, the ADF's interests became more focused on consolidating their place in the borderland, pursuing their economic interests there, and generally maintaining working relationships with the Grand Nord population.

This more positive cohabitation arrangement was pivotal. It allowed the ADF to become a part of borderland economic networks to such a degree that the dividing line between who was and was not ADF was often difficult to distinguish. This was crucially important for many of their business ventures, the vast majority of which would have been difficult to pursue had it not been for local support, labor, market access, and so on. The area's economic environment, which was dominated by the Nande trade networks, very much relied on informal economic structures and local networks (for example, there was little of a formal banking system): informal systems in the trading and mining sectors were much stronger than formal structures. As such, connections—especially cross-border ones, such as with the Konjo commercial class—were everything. The ADF's embedded position in the borderland and thus access to the lucrative economic networks was key to their material resource success.

One dimension of the group's economic activities was geared towards producing or acquiring goods for their own consumption. This took a variety of forms, including direct shopping by their network agents, deliveries from network agents in nearby urban areas of goods, sending female members of the group out to the forest to gather items, exploiting locals, and growing their own products. Indeed, because the ADF were so territorially established, they were able to engage in various agricultural activities. Throughout their areas of control—much of which comprised highly fertile land—large plantations of rice, maize, manioc, sugar cane, coffee, and bananas were managed (Interview Sixty-Three). Indeed, some of their food, which according to former combatants usually included bananas, cassava bread, rice, and beans, was locally produced by the ADF themselves and/or coercively acquired from the surrounding communities (MONUSCO Document Six). Of course, after Operation Rwenzori it was more difficult to collect foodstuffs, and thus 'squads' would be dispatched nightly at 03:00 for this purpose (MONUSCO Document Six). While some of the agricultural labor was done by those directly in the ADF, a great deal was carried-out by local farmers in the area, who would sometimes receive a part of the yield in exchange for their work (Group of Experts on the Democratic Republic of the Congo 2011). Those products that were not consumed by the ADF themselves were sold in local Beni-area markets, and ADF members would frequent local markets, dressed in civilian clothing. Mondays tended to be 'market day' for the ADF, when members were allowed to visit the markets and purchase food and non-food items (MONUSCO Document Ten).

Another dimension of the ADF's economic activities were those pursued for profit. Gold mining was a significant part of this. The group controlled several mines around the Semliki River in Kaynama, east of Eringeti in Chuchubo, as well as in Kikingi (MONUSCO Document Ten). The ADF also collected taxes from two larger mines along the Losselosse River, which were owned by two Congolese businessmen, Donat Bulumosi and Mao Manaki (MONUSCO Document Eighteen). Approximately half of these taxes went to ADF officials, and the other half to Congolese authorities (MONUSCO Document Five). According to the UN Group of Experts, by 2011 the ADF were taxing local miners approximately 1,000 Congolese francs per person, per week, and "All gold production taxed by the rebels is initially sold in Beni and Butembo and subsequently sold in Kampala and beyond" (Group of Experts on the Democratic Republic of the Congo 2011, 29). Coltan was another mineral mined by the ADF (albeit minimally), specifically in the area of May-Moya, again near Eringeti (IRIN News 2006b). Still other economic activities practiced by the rebels included trading in fish, fuel, vehicle spare parts, and reconditioned motorcycles, as well as poaching in Virunga National Park (Kavanagh 2010; De Temmerman 2007a; Wasike 2005; Interview Sixty-Three). One rebel's DDRRR report sheds light on typical procedures for some of these practices: "He [the rebel] said that February 2009, a team of 6 persons including himself together with their commander, colonel Odomo went to Goma via Kyondo, Butembo for selling their Okapi's skin and leopard's ivory which were sent to them by Colonel Musayo Kasereka from Richard mountain" (MONUSCO Document Seven).

The group's most lucrative endeavor was their participation in the regional timber trade. As part of the wider Nande-managed cross-border commerce networks, the timber trade blossomed during the Congo wars of the late 1990s and early 2000s. The conflict environment, including lack of official regulatory authorities to manage forested land, facilitated the plundering of North

Kivu's forests by national and foreign armed groups.[10] After the official end of the Congolese wars in 2003 the timber trade continued relatively unabated (and in fact increased), and the ADF were territorially in an ideal location to take advantage of this (Forests Monitor 2007).[11]

Logging in the Grand Nord area of North Kivu principally took place in Beni's northern territory, with the key sites being the Mabalako forest and the area around Oicha and Eringeti (Spittaels and Hilgert 2008). Not only did the ADF control some of the most timber-rich areas of North Kivu (Beni territory was in fact known as 'the lungs of North Kivu'), but two of the timber market's main trade routes and border crossings—Kasindi-Mpondwe, and Kamango-Bundibugyo—traversed ADF-infiltrated space (Chishweka 2007). In fact, according to a report by Forests Monitor (2007, 51), "The largest single exit point for timber from eastern DRC is located between the towns of Kasindi and Mpondwe. This route is on an almost direct line between the main source of DRC timber (Ituri forest) and the main markets of Kampala and Nairobi." Furthermore, when it came to the timber trade, several local chiefs, including Kamango's Saambili Bamukoko and Chuchubo's Mr. Mundeke, were established collaborators with the ADF (Group of Experts on the Democratic Republic of the Congo December 2, 2011; MONUSCO Document Five). The Kamango-Bundibugyo route was smaller in scale, but tended to source timber specifically from the Rwenzori range—namely, the ADF's zone (Forests Monitor 2007).

Not only were the ADF well-positioned in Congo to exploit the timber trade, but they were also strategically connected to relevant personnel on the Ugandan side of the borderland too. Konjo business contacts in Mpondwe, for example, advised on which taxi services to use, the best locations to store timber-related goods, and so on. When moving timber products out of Congo, Congolese members fronted the group; when operating on the Uganda side, vice-versa. Among other things, this cross-border economic presence helped them to traverse or take advantage of customs and the astoundingly large number of border taxes.[12] Spittaels and Hilgert (2008, 23) describe the timber borderscape as the following: "Many teams of loggers are financed and equipped by Ugandan businessmen who organize the logging through Congolese intermediaries. The trucks drive the timber to the border crossing at Kasindi. On the Ugandan side of the border (Mpondwe) there is a trade zone where foreigners can do business without needing to go through any border formalities. It is in this area that the timber market is located." The ADF's historic connections with the Nande-Konjo cross-border economic and trading community enabled them to be a part of the scene described above. Moreover, as an Office for the Coordination of Humanitarian Affairs (OCHA) employee in North Kivu explained, "because they have been settled in the area for so long, they can work in agriculture, they can work in wood—they've mastered the forest" (Interview Five).

The rebels not only generated revenue from exporting timber; they also taxed others felling wood in the forests under their control. Community leaders in Eringeti reported that the ADF taxed chainsaws USD $200 per year and issued fines of USD $500 to those accessing such areas without their permission (Group of Experts on the Democratic Republic of the Congo December 2, 2011). Interestingly, even FARDC officers were known to pay the taxes for chainsaw access to ADF forests.[13] To uphold their relationship with the surrounding communities, a significant proportion of the profits accumulated from their timber-related businesses went to local leaders. This likely amounted to as much as half of their revenue going to Congolese officials in Eringeti (MONUSCO Document Eighteen).

Their extensive local commercial contacts throughout the Grand Nord area, including with important Nande traders and the politically-connected like former warlords from the Congolese wars, helped in other fields as well. They allowed members to set up various small businesses, for example (Mwanawavene 2010; Interview Sixty-Eight). ADF-operated retail shops and pharmacies could be found in urban centers like Butembo. They also ran larger ventures, such as 'pikipiki' (motorcycle taxi) companies throughout urban areas along the Uganda-Congo border, as well as petrol and transport cargo services. They initiated a scheme to enmesh themselves further into the business scene in the region (and thereby also acquire more collaborators): they made agreements with various traders whereby in exchange for providing some of the necessary goods for their business, profits would then be shared with the ADF (Titeca and Vlassenroot 2012; Group of Experts on the Democratic Republic of the Congo December 2, 2011).

These business ventures helped with not only providing supplementary sources of income for the rebels, but also aided in their intelligence efforts. Many of the ADF's pikipiki businesses, for example, were directly manned by ADF intelligence operatives (MONUSCO Document Seventeen). They also had agents/middle men strategically placed in Goma and Beni, among other cities, to transfer finances (in addition to people) from various areas (including abroad) to ADF camps. According to senior ADF defectors, a Konjo brother and sister team, Twaha and Yalala Kisendo, led the Goma financial 'bureau' (MONUSCO Document Four). Likewise, a husband and wife team, Donatien Kampale Manzameli (eventually arrested) and Abigail Mbambu Sirimirona—both relatives of original NALU founders—headed the Beni financial sector (MONUSCO Document Four). Such cases of integration into the economic life of the borderland were pivotally important factors in the ADF's material sustainability.

Territorial Control Practices

Apart from during the two attacks suffered in 2005 and 2010 (to be discussed in the third part of this chapter), ADF influence was felt throughout a significant area of North Kivu. At times they pursued semi-ruthless practices to sustain this influence. They regularly threatened Virunga National Park rangers who ventured into 'their' forests, for example, and would often not hesitate to use violence in order to keep outsiders at bay (Romkema 2007). Nevertheless, the result was that a relatively small, but strategically located (with prime access to the border) and resource-rich territory was theirs.

It is important to clarify the different types of ADF influence and control that existed. First, the ADF had infiltrated a large part of Grand Nord territory. ADF-infiltrated territory during this time period ran in the north from close to the North Kivu-Ituri provincial border, to the south on the northeast shore of Lake Edward. It then stretched in the west from the area immediately surrounding Beni town, to the east up to the Uganda-Congo border. Population centers in this zone are found on the Lubero-Eringeti axis, such as Butembo, Beni, Mbau, Oicha, and Eringeti, and along the string of border posts following the Uganda-Congo border, including Kasindi and Kamango. ADF members moved freely (but still undercover) in the urban centers, could access medical care, and buy supplies. It is interesting to point out that regular foot soldiers were not permitted to carry cash on themselves; all funds were stored in headquarters, where there was a sort of 'ADF bank' controlled by Sharif Twebo. If an ADF member wished to purchase goods, they simply made a request to the bank, and designated financial agents would travel to town (usually Butembo or Beni) to make the acquisition (MONUSCO Document Four). The ADF financial personnel were known to purchase goods in these urban centers on a regular basis, often using USD $100 bills (Mwanawavene 2010). Thus, ADF infiltrated territory was an important parcel of Grand Nord land, where the rebels did not necessarily govern the population, but nevertheless were largely supported by the population, could move around quite freely, carry-out their business practices, and so on.

Crucially, however, when referring to the rebels' zone of infiltration, the Kasese, Bundibugyo, and Kabarole districts of western Uganda have to be included as well. The principal towns in these areas—Kasese, Bundibugyo, and Fort Portal—were all infiltrated by ADF, and acted as key transit centers for the movement of personnel, goods, and information (The Independent Team 2010b). Even as far east as Fort Portal, for example, certain bars were used by ADF to conduct money transfers (delivering funds to be spent on food, for example) and hold meetings (Interview Twenty-Nine). A declassified JATT intelligence file described a typical scenario of ADF cross-border movement:

> Around March 2007, a group of 52 ADF rebels including subject were ordered by the late ADF commander Bosco Balau Isiko to move into Uganda. They were dispatched under the command of Kawooya, deputized by Mukwaya and Kijjambu, and were briefed not to harass the population nor interfere with their property. They infiltrated the Semuliki NP [National Park] to Kalambi hills from where they linked up with commander Kato and another group which the subject could not ably establish (The Independent Team 2010a).

Former combatants have told how their officers would regularly travel to Uganda for periods of two weeks at a time, presumably for meetings, collection of information, and so on (MONUSCO Document Thirteen). While eastern Congo was the ADF's principal theatre of operation between 2004–2013, the ADF's infiltration and economic penetration of western Uganda was crucial to their material sustainability as well.

Within the infiltrated zone, however, there was a section actually controlled by the ADF: they were the authority in that area, and as such, governed the population. Referred to unofficially as the 'Kamango zone,' this is where the majority of the ADF's principal camps were, including their headquarters, and consequently where most of the force and their dependents resided. This area of control was in Virunga National Park, and was a sparsely populated space consisting for the most part of virgin forest. This helped to make infiltration and penetration by outsiders difficult. As an OCHA employee in Beni explained, "The Kamango zone is an enclave within a wider area of insecurity" (Interview Five). Essentially the whole of Virunga was occupied by 'negative forces,' and actually getting from urban centers such as Beni, to Kamango, was highly dangerous for outsiders.[14] Their headquarters were initially situated in the village of Nadui, within extremely dense forest and a deep valley, but were later moved to Chuchubo.

Other main bases were located in Bundiguya, Mwalika, and Makayoba, with smaller groups of usually no more than 50 ADF positioned in Mavivi, Ilungu, Motara, Bumbuli, Kambi, Kambiyajua, Nobili, Kaylama, Maisafi, and Kikingi (Wasike 2005; De Temmerman 2007b; The Independent Team 2010a; Wakabi 2005; MONUSCO Document Seventeen; MONUSCO Document Eighteen). Often supplies and new recruits were first sent to Mwalika, which was partially used as a transit center. Training was principally done at the Mwalika camp as well, frequently for periods of two to three months, although more specialized training also took place at Nadui and Chuchubo (the latter is said to have had an 'Advanced Training Center') (Group of Experts on the Democratic Republic of the Congo December 2, 2011, 26). Depending on whether the ADF were engaged in fighting, a new recruit's typical journey involved arriving in Mwalika (either from a transit site in western Uganda or other locale in Congo), undergoing basic training, and then being dispatched to either one of the force's operational sites for purposes of reinforcement, or if during quieter periods, to Nadui or Chuchubo for additional learning of specialized military techniques.

Government Responses

The nature of the Congolese and Ugandan governments' presence in the borderland also influenced the ADF's capacity to acquire material resources. With regards to this, it is important to consider the influence of both acts of commission and acts of omission on the part of Kinshasa and Kampala. In other words, it is necessary to look at their active and inactive roles in the borderland, which had bearings on the ADF. For a significant portion of the 2004–2013 time period the force had a relatively cordial, albeit unstable, relationship with the national Congolese government. The two actors had made a 'gentleman's agreement' on a line of demarcation. Occasionally this was breached—for example in April 2008 by FARDC soldiers who were hunting monkeys and crossed the unofficial boundary—but generally this line was upheld. Indeed, in between the two attacks waged on the ADF (essentially from 2006 to the first half of 2010, during which ADF-Ugandan government negotiations also took place), the two actors derived certain benefits from each other, and thereby were able to maintain somewhat of a loose alliance. Most importantly for the ADF, they received what could be called a 'protected status' from Kinshasa: they were allowed to maintain their control over a valuable and strategically important space of North Kivutien territory (Interview Thirty-Four).

From Kinshasa's perspective, the ADF represented—especially when compared to FARDC—a militarily capable, robust, and disciplined force that could repel threats such as the CNDP. In fact, the ADF played a decisive role in 2008 in helping to halt the CNDP's advance on Goma. While they were very much a 'useful enemy' for a period of time, ultimately, the relationship between the Congolese government and the ADF—for reasons to be discussed in the third part of this chapter—dramatically dissolved by mid-2010. However, although Kinshasa for a time helped the ADF with territorial access and control, the government's most important 'contribution' to the group, especially when it came to land, was actually its lack of capacity to govern the borderland in any meaningful way. Facilitated by Kinshasa's effective absence from the Grand Nord of North Kivu, the ADF were undoubtedly the authority in the space they occupied. They taxed people, manned roadblocks, and controlled the general politico-economic atmosphere (Interview Thirty-Four). Periodically throughout this time period the number and strength of Uganda's UPDF in the borderland increased, during which the ADF temporarily shifted camp to the western side of the Oicha-Eringeti road, away from their more permanent bases on the eastern flank next to the border (Interview Sixty-Three). However, for the most part the ADF did not have to contend with a heavy UPDF presence. Indeed, western Uganda's continued marginalization meant that access to the border and movement into Uganda was a constant feature of ADF activity.

It was not only territorial control that was enabled by the lack of borderland governance on the part of Kinshasa and Kampala, but also access to weapons, as arms networks continued to have essentially free rein. The unique economic atmosphere that existed in North Kivu's Grand Nord facilitated the networks. As Kabamba (2008, 198) notes, "All the rebels in eastern DRC are selling gold, cassiterite, wolfram, and sometimes coltan to Nande traders in exchange for cash or weapons." The Grand Nord towns of Eringeti, Oicha, Mavivi, and Mutwanga together constituted a regional weapons hub. They were well-positioned to service a variety of violent groups, and intersected key trade routes—notably those coming from Uganda, for which the towns of Kanyatsi and Kitoma in western Uganda served as principal entry points for weapons and ammunition (Mwanawavene, Baheteet, and Bilali 2006).

According to a report by la Groupe de Recherche et d'Information sur la Paix et la Sécurité, civilians in these borderland towns were well aware of the militarized nature of their area. Many were cognizant of the frequent arms transactions, weapons seizures, transport routes used to move the goods, and locations of weapons caches (often at the foothills of the Rwenzori Mountains) (Mwanawavene, Baheteet, and Bilali 2006). The militarization of these communities was an entrenched phenomenon, fuelled by years of conflict or negative peace. Many of those who had been actively involved in the Congo wars kept their weapons post-2003 because of the lack of effective disarmament programs. According to a DDRRR Specialist at the UN Development Program (UNDP) in Goma, there were 300,000 arms in eastern Congo as of 2011, with 95 percent of those held within communities by civilians (Interview Fifty). It was not only the accessibility factor that made weapons so attainable for the ADF. The low cost was important as well; a Kalashnikov could be bought for USD $20, and a hand grenade for 50 cents (Thakur 2008).

Wider eastern Congolese dynamics, such as the influence of ongoing violence in Ituri, and the arms dealings to other rebels by Lendu militias, also played into the ease with which arms were acquired (Mwanawavene, Baheteet, and Bilali 2006). While the 'wild west' nature of the arms trade that had existed in the late 1990s was largely gone by the time period of this chapter, the region was nevertheless inundated with weapons. The ADF became known for having large arsenals of weapons. They thus often had groups such as Mai Mai, as well as poachers approach them to do exchanges: weapons for money, minerals, or ivory (Mwanawavene, Baheteet, and Bilali 2006).

Just as key, however, was collaboration with certain Congolese and Ugandan government officials, especially in key border locales such as Kasindi. For FARDC and Ugandan officials, their meagre incomes made them susceptible to involvement in arms trafficking. But perhaps the most pivotal source of weapons, and increasingly so with time, were those acquired from FARDC (if not by illegal diversion, then via capture). The ADF were skilled in manipulating the liminal nature of the borderland—the blurry categories between government official and civilian, illegal and legal activity, and so on—and this proved helpful for their acquisition and control of material resources.

Some analyses of the group have argued that such examples of collaboration with Ugandan officials were symptomatic of a much bigger issue: namely, that the Museveni regime actually found it beneficial to keep the ADF alive. Among the advantages the Ugandan government could accrue, proponents of this idea argue, is an alibi to re-enter the Congo, the excuse to sustain high military spending, but most of all, a reason to continue to receive US aid for fighting terrorism. According to Titeca and Vlassenroot (2012, 168), for example, "Although the ADF was in 2005 removed from the US 'Terrorist Exclusion List,' the Museveni regime is doing everything to show it is not a 'dormant' force, but a direct terrorist threat: the assumed links of the ADF with Al Qaeda and Al Shabab are therefore geo-politically useful, as it allows Uganda (again) to identify itself again as a key ally for the US [. . . and] to receive US support for its 'war on terror.'" It is likely that the Museveni regime in the past found certain conflicts useful for its economic/business or geo-strategic interests.[15] It is also the case that the Ugandan government failed to wholeheartedly pursue negotiations that were initiated with Kinshasa and the ADF in 2009. These negotiations were to be held under the auspices of MONUSCO and the International Organization of Migration (IOM) in the city of Kisangani. They never went beyond the preliminary stages, however.

Yet to conclude that Kampala was purposely keeping the ADF alive is going too far—not to mention that such a scenario credits Kampala with far more power and capability than it deserves in this regard. For one thing, none of the parties to the 2009 negotiations appeared committed or enthusiastic to the peace talks.[16] More importantly, though, President Museveni's emphasis on the ADF's Islamic and terrorist dimension did not equate to him supporting the group—it was simply the frame through which the government chose to understand (for strategic reasons or otherwise) the ADF. Furthermore, the politics of this situation have to be kept in mind: this argument was perhaps expressed most frequently by Congolese politicians, who clearly had an interest in deflecting criticism about the ADF's continued existence off of themselves, and on to Uganda. "This group is just sustained by officials in Uganda," a Congolese official in Butembo argued (Interview Fourteen). In the end, this argument rests on extremely dubious evidence, and is simply one more dimension to the extensive political rumor mill in existence in the Great Lakes area.

With regards to the ADF's capacity to acquire material resources between 2004–2013, funding from various outside Islamic national and regional actors played a part at times. However, this support cannot fully account for the group's resiliency in terms of access to, and procurement of, material resources—including their control of a significant parcel of North Kivutien land. What also proved sustainable and lucrative for them were their economic endeavors at the micro-level in the borderland. The ADF were able to a degree to become a part of the local agricultural scene: they farmed a variety of products, used their produce to feed the ADF community, and traded their goods at local markets. They also became involved in gold mining, controlled timber forests, and set up businesses in local urban centers. These are endeavors that can only sufficiently be appreciated through a borderland perspective.

These economic pursuits were facilitated by the ADF's changed relationship with, and approach to, the surrounding civilian population in North Kivu. Negative peace and structural violence still underpinned this relationship, but there were less overt attacks. Moreover, the Konjo-Nande segment within the force enabled them to maintain more positive relationships with segments of the western Ugandan population as well, especially those involved in cross-border economic activities. The ADF's increasing commercial achievements encouraged them to uphold this changed relationship with the surrounding public. In essence, their financial 'success' made them dependent on the borderland and borderlanders. In fact, one conflict resolution practitioner called the group "rebels slash businessmen," but "increasingly on the business side of things" (Interview Twenty-Seven). It helped for example in their involvement in cross-border trade. Principally this revolved around timber and gold, but it also included other resources such as ivory and diamonds. Without the borderlanders' trust, they would not have been able to gain access to these trans-local trades, let alone the opportunity to advance and further develop them.

Perhaps most importantly though, it would have been impossible for the ADF to partake in these trade networks had it not been for the Rwenzori borderland's economically independent, rebellious, and anti-state character. For all of their complaints of being marginalized and ignored by Kinshasa, the Nande of North Kivu were effectively 'state runaways' to use Scott's terminology, and valued their independence and distance from central authority. Prunier (2009, 325 and 457) described the economic hub of the Nande zone, the 'Autonomous Republic of Butembo,' as the following: "For the past eight years, the Butembo area and the surrounding countryside has, for all practical purposes, been an independent political and economic unit." In fact, it is often rumored that the Nande traders 'bribed' Kabila with significant sums of money to leave them alone, so to speak. A similar sentiment existed amongst western Ugandan residents, who were economically far more oriented towards eastern Congo than their own state. It is telling, for example, that Kasese district with its Konjo majority, consistently voted for the opposition during this time period.

In economic terms, all of these factors meant that there was enough distance from the state for cross-border illicit activities to thrive. And due to the ADF's enmeshment in the socio-political milieu of the borderland, it was possible for them to become deeply involved in these cross-border economic trade networks. Far from being the marginal or peripheral zone many analyses assumed it to be, the Rwenzori borderland and its borderlanders demonstrated a great deal of agency and influence during this time period. Overall, therefore, while there were outside sources of material support for the ADF, it is impossible to understand the force's ability to materially survive (indeed, thrive) without also considering their place in the borderland's economic networks.

PART III: EXECUTION OF VIOLENCE

MISGUIDED EXPLANATIONS OF THE ADF'S EXECUTION OF VIOLENCE

The majority of analyses understood the ADF's violent actions through the lens of terrorism. In 2007 Uganda's Defense Minister, Crispus Kiyonga, declared, "The people of Uganda must be re-assured that the government will not allow its territory and people to be attacked by these terrorists. We reserve the right to self-defense, including pursuing terrorists to their points of origin" (Allio 2007).[17] A 2010 internal JATT intelligence memo is typical in this respect: "The situation has been generally calm with no terrorist incidents reported in and around Kampala. However, ADF remains active and nurses intentions of revamping its urban terror operations" (The Independent Team 2010d). Of course, the ADF did commit various terrorist acts throughout this time, most notably in terms of their involvement in the Al Shabab 2010 twin Kampala bombings, described earlier. It was also alleged that they had planned to sabotage the 2007 Commonwealth Heads of Government Meeting in Uganda, through bombing various venues; however, this was supposedly foiled by UPDF intelligence agents (Matsiko 2007; Mwenda 2010a).[18]

Due to this preoccupation with terrorism, it appeared to many as though the ADF were active on only a sporadic basis. The group was seen as largely dormant, periodically coming alive to terrorize Uganda. Especially amongst Ugandans, there was a widespread opinion that the ADF were composed of mainly inactive remnants of a past group. This was the opinion of not only the general public, but surprisingly UN organizations, NGOs, and so on (Interview Twenty-Five; Interview Forty-Seven). There appears to have been little awareness that the rebels were in actual fact consistently active—and not usually in terms of terrorism.

The Uganda Human Rights 2006 Report stated, for example, "The period under review witnessed the resurgence of the long-dormant ADF rebel group, which had been quiet since the UPDF flushed them out of their bases in eastern DRC in 2000–2001 [. . .] Recently, however, they had started showing signs of regrouping in their former bases in the DR Congo and also made attempts to re-enter Uganda and destabilize the country again" (Uganda. Human Rights Commission 2006, 51). Likewise, *The New Vision* reported in 2005, "Reports from the eastern jungles of the DRC reveal that the ADF have reopened camps. The rebels are reportedly reorganizing their command structure and training in preparation for an assault on Uganda" (Wasike 2005). *The Daily Monitor* in 2011 wrote, "There are reports that ADF rebels are regrouping in the DRC and have intentions of attacking Uganda again. The Inspector General of [Ugandan] Police, Maj. Gen. Kale Kayihura, a fortnight ago issued a terror alert" (Bagala 2011). And the *Think Africa Press* article referred to earlier stated in 2012, "The ADF appears to have been largely dormant for the past decade, and it is believed its sudden revival is related to the shifting geopolitics in the region" (Muhumuza 2012).

Interestingly, despite believing the ADF to have been sleeping for a large part of the 2004–2013 time period, the 'misguided explanations' of the group portrayed their threat level as quite significant. The 2010 JATT memo concluded with the following: "The threat is very imminent. It calls for gallancy and vigilance with each member of society/security conscious of his/her own security" (The Independent Team 2010e). Especially from 2009 onwards, the UPDF was very vocal in its concerns, maintaining that the potential danger from the ADF was far more serious than that of the LRA. A picture was painted of a group on the offensive, with the potential to strike Uganda at any time. Compounding this scenario was the force's supposed fundamentalist ideology and consequent irrationality. In a speech to Bundibugyo residents in 2010, President Museveni described the ADF's agenda as one of attempting to "re-organize their confusion," and "wasting time in the bushes" (Bariyo 2010). And speaking of Mukulu, Mugira said, "We know he's going to be a very, very dangerous person [. . .] We think he'll become the next Bin Laden of Africa" (Sheikh 2005).

Yet in numerous ways, as the following sections will demonstrate, these understandings do not reflect the situation on the ground. They were based on outdated concepts of the group's objectives, capabilities, and military agenda. Or, as a DFID employee in Kampala argued, "the ADF keeps being judged on past form" (Interview Forty-Eight). As discussed earlier in this chapter, while the group still proclaimed long-term interests in destabilizing Uganda, their more immediate concerns and in fact overriding objectives, were far more related to maintaining their position in the borderland. Thus, rather than being a force made up of remnants of have-been rebel groups, coming together only occasionally to launch terrorist raids on urban Uganda, the ADF were firmly and actively rooted in their transnational territory and networks, attacking those whom they perceived to be threatening their borderland community and interests.

Military Strategies and Tactics: Operation North Night Final and Operation Rwenzori

On 24 December 2005 a combined FARDC-UN force launched the largest operation ever conducted against the ADF until that point, Operation North Night Final, in the group's North Kivu territory. Approximately 3,500 FARDC soldiers were involved, supported by 600 Indian MONUSCO peacekeepers. The ADF had prior to that been relatively quiet, concentrating on regrouping and re-establishing themselves after their 2003 exit from Uganda. The rebels had continued to reject offers of repatriation and amnesty from the Ugandan government (how genuine these offers were can be questioned), and Kampala had been putting pressure on Kinshasa and MONUSCO to do something about the negative forces which they argued were a threat to Uganda. It is also likely that MONUSCO was worried about 'foreign' groups such as the ADF disrupting Congo's upcoming 2006 elections (BBC 2005). Earlier in the year, in a comment directed at Kinshasa and MONUSCO, President Museveni had disparagingly stated, "You give a terrorist group two years of holiday; this means that you are supporting terrorism. The ADF has been there for two years, growing food and resting" (IRIN News 2005). Indeed, Uganda had likely been a driving force behind the operation, with the UN at least partly spurred to action in order to take away any excuse President Museveni might make to enter Congo.[19] The campaign only lasted a few days. By 26 December FARDC declared most of ADF territory to be back under its control. On 28 December the ADF's last bastion, Mwalika, fell and FARDC celebrated victory over the ADF. In the end, over 90 ADF rebels, several Congolese soldiers, and one Indian MONUSCO peacekeeper were killed.

MONUSCO's Lieutenant-Colonel Frédéric Médard warned, however (and accurately as it turned out), against declaring the rebels a spent force:

At this stage all the known ADF camps in the region are occupied and dismantled. The Mwalika camp fell today. It was in a way the last ADF bastion, which could engage in fighting. The rebel fighters fled to the Ruwenzori massifs. It will be important to carry on with patrols to look for armed elements who could have found refuge in the forested areas. Therefore we can say that the operation is not really over yet. The objective is to capture all the armed elements with a view to ensuring total security in the area to ensure there will be no reprisals against the populations (Radio France Internationale 2005).

As was also common between 1996–2003, predictions of operational success against the ADF proved to be premature. The rebels were undoubtedly greatly disturbed: camps were ruined and they were ultimately substantially uprooted by the offensive. But importantly, their command structure was left intact, at least partly owing to numerous ADF units vacating the area in the weeks prior to the offensive (Titeca and Vlassenroot 2012). It was not long before the ADF were regrouping and recommencing military action, with regular reports—as early as April 2006—of skirmishes between UPDF, FARDC, and ADF (Esiara 2006; Radio Uganda 2007; Xinhua 2007; Karugaba 2007; Mugerwa 2007).

Nevertheless, the 2005 offensive had weakened the ADF, and they could no longer be considered a threatening military force. But perhaps one could say that such an objective was not necessarily of overriding concern to them. Rather, of more importance was re-establishing their place in the borderland: re-securing their socio-political networks, economic activities, and community space in general. In fact, throughout the entirety of this time period the ADF's military activities were overwhelmingly defensive in nature. When their interests were threatened, they used force to rectify the situation. If their territory, or business interests, or access to western Uganda were put in jeopardy, the ADF did not hesitate in dealing with such matters violently. The rest of the time, though, the force were largely leading a settled, quiet, even peaceful existence.

This is why the 2010 Operation Rwenzori came as such a surprise to so many actors. Launched in late June 2010, Operation Rwenzori was militarily undertaken solely by FARDC, with MONUSCO believing the threat posed by the ADF was not significant enough to warrant such a campaign. According to the MONUSCO spokesman, Madnodje Mounoubai, FARDC "did not approach us to prepare this operation. It's something they did on their own" (Kavanagh 2010). While the UN did not provide military support to the Congolese Army, its mandate was still nevertheless one of state-building and helping the national government to consolidate control over its territory. Resultantly, the peacekeeping force contributed to the endeavor in more passive ways, such as helping with logistics, dissemination of intelligence, strategy, and so on (Radio Okapi 2012c). In light of this, MONUSCO led the 'Joint Coordination Centre' in Beni, which was tasked with facilitating the sharing of information between MONUSCO, FARDC, and UPDF personnel (Radio Okapi 2012c).

A variety of reasons have been put forward as to why the ADF-Kinshasa relationship disintegrated so dramatically and quickly in 2010. Some suggest that Kinshasa wanted to demonstrate military capability in the east and thus chose to attack a relatively easy (or so it thought) target. A further incentive for Kinshasa to dispel the rebels, according to another line of thought, had to do with the resource-rich and extremely fertile land the ADF controlled. Other sources close to the group argued that it stemmed from pressure applied by Kampala, specifically with respect to the approaching 50th anniversary of Congolese independence: President Museveni had apparently said he would not attend the festivities if the ADF situation had not been taken care of (Interview Five; Interview Nine). In a blog by Stearns (2010a), it was pondered as to whether President Museveni had been tipped-off about the forthcoming July 2010 Kampala bombings, and thus had urged Kinshasa to launch an operation. Whatever the reason, the offensive initially was somewhat successful, dislodging the rebels from many of their entrenched bases, including the Nadui camp. The first phase of the operation, which concentrated on southern Beni territory, ended in August 2010. That month Lambert Mende of FARDC declared, "Most places in the territory of Beni previously controlled by this militia have been liberated" (Agence France-Pressse 2010). He went on to claim that the ADF had been forced to return 'home' to Uganda: "The residual elements of this armed group fled in disarray towards the heights of Mount Ruwenzori, which is incontestably the right direction for their country" (Agence France-Pressse 2010).

Yet, the ADF in fact did not have to flee their territory. They were able to quickly regain their eastern Congolese Rwenzori borderland space, and all the while maintain their western Ugandan networks and connections. If anything, they had to slightly shift their operating theatre to more remote territory. This was similar to the scenario which transpired in the aftermath of FARDC-FDLR battles, as elucidated by the Pole Institute (2010, 9): "The helplessness of the Congolese authorities becomes ever clearer when Congo's army, the FARDC, takes military action against the FDLR in South or North Kivu [. . .] Each time, the attacks have only resulted in spreading the FDLR further into the bush, thus giving them more protected territory to operate from." The rebels launched an extremely aggressive campaign to counter Operation Rwenzori, which included reprisal attacks against the population (to be discussed in the next section) and assaults on FARDC posts. As the UN Group of Experts stated, "during 2011 the rebels have implemented an aggressive strategy, pre-empting any subsequent operations with attacks on FARDC positions, through which they have regained control over all of their previously lost camps, including Nadui" (Group of Experts on the Democratic Republic of the Congo 2011, 27).

FARDC was ill-prepared for such a strong comeback from the ADF, and suffered heavy casualties, despite its persistent claims to the contrary (Sole 2011). It was soon apparent that the ADF out-equipped, out-skilled, and ultimately was out-fighting, the Congolese army. The longer the operation carried on, the more obvious it became that FARDC simply did not have the capacity or resources to take on the ADF. As a UNHCR representative commented, "The ADF controlled FARDC—not the other way around" (Interview Four). The rebels sustained this aggressive strategy up to the summer of 2011, as the following by the UN Group of Experts shows: "Prior to the start of a fourth phase of operations scheduled for 30 April 2011, according to FARDC officers, ADF ambushed FARDC at Makayova, killing three army soldiers and injuring 21. When word of another round of potential operations reached ADF, the rebels attacked FARDC positions east of Eringeti on 1 July at Chuchubo and Makembi, where they killed nine FARDC soldiers" (Group of Experts on the Democratic Republic of the Congo December 2, 2011, 27).

Political Geography Factors

The rebels had several interesting factors working on their side. For one thing, FARDC was an extremely weak, militarily incapable, and notoriously undisciplined army (Lwamba 2011b). Its intelligence capabilities were profoundly flawed, with the result that "the army can only report in general terms on the various security threats in the respective provinces" (Romkema 2007, 26). Their practice of human rights abuses towards Congolese civilians was prevalent and widespread. This also put MONUSCO in an awkward position. As Raeymaekers (2011, 8) describes the Kinshasa-MONUSCO relationship, "it [MONUSCO] was supposed to 'stabilize' insecurity and integrate warring parties into a new security framework. In practice, however, it often found itself operating side by side to an abusive security apparatus that used this external cover to support claims of territorial sovereignty and sustain violent modes of predation." As such, the ADF increasingly came to regard MONUSCO as just as great a foe as FARDC, hence the large number of assaults on peacekeepers by the rebels (Radio Okapi 2012a). Militarily-speaking, the ADF worked in almost total contrast to FARDC. Not only were they extremely disciplined, but the combatants were simply much more skilled and trained in military strategies and tactics (Interview Twenty-Two). With regards to their technique, CRC staff in Beni explained, "When they fight, if they want to shoot you in the eye, then they will shoot you in the eye" (Interview Sixty-Eight). Their command structure was "cohesive and coherent" and "difficult to penetrate" (Interview Nine). And at the top, ADF leadership were not only competent and proficient, but perhaps in most stark contrast to FARDC, they were motivated.

Compounding the above was FARDC's unfamiliarity with the Grand Nord area, and thus its attempt to operate on what could essentially be thought of as foreign soil.[20] It did so in a conventional manner, in contrast to the ADF, which used relevant guerrilla warfare techniques. As described by a UN fieldwork report, "The terrain supports guerrilla warfare and is not conducive for large scale movement/conventional operations. Thick forests/vegetation hinders effective aerial view/recce unless flying low. The gorges, caves and thick jungles in the mountainous area of Makayoba 3, Nadui and Kyalama (northeast of Beni) make this area suitable for asymmetric operations" (MONUSCO Document Seventeen). It goes on to note, "Existing communications (roads and riverine) naturally presents a lot of potential choke points which may be exploited by ADF; whilst the jungle makes any landward advance towards ADF strongholds a Command and Control nightmare" (MONUSCO Document Seventeen).

Even more important than their strategic use of the terrain, however, was the ADF's manipulation of the borderland's position. Because of their territorial control and intimate familiarity with the terrain, it was easy for the ADF to attack in small groups, usually of about one dozen fighters, and then slip back into the forests or villages (Sole 2011). Indeed, while the group's small size had its limits—it was impossible for example to expect that they would wholly defeat the Congolese army—they could nevertheless succeed in enough battles to maintain an advantage in their operating area. Post-Operation Rwenzori the ADF re-established and expanded upon many of their previous camps (living in these until early 2014). Still, from the summer of 2010 onwards, there were some smaller factions of the force that maintained a very mobile existence. They constantly moved camp so as to both evade detection, and to carry-out ambushes on FARDC (Interview Twenty-One). As the UN Group of Experts noted, "Taking advantage of the regimentation process, ADF has become increasingly mobile, often changing positions during the course of 2011 and even seeking to make inroads in Ituri" (Group of Experts on the Democratic Republic of the Congo December 2, 2011, 26). While in mobile form, living conditions could be difficult. They had to travel lightly and sleep under banana leaf tents.[21] In these small groups they were able to cross the border frequently, and the ADF used their contacts and networks to move around Kabarole, Kasese, and Bundibugyo districts in western Uganda. Going to Uganda so frequently allowed them to not only escape FARDC and MONUSCO, but to replenish weapons stocks and gather intelligence. FARDC had great difficulty curbing the ADF's constant movement across the border both in the Grand Nord area, as well as in several other ADF border hotspot locales, such as Rutshuru and Bunagana (Interview Fourteen).

Cross-border mobility had also played an important part in their surviving the 2005 offensive. Immediately after the attack, Mukulu had ordered for important personnel to seek safety in small groups in western Uganda. While some were ultimately intercepted by Ugandan intelligence, several groups of rebels were able to find temporary refuge there (MONUSCO Document Four). Regular infiltration into western Uganda continued after 2005. A DDRRR debriefing note on an ADF rebel provides an example of this: "He [the rebel] was taken to Chuchubo camp for 6 months training under Maj. Katusa Chief Instructor. Total of trained recruits was 38 (Ugandans and Congolese). They stayed at Chuchubo from 2003 to 2005. Then he was sent along with 56 others among them 15 Ugandans to fight against UPDF in areas located between Lamia River [in Bundibugyo District, western Uganda] and Mubendi village [in Mubendi District, western/central Uganda] near Kampala" (MONUSCO Document Fourteen). Their mobility helped them in taking back their bases so quickly in 2011, which was pivotal to the group's success. It not only allowed them to re-establish command and control, but camps such as Makayoba housed important and much-needed arms caches (weapons were frequently buried in large covered pits).

The ADF's numbers were nowhere close to those of other groups based in the borderland. In 2008 Mukulu told facilitators of the Kisangani peace talks that he had "1,200 soldiers well-trained"; by 2011, it was estimated that the ADF's numbers were approximately 1,500 (MONUSCO Document Twenty). By later in this chapter's time period numbers were reduced to just over 100 fighters. The FDLR, in contrast, were around 6,000 pre-2008, and post-2008 were reduced to a still significant 3,000. Despite the ADF's relatively low numbers, sources emphasized that it was their contacts and networks that really made them threatening. Their combatant community was relatively small, but the support structure was extensive. Furthermore, they maintained sleeper cells and a complex network of safe houses throughout Uganda—notably in the west of the country and in Kampala—and thus had the ability to move large numbers of personnel (MONUSCO Document Eighteen; Interview Thirty-Four; Interview Twenty-Two). When conditions became too precarious in one state (Uganda or Congo), it was undoubtedly a major asset having access to the other. With territorial control in Congo, infiltration of western Uganda, and safe houses in Kampala, the ADF had numerous safe haven options that could be taken advantage of.

Finally, all of the above factors were helped by the ADF's relationships with many of the other non-state actors in the borderland. Not only did the ADF and groups such as the Mai Mai cooperate in terms of exchanging training for minerals (or access to minerals), but they would also liaise with each other over communications, transportation of personnel and/or supplies, and ultimately coordination of attacks (Interview Five).²² ADF space overlapped with that of various Mai Mai groups, specifically 'Mai Mai Rwenzori,' and thus cooperation with them was essential to maintaining full mobility throughout the territory. The FDLR were the only other rebel group in close proximity to the ADF, but with the FDLR it was more a case of small numbers coming into Butembo, and so on, and not actually occupying territory in the area (Interview Fifty-Four). With time the ADF only became more effective in responding to the FARDC offensive. They grew bolder, bringing their attacks to urban areas like Beni, and even to the Congolese army's bases (Radio Okapi 2012d; Radio Okapi 2012e; Lwamba 2011a).

Civilian Collaboration

Arguably the ADF's most pivotal resource in terms of their ability to succeed militarily derived from the borderland public's poor relationship with central authority. In both the ADF's main theatre of operation during this time period, eastern Congo, but also in western Uganda, this dynamic was important. In terms of Congo, the Grand Nord area of North Kivu had of course historically been distanced from the central government (as discussed extensively in previous chapters). More recently its inhabitants had grown frustrated over what they perceived to be the exploitation of their territory's minerals by Kinshasa. More specifically, it angered the Nande that Kinshasa was interfering with their ability to (illegally) exploit minerals from the region. But the nature of the government's response to the presence of the ADF also greatly fed into the area's animosity, beginning with Operation North Night Final in 2005. The offensive had caused 150,000 civilians to flee their homes because of the fighting, subsequently live in extremely harsh conditions and makeshift shelters, and suffer economic loss due to not being able to attend to crops and fields (IRIN News 2006a).²³ Is it also important to remember, of course, that Operation North Night Final came after years of instability in the region, followed by foreign control on the part of the UPDF and Rassemblement Congolais pour la Démocratie-Kisangani/Mouvement de Libération (RCD-K/ML), and then finally a (what would turn out to be very brief) reprieve. The campaign and its aftermath shattered the optimism beginning to brew in the area of a more peaceful future.

The abuses meted out by FARDC were even more distressing to the area's inhabitants. As IRIN News (2006b) stated in May 2006, the IDPs "say that if they were to return home they would face greater persecution by their own army than by the rebels." A local village leader further explained: "Those of us who have tried to return to our villages have been forced to work for the [government] soldiers and give them food [. . .] Sometimes, they have gotten violent. If it were not for the abuses by the soldiers, we would have returned home by now" (IRIN News 2006b). Compounding this, according to a MONUSCO official, were "soldiers [. . .] going out of the conflict area at night along the main road north of Beni to attack the displaced population" (IRIN News 2006b). Their human rights abuses were extensive, and included regular looting, raping, maiming, and killing of the people they were supposedly there to protect.

Several postings from Ernst's blog shed an interesting light on FARDC's reputation in the area. Describing the beginning of Operation Rwenzori, for example, Ernst (2010–2012) wrote,

> There's a military confrontation in Isale, about 25 km from Butembo, which is one hour by car [. . .] The FARDC-Congolese 'governmental' forces—are fighting the NALU—Ugandan rebel forces [. . .] One would assume that the FARDC, being 'governmental' forces would be on the side of the Congolese people, yet Maman Marie and I receive word that in Isale the FARDC have pillaged several villages around Isale, raping at least 3 women and at least one man. The only consistent enemy in this war are the regular people, children especially.

On 9 July 2011 she (2010–2012) posted, "With all of the rebel forces in Congo, the governmental forces frighten me the most. They have the 'law' behind them, no matter how corrupt or non-existent that law is and thus they have more power than simply the power of a gun. They cause more chaos in this country than any rebel, but much less than any politician." The local Islamic population around Oicha and Eringeti especially suffered, being subject to arbitrary attacks by FARDC on the basis that Muslims were traditionally a large part of the ADF (Interview Eight). FARDC's popularity plummeted even more when ex-CNDP forces (as part of FARDC) were deployed in the Grand Nord—particularly when ex-CNDP member Eric Ruhorimbere was made Commander of the 81st sector in Beni.

While the inhabitants of ADF-controlled territory had prior to the offensive been living in relative harmony with the rebels, Operation North Night Final and its aftermath further encouraged the public's inclination for ADF rule over FARDC's—neither of course were optimal, but the ADF were arguably the lesser of two evils for some. Even the UN appeared to have serious doubts about FARDC's agenda and actions: "Of course, all the territory of the DRC should be under the control of the government, but the result [of the offensive] has not been positive from a humanitarian point of view" said one MONUSCO official (IRIN News 2006b). For the subsequent five years the rebels and North Kivutiens were able to resume their cohabitation living arrangement, and the area was comparatively calm. In fact, it was classified by international actors as 'stabilized.' But with Operation Rwenzori, this scenario was once again violently disrupted. Perhaps even more so than the previous time, the public was strongly against the offensive. They only grew more adamant in their stance as the violence continued. "The operation was bad news; they knew they would suffer," Solidarités explained (Interview Fifty-Five).

An estimated 100,000 people were forced to flee in the first month of Operation Rwenzori alone (Mumbere 2010). Many went to western Uganda as refugees, or moved west of the Beni-Oicha road and settled in makeshift shelters as IDPs, or moved in other directions such as towards Butembo (Interview Nineteen; Interview Sixty-Seven). "The people who fled live in sub-human conditions. Most of them sleep outside, some of them on the bare ground. Others have nothing to eat or need urgent medical treatment that they cannot get," reported Beni civil society leader Omar Kavota (IRIN News 2010).[24] FARDC made no evident attempts of trying to win over the hearts and minds of the local population. In fact, it appeared (or attempted to appear) quite oblivious to the problematic situation, as the following comment by a FARDC official exemplified: "The supposed threat to civilians is a fake problem" (IRIN News 2010).[25]

FARDC furthermore accused anyone left in the fighting areas of being an ADF collaborator, and then would issue brutal punishments (Interview Fifty-Five). Those who had been cohabitating with the ADF were especially vulnerable in this respect (Interview Nineteen). But what seemed to be most upsetting to people was their inability to return to their farming livelihoods. For some, it was simply impossible to access their fields anymore. Others, however, were in IDP gatherings that were located relatively close to their homes, and thus they would try to travel to their plots. Yet when they attempted this, FARDC charged them to access their fields, often as much as several hundred francs (Interview Fifty-Five; Interview Five). Indeed, civilians perceived one of the most key differences in terms of the control meted out by FARDC as compared to that of the ADF, to be their ability (or lack thereof) to practice agriculture.[26] It was not only the obstructed access to their fields that was distressing, however. As the UN Group of Experts noted, since "many local farmers work on these ADF-controlled plantations in exchange for a part of the yield, counter-insurgency strategies by FARDC impeding access across enemy lines are widely unpopular" (Group of Experts on the Democratic Republic of the Congo December 2, 2011, 30). Business leaders in the area were highly opposed to the operations as well, in light of their vested economic interests in the ADF's presence (Romkema 2007).

The relationship between the ADF and borderland residents, however, was by no means entirely positive after 2003. In some villages traditional leaders (chiefs) were unhappy with having to submit to ADF authority, and thus were forced to leave (Mwanawavene 2010). But it was not really until Operation

Rwenzori that problems developed between the rebels and civilians. With the offensive, the ADF were uprooted and forced into 'survival mode.' As pressure was exerted on them by FARDC, they in turn tended to exert pressure on locals, and were often described as an intimidating group (Reuters 2011). There were several reasons for this, including to demonstrate the government's inefficiency in protecting civilians (as during the previous time period); revenge for villages they suspected of collaborating with FARDC (reprisal attacks); and sometimes to (forcefully) acquire food and supplies (Interview Forty-Four; Interview Nine). The ADF often warned villages via leaflets of impending attacks on FARDC bases, inducing the inhabitants to flee, and thereby contributing to the extensive number of displaced (Beni Lubero Online 2011c; Beni Lubero Online 2011b). In a 2 February 2011 letter addressed to the Mayor of Beni, for instance, which was distributed throughout the Grand Nord area, the ADF warned ("respectfully") that they would soon be fighting FARDC in the villages of Beni, Ngadi, Halungupa, Mamove, Eringeti, Mutwanga, Loulo, Mwenda, and Musimbila (MONUSCO Document Two). Such warning letters definitely attempted to portray the ADF as not only the friends and protectors of the population, but also as a community experiencing similar victimization from the government as the civilians. A letter written on 2 July 2010, for example, reads, "Dear brothers, dear sisters and Congolese brothers in-laws. We don't have any problem with you because we came in DRC to be protected and the government of DRC accepted to protect us [. . .] So we don't need to shed your blood because you are not our enemies and we request you not to shed our blood as well [. . .] Until now many of our brothers have been killed [. . .] We confirm that DRC government wants to put your lives in danger" (MONUSCO Document Three). The public in many locations were essentially trapped between the two forces.

However, the following description of the reaction to conflict by northern Uganda's population, provided by Finnström (2008, 129), bears a striking resemblance to the response of Grand Nord residents:

> It is not surprising that the logic of war alienates people in the war-torn region from the central government. To put it simply, the more violence the rebels commit against the noncombatant population, the more the government will be blamed by the noncombatant population, the more the government will be blamed by the same exposed people for its failure to protect and provide for its citizens.

Indeed, discussions with civilians, local NGOs, and civil society members all displayed the same disdain towards the government for 'disturbing' the area. The only dissenting views came from international conflict management actors, such as MONUSCO employees, who argued that FARDC's actions were necessary for the central government to 'regain' control of its territory.

Nevertheless, even MONUSCO largely agreed that outside of Operation Rwenzori, the ADF coexisted well with the borderland population. As a Food and Agriculture Organization (FAO) representative in Beni stated, "The NALU will only attack the population if they are provoked" (which relatively speaking, is quite a positive arrangement in light of the civilian-rebel relationship of other groups) (Interview Sixty-Nine). Even during the offensive, they ultimately gained the upper hand in large part due to collaboration and support from the population. When being pursued, they were able to disperse into the villages, where FARDC essentially had no way of detecting who was or was not ADF (Interview Eight).

Villagers provided the ADF with intelligence on FARDC.[27] When the rebels found themselves in a precarious position and for example were stuck 'in the bush,' civilians were crucial in accessing food, weapons, and other materials from the urban centers for them (MONUSCO Document Four). The surrounding population also helped to insulate them from potential outside threats, as explained by Romkema (2007, 19): "Some local Congolese military and civilian officials, who benefit financially from the presence of the ADF/NALU rebels in the Rwenzori Mountains and the southern parts of Ituri, use (former) Congolese militia and security personnel to prevent outsiders from contacting the ADF/NALU, as well as from talking with Congolese civilians or military who could provide information that could lead to the repatriation or dissolution of these Ugandan rebels." There were repeated requests by FARDC to civilians in places such as Beni to cease assistance to the rebels (usually this was to do with the supply of arms).[28] This was likewise the situation in western Uganda, where the UPDF called for an end to collaboration with the ADF: "Although we defeated and repulsed them, there are some collaborators who remained here and are actively mobilizing for armed struggle," the UPDF's second division spokesman, Lt. Tabaro Kiconco declared in 2008 (Mugerwa 2008). In the end, the borderland population blamed their predicament on the governmental soldiers, and the ADF were able to leverage this to their advantage. As an employee with MONUSCO's Movement Control division clarified, "The locals are against the way the operations are run, because there is no mechanism in place to protect them. They blame the government for this" (Interview Forty-Four). And it should also be noted that the public demonstrated frustration over the lack of government assistance when it came to rebuilding and recovering from Operation Rwenzori (Radio Okapi 2011).

While factors at the national and regional levels played a role in the ADF's ability to effectively execute violence (such as assistance by outside Islamic actors with terrorist attacks in Kampala), in the end their integration at the translocal level into the Rwenzori zone's political and socio-economic networks proved more rewarding. Crucial to their ability to withstand FARDC, MONUSCO, and the UPDF were strategies at the micro-political level. Their cross-border mobility, alliances with other borderland actors, intelligence and safe house networks throughout western Uganda (and Kampala), wider support structure from the borderland community, and 'collaboration' with civilians, were some of the assets they derived from understanding the borderland milieu and manipulating its liminal nature.

To a sizeable portion of the borderlanders living within the ADF realm of control, the rebels were the lesser of two evils (the other being FARDC). In fact, with the commencement of Operation Rwenzori, the ADF were perceived as an actor that could weaken the predatory state in that area. Dislike of FARDC was further heightened when the 'Tutsi' CNDP began to be integrated into FARDC. But the ADF's status within the area was more than one of just another rebel group fighting FARDC. To some they were also a business partner, an active member in the community, and an employer of family and friends. With reference to the FDLR's societal embeddedness, the Pole Institute (2010, 15) notes, "Today they are seen as sons-in-law by the Congolese, if not uncles. Any military attack on them causes concern and fear in the local population. They think about the future widows, nephews and nieces that would have to be supported." The same could be said of the ADF. As similarly noted by Romkema (2007, 28), "The AGs and their dependents are, cheap laborers, subjects, buyers and sellers, spouses, friends or enemies, killers, looters, rapists, and 'those in charge.' The lives of the foreign AGs and the host communities have become intertwined and cannot be disentangled easily." This was the situation for many within the ADF's realm of influence as well.

For some members of the Nande community that were not in full agreement with the ADF's goals or mode of operandi, they still largely chose to be under ADF rule than FARDC 'protection.' Importantly, even during those periods when the ADF attacked civilians (which as explained previously, tended to be when the rebels were in escape mode), the Nande did not express support towards the Congolese army. A similar, though much more extreme, situation characterized the northern Ugandan periphery during the LRA rebellion. As Paul Nantulya (2001, 88) explains, "Coupled with its strategy of abducting underage children and forcing them into its ranks, the LRA has not endeared itself to the population. But this has not automatically translated into support for the NRA. This is a clear indication that the North-South schism is much more profound than it usually appears."

Arguably there was a higher degree of acceptance of the ADF's presence and activities in the Grand Nord territory than would likely have been the case in a non-borderland zone. The same was true of the western Ugandan portion of the borderland. Although the ADF did not control that territory, they used it for a variety of purposes and were heavily infiltrated throughout. This infiltration was made that much more practicable because of the distrust of the UPDF and overall disdain for the central government.

The Rwenzori borderland was a different place during this phase of the ADF conflict as compared to the 1996–2003 period, and the ADF were confronted with a new set of challenges and enemies. Nevertheless, the borderland was still a profoundly anti-state and liminal space, characterized politically by a tradition of resistance against central authority, socially by the predominance of a borderland identity, and economically by a system built around independent cross-border trade. Through taking advantage of these features, and building upon and deepening their enmeshment in the area's cross-border networks, the ADF were able to successfully traverse the borderland. The ADF were initially disturbed by Operations North Night Final and Rwenzori, but were ultimately able to regain their territory, and re-consolidate their socio-political and economic place in this micro-region (Interview Sixty-Eight; Interview Fifteen). In contrast to the image projected by many analyses—namely, the ADF as a disorganized, weak, puppet rebel group, operating in the backwaters of Uganda and Congo—the rebels actually displayed enormous skill in manipulating and extrapolating from what has been shown to be a very *non*-marginal, influential, and dynamic space.

NOTES

1. This chapter includes material previously published in "Prominent Peripheries: The Role of Borderlands in Central Africa's Regionalized Conflict," Lindsay Scorgie, *Journal of Critical African Studies*, copyright © 2013 Centre of African Studies, University of Edinburgh, reprinted by permission of Informa UK Limited, trading as Taylor & Francis Group, on behalf of Centre of African Studies, University of Edinburg.

2. 1,500 is the number strictly for combatants (namely, exclusive of dependents such as women, children, and the elderly). It is estimated that if factoring-in additional militia that they would be able to mobilize (from sympathizers), 1,500 would rise to 1,800.

3. DDRRR was organized largely by MONUSCO, and directed towards the so-called 'foreign' armed groups on Congolese territory. The most prominent groups targeted for this scheme included the Conseil National Pour la Défense de la Démocratie–Forces pour la Défense de la Démocratie, Forces Démocratiques de Libération du Rwanda (FDLR), and LRA. For more information on Congo's DDRRR process, see Thakur (2008).

4. In the last several years there was also a noticeable shift from a concentration on Tabliq mosques, to those more oriented towards Salafism (MONUSCO Document One).

5. The ADF were apparently even having success with recruiting graduates who were unable to find work (Interview Twenty-Six).

6. Mukulu's children resided in Belize (Group of Experts on the Democratic Republic of the Congo December 2, 2011).

7. Most of the women in the video appeared in hijabs. While this would seem to give credence to the Muslim orientation of the ADF, it is also important to consider the possibility that this was a kind of promotional tool that would be shown to potential Islamic donors (a practice not unheard of with the ADF) (Interview Thirty-Five).

8. Titeca and Vlassenroot (2012, 163) argued that ADF members had become "'naturalized' and part of Congolese society."

9. It should be noted, however, that HRW (2009) has documented the use of torture to coerce suspected ADF members into making alleged 'confessions,' and thus such information must be considered within such a context.

10. For more on the relationship between conflict and timber, see for example Forests Monitor (2007).

11. For an interesting discussion on the introduction of the chainsaw to North Kivu's forests, and the influence this had on accelerating (illegal) deforestation, see Chishweka (2006).

12. It is commonly acknowledged that the enormous number of taxes levied on traders at the border in fact encourages smuggling.

13. The complicity of FARDC personnel in the timber trade extended to various dimensions and levels. As Spittaels and Hilgert (2008, 23–24) note, "FARDC units are stationed at the border crossings of Kasindi and 'Kasindi Vieux.' Their position at border crossings gives the FARDC a lucrative asset in conducting business. Less than 100 meters across the Ugandan border at Kasindi, a large timber market is located. It is the center of illegal timber export from the territory of Beni." They furthermore note, "The involvement of the FARDC soldiers in the profitable illegal trade lies in facilitating the transport of the timber and organizing transports for their own account. Trucks commissioned by FARDC officers can pass the border without any customs or migration official daring to stop them. The soldiers also use intimidation throughout the other stages of the timber production process, for example to get access to rare species of timber."

14. The degree of insecurity in the Grand Nord area of North Kivu was indicated by the 'threat level' assigned to it by MONUSCO. During the summer of 2011 for example, in the aftermath of Operation Rwenzori and follow-up operations in early 2011, it was designated as a 'phase 3, threat level 4,' which at that time was the highest rating in the country. The Beni-Oicha road was coded 'red,' meaning a military escort was needed for travel. The northern part of Beni territory was classified as an 'emergency zone' (Interview Fifty-Three).

15. See Fahey (2009) for an interesting discussion on this subject. See also Omach (2009) for a related discussion on the Museveni regime's practice of linking opposition candidates to involvement in rebel groups.

16. Sources intimately familiar with the negotiation process informed me that Kinshasa was actually more problematic than Kampala, and that the rebels were slow and unenthusiastic in responding to the preliminary negotiation meetings. Furthermore, Kampala was unhappy (and not unjustifiably so, many argued) with the ADF's choice of mediator, a former leader of the Kosovo Liberation Army (Interview Twenty-Seven; Interview Thirty-Four; Interview Fifty-One).

17. See for example, Mwenda (2010b), for more about JATT's focus on the ADF's terrorism dimension.

18. It is worth mentioning, however, that "Extensive searches of the vans (which it was argued were going to be used to deliver the bombs) by the Presidential Guards Brigade turned up nothing, but the security services claimed a success" (McGregor 2007, 4).

19. For more on Uganda's political and economic agendas in Congo, see Fahey (2009) and Prunier (1999).

20. The fact that FARDC did not deploy until 2004 only furthered its limitations in this respect.

21. While former combatants' accounts of camp life varied, it would seem on the whole, however, that 'mobile form' greatly differed from their conditions pre-Operation Rwenzori, when they had satellite television with international channels, for instance (MONUSCO Document Six; Interview Twenty-Two).

22. As Spittaels and Hilgert (2008, 13) point out, throughout the majority of eastern Congo, the proximity of the various non-state actors to each other suggested more cooperation between them than perhaps was commonly known: "If we take a closer look at our positional maps, it is difficult to imagine that the FARDC, PARECO [Patriotes Résistants Congolais] and the FDLR would not be coordinating their efforts. On our maps we can find several places where PARECO and the FDLR are quartered in the same village. The same goes for the FARDC and the FDLR. If we take the road between Goma and Rutshuru (and beyond) for example, the positions of the FARDC and the FDLR seem to alternate."

23. Most IDPs set-up camp in and around the village of May-Moya, north along the Beni-Oicha road, about 9–12 miles from the area they fled. They were largely able to return home in April 2006 (Interview Five).

24. See also Mumbere (2010) for the difficult conditions faced by the displaced.

25. The significant fear civilians had of FARDC was noted by many sources (Interview Thirty-Three).

26. FARDC in fact went so far as to implement a forced labor scheme whereby the IDPs were made to provide food and build houses for the soldiers (Raeymaekers 2007).

27. It is once again important to reiterate here that a significant degree of fear was undoubtedly involved in such actions; civilians were aware of the serious consequences involved with not aligning with the ADF's agenda.

28. See for example, Radio Okapi (2012b).

Chapter 6

Transformations or Continuities? The ADF 2014–2021

In the 2020 midterm report by the United Nations Group of Experts (S/2020/1283) they note, "In North Kivu, operations of [FARDC] scattered the [ADF] into several mobile groups and extended the ADF area of operations. While supply chains were disrupted, ADF continued to attack FARDC and civilians." They go on to state six months later in the 2020 (S/2021/560) final report "[. . .] despite operations of FARDC, the ADF armed group rebuilt and intensified its attacks, particularly in the Rwenzori sector." Indeed, this has been the story of the ADF's existence, as the previous two chapters have demonstrated. While military incursions—whether from the UPDF, FARDC, or MONUSCO—may inflict damage, the ADF have proven time and again that a weakened status is only temporary. Each time, without fail, they recover.

Chapters Four and Five argued that the sources behind this resiliency were fundamentally intertwined with the borderland and its anti-stateness and liminal qualities. Indeed, by 2014 the ADF had been in existence for nearly two decades, representing one of the oldest and most durable rebel groups in eastern Congo. Throughout these two decades they had consistently drawn on the political, social, and economic resources of the Rwenzori borderland to sustain themselves. This continued to be the case for the time period under focus in this chapter, roughly 2014 to mid-2021.

2014 to 2021 warranted its own chapter for several reasons. First, the conflict 'landscape' in eastern Congo was changed. Armed groups were fragmenting and proliferating: in 2017 the estimate was approximately 120 rebel groups in existence in the Kivu provinces alone (Kivu Security Tracker December 2017). Violence was increasing, resulting in some of the highest levels of internal displacement ever for the Congo, with 4.1 million displaced in 2017 for example (Kivu Security Tracker December 2017). President Joseph Kabila delayed the national elections that had originally been scheduled for November 2016, until December 2018, and Félix Tshisekedi ultimately won. Kabila's unconstitutional actions sparked unrest and uncertainty, which armed groups both took advantage of, as well as reacted to. Their behavior, rhetoric, and relationships with politicians and/or businesspersons were noticeably affected by the political climate, and rebels in turn only further contributed to the political turmoil.[1] Whereas previously opposition and antipathy towards Rwanda was one of the main mobilizers for armed groups, during the first several years of this period that was outdone by antagonism towards Kabila.

By 2014 the ADF were not only one of the oldest rebellions, but also one of the most powerful and certainly well-trained and equipped in eastern Congo. They increasingly came to be considered one of the most dangerous and deadly groups, largely owing to their being blamed for a series of mysterious and horrifically violent civilian massacres that engulfed the Beni area from 2014 onwards. Occurring in waves, the killings resulted in thousands dead, with no easily identifiable rationale or perpetrator. Nevertheless, the violence was overwhelmingly written-off as senseless and the work of the ADF. And this is despite any claim of responsibility from the rebels, the presence of many other armed groups in Beni during this time, and indeed a great deal of evidence to suggest that the ADF worked with a *multitude* of parties—and were certainly not behind every attack.

Second, 2014 marked the beginning of a more aggressive stance towards the rebels on the part of FARDC and MONUSCO. Particularly during the first half of 2014, the ADF were determinedly pursued as FARDC—with limited logistical support from MONUSCO—waged a campaign against them known as 'Sukola I.' While exact numbers are always difficult to calculate with the ADF, it is estimated that hundreds were killed, and around 200 more (mostly dependents, the majority being children) succumbed to starvation as they were driven out of the camps and deep into the bush (S/2015/19). Sukola I undoubtedly had a drastic impact on the group, not only in terms of the force being reduced in size, but also in light of many of their camps being destroyed and/or captured by FARDC, some of their leadership fleeing abroad—including Mukulu—and the force splintering. In fact, some sources put the number of combatants left by late 2014 at only 60–70. On top of that, Mukulu was captured in Tanzania and sent to Uganda for trial, causing the group to undergo a leadership change, with Musa Seka Baluku taking up the helm.

Nevertheless, it was not long before the ADF yet again began to rebuild themselves. When Sukola's commander, General Lucien Bauma, was killed in August 2014, the military operations slowed down, giving the ADF an important reprieve. The ADF were soon in recovery mode, not only in terms of reconstituting their numbers, but also rebuilding their camps, restoring economic relationships, and so on. ADF command-and-control, it turns out, largely survived, as did their embedded borderland recruitment networks (S/2015/19). While for a period of time they remained more scattered and decentralized than previously, by 2019 the group were securely under one centralized command-and-control and had for a couple of years by that point maintained an estimated strength of at least 450 combatants (S/2018/531; S/2019/469). FARDC operations of course continued, most notably in early 2018 under the leadership of General Marcel Mbangu, in late 2018 in coordinated operations with MONUSCO, and then again in late 2019 (and continuing).

More recently FARDC's operations have had the effect of splintering the rebels into smaller groups over wider territory. And while that seemed to, in the first half of 2020 for example, cause disruptions to their supply chains, by early 2021 it was quite clear that they had recovered. In fact, while according to FARDC more than 370 ADF militants were killed and 70 captured over the course of October 2019 to October 2020, this only seemed to intensify the ADF's drive to recruit more combatants (S/2020/1283; S/2021/560). And their splintering arguably even gave them an advantage: as the Group of Experts (S/2020/1283) notes, it "further increased the unpredictability of ADF movements and attacks and extended the armed group's area of operations." It was thus obvious by early 2021 that the ADF had yet again largely outwitted and outmaneuvered FARDC. While operations against them continued, ultimately the "ADF rebuilt itself using intensified recruitment, a well-organized support system and superior command over terrain, including increased use of improvised explosive devices, that outstripped FARDC capabilities" (S/2021/560).

Finally, from 2014 onwards there was an increasing chasm between the ADF on the ground, versus the ADF as discussed in the media, by regional governments, and amongst international conflict management actors. During this time period claims of ADF association with international Jihadist terrorist groups markedly increased, to the point that the rebels became divorced from any meaningful association with the Congolese conflict, let alone Rwenzori borderland, in most analyses. And yet, while the narrative surrounding the ADF was more detached than ever from their borderland environment, the rebels were arguably further enmeshed in this cross-border micro-region than at any previous point in their existence. While such a divide clearly existed previously, the gulf between reality and rhetoric was never greater. The result was ineffective attempts at quelling hostilities, let alone defeating the rebels.

An important development to occur shortly before this book went to print—and one that will likely only further hinder attempts at subduing the violence—was the U.S. designation of the ADF (who the State Department termed 'ISIS-DRC') as a Foreign Terrorist Organization (U.S. Department of State 2021, International Crisis Group 2021). While it remains to be seen of course how exactly this will affect the ADF, the repercussions in terms of conflict management should not be underestimated (Flummerfelt and Verweijen). As Stearns explains, "If the threat is perceived to be from an armed Islamist extremist group, one is more likely to use a purely military approach to resolve the problem" (Gras 2021). This could take the form of, for example, encouraging, assisting, or relying on actors like FARDC or the UPDF to deal with the rebels, while inevitably sidelining or negating other types of responses. Stearns goes on to note how "The more IS is perceived as the enemy in eastern DRC, the more other factors contributing to the conflict there are neglected" (Gras 2021). This not only serves in "undermining the state's accountability towards it citizens," but—and as will be discussed later in this chapter—"there is a very strong correlation between military operations against the ADF and reprisals against the population. The more we focus on the military aspect, the more we risk reinforcing this dynamic" (Gras 2021).

This chapter does not follow the same structure as the previous two, and instead explores the ADF's continued resilience through specifically focusing on those factors mentioned above, that are markedly different throughout the 2014–2021 time period. It starts by examining the alleged global Islamist terrorist connections, and then questions those allegations given the local reality of the group. The chapter then looks at how the Rwenzori borderland has changed—and yet retained and even amplified its anti-state and liminal qualities. Next the chapter considers the multitude of actors interested in mimicking the ADF, and the heightened confusion this has generated about the violence in the region. Finally, the actual identity of the ADF will be considered, with a particular look at their economic interests, to better understand their survival in the borderland.

A NARRATIVE OF JIHADIST TERRORISM IN THE CONGO

The ISIS-ADF Connection

In April 2019 the Islamic State of Iraq and the Levant—more commonly known as ISIS—announced its first operations in the DRC. Via its news and propaganda channel, *Amaq*, ISIS claimed responsibility for deadly attacks committed by the ADF on the villages of Kamango and Bovata in Beni. Immediately numerous local, regional, and international media sources picked-up these developments. *The New York Times* on 20 April 2019, for example, ran a piece entitled "ISIS, After Laying Groundwork, Gains Toehold in Congo" (Callimachi 2018). At a time when ISIS' territorial and military prowess was at a record low, the potential that it was possibly shifting focus geographically was significant. And the idea that an obscure, shadowy, relatively unknown rebel group in the Congo was key to this development was intriguing to many. The following from *The Defence Post* was thus typical of many reports at the time: "In the jungles of the Democratic Republic of Congo an old insurgency may have a new trajectory, giving rise to the possibility of ISIS expanding its global conflict there" (Postings 2018).

Shortly after the Beni attacks, ISIS leader Abu Bakr al-Baghdadi officially recognized the ADF and their territory as an ISIS province: the 'Central Africa Province of the Caliphate' (ISCAP)—or *Wilayat Central Africa*. The ADF were supposedly renamed *Medina wa Tawhid wal Muwahdeen* (MTM), or 'The City of Monotheism and Monotheists' (West 2019). Attacks in Mozambique in June 2019 were attributed to ISCAP, and ISIS began to cultivate the image of an extremely active *Wilayat* (ISIS province) (Beevor and Berger). There also began to appear an increasing amount of ADF propaganda videos featuring religious instruction, members visibly dressed in Islamic attire, and displays of the MTM logo (S/2019/469).

To many observers, the April 2019 attacks and subsequent developments appeared to validate earlier claims that the ADF were not only primarily a Jihadist-oriented organization, but that they had indeed always strongly been allied to various Islamist forces. As was noted in Chapters Four and Five, such claims date back over a decade and a half, and include alleged affiliations and/or alliances with such groups as Al Qaeda, Al Shabab, Hezbollah, Boko Haram, the Taliban, and more. However, the suggestions of an ISIS connection, specifically, have generated more interest regarding the ADF's Islamic dimension than has ever been the case previously. In fact, the ADF arguably became the focus of more attention from regional governments, conflict analysts, and the media than at any previous point in their existence (O'Dwyer 2019).

Before delving into the motivating factors behind this, and the veracity of the alleged connection, it is worth addressing one of the most influential sources behind the popularity of the ADF-ISIS narrative, namely the Bridgeway Foundation. The CEO of the Bridgeway Foundation—which is the charitable arm of the multibillion-dollar hedge fund Bridgeway Capital Management—is Texan Evangelical lawyer Shannon Sedgewick Davis. Prior to Bridgeway, Davis was active with the troubled NGO Invisible Children, which gained notoriety for its misleading and inaccurate 'Kony 2012' campaign. Calling for a military solution to the LRA conflict, Kony 2012 wholly misconstrued the nature of the violence (and simple facts on the ground such as where the LRA were actually located at the time), and helped to convince the Obama administration to get involved in what was ultimately a failed mission to try to take out the LRA.[2]

Davis is not the only former Invisible Children member to be involved in Bridgeway though: one of the NGO's founders, Lauren Poole, is Chief Operations Officer of Bridgeway. Poole appears to have oriented the Foundation towards the ADF conflict owing to close connections with UPDF officials who had—as this book has extensively discussed—been attempting for years to construct a narrative of ADF-Islamist connections. Bridgeway's focus on the Islamic character of the ADF, and the need to defeat the rebels, is significant, and is apparent in their recent report, "The Islamic State in Congo" (Candland, et al 2021). This drew on interviews conducted by not only Bridgeway staff, but Ugandan authorities. Many of the Ugandan-conducted interviews were done by officials reporting to the 'director of counterterrorism,' which refers to the head of JATT (Epstein 2021). As Helen C. Epstein (2021) explains, 'the summaries of the Ugandan officials' interviews conclude with the words, 'For Interrogation,' or 'For Joint Interrogation' in bold type. At first glance, it's not obvious what this means—unless you know something about the methods of the [JATT]." Indeed, the kidnapping and torture by JATT (whose director it should be noted "appears to be involved in Bridgeway's research") of alleged ADF members, and coercing them into confessions stating their supposed secret affiliation to ADF, has been documented thoroughly by HRW (2009; Epstein 2021). The fact that Bridgeway has relied on information gleaned from such methods is therefore highly problematic, and ultimately has led them to peddle naïve and what are arguably unsubstantiated claims about the group's ISIS links.

Unfortunately the ramifications of Bridgeway's work have been substantial. The organization has provided funding to bodies heavily involved in reporting on and analyzing the ADF, including the Congo Research Group (CRG) and Kivu Security Tracker (KST). This is not to say that the work coming out of CRG and KST is inaccurate; both are staffed with some of world's leading experts on eastern Congo. Nevertheless, it perhaps helps to explain the gulf in understandings of the ADF between Bridgeway, CRG, KST, *The Defense Post*, and various other media outlets (whose journalists have connections to Bridgeway) on the one hand, and the UN Group of Experts (among other analysts) on the other. In particular, it sheds light on the chasm in interpretations of issues such as the Beni massacres (to be discussed later in this chapter), and of course most substantially, the alleged ADF-ISIS connection.

REGIONAL GOVERNMENT INTEREST—CONGO

Governments in the region appeared more eager than ever to not only draw attention to the ADF, but particularly to frame them as part of the wider global terrorist threat. In April 2019, for example, and just prior to the attacks discussed above, Congo's President Felix Tshisekedi stated, "it's easy to see how the defeat of Daesh, the Islamic State, in Syria and Iraq could lead to a situation where these groups will now come to Africa and take advantage of widespread poverty and chaos" (O'Dwyer 2019). Kinshasa, in a joint statement with the US government, announced on 12 April 2019 that it would be joining the international fight against ISIS (O'Dwyer 2019).

And while not going so far as to conceptualize the ADF in an 'international Jihadist' lens, Kabila had been steadfast in equating the ADF with terrorists. "There is no question of negotiation with terrorists," he said in 2014, when attempting to explain the government's plan for defeating the ADF (Reuters 2014). It is also worth remembering that, as Christoph Vogel and Stearns (2018, 700) explain, "The Congolese government [. . .] has shown little interest in ending peripheral wars that do not threaten its survival." Thus, the ADF were a politically convenient enemy for Kinshasa in many ways: not sufficiently powerful to seriously threaten the government, and misunderstood, unknown, and mysterious enough to enable control of the narrative surrounding the rebels.

REGIONAL GOVERNMENT INTEREST—UGANDA

For Uganda's part, despite an absence of any attacks on the country in years, the government maintained the storyline of a grave (and growing) terrorist threat from the ADF. Defence Minister Adolf Mwesige stated in March 2020, "The threat of terrorism, mainly by al-Shabaab and Islamic State Central African Province (ISCAP) elements persists" (Kyeyune 2020). He went on to note, "The Allied Democratic Forces has continued to be a regional security threat and has further established contact with another terrorist organization Ahlu Sunna Wa Jama'ahin Mozambique" (Kyeyune 2020). Even before the supposed ISIS connection, Kampala was sure to continually emphasize the potential danger the country faced. As the UPDF stated in December 2017, "Shared intelligence between Uganda and the DR Congo confirmed that the Allied Democratic Forces (ADF) terrorists which recently carried out attacks on UN peacekeepers. . . were planning to conduct hostile activities against Uganda" (Admin 2017).

As discussed previously, Uganda has long been interested, and often very successful, in aligning itself with the US—and more broadly Western—anti-terrorist agenda. Its motives for doing so vary, but arguably at the forefront has been a funding-related agenda. Throughout the time period covered in this chapter, while not necessarily always linking the ADF to ISIS, Museveni has consistently used the terrorist descriptor when discussing the ADF (Oteng 2018). As Titeca (2016) aptly states, "by exaggerating the Jihadi threat, the Ugandan government can tap into international discourse on—and resources of—the 'war on terror.'" These resources have included not only tremendous amounts of aid towards the government budget, but also military hardware supposedly needed in the fight against terrorism, as well as military training.

But it is important to recognize that the ADF served a *multitude* of useful functions for the Ugandan government.[3] Museveni continued his earlier practice, for example, of pinning domestic issues on the ADF while simultaneously maintaining that the group has been defeated. In late 2014 and early 2015, for example, there was a string of assassinations of Muslim clerics in Kampala, followed by the murder of senior state prosecutor Joan Kagezi and other high profile individuals (Mwesigwa 2018). Without evidence being provided, the ADF were blamed and several supposed ADF agents arrested (AFP 2015). In a wholly unsubstantiated statement, for example, Police Operations Commander Andrew Felix Kaweesi stated, "These (Muslim) killings are a broader project of the ADF. They are trying to use diversionary means to limit our investigations and operations. But we are taking a holistic approach in investigations" (Vision Reporter 2015).

Yet, the ADF not only aided Kampala in becoming a successful recipient of US counter-terrorism funds and provided the government with an easy scapegoat for a multitude of tricky domestic issues, but they additionally helped to deflect criticism related to the country's poor human rights record, its substantial defence budget, and demands for democratic change (Fisher 2014b). Indeed, scholars such as Fisher (2012) and Whitaker (2010) have pointed out just how successful the Museveni regime was in securing substantial foreign aid without the usual strings attached for reform. And while Uganda's significant involvement in AMISOM in Somalia most definitely contributes to this situation, there is no doubt that the country's strategic framing of its determination to quell supposed terrorism at home was pivotal. As described by Fisher (2012, 415), "Through lobbying activities, speeches, and interviews with the US, UK, and other Western media organizations, the regime has promoted the idea to donors that it is not only a key ally against international terrorism, but just as much a victim of terrorism as they are." It worked hard to control information and access for donors to the peripheral zones of the country where its terrorist groups allegedly are (namely western Uganda for the ADF and northern Uganda for the LRA).[4] As such, as Jonathan Fisher (2014b, 328) describes, "donors have become personally familiar with the 'strong' Ugandan state, while their encounters with Uganda's 'fragile' periphery have been largely indirect, mediated and impersonal." And thus, through such 'image management' tactics, Museveni's government has been accorded far more agency than others in similar positions when it comes to the donor-recipient relationship (Fisher 2014b). This has meant that despite its status as an anti-democratic, aid dependent nation, Uganda did not receive nearly the same degree of criticism that others in similar positions were subject to from international donors (Fisher 2012).[5] And in fact, one could argue that many of the Museveni regime's anti-democratic practices were aided by his commitment to the fight against terrorism. Anti-terrorism legislation was used, for example, to silence not only critical media, but political opponents as well.

VIOLENCE MISCONSTRUED?

Practical Reasons to Doubt the Connection

However, despite increased attention on the ADF during the time period covered in this chapter, and particularly over the past couple of years as ISIS entered the ADF fray, understandings of the ADF—such as their structure, goals, and operations—were arguably never weaker. Part of that weakness stems from the misinformation campaign put out by ISIS. As reflected on by Eleanor Beevor and Flore Berger (2020), "the picture on the ground is very different to what ISIS portrays," with the ADF much more accurately representing a group whose motives "are predominantly shaped by their local surroundings."

Indeed, there are some very practical reasons to doubt the quality and strength of the ADF's connection with ISIS. The ADF did not publicly make known their intention to become an ISIS affiliate until July 2019 when Baluku made a pledge of *bayah* (loyalty) to ISIS.[6] Interestingly however, as the Group of Experts (S/2021/560) notes, while ISIS apparently accepted the pledge, unlike with other affiliates of theirs such as Boko Haram, they refrained from attaching public recognition of such. Nevertheless, ISIS went on to increasingly claim responsibility for ADF violence, with particularly frequent declarations made in this regard in late 2020 and early 2021. However, there appear to be errors or discrepancies in many of ISIS' statements concerning ADF attacks. For example, in relation to an assault that occurred in January 2020 against FARDC—and for which ISIS claimed responsibility—ISIS declared there to have been casualties and the location to have been Eringeti. In actual fact, however, there were no casualties or even injuries, and the violence occurred in Kithekya, about six miles south of Eringeti (S/2020/482).

The opaque and murky nature of the ISIS-ADF relationship does not only stem from ISIS' actions, however. There appears to have been a degree of internal division within the ADF over whether their loyalty should be directed towards ISIS or Al Qaeda.[7] The extent to which the group even wants close ties or integration with ISIS has to be questioned. Indeed, it seems clear that there is at least one faction within the ADF—reportedly with around 30 combatants—that has resisted the ISIS allegiance and instead remained loyal to Mukulu's vision for the group, namely to fight the Ugandan regime.

Undoubtedly the most important reason to doubt the connection, however, is the fact that the UN Group of Experts has yet to find "any direct links between ADF and Islamic State in Iraq and the Levant" (S/2020/482, 2). In their most recent report (S/2021/560), they definitively state that they were "not able to confirm any direct command-and-control of ISIL over ADF nor any direct support of any kind to ADF." Indeed the Group of Experts have been consistent and clear in denying evidence of any meaningful kind of link between ISIS and the ADF. With regards to the videos featuring the MTM logo, for instance, the Group notes "they [the videos] did not in themselves offer proof of direct contact or association with other Islamist groups" (S/2019/469, 9). In fact, the Group has also stated that several ex-combatants captured by FARDC from two of the ADF's principle camps, Madina and Mwalika, "had never heard of ISIL" (S/2020/482, 11). In a similar vein, the CRG found confusion amongst recent defectors over the 'MTM' slogan, with some reporting that MTM is actually the name for the Madina camp (Congo Research Group 2018b).

Finally, it is significant that FARDC has yet to recover any evidence during its ADF operations that could confirm connections with ISIS (S/2020/482). Also noteworthy is the lack of substantial change in the ADF's overall modus operandi since the apparent affiliation began. While an increase in the use of slightly more sophisticated improvised explosive devices (IEDs) has been noticed—a practice that various observers have attributed to ISIS influence over the ADF—this is in fact due to an increase in membership from foreign combatants, especially from Burundi, Kenya, and Tanzania (S/2020/560). In other words, there is thus far no evidence that ISIS has anything to do with the making, supply, or operation of the IEDs used by the ADF.

THEORETICAL REASONS TO DOUBT THE CONNECTION

On a more theoretical level, it is worth remembering that alliances of the type suggested between the ADF and ISIS have to bring benefits to *both* parties to be viable. And yet there is little evidence of such a symbiotic relationship in this case. Only around 3 percent of the population in North Kivu is Muslim, and of that population, radicalism is almost non-existent (Congo Research Group 2018b). Thus, there is little chance of Sharia Law or a global

Jihadist agenda gaining traction. Related to that is the fact that for a supposedly Islamist organization, the ADF seem to have no qualms about allying themselves with non-Muslim groups. Indeed, the various other forces that the ADF collaborate with are almost entirely composed of non-Muslims, and certainly do not espouse any kind of Islamic agenda. As well, it is important to take into account the civilian population that the ADF exists amongst. Not only are they overwhelmingly Christian, but their political and cultural traditions vastly differ from those of the 'foreign fighters' that an alliance with ISIS would presumably involve. Given the ADF's dependence on integration with the borderland for their socio-economic existence, it is highly unlikely that they would risk the alienation and backlash that would come with inviting a global Jihadist group to the area. Such a move would also likely attract increased attention from the ADF's enemies, particularly the UPDF. It is not unreasonable to wonder whether the Ugandan government would become more serious about eradicating the ADF if they appeared to truly be rebels with a global Jihadist agenda. And yet despite all of the above, analysts are still likening the North Kivu milieu within which the ADF are positioned, as one akin to areas of the Middle East that ISIS roamed. "Rebel violence in eastern DR Congo has largely been sustained by a lack of strong government institutions and mistrust in military intervention. These are ideal conditions in which IS can expand, as evidenced by its surge across Iraq and Syria in 2014," the BBC (2021) stated for example.

Furthermore, the ADF are almost exclusively focused on targeting the 'near enemy'—whether that is the UPDF, FARDC, MONUSCO, or other borderlanders such as rival rebel groups or 'traitorous' civilians. Offensive behavior tends to be practical or transactional in nature—not of an ideological or religious character. Indeed, while much of the fighting with FARDC and MONUSCO was defensive in nature, of the violence that *was* offensive, it tended to be for the purpose of encouraging the army and peacekeepers to leave their territory and interests alone, or to seize weapons and ammunition (S/2018/1133). An August 2018 attack against FARDC in Ngadi for example, was typical in this regard: "the assailants [ADF] had taken 17 AK-type assault rifles, 2 60 mm mortars, a box of rockets, 7 PK machine guns, 1 recoilless B10 rifle and an unknown quantity of ammunition" (S/2018/1133).[8] In terms of civilians being attacked, there tended to be three potential reasons: to punish civilians for collaborating with an enemy, or to warn them of the dangers of doing so; to abduct people into the force (including sometimes only for very short durations in order to help with the carrying of supplies back to camp); or to collect needed foodstuffs and other supplies via looting. In February 2017, for example, the ADF released a group of farmers and their children with the following messages: "tell the Government that they can never chase us from this forest. Waging war with us will not lead to anything, if there are no talks, nothing will change" (S/2017/672, 14). And to the abducted farmers themselves, the ADF warned, "If we kill you it is because you talk too much and inform the FARDC of our whereabouts" (S/2017/672, 14). Meanwhile, a 2019 assault on the Mamove area was typical of the third reason. In this attack, Mamove's health center, shops, and various houses were ransacked, and 24 civilians abducted to help the rebels with the transportation of looted materials (most of the abductees were then later released). An ADF participant in the Mamove attack explained that the village had been targeted "owing to a lack of medical supplies after an operation conducted before Christmas 2018, after which many ADF elements had returned wounded" (S/2019/469, 24). While the above factors constitute the primary motives for civilian attacks, it is worth noting the ever-present existence of a secondary motive: to demonstrate the inadequacy and unreliability of FARDC and MONUSCO's protection capabilities. And indeed the two forces' incompetency's were continually on display, as will be discussed later.

Thus, the ADF were overwhelmingly a strategic actor, in that their overriding objectives were concerned with maintaining their space in the Grand Nord, and everything that entailed (i.e. maintaining the ability to pursue their lucrative economic ventures). They have never exhibited a serious interest in—or any kind of action against—the 'far enemy' of the sort that ISIS is focused upon. This is not to say that both parties derive naught from the relationship; the ADF could benefit from attaining better knowledge in areas such as the use of improvised explosive devices, for example, while ISIS could keep itself 'newsworthy' and cultivate the image of a group with global reach. Nonetheless, an alliance between the ADF and ISIS brings relatively minimal meaningful benefits to either party (Weeraratne and Recker 2018).

STRATEGIC REASONS BEHIND THE DOUBTFULNESS OF THE CONNECTION

Understandings of the ADF have also arguably never been weaker due to the power of the narratives coming from external actors. States such as Uganda and Congo, for instance, have greatly shaped the discourse around the group—as discussed above—and have framed it according to their own priorities rather than factual analysis. As Titeca and Fahey (2016, 1189) so pertinently note, descriptions of the ADF "may reveal more about the intentions of the actor framing the group than the group itself." Unfortunately, the main actor who had the power to correct such framing, MONUSCO, was plagued with severe inabilities to properly collect, analyze, and act upon, high quality information. While traditionally MONUSCO had written the ADF off as a mere nuisance, and one of the more minor rebel groups in a sea of much more significant armed actors—it had focused primarily on the CNDP, M23, and FDLR for the bulk of 2008–2013 for example—there was a sizeable shift in its stance beginning mid-2014. Precisely because it had largely ignored the ADF for so long, MONUSCO had a dearth of information and expertise on the group. This was compounded by MONUSCO's tendency to rely on minimal numbers of informants, and staff its intelligence units with individuals unfamiliar with the conflict and untrained in intelligence practices. Its military intelligence unit, G2, for example, was staffed with officers who could not speak French or local languages, had no prior knowledge of Congo, and had not served in an intelligence capacity previously (Fahey 2016). Moreover, the number of officers actually based in Beni was minimal, and for those who were, movement beyond the MONUSCO base was severely restricted. Interaction with the local community was thereby minimal, influencing intelligence collection abilities and eventually MONUSCO's overall understandings of the ADF (S/2014/428).

Perhaps the most blatant example of the consequences of such practices concerned the case of 'Mr. X'—a man who fooled MONUSCO into believing that he had insider information on the murder of beloved national hero of the Congolese army, Colonel Mamadou Ndala. After leading FARDC to victory against the *Mouvement du 23 Mars* (M23), Ndala had been put in charge of FARDC's campaign against the ADF in late 2013. On 2 January 2014 he was then killed in an ambush, which the Congolese government pinned on the ADF. Presenting himself as a 'dashing special agent,' Mr. X approached MONUSCO in Beni, claiming to have been a senior ADF commander. He supposedly had insider information not only on this case, but also upcoming attacks on MONUSCO by Taliban-trained terrorists, who were soon to be *en route* to Congo from Afghanistan. While none of this was true, and Mr. X had fabricated the entire scenario, a convincing enough picture was painted of an ADF in league with multiple international terrorist groups, including Al Qaeda, Al Shabab, Hezbollah, Boko Haram, the Taliban, and more.

Unfortunately, MONUSCO swallowed it up. In a profound case of confirmation bias, analysts within the force saw Mr. X's narrative through the lens of what they had already heard from actors like the Ugandan and Congolese governments. According to former Group of Experts analyst Fahey (2016, 99), "groupthink took over [within MONUSCO], dissenting views were not welcome. They interpreted each new event—an attack on a village, people throwing stones at UN vehicles—as evidence of Mr. X's credibility and as something he had predicted." The consequences of this were profound, and meant that violence such as the Beni massacres were not only inadequately analyzed, but ultimately misattributed as wholly the ADF's doing. As will be discussed later, the Beni killings indeed had ADF involvement, but they also included the work of a multitude of others, including many FARDC officers.

Not being properly investigated, many of the perpetrators were let off the hook, and the killings were able to continue. The violence was allowed to be explained through a terrorist lens: the ADF were seen to be randomly and irrationally killing civilians, with no political purpose to speak of, and all the while being supported by foreign terrorist entities.

MISSING THE FOREST FOR THE TREES

One can see how using the global terrorism narrative profoundly misconstrues the ADF's violence at an even more elementary level. Take the April 2020 article on the military news site SOFREP, entitled 'A Religious War: Jihadists in the Sahel Target Christians,' for example. The ADF's violent actions are described in the piece as "attacking the mostly Christian population of the region," with the aim of establishing "'a caliphate' in the region" (Balestrieri 2020). While of course technically speaking the majority of people who have been subject to ADF attacks are indeed Christians, it is wholly inaccurate to suggest that the victims were targeted *because* of their Christian affiliation. The ADF kill for the reasons discussed previously throughout this book, and particularly during this period for objectives such as abduction, stealing food and other goods, attaining FARDC weaponry, and diverting FARDC. They do not kill for the sake of punishing or eliminating non-Muslims. Unfortunately, however, the more the ISIS connection is invoked, the more frequently a sectarian or religious lens is used to explain the violence. Even the BBC (2021) appears to be falling into this trap. In a June 2021 in-depth article on the ADF, problematically entitled 'The Ugandan Rebels Working with IS in DR Congo,' the BBC (2021) states that the "vast majority of these [attacks] are on military targets, but the deadliest attacks are on Christian civilians." Similarly being misconstrued is the issue of conversion, and particularly Islamicization. On 8 April 2021 a number of prominent Congolese Catholic bishops issued a statement which included the following: "The assailants use the weak points of the regular armed forces to achieve their political or religious goals: occupations of land, illegal exploitation of natural resources, unjust enrichment, Islamization of the region in defiance of religious freedom" (Atemanke 2021). While conversion is indeed practiced by the ADF, it is done so to those being forcibly brought into the group (or to other members who are not already Muslim). To describe the ADF agenda as one focused on conversion of the surrounding population or the killing specifically of *non*-Muslims is misguided.

Yet it is important to recognize that the ADF are by no means the only group where analysts, the media, governments, and international actors have jumped on the explanatory bandwagon of global Jihad. Boko Haram is another African rebel group that has more often than not been depicted as evidence of the spread of Islamist terrorism in Africa. And yet, the targets of their violence are local, they draw recruits from Nigerians fed up with the endemic poverty and corruption in their state, and they maintain deep ties with the borderland population they are situated amongst. "Boko Haram is not the imported, 'foreign' menace Nigerian authorities depict it to be," *The New York Times* rightly states (Nossiter 2012). Sometimes, of course, rebellions "give themselves a global gloss" (The Economist 2013). Currently global Jihad is an easy and convenient label to adopt for groups looking for a boost—be it a political, financial, or other kind of advantage. And of course this is not to deny the existence of groups that truly do identify as Islamist, and act according to a global Jihadist agenda. Yet that should not confuse observers into believing that all forces with an Islamic dimension are necessarily global or even regional rebellions. As *The Economist* (2013) writes with reference to so-called Islamist violence in African states such as Mali, Niger, and Tunisia, "the direct threat is overwhelmingly local."

Indeed, for so many of the rebellions in Africa that have been seen through the lens of global terrorism, the impetus for their cause emanates from the local environment. As Hilary Matfess (2019) cautions in her article entitled 'In Africa, All Jihad is Local,' "Analysis that characterizes local groups primarily as subsidiaries (or potential subsidiaries) of a global Jihadi movement fundamentally misrepresents their nature. This sort of analysis is not merely a distortion of the armed groups' activities—it also has tangible and dangerous policy implications." Most importantly, using the wrong lens to understand these violent actors leaves their local networks unaddressed. Thus, the remainder of this chapter will consider the most pertinent factors behind the ADF's strength and survival between 2014 and 2021—and this begins with the local borderland milieu in which they were operating.

A BORDERLAND OF DISCONTENT

Frustration with 'Protection' Forces in Eastern Congo

The borderland remained an extremely restless and violent one throughout this time period. As discussed in Chapter Two, there are often references to discourses of marginalization, hidden transcripts of discontent, and of course unresolved political issues in such spaces. The western Uganda/eastern Congo borderland was rife with all of these factors during this time period. And rather than having anything to do with the Jihadist agendas of a global terrorist network, such sentiments were much more locally-induced. One of the most significant sources of grassroots anger concerned the actions (or rather lack thereof) of FARDC and MONUSCO, two forces ostensibly in place to protect the residents of the region. As the killings of civilians (discussed previously) continued and increased, the residents of Beni grew frustrated with the apparent inability and complacency displayed by FARDC and MONUSCO in responding. As the Group of Experts notes (S/2018/1133, 8), "The terror, along with the exasperation of the population, has triggered a growing and worrying distrust towards local and national Congolese authorities, FARDC and MONUSCO." Indeed, the frustration and anger manifested themselves into an overwhelming consensus amongst the borderlanders that they were being left to fend for themselves—in other words, the area's discourse of marginalization became more heightened and profound than ever before.

With regards to a September 2018 attack in Beni town, for example, in which 14 civilians were killed, one resident described the horror of the violence, and confusion and anger over FARDC's reaction:

> When the attack started, I was in the east of the town, in the Mupanda neighbourhood. I heard gunfire, and so I immediately took cover in a cafeteria. I saw people running towards the town center, so towards the west. It was a stampede. I think that the FARDC only came around 6:30pm, because it was then that we heard gunfire being returned. [. . .] The fighting carried on until about 11pm. I waited until the following morning to go out and went straight to the morgue. It's what we always do after an attack, to see if we know anyone who died. [. . .] People are angry, because they have the impression that our leaders and the military are barely doing anything, even though people have been massacred in the area since 2014. We feel like the military always arrives too late. Politicians make promises, but it hasn't stopped the massacres from happening. Saturday was the first time that the attackers came right into the center of town. And we were surprised, because they attacked in the east of the town, which is a place where the Democratic Republic of Congo army is stationed (Lauvergnier 2018).

Similarly, as the local news source *Le Nouvel Observateur* reflected, "How can these murderers operate freely and easily in a town that is supposed to be patrolled day and night by the Congolese army and thousands of Monusco peacekeepers? It seems that the aim is to create a climate of fear and terror in order to discourage the holding of elections in this part of the Democratic Republic of Congo" (Lauvergnier 2018).

Beni's civil society was active and vocal in attempting to draw attention to the matter, with demonstrations, strikes, and calls to national politicians to address the violence (Lauvergnier 2018; Radio Okapi 2019a). Protests were frequently tense and violent, and local government-affiliated businesses and buildings were often targeted (i.e., torched or outright destroyed), health workers' vehicles pelted, and MONUSCO facilities attacked (Radio Okapi

2019b). As Day (2017b) notes, "Anti-Kabila protests in Beni are now distinctly anti-UN as well, as residents express frustration at both the government and the UN's shortcomings." It was indeed not difficult to understand their dissatisfaction, as the security and humanitarian state of affairs steadily grew worse.[9]

MONUSCO'S FAILINGS IN-DEPTH

Given its corruption, human rights abuses, and collaborations with armed groups, FARDC has always been a particularly problematic force (as discussed earlier in Chapters Four and Five). And given the population's anger over increased evidence of FARDC officer involvement in the Beni massacres, FARDC's competencies certainly did not seem to improve 2014 onwards (Lukinga 2021). Indeed, there were calls from civil society representatives for there to be increased evaluation of FARDC's Sukola operations against the ADF, and in particular an addressing of the unrelenting insecurity environment (Radio Okapi 2021a; Radio Okapi 2021b). However, it was MONUSCO's inadequacy during this time period that seemed to reach new levels. Not only was it failing to identify the perpetrators of the attacks, but it frequently seemed completely incapable of defending the residents of eastern Congo. Attacks could occur as close as just over half a mile away from a MONUSCO camp, and yet civilians were still killed. Civilians were regularly having to flee Beni and its environs for fear of attacks and no protection (Radio Okapi 2018a). In fact, MONUSCO increasingly became the target of assaults itself. On the evening of 7 December 2017, in what has become known as the 'Semuliki attack'—and in what UN Secretary-General Antonio Guterres termed "the worst attack on UN peacekeepers in the organization's recent history"—15 peacekeepers were killed, over 50 injured, and armored personnel carriers, an ambulance, and truck all destroyed (Burke 2017; DW 2017). The strike caught the force completely off-guard, and then appeared to paralyze them into inaction. The four-hour assault saw MONUSCO's attack helicopters grounded, for example, despite their being equipped with night-vision capabilities.

Perhaps somewhat ironically, the Semuliki base targeted in the assault housed some of MONUSCO's Force Intervention Brigade (FIB), a contingent meant to act offensively to 'neutralize and disarm' rebel groups.[10] Established in 2013 after MONUSCO's astounding failure in securing Goma from invasion by the M23 rebel group in November 2012, the FIB had initial success with its campaign in defeating M23. Yet its campaign against the ADF has on the whole not only been ineffectual, but has also made obvious the faulty conflict analyses driving the FIB mission. As Rachel Sweet (2019) explains,

"The strategy behind the FIB assumes a world in which rebels fight the government on clear sides. [. . .] But in reality, the separation between armed groups and state forces is often less meaningful. Weak states produce more complex wars." MONUSCO's foe in this conflict was certainly a complex one. Similar to the Beni civilian massacres, the attack was likely a blend of ADF and other rebel forces (as will be discussed in the next session), who had interest in controlling the Mbau-Kamango road on the way to the Ugandan border (Congo Research Group 2017b). Attacks on MONUSCO only continued after that. They were frequently subjected to ambushes along the Mavivi/Boikene road, for instance, their armored personnel carriers often shot at, and they were called on to depart the Congo on an increasingly frequent basis from the population (S/2018/1133).

The sub-par performance of MONUSCO only played into the discourse of marginalization and discontent amongst the borderlanders. It appeared to them that not only Kinshasa, but even members of the international community that were supposed to be interested in their well-being and protection, were willing to write-off the borderland as an endemically violent and insecure one. They felt abandoned (Kahindo 2018b; Sematumba 2016). In fact, MONUSCO in many ways only entrenched the peripheral status of the area. Its concentration in urban centers such as Goma left regions like that of the Grand Nord more unprotected. Its very existence also meant that Kinshasa had little motivation to take more responsibility in tackling the insecurity. MONUSCO's support of FARDC only added to its poor reputation.[11] Some 65 percent of all human rights abuses in the Congo are committed by FARDC, and MONUSCO has not only been unable to rein in this behavior, but by cooperating with FARDC has been seen to be thereby condoning the abuses (Day 2017a). MONUSCO has often appeared naïve and somewhat tone deaf in this respect, as the following press statement suggests: "With regard to cooperation with the FARDC, MONUSCO is confident that the measures put in place with the Government to mitigate risk and provide appropriate monitoring where necessary will ensure that MONUSCO-supported operations against ADF, FDLR and other armed groups are undertaken in line with the United Nations Human Rights Due Diligence Policy" (MONUSCO 2016). Perhaps it is not surprising then that less than 50 percent of eastern Congo borderlanders perceive MONUSCO to be providing any form of protection, and roughly half in fact believe the force should no longer exist at all (Day 2017a). In August 2018 for example, Riginal Masinda, a leader of Beni student associations, declared "MONUSCO has proved its uselessness and its negligence in protecting civilians" (Claude 2018).

Some analysts have also suggested that MONUSCO's presence has led to the interesting phenomenon where no one rebel group can become truly dominant. In other words, as Léopold Ghins (2019) writes, "it could also be 'condemning' myriad rebel formations to coexist indefinitely." MONUSCO itself, of course, is not behind the proliferation of rebel groups in the east. During the Congolese war years and for approximately a decade afterwards, the rebel landscape was one of much fewer, but substantially larger and more dominant, rebel groups. Yet in a process termed the 'democratization of militarized politics,' armed actors proliferated (Verweijen and Wakenge 2015). There are several reasons for this, including a low risk threshold to start an armed group (either 'from scratch' or due to splintering an existing one) given the tremendous culture of impunity, as well as advantages for provincial and local level politicians, businesspersons, or even customary authorities to be associated with an armed actor and have the ability to manipulate them.[12] MONUSCO's contribution to the entrenchment of this status quo left the borderlanders as frustrated and unhappy as ever.[13] Ultimately, though, perhaps the most serious mistake made by MONUSCO was assuming that a military solution is needed for the rebel group problem in eastern Congo. As the ADF have demonstrated time and again, military assaults may temporarily diminish their capacity and strength, but if the grassroots foundations of their existence—their enmeshment in the borderland—are allowed to survive, then so too is the group.

TURMOIL IN WESTERN UGANDA

While perhaps not as integrally intertwined with eastern Congo as previous eras discussed in this book, western Uganda was nevertheless still a pivotal component of the Rwenzori borderland between 2014 and 2021. The ADF were not active in terms of attacks in western Uganda during this time period, however they continued to rely on the space for the successful operation of their economic activities, recruitment networks, and so on. And to a certain degree, of course, such ventures are easier for the ADF to pursue the more chaotic an environment there exists in that space, and the less solidified the Ugandan government's control there.

Interestingly, western Uganda experienced a significant resumption of turmoil starting in 2014, as the sensitive issue of the Rwenzururu Kingdom was reactivated. In July 2014, after several groups of Bakonzo youth attacked various government installations (which they attest was to draw attention to their historically marginalized status), mass retaliatory violence engulfed the districts of Kasese, Ntoroko, and Bundibugyo (Human Rights Watch 2014). The exact death toll is still unclear, but it is estimated that well over 100 Bakonzo civilians were killed by members of other ethnic groups and the security forces (Mugabe 2016). Bakonzo youth were accused by the government of being Rwenzururu Kingdom members: of essentially acting in the name of the Kingdom. HRW (2014) conducted lengthy investigations into the violence, and were particularly disturbed by the involvement of state forces:

> HRW is deeply concerned by credible allegations that in Bundibugyo district, Bakonozo civilians were attacked, detained in private homes, mutilated, tortured, killed, and burned or buried in mass and unmarked graves. Witnesses and community leaders told HRW that these reprisals allegedly occurred under the supervision of local leaders and members of the security services. [. . .] In Kasese district, police and military swiftly countered the initial attacks with cordon and search operations, beating and arresting many Bakonzo people. Victims and witnesses told HRW that alleged suspects were again beaten in police detention and denied access to lawyers and their families.

Thereafter a pattern evolved of the government making repeated accusations against the Rwenzururu Kingdom, usually along the lines of alleging that Bakonzo youth were harboring violent intentions and plans to establish an independent state. In October 2014, for example, it was suggested that a new rebel group, comprising Bakonozo involved in the attacks earlier that year, had been formed with bases in the Congo (Ninsiima 2014). While such claims were not substantiated, the government was nevertheless persistent in its messaging to the Kingdom. "I want to warn you to go back to your people and reorganize them in advance before the situation gets out of hand. You can joke with politics but you will never joke with the security of the country. We shall use the coercive forces to defend the state," stated Major James Mwesigye, chairperson of the Kasese district security committee (Ninsiima 2014).

Then in 2016 violence reached a level not seen in western Uganda for years. The government claimed the Rwenzururu Kingdom's Royal Guards had ties to a supposed rebel group, *Kilhumira Mutima* (the Strong-Hearted), which wanted to pursue independence for the Kingdom. Not only did this force apparently have support from various socio-politically and economically influential Nande individuals in Congo, but it also allegedly had links to the ADF. Peter Elwelu, a regional UPDF army commander, attempted to explain the supposed ADF ties: "The strategy of using Improvised Explosive Devices (IEDs) is an ADF tactic. We have intelligence that the king had started to establish military camps in the mountains" (BBC 2016). While the Kingdom and its leader King Mumbere vehemently denied all allegations, it was not enough to save the Palace from being attacked and burnt to the ground. Over 100 ceremonial guards of the Kingdom were arrested on charges of terrorism and treason, around 150 people were killed, and the King himself was arrested and is still facing strict bail conditions (Leni 2019).

Museveni has continued to manipulate the politics of the area, funding opposition politicians, cozying up to Mumbere's mother, Queen Christina

Mukirania (who is friendlier to Kampala than most in the region), and delaying investigations or any kind of justice from occurring over the 2016 attacks (Beevor and Titeca 2018; Reuss and Titeca 2016). In a region of the country with a long history of opposition to President Museveni, the events from 2014 onwards have done nothing to quell such sentiments of animosity amongst the borderlanders towards the central government. The restlessness, violence, and distrust of central authority, have all steadily increased—playing right into the ADF's hands.

THE ADF LOGO

Confusion Around the Beni Massacres

It is clear, then, the degree to which not only the ADF and their actions, but the violence in the borderland as a whole, was being misunderstood, misconstrued, and sometimes even hijacked by others during this time period. And it is important to note that the population of the region recognized this. Indeed, they were aware that those not living in the 'periphery' were failing to pay sufficient time and attention to their plight.

However, it is also the case that the violence in the borderland, and particularly that associated with the ADF, was truly difficult to comprehend. As was discussed extensively in Chapter Two, not only do borderlands tend to attract a wide array of actors, but the societal composition and organization of many borderland populations is highly heterogeneous, polymorphous, and shapeshifting. And if violent actors are skilled in 'boundary activation'—knowing which qualities and identities of the population to emphasize or utilize—then the borderland violence becomes all the more ungraspable and unconquerable to outside actors.

Arguably nothing epitomizes all of the above more than the Beni massacres. The first wave occurred largely between October 2014 and December 2016, when an estimated 800 people were murdered and 180,000 internally displaced. The killings then continued on a more sporadic basis—but still as astoundingly violent and ultimately deadly—in the years following. The brutal slayings of civilians in Beni provoked mass fear, anger, and confusion amongst the population. The killings tended to occur openly in the streets of Beni, in broad daylight, and in an extreme and barbarous nature, featuring such measures as decapitation and disembowelment. Senior Catholic clergy in the area described the violence: "The criminals kill brutally with machetes, knives or axes. The throats of some victims are cut, the arms of children mutilated, the bellies of pregnant women cut open, and whole families wiped out" (The New Humanitarian 2015).

Numbers of fatalities varied, but could often be extensive. A 2014 massacre left 80–200 civilians brutally killed, for example, and a 2016 massacre in the Rwangoma area of Beni city resulted in 36 civilians killed. While the knee-jerk reaction of authorities, including MONUSCO, was to blame the ADF, the identity of the perpetrators was by no means monolithic, and locals certainly had their doubts about the ADF being the sole perpetrators (Flummerfelt 2020). For one thing, witnesses and victims often noted an array of languages being spoken by attackers, including a substantial amount of Kinyarwanda (a language almost never associated with ADF, and leading to rumors that M23 was actually a significant force behind the ADF) and Lingala (Tsongo 2021). Furthermore, it makes sense that the ADF would target civilians in order to scare them from collaborating with FARDC during Sukola I. But why then, did the attacks escalate precisely when FARDC's targeting of the ADF dissipated? Finally, there is clear evidence of involvement of both FARDC officers and soldiers "in not only facilitating, but in actively organizing mass killings" (Congo Research Group 2017a, 12). One participant's account of FARDC's contribution to the attacks reveals just how significant a role they played:

> When we go to kill, we are surrounded by soldiers of the 31st brigade [within FARDC] . . . We could not only kill with firearms, we also used machetes and axes. The soldiers know how to tie up victims: first they tie up the people, then the people who are paid do the killing. Mundos or his assistant, Colonel Muhima came to verify the killing. . . . Every time there was a massacre, the 31st brigade secured the area so that no one could flee (Congo Research Group 2017a, 45).

THE ASSAILANTS

The most comprehensive examination of the Beni massacres to date was undertaken by the CRG. It is worth quoting their report at length when attempting to account for the perpetrators:

> While the ADF participated in many of the massacres, it is clear that several overlapping networks of actors were also involved, waxing and waning in prominence, sometimes collaborating and other times competing with each other. Specifically, it is clear that ex-APC officers initiated the massacres that began in 2013, in conjunction with partners, including the ADF and Kinyarwanda-speaking combatants. At some point in mid to late 2014, government agents were able to penetrate these networks that organized attacks. Instead of bringing the perpetrators to justice, however, they appear to have coopted these networks and continued the violence. All sides benefitted from

being able to blame a foreign, Islamist organization for the killings (Congo Research Group 2017a, 13).

The CRG furthermore found that "the killings feature mixed groups of combatants instead of cohesive groups with singular political agendas. These networks included former members of the APC [. . .], the Congolese army, local militias (namely, Mai-Mai Mayangose and the Vuba militia), and Kinyarwanda-speaking combatants.[14] They also involve FARDC officers from within Operation Sukola I" (Congo Research Group 2017a, 13).

When considering the motives of this array of assailants, most tended to have their own (often opportunistic) agendas. Former APC officers, for example, were interested in new avenues to maintain their economic and political power in the area, while the Vuba militia were seeking benefits specifically for the Vuba ethnic minority community, such as land and leadership opportunities (Congo Research Group 2017a). Perhaps one of the most difficult agendas to discern was that of the FARDC personnel who took part in the killings. Again, it is worth directly referring to the CRG (2017a, 16): "While it is difficult to know the exact thinking of the decision-makers, sources close to them describe that the leadership of Sukola I was more intent on neutralizing political opposition to the government than bringing an end to the violence." Some actors it seems can only best be described as mercenaries: hired to enact violence, without any actual political motive. The ADF for their part, were of course partially retaliating to the Sukola I mission. They were also likely attempting to protect their camps from FARDC attacks by drawing the national army away from their bases and towards National Road #4, where many attacks took place (Congo Research Group 2017a). Furthermore, they were seeking to protect their economic interests—particularly access to trade routes—in the area. They also sought to discourage civilian collaboration with FARDC, and strengthen ties with other violent groups in the region. Perhaps most basically, however—as Stearns succinctly notes—"It is a way of putting pressure on [FARDC] and their Western allies by saying: 'If you attack us, we will take revenge on the civilian population'" (Gras 2021). And thus while such a myriad of analysts and observers have tended to look at the beheadings and other brutally violent acts against civilians through the extremist Islam lens, that would be a mistake. This was overwhelmingly not ideologically-motivated violence: it was tactical, strategic, and ultimately locally-driven.

The degree of collaboration and cooperation amongst actors varied. Between ex-APC and ADF, for example, it could be relatively tight, considering that they sometimes shared camps and launched attacks together. The ADF and Vuba leaders, likewise, had a relatively close relationship. The ADF had a history of exchanging arms for resources with them, and they were said to often partake in economic ventures such as mineral trafficking together (Congo Research Group 2017a). Working jointly with regards to the Beni massacres was thus part of a longer working relationship. However, between the ADF and various other local militias, the relationship was more fleeting and opportunistic (Radio Okapi 2018b). As a Mai Mai member explained, "We [Mai Mai] received the enormous support of the ADF/NALU elements, who asked us to rally to them given our close knowledge of the area" (Congo Research Group 2017a, 41). In terms of the ADF and FARDC, meanwhile, there was a history of various officers and foot soldiers collaborating with the rebels. Indeed, this was well known amongst the borderland to such an extent that locals would often make reference to the 'ADF FARDC' (Tilouine 2017). It was not uncommon for local media, for example, to report civilians finding slain FARDC personnel dressed as ADF fighters (Kahindo 2018a; Lukinga 2021).

MUTUAL INTEREST IN THE 'BRAND'

While the backgrounds, motives, degree of participation, and so on clearly varied enormously between participants, what they all appeared to share was an interest in using the ADF 'brand' to achieve their respective agendas. In other words, as the Congo Research Group states, "All the groups [. . .] had an interest in deflecting responsibility onto the ADF, reinforcing the misleading notion that the killings were the sole result of a radical Islamist group" (Congo Research Group 2017a, 70). It is important to note that by no means was this a phenomenon only tied to the Beni massacres. In general, nearly all attacks committed in the ADF's general territory—i.e., not necessarily just the territory strictly controlled by the ADF, but more broadly their operating environment—were attributed to them. It is also interesting to consider that this practice had been in place for several years prior to the Beni massacres. In 2010, for example, leaders of local militias signed written threats with "We, Commanders of [ADF] NALU army in Beni Territory" (Congo Research Group 2017a, 27).

Nevertheless, the use of the ADF brand became far more commonplace from 2014 onwards. Groups found the lawless and chaotic environment advantageous, and discovered that mirroring the ADF's habits, modes of violence, and even Islamic attire was not entirely difficult. Indeed, the elusive, secretive, and mysterious origins and nature of the ADF made this relatively easy to pull off. The following from non-ADF participants in the Beni Massacres is revealing of the mimicry tactics used: "We adopted the *mode opératoire* of the ADF; to dissimulate, we adopted their method . . . women and children were included in the group. They killed, because this is the style of the ADF ... children killed, because we knew that when the ADF travels, they bring these people" (Congo Research Group 2017a, 11).

Not only was it useful for armed actors to have the ADF as a scapegoat for so much of the violence (Radio Okapi 2018c), but political actors found it helpful to discredit their opponents via casting accusations of ADF connections upon them. As an anonymous posting on the Suluhu Blog discussed in late 2014, "Rumors circulated in Beni last week that two captured ADF members confessed to ties to Mbusa Nyamwisi. These rumors preceded Governor Julien Paluku's press conference on November 12 during which he accused Mbusa of instigating a new rebellion in Beni" (Anonymous 2014). Likewise, civilians found advantages to invoking the ADF brand as well. In an area where paths to pursue justice are almost non-existent, it proved expedient to settle scores with others by lobbing allegations of ADF ties at them. Even the lowest level of bureaucrat in the region could benefit: referencing and heightening fear of the ADF allowed them to implement more check points and roadblocks, for example (Sweet 2015). Essentially there were constant rumors, but few confirmed facts, when it came to responsibility for many of the killings.

For a group that had previously tended to live in the shadows, suddenly they appeared to be front and center in the violence landscape of the Rwenzori borderland. And yet, as the above demonstrates, it was more difficult than ever to know who the ADF really were. In fact, the lines between civilian and militant, collaborator and adversary, were not only difficult for outsiders to decipher—it was a challenge for borderlanders as well. Living in a state of constant insecurity and heightened fear, residents were often forced to rely on the ever-present rumor mill and unreliable cues and indicators to determine whether they were in danger. An incident in Beni in October 2014 demonstrates this well. A man travelling on a bus in the city was killed by his fellow passengers when they discovered he was not speaking the local language, and was transporting a machete (which it should be noted is not an unusual practice). They stoned him to death, burned his body, and apparently cannibalized him—all because they assumed him to be one of the perpetrators of the recent spate of civilian massacres in Beni (Reuters 2014). And unfortunately as the killings not only continued, but went unresolved, the climate of insecurity and impunity induced residents to take matters into their own hands. Armed and unarmed self-defence groups emerged, which only furthered the blurring of lines between civilian and militant (Claude 2018).

THE ADF IDENTITY

Internal Structure of the ADF

Part of the difficulty in understanding the violence also undoubtedly stemmed, however, from lack of information on the ADF's structure and motives. For the most part, the ADF continued to refrain from issuing public pronouncements or communications in general. There were some exceptions to this, including those mentioned previously in this chapter such as warnings to the government and civilians. Also, there was an increase in activity from 2016 onwards on social media. The CRG notes for example that there were around 35 videos posted by an ADF member between 2016 and 2017 (although many of the videos were from several years prior), depicting "ADF attacks, medical care for their wounded, martial arts exhibitions, indoctrination of children, and propaganda messages" (Congo Research Group 2018b, 3).

Nevertheless, largely owing to information gleaned from (the albeit small number of) defectors and escapees, it is possible to gain a general idea of the ADF's organization during this time period. The ADF maintained their segmented leadership structure, with intelligence, recruitment, armory, finances, and health care all constituting individual steams with their own commanders.[15] They also similarly maintained the regimented social hierarchy. Nearly all leadership positions were held by Ugandan-born men with long-time affiliations with the group. Under them were the foot soldiers, whose numbers varied quite widely throughout this time period, but whose basic positions and rights remained the same. The foot soldiers, for example, received access to the ADF's 'health care,' and they also had the opportunity to acquire 'wives.'[16] While rape was apparently considered a punishable offense by the ADF, females were nevertheless subjected to this forced marriage system within the group. Women retained few rights, although they were expected to participate in the violence enacted by the ADF. They also served in various other roles, similar to the previous time periods, such as cooks, guards, and so on. It is also worth mentioning that exceptions could be found amongst the wives of commanders, who frequently occupied more significant positions. Residing at the bottom of the ADF pecking order, with essentially no rights at all, were the *bazana*—namely, the abducted Congolese civilians (mostly women and children), who the ADF considered to be essentially slaves.[17]

THE BROAD SPECTRUM OF ADF MEMBERSHIP

Similar to the previous time periods considered, the ADF's composition—namely, its incorporation of various borderland communities—certainly engendered it with a multifaceted identity, which continued to be used strategically by the force. Their heterogeneity allowed them to blend into different segments of the population, while also maintaining the general confusion amongst outsiders about who they really were.

The significant Nande presence in the group, for example, continued to facilitate their operations and ability to be embedded in the Grand Nord, much to the frustration of their enemies. As a former member states, "The ADF is no longer a visitor [in Congo]. It's not considered a foreign entity because it has married, had kids and set up businesses in Congo. The shopping centers are filled with ADF. Even the taxis in the park—some are owned by the ADF. The civilians in Congo are in-laws, grandchildren" (Anderson 2018). Or as the Director for the Centre for Geopolitical Study and Research of Eastern Congo, Nicaise Kibel Bel'Oka similarly explains, "the leaders and supporters of the ADF are among the local [Congolese population]" (The New Humanitarian 2015).

The above highlights how inaccurate it would be to consider the ADF a discrete entity in the sense of membership being restricted to only those living in their camps. For the time period of 2014 to 2021, membership could be thought of in more fluid terms: there certainly existed the leadership, foot soldiers, and families that lived in the group's series of bases. But in important respects membership extended beyond those roles. It could arguably be said to include the local militias that lived and operated on the periphery of ADF territory, and with whom the ADF "maintained relations"—in part because some of the militias were the kin of various ADF leadership (S/2017/672, 14). Membership could also arguably extend to the numerous supporting personnel throughout the borderland that facilitated the group's economic activities, intelligence functions, and perhaps most importantly recruitment. And lastly it is important to not forget those beyond the borderland, who contributed in similar ways, especially financially.

RECRUITMENT TRENDS

Indeed, to better understand the liminal nature of membership it is useful to look at recruitment practices during this time period. The majority of recruitment continued to be focused on Uganda, and to a lesser extent Congo, with recruits often lured in through false promises of employment or opportunities to study abroad, having family members already a part of the force tricking them into joining, or simply through abduction (which most often occurred during attacks) (S/2018/1133; S/2019/469). The ADF undertook some dramatic one-off recruitment events, perhaps most notably their October 2020 attack on the Kangbayi Beni prison, which freed 1,300 prisoners—many of whom thereafter joined (or rejoined in some cases) ADF's ranks (S/2021/560). It is important to not overlook some of the more mundane incentive factors in recruitment as well though. While talking more specifically about the Mai Mai, the general sentiment of the following quote from Caroline Hellyer (2014) bears much relevance for the ADF as well: "what is also visible in Oicha are the large groups of unemployed young men hanging around aimlessly with little or nothing to do. These young men are often the fodder for local Mai Mai groups [. . .] Sometimes these groups of young men organise to protect their villages but too often economic necessity and the entangled politics of the region suck them into the networks of militias that shift and change sometimes on a weekly basis." It should also be noted that the ADF appeared to develop an increasing interest in drawing Ugandan demobilized/former members of the ADF back into the force (S/2019/469).

For those recruited in Uganda, the most common mode of being transferred into the ADF's domain involved crossing the border at Kasindi and Mpondwe, then being held in the Mwalika camp, before finally being moved en masse with other new recruits to Madina (S/2019/469). It is when examining the ADF's well-organized and quite solidified recruitment network from Uganda to Beni territory that the vast network of membership becomes so apparent. At key urban centers along the route were 'focal points'—namely, individuals "in charge of the recruits travelling through their respective areas of responsibility," whose task it was to "provide them with the necessary support and identity documents" (S/2018/1133, 5). Working with the focal points were other important facilitators. These included for example motorcyclists that would transport the new recruits from one node in the system to the next, as well as individuals that provided fraudulent Congolese electoral cards to Ugandan recruits (S/2018/1133). In terms of the later, the ADF had contacts within the Commission Électorale National Indépendent that would make (at a cost of USD $30/person) a card with the new recruits' picture and fake name in one to two days (S/2018/1133).[18]

While certainly the majority of the force continued to be Ugandan and Congolese nationals, other countries were recruited from as well, and several of these—including Burundi, Tanzania, and South Africa—had active and well-established recruitment cells. For those joining the ADF from states such as the above, passing through Goma and then travelling via road to Butembo was the most common route (S/2018/1133). Once in Butembo, the ADF had a motorcyclist that would transport them north-east, before being finally led into the bush by a group of armed ADF militants. Indeed, this method has been a long-standing transit and delivery mechanism for the ADF. It is important to note as well that the ADF clearly worked hard to maintain strong relationships with key figures and the wider community in the areas (i.e., Butembo and its environs) deemed crucial for their operations. In other words, the civilian massacres discussed above tended to occur in specific locales—areas where such attacks would not jeopardize their key interests. As the CRG explained in its 2018 report, "Few of the killings of civilians since 2014 have taken place in this [the Mwalika area] southern sector, suggesting that the ADF is intent on keeping a low profile here and maintaining good relations with local communities" (Congo Research Group 2018b, 12).

THE ISLAMIC DIMENSION

The ADF's extensive membership and support circle was therefore not only unquestionably important for their resilience and sustainability, but it also contributed to the difficulty of outsiders deciphering who they really were. Perhaps the feature of the group that generated the most confusion about their identity—as touched upon earlier in the chapter—was the Islamic dimension. For while the ADF were undoubtedly enmeshed in the borderland, they existed in an area where only a small minority of the population practices Islam. These two facts at first glance would appear to contradict each other. But in fact they do not, if one takes into account how adept the ADF have been at emphasizing or activating different components of their identity for different purposes. And drawing attention to their practice of Islam served some very critical functions during this time period.

First, it certainly contributed to their recruitment efforts. The ADF voluntarily recruited Muslims via three methods: having Muslim ADF members convince relatives to join the force, having Muslim ADF members appeal to non-relatives, and using mosques or Muslim schools as recruitment avenues, particularly through Muslim clerics appealing to their congregation in Uganda, Congo, and additional countries (S/2015/19; S/2019/469). While the ADF certainly employed abduction extensively, it is thus important to note that some recruits indeed joined the force voluntarily (S/2015/19). Nevertheless, it would be inaccurate to think of the voluntary recruitment of Muslims as something akin to the way ISIS or Al Qaeda attracted droves of people from around the world to join their efforts. Despite the inflammatory statements from regional governments, various media, and certain analysts suggesting otherwise, ADF territory was simply not an attractive destination or even known to many Muslim communities outside of the region. It is thus important to seriously question and investigate claims such as the following (this from *The Defence Post*): "Since 2017, ADF in the DRC has become a destination for Islamic State recruits from Kenya, with would-be ISIS members detained while attempting to join the ADF, according to the Hiraal Institute report. This suggests that some regional radical Islamists view ADF ideology as similar enough to ISIS's for it to be attractive to would-be foreign fighters" (Postings 2018).

The practice of Islam within ADF camps furthermore helped the group maintain internal control. The ADF have long practiced strict codes of conduct for members, particularly those living in the camps, but it appears that over time behavior became increasingly regulated in a quasi-religious manner. The ADF forced most new recruits to convert or risk being killed. New recruits received detailed instructions from the religious leader of Mwalika camp, 'Sheikh Koko,' and the ADF did not hesitate to follow through with punishments for bad behavior. It seems that often religious teachings were used as the basis for what they deemed to be punishable violations, and that many within the group considered themselves to be following and subjected to Sharia Law. The Baluku group was particularly strict in this sense, with punishments of anywhere between 60 to 500 lashes and potentially 'jail time' for "infractions such as leaving a camp without permission, making a fire in the morning, being lazy, engaging in idle chatter, disobeying orders, talking during prayer and sleeping while on watch" (S/2016/1102, 11). Defectors have talked of stoning being used as a punishment for adultery, people having their mouths sewn shut for offensive talk, having limbs amputated for rape, decapitations, and the infamous 'Iron Maiden'—a casket lined with nails (Congo Research Group 2018b). Refusal to convert to Islam was punishable by death (specifically death by throat being slit or crucifixion), as was attempted escape (S/2015/19). Killings were usually inflicted upon men, whereas women would more often be kept in slavery, in such circumstances.

This is not all to suggest, however, that Islam should be reduced to a purely instrumental role for the ADF. It is unquestionable that, as Hellyer (2014) says, "the ADF has a very solid nucleus that operates according to its own self-defined Tablighi influenced vision." Indeed, children in the ADF camps were taught the Arabic alphabet, learned about the Koran, and were instructed on how to pray in Islam, for example. Members were forbidden from worshipping another God, saying 'Jesus,' or eating pork (S/2019/469). And numerous former members have described undergoing a conversion process from Christian to Muslim, as the following from one ex-ADF militant sheds light on: "After six months of training, they taught me how to be a Muslim. First they taught us the Quran, then how to pray. When you are a Muslim, if you kill you must say the prayer that says bismillah (in the name of God) to be sure that the spirit of the one you are killing doesn't attack you" (Anderson 2018).

Yet the significantly varying accounts from defectors of life within ADF camps suggests a highly segmented organization. For one thing, there seemed to be minimal flow of information between commanders and their subjects, as well as between the ADF's different departments and bases. This helps to explain why such a high number of defectors have been so ill-informed on the group's objectives, strategies, and so on. Although, an additional critical component behind the lack of informed defectors is simply due to the fact that leadership tended to not leave the ADF: defectors were overwhelmingly from lower ranks who knew little about the group. It also appears that experiences varied widely amongst ADF members. Some certainly appear to have been subjected to a far more religious environment than others, just as some units during attacks appeared to be following stricter behavioral codes than others. Whereas some camps experienced the strict codes of conduct discussed previously, others—in particular that under the command of 'Major Efumba'—were considerably more 'liberal.' In Efumba's group, men and women were free to interact with each other, they were permitted cell phones, and apparently women only donned headscarves when "on mission, as if it were an act" (S/2016/466, 16). In fact, the varied and even fractured nature of the group has led certain analysts to question at times "whether the ADF could be considered a unified group" (Congo Research Group 2017). A pivotal consideration to take into account when analysing the ADF's Islamist dimension is the fact that ultimately, Islam was *intermittently* used or adhered to. When committing attacks, there certainly was often evidence of Islamic symbols, whether it was militants' dress, use of Arabic phrases, or references to 'Allah.' However, this was wholly absent in so much of the ADF's other ventures and interactions, and especially in their economics-related activities. It all points to the multifaceted structure and agenda of the organization. As Hellyer (2014) states, "like a set of Russian dolls it is highly compartmentalised. This enables the rebels to maintain a multi-level network that provides it with sources of finance and support that extend to the transnational." And it is to their economic activities that this chapter turns to next.

THE REBELS' SUSTENANCE

The Economic Milieu of the Borderland

Nothing showcases the ADF's astounding resiliency more than their economic ventures. Indeed, it was the ADF's economic networks that were most embedded in the borderland. And perhaps it should not be surprising, then, that after two and a half decades—and facing numerous setbacks such as most recently the Sukola II operations—the group not only maintained such networks, but actually were able to "*build* its financial capacity" [emphasis added] (S/2020/482, 11). Before delving into the specifics of such financial operations, it is worth briefly discussing the economic milieu of the borderland during this time period. Above all, this cross-border micro-region remained a space best conceptualized, as the Social Science in Humanitarian Action (2018) noted, "as an entity (or group of entities) in itself rather than to define areas as being associated with DRC and/or Uganda."

The porosity and inability of state agents to effectively monitor much of the border(land) was more apparent than ever throughout this time, owing to an outbreak of the Ebola virus in North Kivu. Fears of its spread across the Congo border into Uganda and beyond, pushed not only regional governments but also relevant international bodies, to more closely monitor and understand the cross-border micro-region. What quickly became apparent to all involved (who were not aware of this prior), was just how intertwined the social, cultural, and particularly economic lives, of the borderlanders in Congo and Uganda were. Not only did it become clear just how extensive cross-border movement was for reasons such as schooling, worship, weddings, and healthcare, but the degree to which those on either side of the state line relied on cross-border access for economic reasons was more apparent than ever. Market days in some border towns were seeing as many as 20,000 people crossing the border, for example, and markets such as that based near Mpondwe could see goods from a catchment area extending to cities like Kasese in Uganda, and of course Beni and Butembo in Congo (Social Science in Humanitarian Action 2018).[19]

Indeed, border crossing data from the International Organization for Migration during this time period highlights the degree to which border crossings between North Kivu and Uganda were routine, daily affairs, for tens of thousands. The majority of all border crossings were done by foot, by people returning to their home country the same day, and for the purpose of conducting economics-related activity (International Organization for Migration 2019a; International Organization for Migration 2019b; International Organization for Migration 2019c). While some of this activity was legal, much of course was not, as discussed previously in this book. Indeed, the degree to which smuggling networks were entrenched in this cross-border micro-region cannot be overstated. It is worth quoting an example of quotidian smuggling by farmers at length here—provided by Elie Kwiravusa (2019)—to demonstrate the embeddedness of the practice:

> Farmers often go in groups of four to six people each carrying on his head more or less 25 kilograms of goods. They travel at night to walk across the plain of Graben (Irungu). In addition, everyone has a person who knows well the trails. They arrive in the early morning in Mpondwe where they are received by the natives of their villages and these host them and facilitate their contacts with Indo-Pakistani buyers at the Bwera/Kasese Mall or other villages in Uganda for trade in coffee for other items (clothing, blankets, radios, sewing machines, salt and sugar).

While officially visa fees were USD $50 for Congolese entering Uganda (and USD $100 for Ugandans entering Congo), not only could borderlanders cross and travel within about 9 miles of the state line free of charge, but many simply crossed at one of the multitudes of informal border crossings (Social Science in Humanitarian Action 2018). Due to potential levying of high taxes, bogus, or ad hoc fees by authorities, not to mention simply the hassle, the incentive to cross 'illegally' was high. This was even more so the case given how easy it was, as well as how many borderlanders believed that it was their right to cross the border. Being denied this represented yet more exploitive and unfair measures from the center, in their opinion.

Not only was the extent of cross-border integration and movement made fully apparent during the Ebola epidemic, but the degree to which the state was 'not felt,' or simply incapable of enacting basic state functions in the borderland was more obvious than ever as well (Kwiravusa 2019). After all, the Ebola outbreak was identified weeks late likely due to a health workers' strike over not having been paid in more than six months (Oxfam 2018a). Indeed, the periphery's response to the outbreak showcased much of their attitude towards, and experience with, the 'center,' which is essential for understanding the economic activities of the area. Their distrust of the government, and particularly the Nande community's suspicion of President Kabila, meant that official messaging about Ebola either fell on deaf ears or was actively countered (Oxfam 2018a).[20] The consequences of this, for example, were a significant percentage (30 percent according to Oxfam) of the population preferring 'self-medication' or traditional healers over health centers (Oxfam 2018a; Oxfam 2018b). Many simply refused to acknowledge the existence of an epidemic, instead believing it be part of a plan by Kinshasa to delay national elections. All of this is to say, then, that the existence of a Congolese state capable of working for the people of the borderland, conducting efficient cross-border surveillance, regulating trade and commerce, and enacting effective cross-border economic cooperation with Uganda, was essentially impossible.

BUSINESS NETWORKS

The ADF certainly took advantage of this state of affairs during this time period. Hoehne and Feyissa (2013, 56) argue for thinking of borders as representing institutions that "can be made use of or appropriated, and borderlands as fields of opportunities." Indeed, to understand the economic resiliency of the ADF during this time it is necessary to perceive the Congo-Uganda border, and Rwenzori borderland overall, not from a constraint or barrier lens, but rather from an opportunity perspective.

Just like their extensive recruitment system, the ADF's economic networks stretched across the border into Uganda. It was rather effortless for ADF operatives and suppliers to blend into the masses of cross-border travellers. A distinction is often made amongst the borderlanders between residents and guests (Social Science in Humanitarian Action 2018). Owing to their enmeshment in the area, the ADF personnel were critically able to fit into that 'resident' category. Also similar to the recruitment system, the ADF's financial support network extended internationally as well, with many money transfers being received from abroad, most notably the UK (S/2015/19).

Nevertheless, it was the group's borderland integration and ability to rely on connections throughout the cross-border locale which was most pivotal for their economic sustainability. They continued to maintain important business relationships with borderlanders. Some factions of the group were particularly well-integrated in this regard due to intermarriage with local chiefs (S/2016/466). The motives of borderlanders participating in business activities with the ADF certainly varied. For many it was simply a lucrative opportunity, while for others there was undoubtedly a degree of fear and coercion involved. Indeed, it is well documented that shop owners in North Kivu with whom the ADF had arrangements would be targeted in attacks should that relationship be abused or reneged upon (Congo Research Group 2017a). In a similar vein, while some Congolese farmers chose to collaborate with the group (i.e., in the form of providing a share of their crops), others were certainly forced. In some areas farmers were made to provide the ADF with monthly payments of USD $10-$25 for each acre they farmed, while in other zones they were forced to give the group a portion of their harvest (S/2020/482).

The ADF also used the borderland's thriving black market to acquire illegal materials to make explosive devices, for example.[21] And their relatively well-established presence in the cities of Beni and Butembo made it easy to purchase and transport needed goods. A recent Group of Experts report notes, for example, "they [two intermediaries for the ADF] had bought motorbikes for new collaborators in Beni and Butembo towns, which they used to deliver foodstuffs and medicines to ADF" (S/2020/482, 11). Butembo in particular was critical to the ADF's financial activities. Butembo continued to be a hub of the informal economy and especially the trade in minerals like gold and diamonds—a trade which in recent years has become more informal and pushed increasingly underground due to international attempts to curb 'conflict minerals.'[22]

FARMING, TRADING, AND LOOTING

During periods when the ADF were 'stable' and living a more established existence in their camps (i.e. not 'on the run' and having to escape FARDC and/or MONUSCO assaults), they were able to maintain a reliable and frequent material support network. Deliveries were made to ADF camps on a regular basis, and tended to consist of clothing, fuel, consumer goods, and money (S/2015/19). Staple food items such as rice, beans, and salt were a vital part of these deliveries, although the ADF were often able to maintain fruit and vegetable gardens, or purchase and/or loot such crops from neighboring communities. In terms of farming for their own consumption, the ADF mainly grew rice, manioc, and beans. These tended to be grown in the vicinity of their camps, and in particular around Mwalika (S/2021/560). Like before, the ADF also continued to raid farmers' fields, but towards the end of this time period such raids could often consist of upwards of 100 people, usually women and children (S/2021/560). It was also still common for the ADF to force farmers to hand-over portions of their harvests—in return for 'protection'—and contribute goods or a monetary 'tax' for the right to access (their own) fields (S/2021/560). With regards to actual purchased items, the ADF used their multitudes of contacts and collaborators throughout the borderland. Most commonly this was done in nearby urban centers such as Eringeti, Oicha, Beni, and particularly Butembo. In a continuation from previous practices, the ADF had pre-established meeting points along the Mbau-Oicha and Mbau-Kamango axes, where a vehicle(s) with the goods would drive to and meet men waiting to help offload the goods. From there, additional personnel ('porters') would ferry everything back to the camps (S/2015/19). Indeed, as the famine experienced by the group in mid-2014 demonstrates, during times when the group was forced to leave their camp settlements and retreat deeper into the bush, the material support network would come to a virtual standstill. From several times a week, the frequency of deliveries dropped to just once a week, for example, during the mid-2014 period (S/2015/19).

What the above helps to demonstrate is how pivotal access to the main arteries leading to critical cities and the border were for the ADF. Indeed, control of trade—and control of the routes, networks, and junctions associated with trade—is just as important to many actors in eastern Congo as control of territory for natural resource extraction. Despite the latter receiving far more attention from international actors and conflict management bodies, trade route access was of central concern for groups like the ADF. Nevertheless, natural resource extraction also continued to play an important role for the ADF, as they were significantly involved in the cacao and timber businesses (S/2016/466). Their engagement in these fluctuated over time, depending on whether they were fleeing their camps, and also varied amongst ADF factions. The Mwalika camp, for example, was quite successful at blending in with locals and thereby being able to concentrate on, and carry-out, these activities (S/2016/466).[23] Having the ability to tap into the timber trade, in particular, was pivotal to the ADF's economic success. Eastern Congo is an important source of timber for East Africa, as well as internationally. In fact, about 80 percent of East Africa's timber derives from eastern DRC, with a commonly used route to ferry the resource being through Beni (with some actually *from* Beni of course), across the border at Kasindi-Mpondwe, and then to Kampala (and usually then beyond) (Chevallier and du Preez 2012).[24]

While the ADF's strategic networks facilitated so much of their economic life, it is undeniable that a great deal of the ADF's actual material supplies, including weaponry and medicine, were obtained simply through looting, as briefly mentioned previously. In many of the ADF's attacks on FARDC, an important objective was to abscond with weapons and ammunition (S/2019/469). They were quite successful in this regard, achieving significant military capacity over time. The ADF were not alone in this practice. The Group of Experts noted in 2018 that FARDC stocks represented the main source of weaponry for armed groups in the Congo (S/2018/531). Interestingly, the ADF were also involved in the theft of FARDC salaries, including in May 2014, for example, stealing a "backpack full of money" (S/2015/19, 11). And many of the group's assaults on civilian targets such as homes, shops, and health centers were carried out with an aim of coming away with looted goods.

This chapter has demonstrated the continued, and indeed by this time period the *entrenched*, disconnect between ideas and conceptions of the ADF, versus the reality of the group on the ground. It discussed how so many actors have chosen to understand the rebels through the decontextualized lens of global terrorism, failing to look into their interaction with the marginalized space of the Rwenzori borderland. It is no surprise, then, that by 2021—after 25 years of existence—the ADF's trans-local political, social, and economic ties were essentially still untouched. For not only have the dominant narratives of the rebels skewed understandings of their identity, activities, and goals, but ultimately have led to ineffectual and irrelevant policy responses towards them. And it is to a brief discussion of conflict management in borderlands that this book turns to in conclusion.

NOTES

1. According to the Kivu Security Tracker (December 2017), "Even though most armed groups are based in remote, rural areas a thousand miles from Kinshasa, their leaders are keen followers of national politics and social media has multiplied the spread of news, tracts and documents. It is not surprising, therefore, that the current political turmoil around the delaying of elections increasingly impacts on conflict dynamics."

2. See Gould 2015, Titeca and Atkinson 2014, and Fisher 2012 (among numerous other scholarly and media articles) for more on the Kony 2012 saga.

3. For a broader discussion on the usefulness of certain enemies, see David Keen's adeptly titled book *Useful Enemies: When Waging Wars is More Important than Winning Them* (2012).

4. For an interesting discussion on the Ugandan government's strategic framing of the LRA conflict, see Fisher (2014a). In a similar vein, Titeca and Costeur (2015) discuss how various actors, including regional governments, lobby groups, and so on, all have their 'own' LRA.

5. For a fascinating comparison of Uganda and Kenya in this respect, see Fisher (2013).

6. Baluku went even further in September 2020, when he asserted that the ADF were no longer in existence—only ISCAP (S/2021/560).

7. See Beevor (2019) for more details on evidence pointing towards discord within the ADF on this issue.

8. This particular attack was also interestingly carried out on a FARDC payday, "indicating that the assailants had benefited from intelligence" (S/2018/1133, 7).

9. While FARDC has proven itself time and again to be ineffectual on the fighting and protection front (Kiro 2019), and highly problematic in its interactions with civilians in that regard, it is interesting to consider that it nonetheless carries out a broad range of other functions such as civilian dispute processing. See Baaz and Verweijen (2014) for a discussion of such 'extra-military' practices by FARDC.

10. For more on the weaknesses of the FIB see Day (2017a), and for a discussion of possible future directions for the FIB see International Crisis Group (2019).

11. For more on MONUSCO's challenges, see Doss (2014), Berdal (2016), and Berdal (2019).

12. See Verweijen and Wakenge (2015) for more on the dynamics of rebel group proliferation and its consequences.

13. It is also worth noting, as Ghins (2019) writes, "the international community does not oppose the status quo as it wants to avoid the disturbances and humanitarian costs that a third Congo war would provoke."

14. APC refers to the *Armée Populaire Congolaise*. This was the armed branch of the RCD/K-ML, which operated in the Grand Nord area of North Kivu during the Second Congo War. As the Congo Research Group (2017a, 15) explains, "There is no armed group officially named 'ex-APC,' but combatants often describe their group this way."

15. It is important to note that the ADF does not use ranks in the traditional sense—thus militants are either 'soldiers' or 'commanders' (S/2015/19).

16. 'Marriages' between the rank and file combatants and abducted women occur only after an application is made to the combatant's commander. Moreover, many of the combatants appear to be allowed to marry several women (Congo Research Group 2018b).

17. *Bazana* is a Luganda word for "slaves captured during war" (S/2015/19, 5).

18. See Verweijen (2016) for a more in-depth look at the multi-layered structure of supporters and collaborators for many Congolese rebel groups.

19. And initiatives such as 'One Stop Border Posts' and 'Border Export Zones' will only further the economic integration of the borderland.

20. In general, the Grand Nord population has tended to sympathize with the opposition over the past decade (Kwiravusa 2019).

21. See S/2016/466 for an interesting account of how the ADF acquired Explogel V6, for example.

22. See Geenen (2010), Geenen (2011), and Geenen (2016) for more not only on the role of Butembo in this, but on the dynamics of the trading regime in particular.

23. For more on the growing prosperity of the cocoa industry in North Kivu, see Kwiravusa (2019).

24. See this source for a fascinating and in-depth look at the timber trade originating from eastern Congo. Furthermore, it should be noted that due to demand both in East Africa and worldwide, the timber trade is only set to increase with time (Chevallier and du Preez 2012).

Chapter 7

Quelling Conflict at the Edge of the African State

CHALLENGES OF CONFLICT MANAGEMENT IN BORDERLANDS

This book has shown the importance of moving beyond a state-centric framework in order to fully understand borderland conflicts. It was demonstrated that traditional understandings of transnational conflict were unable to capture the dynamics behind the ADF's resilience in the western Uganda-eastern Congo micro-region. More specifically, they were insufficient in explaining the ADF's success when it came to the recruitment and retention of personnel, acquisition and organization of material resources, and strategic and tactical execution of violence. Ultimately, it was demonstrated that the ADF's ability to withstand a hostile operating environment for 25 years (with no signs of currently weakening) cannot be explained without consideration of their connection to the Rwenzori borderland. Their enmeshment into this space, manipulation of its anti-state and liminal qualities, and extrapolation of its political, social, and economic 'resources,' provided the ADF with the necessary tools to maintain their position and interests in the Rwenzori borderland.

This study has furthermore shown that political science and its sub-field of conflict studies are currently ill-equipped for understanding borderland rebellions. In fact, it points to the idea that perhaps many of our current conflict categorization schema are altogether outdated or inapplicable. The conventional division between intrastate and interstate conflict, for example, is rendered wholly irrelevant and obsolete in Central Africa. However while borderland conflict remains an insufficiently comprehended phenomenon in conflict studies, international conflict management is arguably even further behind. There is increased recognition amongst policymakers today that conflict does not respect territorial boundaries, and that wars are increasingly marked by refugee flows, cross-border weapons networks, and regionalized war economies. Yet, international efforts to resolve such conflicts—especially those of a borderland character—have continued to use conventional approaches.

Part of the problem has to do with the historic neglect of borderlands and the long-established tradition of viewing these spaces as marginal backwaters. As Goodhand (2009b, 240) says, "Borderlands are central to the dimensions of war and peace, yet they tend to be peripheral to policy discourse and practice." Likewise, Jackson (2006, 443) argues that "international frames of reference regrettably still neglect borderlands in much the same way as states have tended to do, suggesting that much work still needs to be done at the advocacy level to win the argument that borderlands are vital elements of focus."

Compounding this neglect of borderlands is the ingrained *structure* of conflict management responses. "Policy is well established—if not always well applied—between states (diplomacy) and within them (governance). But there is a policy gap across borders and in borderlands where governance and diplomacy can struggle to reach, as conflict response strategies still focus on the nation state as the central unit of analysis and intervention," argue Alexander Ramsbotham and Zartman (2011, 5). Conflict management actors tend to pursue strategies organized around national political boundaries. While they may recognize the role of cross-border actors, they tend to do so superficially, as their strategies rarely transcend the level of individual countries. In essence, they usually target problems through the realm of the *state*, rather than the conflict *system*.

The most obvious problems that arise from this are what Jackson (2006, 434) calls 'edge effects': "the radical contrasts and discontinuities experienced by citizens on either side of a border [. . . which] may arise from differences in legal frameworks between countries [. . .] or they may result from differences in other kinds of international intervention." Edge effects stem from policies that fall short of seeing the borderland as an integrated whole—or more specifically, policies that fail to understand how initiatives confined to the boundaries of a state will be made redundant if the political dynamics linking one side of a border to the other are not taken into account. The edge effects brought on by inadequate strategies for DDRRR and the curbing of war economies have been especially common. The UN's involvement in the regional conflict in West Africa was particularly illustrative in this respect. Due to different levels of cash payments offered to ex-combatants in Liberia and Côte d'Ivoire, the UN effectively created an incentive scheme for fighters to attempt demobilization in both states (Jackson 2006, 434). When a domestic certification scheme for diamonds was introduced into Sierra Leone, the result was simply a reversal of the direction of diamond flows to Liberia. Similar policies have been applied to transnational conflicts around the world. Banning poppy production in Afghanistan, for example, translated to a marked increase in poppy cultivation in neighboring areas (Studdard 2004). These examples help to highlight just how awkwardly the liminality of borderlands fits with traditional approaches to conflict management.

In addition to the historic neglect of borderlands and the structural focus on responses to the individual nation state, international conflict management in borderlands has also been marred by a lack of attention to factors at the micro-political level. Autesserre (2010, 430) writes, "standard analyses stress high-level international politics, elite interactions, and diplomatic history. They infer local and individual identities and action from the war's master cleavage, meaning the overarching issue dimensions (such as government versus rebel, Hutu versus Tutsi, or Christian versus Muslim), which analysts usually use to explain a crisis." Although referring mainly to civil wars, Autesserre's observations are just as relevant to international involvement in borderland conflict, and arguably even more so. It is a rare occurrence that trans-local actors and dynamics are given the attention they warrant in such cases.

Finally, as was discussed in Chapter One, there has been a superficial engagement overall with the realm of the 'transnational.' Indeed, transnational with regards to an armed group or conflict in general, can infer such a range of different practices and dynamics. It can point to the involvement of outside actors in a conflict, or a rebel group that uses a neighboring state for safe haven, or a war taking place at the regional level on the territory of multiple states (among other scenarios). Too often conflict management responses (and academia) fail to properly investigate which type of transnationalism is actually taking place (Checkel 2013; Wood 2013; Oftedal 2013). As Dowd (2018) notes with regards to Boko Haram, for example, while indeed the rebel group operated across borders, this was more a symptom of being militarily pursued out of Nigeria than enacting a truly transnational agenda. Likewise for the LRA: when chased out of Uganda and forced to relocate to the borderlands of neighboring states, this was not the materialization of a transnational strategy, but rather a group's actions being dictated by restrictions on its operations. The tendency to apply underexplored theories of transnationalism is arguably greatest when it comes to supposed Islamist actors—groups that often espouse rhetoric replete with global goals and alleged international connections with other like-minded groups. Yet as this book has demonstrated, sometimes such rhetoric is bult upon flimsy foundations, and represents nothing more than an attempt at intimidating opponents—or perhaps even just wishful thinking. The growing attention to the 'transnationalization of political violence' is a welcome development—but let us be sure we are applying it correctly.

INTERNATIONAL RESPONSES TO THE ADF

Conflict management efforts with respect to the ADF rebellion were certainly marred by the above practices.[1] More specifically, interventions tended to mirror those understandings and interpretations of the conflict displayed in the 'misguided explanations' discussed throughout this book. For one thing, the overwhelming focus on the Islamic angle of the group dictated the shape of the international response. As this book has demonstrated, the ADF are a multi-faceted actor, with a variety of internal strands and component bodies, some of which are inextricably bound-up with borderland dynamics. The diversity of the group, however, went largely unrecognized by not only analysts, but MONUSCO as well. Only one strand was essentially picked-up—the extremist Islamist one—and hence this tended to be the only element acted upon. As a DFID employee in Kampala noted, "There was an underlying stereotype with this conflict," which prevented attempts at digging deeper, and promoted responses that "blamed it [the conflict] on Islam" (Interview Forty-Eight).

In terms of recruitment, there was little consideration of the role of borderland grievances, for example, and instead an almost exclusive focus on attempting to monitor and curb Islamic networks. Likewise for the UN's approach to the ADF's acquisition of material resources: external Islamic sources of funding and supplies, their transit routes into ADF territory, and so on, received far greater attention than the ADF's borderland material lifelines. Indeed, the idea of the ADF serving as a proxy force for Sudan (in earlier stages) and later for various other Islamic actors such as Al Shabab and ISIS, significantly shaped the nature of responses. And with regards to the execution of violence, the Islamic focus steered conflict management personnel towards viewing the ADF's actions through the lens of Jihad and other extremist terrorist motivations, and becoming concerned with preventing terrorist attacks in urban locales often to the exclusion of their more prevalent and sustained activities in the Rwenzori area. The situation was clearly very influenced by the global discourse on terrorism, but more interestingly, it equated to somewhat of a self-fulfilling prophecy: if one *looked* for an extremist Islamic dimension to the group, one was undoubtedly likely to find *something*. There were other ways the scenario was leading to a self-fulfilling prophecy: there are burgeoning signs that the overwhelming focus on Islam is leading to a demonization of the Muslim community in the area. In other words, the inaccurate framing of the conflict is spawning the seeds for future violence in the creation of a Muslim-Christian rift where there was none before. Seeing the ADF as foremost or overwhelmingly a Muslim group is inaccurate, and has meant that other pivotally important strands of the group have been side-lined, if not ignored altogether.

Yet, also important to remember is the faulty interpretation of the ADF as a *Ugandan* group. Their connection with the Congo was understood to be merely territorial, and this was pivotal in shaping why and how MONUSCO took the kind of action it did against the rebels. When asked what the rationale behind MONUSCO's involvement in Operation North Night Final was, for example, a Political Affairs Officer with the peacekeeping force explained that the ADF's foreign status necessitated their removal from the Congo (Interview Fifteen). While the UN refrained from directly fighting the ADF in Operation Rwenzori, the peacekeepers nevertheless supported the campaign in other ways. The ADF were understood to be just another 'negative' (read, foreign) force on Congolese soil, and simply one more rebel group to be dissolved or expelled. The following quotation by Romkema (2007, 15) displays this mindset: "The continued presence of armed groups that operate across borders is an immediate threat to the consolidation of peace in the Great Lakes Region of Africa. As long as these groups remain active, it will prove difficult to implement peace in the sub-region." Similarly, in a 2009 article on rebels in the Congo, the Institute for Security Studies stated, "The presence of so-called 'negative forces' in the Great Lakes Region, especially eastern Democratic Republic of Congo, has long been recognized by major stakeholders such as the African Union, the International Conference on the Great Lakes Region and the United Nations, as one of the major impediments to stability in the region" (El Abdellaoui 2009).

There were two serious problems with this interpretation of the ADF, however, and they both negatively affected international attempts to respond to the rebellion. The first was that the rebels did *not* represent a Ugandan—and hence foreign—group. Of course, neither were they strictly a Congolese force either. As this book has shown, they were fundamentally translocal, and most of all, constituted by the borderland. Because they were so deeply politically, socially, and economically embedded in this micro-region, military action against them was largely ineffective. Their ties and networks in the borderland, including substantial local support, were too strong and developed to allow them to simply be thrown out of this space. Their ability to move to the other side of the border in times of crisis of course significantly helped them as well. Their borderland integration was also why the ADF's responses to DDRRR initiatives were generally so lacklustre. For a large part of the force, returning 'home' to Uganda made no sense, nor was it necessarily desirable (Interview Thirty).[2] In essence, the rebel group could not be separated from the borderland community: the ADF represented how this area expressed its politics. It is also worth considering that the ADF provided a means to express discontentment with central authority in a space historically abandoned by the state; they provided a degree of security to individuals and/or communities with nowhere else to turn for protection; they provided a way to act out various micro-agendas—whether related to issues of justice, or humiliation, or revenge—for people with no other viable avenues to do so.

Second, not only did MONUSCO fail to recognize the above factors, but the military operations they supported against the ADF set in motion additional conflict dynamics. In fact, operations such as North Night Final and Rwenzori arguably contributed to *further* destabilizing the area. For obvious reasons (most prominently being the international community's commitment to state sovereignty), the UN's position was one of helping the Congolese government retain (or perhaps attain for the first time) control of its territory. The UN therefore took the stance that any actor other than the central government exercising power over any parcel of Congolese land, needed to be expelled. This position on the part of the UN is understandable. However, especially given the nature of the Congolese state, and FARDC's record of human rights abuses, this position should have been adjusted.

A first step towards a more effective response would be appreciating the substantive differences in origin, development, motives, and structure of the various rebel groups operating in the Great Lakes area, rather than conceptually lumping them together. The ADF bore little commonality to groups such as the FDLR or LRA. They had the cooperation of many of the people in their locale (obviously not at all times of their existence), and even those who did not wholly support the force still tended to prefer ADF rule to FARDC 'protection.' Most importantly, the ADF were a *borderland* force. As such, they had particular modes of recruiting, acquiring material resources, and executing their violence. They harbored specific borderland grievances, and correspondingly held particular borderland goals. The ADF were in many ways a reflection of the political, social, and economic conditions of the borderland. While they of course contributed to its further militarization, they also were very much a product of its ills.

What needs to be addressed, therefore, are the deeper structural problems of the borderland: the governance shortfalls and political marginalization; the societal networks of unemployed young men or non-demobilized or non-reintegrated former combatants; and the economic cross-border systems that have come to revolve around war economies. Restive borderlands all too easily can become 'neuralgia points' in larger, region-wide conflict systems (Garrett and Seay 2011). It is their overall militarization, therefore, that needs to be accorded particular attention. The networks of the borderland need to be reclaimed and ultimately reoriented towards more peaceful purposes. Borders and the borderlands around them have to be transformed from sources of insecurity to spaces of security. Political settlements that primarily have the center in mind, or that assume peace will 'trickle down' and spread from the metropole to the periphery, will not work. While local states will likely push for securitized responses and increased border controls, such approaches are not likely to bring about the required change. "Violence often looks different in border regions," as Conciliation Resources (2017) notes. Operating from that recognition is crucial, as failing to appreciate the unconventional practices and actors within the borderland, could simply bring about yet more insecurity for the micro-region (Jones 2011).

There are some emerging examples of appropriate international efforts at borderland conflict management. DFID initiated a 'Trading for Peace' scheme at several borderland points along the Congo-Uganda border, with the aim of encouraging more benign cross-border trade practices. As a Ugandan NGO worker explained specifically in reference to the Kasese-Kasindi locale, "The trade has become monopolized by war elites. The whole cross-border trade environment has become militaristic, and so the whole community has too" (Interview One).[3] Of course, some might argue that borderlanders will inherently resist such approaches, given their traditional anti-state lifestyle and tendency to pursue state-evading practices. But a reduction in the militarization of the borderland does not have to equate to an *increased* state presence. Rather, a reorientation of the borderland towards the more peaceful end of the spectrum should simply coincide with a *better* state presence. This would include a recognition that this translocal space houses people who interact with state authority in alternative ways and that state authority itself has a contentious history in this space.

In the end, a scenario whereby the ADF are removed from the borderland, but the structural problems of the cross-border space are left unaddressed, will accomplish little. As the history of the Rwenzori micro-region has shown, eventually another rebel group will simply fill the void. Indeed, given the lack of focus on the structural problems of the Rwenzori borderland, it is not surprising that the ADF are currently as strong as they are.

CENTRAL AFRICA AND BEYOND

While this book has been primarily concerned with Central Africa (and restive African borderlands more generally), the salience of borderlands is of course not confined to this region. If one is to take only a cursory glance at the world's current conflict 'hot spots,' it is readily apparent that borderlands are playing a critical role in not only shaping the violence, but also reshaping the states involved. Syria's various borderlands, for example—shared with Jordan, Iraq, Turkey, Lebanon, and Israel—have been instrumental to the conflict, whether it be with regards to illicit trade; the movement of weapons, refugees, and violent actors; or even the spread of various ideologies (Accord

2018). Many of these borderlands are undergoing processes of rebordering ('the mutation of border features'), and all states involved have had to reorient significant time, resources, and in some cases personnel, to deal with these peripheries (Vignal 2017).

It is also worthwhile remembering that it is not only historically weak states that are experiencing borderland violence today. Some of the strongest and politically most significant states still struggle with their peripheries—and indeed many provide a cautionary warning of arguably how *not* to engage with borderlands. Russia, for instance, has a number of restive borderland areas, particularly in the Caucasus, where it has employed controversial counter-insurgency strategies. The contentious nature of Russia's policies towards its peripheries (both those inside and outside of its borders) has in recent years received even greater scrutiny in light of its actions in eastern Ukraine. China's political relationship with its borderlands has varied over the years, with significant changes having taken place quite recently. While the benefits of the country's rapid economic growth were originally largely confined to its urban centers, Beijing has started to more seriously pursue development initiatives—especially in sectors such as education—in its historically neglected peripheries. Nevertheless, Beijing continues to practice heavy-handed and ruthless tactics to subdue and forcibly integrate separatist and/or restless borderland spaces such as the Tibetan and Xinjiang regions, into the national framework. And while the Kashmir borderland between India and Pakistan is perhaps one of the most well-known borderland disputes in the world, India also hosts a number of other conflictual peripheries, particularly in the north-east of the country. Non-state actors of religious, nationalist, and separatist orientation, along the state's borders with China, Nepal, Bhutan, Myanmar, and Bangladesh, have posed serious challenges to the Indian leadership. And in Brazil, there are struggles with its Colombian border in terms of the continued presence of violent non-state actors and the effects of drug trafficking and coca cultivation. The tri-border area of Brazil, Paraguay, and Argentina—a safe haven for terrorists and criminal organizations—also poses significant challenges to Brazil's ability to maintain and consolidate political control over its entire territory.

The above are just a tiny sampling of ongoing borderland struggles around the world. However while borderland conflict is truly a global occurrence, there is a particular urgency to better understanding the phenomena in the African context. The vast majority of wars on the continent have their origins in borderlands (Bøås 2014) and as the Central African example illustrates, some of these can simmer, if not boil, for decades. In fact, again as the Great Lakes case demonstrates, the borderlands are often not only the originator, but the *epicenter*, of the violence. To solve the Rwenzori conflict and others like it, then, it is imperative that a borderland lens be used. For the ADF, this means an acknowledgment of both the complexity of the warscape they are fighting within, and the complexity of the group itself. The ADF have a multitude of 'faces'—Islamist Jihadis, apolitical rebels without a cause, greedy profiteers, among many others. The trick is to not fall into the trap of simplistic narratives that erase their translocal embeddedness. Only through embracing the 'central peripherality' of borderlands, and recognizing the limits of a state-centric lens, can we begin to address the violence enacted by the ADF and groups like it—actors that have long proven far more adept than their adversaries and analysts at recognizing and taking advantage of the resources on offer from borderlands.

NOTES

1. The ADF conflict never received a great deal of international attention, and hence was not a priority in the conflict management field. Essentially the only actor of relevance in terms of conflict management in this respect was the UN—specifically its peacekeeping operation in the Congo, MONUSCO. Thus, the following section is written largely with reference to MONUSCO's actions in the conflict.

2. Personnel working in the Kampala, Kasese, and Beni amnesty commission offices all described the number of ADF members going through the amnesty process as extremely minimal. In fact, the Kampala representative described their numbers as "a trickle," and the Beni representative noted that his office received "one or two, every now and then" (Interview Twenty-Seven; Interview Thirty-One; Interview Twenty-Six; Interview Fifty-One).

3. See Rokhideh (2021) for an interesting discussion on current research with regards to understanding cross-border traders as actors with the potential to contribute to peacebuilding in the borderland.

References

Acuto, Michele. 2008. "Edges of the Conflict: A Three-Fold Conceptualisation of National Borders." *Borderlands E-Journal* 7 (1). Accessed August 13, 2020. http://www.borderlands.net.au/vol7no1_2008/acuto_edges.htm.

Admin. 2017. "UPDF Attacks ADF Rebel Hideouts in Congo." *The New Vision*, December 22, 2017. Accessed August 15, 2020. https://www.newvision.co.ug/news/1467986/updf-attacks-adf-rebel-hideouts-congo.

African Rights. 2001. *Avoiding an Impasse: Understanding the Conflicts in Western Uganda*. Kampala: African Rights.

AFP. 2015. "Uganda Charges 18 for Murder of Muslim Clerics." *AFP*, January 30, 2015. Accessed August 15, 2020. https://news.yahoo.com/uganda-charges-18-murder-muslim-clerics-115346498.html.

Agence France-Presse. 2010. "DR Congo army takes Ugandan rebel base: government." *Agence France-Presse*, August 3, 2010.

Agnew, John. 2008. "Borders on the Mind: Re-Framing Border Thinking." *Ethics & Global Politics* 1 (4): 175–191. https://doi.org/10.3402/egp.v1i4.1892.

Ahimbisibwe, Tom. 2004. "Problems and Coping Mechanisms of Internally Displaced Persons: The Case of Former IDPs in Bundibugyo District, 2000-2003." Master's thesis, Makerere University.

Albere, Kambale Ezron Muhumuza. 2007. "Trends Towards Monarchism: A Case Study of the Bakonjo of Western Uganda, 1962-2001." Master's thesis, Makerere University.

All Party Parliamentary Group on the Great Lakes Region. December 2004. "Arms flows in Eastern DR Congo." Accessed August 13, 2020. https://ipisresearch.be/wp-content/uploads/2015/06/Armsflows-1.pdf.

Allio, Emmy. 1996. "Bakonjo king planned." *The New Vision*, November 22, 1996.

Allio, Emmy. 1997. "Kabila troops head for ADF hideouts." *The New Vision*, June 23, 1997.

Allio, Emmy. 1998a. "3,300 want return." *The New Vision*, February 10, 1998.

Allio, Emmy. 1998b. "The 1997 cancer in Uganda." *The New Vision*, January 7, 1998.

Allio, Emmy. 2007. "Uganda threatens to enter DRC." *The New Vision*, April 1, 2007.

Alnaes, Kirsten. 1969. "Songs of the Rwenzururu Rebellion: The Konjo Revolt Against the Toro in Western Uganda." In *Tradition and Transition in East Africa: Studies of the Tribal Element in the Modern Era*, edited by Gulliver, P. H., 243–272. London: Routledge and Kegan Paul.

Alnaes, Kirsten. 2009. "Rebel Ravages in Bundibugyo, Uganda's Forgotten District." In *Crisis of the State: War and Social Upheaval*, edited by Kapferer, Bruce, and Bjorn Enge Bertelsen, 97–123. New York: Berghahn Books.

Amooti, Tusiime Faisal. 1999. "Mukono Youths top ADF ranks." *The Crusader*, March 4, 1999.

Anderson, Ben. 2018. "'They killed people until they got tired.'" *Vice News*, September 7, 2018. Accessed August 15, 2020. https://www.vice.com/en_us/article/xwkenw/they-killed-people-until-they-got-tired.

Anderson, James, and Liam O'Dowd. 1999. "Borders, Border Regions and Territoriality: Contradictory Meanings, Changing Significance." *Regional Studies* 33 (7): 593–604. https://doi.org/10.1080/00343409950078648.

Anderson, Malcolm. 1996. *Frontiers: Territory and State Formation in the Modern World*. London: Polity Press.

Angurin, O. 1997. "Rebels capture Bundibugyo town." *The Crusader*, June 17, 1997.

Anonymous. 1999. "The ADF: Rebels without a cause." *The Monitor*, December 10, 1999.

Anonymous. 2014. "Misinformation and Misdirection in Beni's ADF Attacks." Suluhu Blog, November 17, 2014. Accessed August 15, 2020. https://suluhu.org/2014/11/17/misinformation-and-misdirection-in-benis-adf-attacks/.

Ansorg, Nadine. 2014. "Wars Without Borders: Conditions for the Development of Regional Conflict Systems in Sub-Saharan Africa." *International Area Studies Review* 17 (3): 295–312. https://journals.sagepub.com/doi/10.1177/2233865914546502.

Asiwaju, Anthony I. 1996. "Borderlands in Africa: A Comparative Research Perspective with Particular Reference to Western Europe." In *African Boundaries: Barriers, Conduits and Opportunities*, edited by Nugent, Paul, and Anthony I. Asiwaju. London: Pinter.

Atemanke, Jude. 2021. "Catholic bishops in DR Congo worried by killings, forced conversions in east." *The Catholic World Report*. April 9, 2021. Accessed June 17, 2021. https://www.catholicworldreport.com/2021/04/09/catholic-bishops-in-dr-congo-worried-by-killings-forced-conversions-in-east/.

Autesserre, Séverine. 2010. *The Trouble with the Congo: Local Violence and the Failure of International Peacebuilding*. Cambridge: Cambridge University Press.

Azarya, Victor, and Naomi Chazan. 1987. "Disengagement from the State in Africa: Reflections on the Experience of Ghana and Guinea." *Comparative Studies in Society and History* 29 (1): 106–131. https://doi.org/10.1017/S0010417500014377.

Baaz, Maria Eriksson, and Judith Verweijen. 2014. "Arbiters with Guns: The Ambiguity of Military Involvement in Civilian Disputes in the DR Congo." *Third World Quarterly* 35 (5): 803–820. https://doi.org/10.1080/01436597.2014.921431.

Bagala, Andrew. 2011. "Uganda: Interpol issues red notice for ADF boss." *The Monitor*, February 14, 2011.

Bagenda, Emmanuel. 2004. "Congolese Refugees in Bundibugyo District: Situation Report." Refugee Law Project, April 2, 2004. Accessed August 14, 2020. https://reliefweb.int/report/democratic-republic-congo/congolese-refugees-bundibugyo-district-situation-report-2-apr-2004.

Baguma, Henry. 2000. "Amnesty won't work—Kazini." *The Sunday Monitor*, January 23, 2000.

Baguma, Raymond, and John Thawite. 2009. "Mumbere crowned King of Rwenzururu." *The New Vision*, October 19, 2009.

Bahati, Obede. 2011a. "Beni: marche des médecins exigeant la libération du Dr Paluku Mukongoma." *Beni Lubero Online*, July 21, 2011. Accessed August 14, 2020. https://benilubero.com/beni-marche-des-medecins-exigeant-la-liberation-du-dr-paluku-mukongoma/.

Bahati, Obede. 2011b. "Les congolais fuient Eringeti à la suite des tracts attribués aux ADF/NALU." *Beni Lubero Online*, July 19, 2011. https://benilubero.com/les-congolais-fuient-eringeti-a-la-suite-des-tracts-attribues-aux-adfnalu/.

Baky, Mariam Abdel. 2018. "Borderlands and Peacebuilding: A View from the Margins." *Accord: An International Review of Peace Initiatives* (4): 56–63. Accessed August 9, 2020. http://148.251.69.135/accord/borderlands-and-peacebuilding-insight.

Bal, Ellen, and Timour Claquin Chambugong. 2014. "The Borders that Divide, the Borders that Unite: (Re)interpreting Garo Processes of Identification in India and Bangladesh." *Journal of Borderlands Studies* 29 (1): 95–109. http://dx.doi.org/10.1080/08865655.2014.892695.

Balestrieri, Steve. 2020. "A Religious War: Jihadists in the Sahel Target Christians." *SOFREP*, April 16, 2020. Accessed August 15, 2020. https://sofrep.com/news/a-religious-war-jihadists-in-the-sahel-target-christians/.

Bamuturaki, Jackie Sharon, and Christopher Busiinge. 2004. *The Effect of Tribal Relations on Socio-Cultural, Economic and Political Development of Bundibugyo: The Case of Bubandi and Harugali Subcounties*. Fort Portal: Kabarole Research and Resource Centre.

Bariyo, Nicholas. 2010. "Uganda President asks ADF rebels to end rebellion, return home." *Fox Business*, July 4, 2010.

Baud, Michiel, and Willem Van Schendel. 1997. "Towards a Comparative History of Borderlands." *Journal of World History* 8 (2): 211–242. Accessed August 13, 2020. http://www.jstor.com/stable/20068594.

BBC. 2005. "DR Congo fighting leaves 40 dead." *BBC*, December 26, 2005. Accessed August 14, 2020. http://news.bbc.co.uk/2/hi/africa/4559718.stm.

BBC. 2016. "Uganda cracks down on 'dissenting' Rwenzururu kingdom." *BBC*, December 3, 2016. Accessed August 15, 2020. https://www.bbc.com/news/world-africa-38169262.

BBC. 2021. "Allied Democratic Forces: The Ugandan rebels working with IS in DR Congo." *BBC*, June 17, 2021. Accessed June 17, 2021. https://www.bbc.com/news/world-africa-57246001.

Bearzotti, Enia, Andrea Geranio, Vivien Katta Keresztes, and Monika Müllerova. 2015. "Containing Boko Haram's Transnational Reach: Towards a Developmental Approach to Border Management." Regional Academy of the United Nations.

Accessed August 9, 2020. http://www.ra-un.org/uploads/4/7/5/4/47544571/containing_boko_haram.pdf.
Beevor, Eleanor. 2019. "The Allied Democratic Forces: the DRC's most deadly jihadist group?" The International Institute for Security Studies, January 16, 2020. Accessed August 15, 2020. https://www.iiss.org/blogs/analysis/2019/01/adf-jihadist-group-drc.
Beevor, Eleanor, and Flore Berger. 2020. "ISIS militants pose growing threat across Africa." International Institute for Security Studies, June 2, 2020. Accessed August 15, 2020. https://www.iiss.org/blogs/analysis/2020/06/csdp-isis-militants-africa.
Beevor, Eleanor, and Kristof Titeca. 2018. "Troubling Times for the Rwenzururu Kingdom in Western Uganda." Africa at LSE Blog, August 29, 2018. https://blogs.lse.ac.uk/africaatlse/2018/08/29/troubling-times-for-the-rwenzururu-kingdom-in-western-uganda/.
Bellagamba, Alice, and Georg Klute. 2008. "Tracing Emergent Powers in Contemporary Africa: Introduction." In *Beside the State: Emergent Powers in Contemporary Africa*, edited by Bellagamba, Alice, and Georg Klute, 7–21. Cologne: Rudiger Koppe Verlag.
Belz, Mindy. 1999. "Life in a War Zone." *World Magazine*, January 23, 1999. Accessed August 13, 2020. https://world.wng.org/1999/01/life_in_a_war_zone.
Beneduce, Roberto, Luca Jourdan, Timothy Raeymaekers, and Koen Vlassenroot. 2006. "Violence with a Purpose: Exploring the Functions and Meaning of Violence in the Democratic Republic of Congo." *Intervention* 4 (1): 32–46. https://10.1097/01.WTF.0000229529.55814.9c.
Beni Lubero Online. 2011c. "Révélation: Les Opérations Ruwenzori, Cheval de Troie de l'occupation de Beni et Mambasa." *Beni Lubero Online*, September 22, 2011. Accessed August 14, 2020. https://benilubero.com/revelation-les-operations-ruwenzori-cheval-de-troie-de-loccupation-de-beni-et-mambasa/.
Berdal, Mats. 2016. "The State of UN Peacekeeping: Lessons From Congo." *Journal of Strategic Studies* 41 (5): 721–750. https://doi.org/10.1080/01402390.2016.1215307.
Berdal, Mats. 2019. "What Are the Limits to the Use of Force in UN Peacekeeping?" In *United Nations Peace Operations in a Changing Global Order*, edited by de Coning, Cedric, and Mateja Peter, 113–132. Cham: Palgrave Macmillan.
Bleiker, Roland. 2000. *Popular Dissent, Human Agency, and Global Politics*. Cambridge: Cambridge University Press.
Bøås, Morten. 2004. "Uganda in the Regional War Zone: Meta-Narratives, Pasts and Presents." *Journal of Contemporary African Studies* 22 (3): 283–303. https://doi.org/10.1080/0258900042000283476.
Bøås, Morten. 2012. "Castles in the Sand: Informal Networks and Power Brokers in the Northern Mali Periphery." In *African Conflicts and Informal Power: Big Men and Networks*, edited by Utas, Mats, 119–136. Uppsala: Zed Books.
Bøås, Morten. 2014. *The Politics of Conflict Economies: Miners, Merchants and Warriors in the African Borderland*. New York: Routledge.
Bøås, Morten, and Kathleen M. Jennings. 2008. "War in the Great Lakes Region and Ugandan Conflict Zones: Micro-Regionalisms and Meta-Narratives." In

Afro-Regions: The Dynamics of Cross-Border Micro-Regionalism in Africa, edited by Soderbaum, Fredrik, and Ian Taylor, 153–170. Stockholm: Elanders Sverige AB.

Bogere, Hussein. 2009. "Al-Shabaab fighters training in Uganda." *The Observer*, December 20, 2009.

Bollingtoft, Marie L. 2006. *Conflict Dynamics in Kasese District: Study on Community Perceptions on Violent Conflicts in Muhokya, Bugoye, Kisinga and Bwera Sub-Counties.* Kasese: NAYODE.

Brambilla, Chiara. 2007. "Borders and Identities/Border Identities: The Angola-Namibia Border and the Plurivocality of the Kwanyama Identity." *Journal of Borderlands Studies* 22 (2): 21–38. https://doi.org/10.1080/08865655.2007.9695675.

Branch, Adam, and Jason Mosley. 2014. "Why East Africa's Borders are Blowing Up." *Foreign Policy*, August 6, 2014. https://foreignpolicy.com/2014/08/06/why-east-africas-borders-are-blowing-up/.

Bright, Richard George Tyndall. 1909. "Survey and Exploration in the Ruwenzori and Lake Region, Central Africa." *The Geographical Journal* 34 (2): 128–153. Accessed August 13, 2020. http://www.jstor.org/stable/1777817.

Bronson, Bennet. 1988. "The Role of Barbarians in the Fall of States." In *The Collapse of Ancient States and Civilisations*, edited by Yoffee, Norman, and George L. Cowgill. Tucson: University of Arizona Press.

Brown, Kate. 2004. *A Biography of No Place: From Ethnic Borderland to Soviet Heartland.* Cambridge: Harvard University Press.

Brunet-Jailly, Emmanuel. 2011. "Special Section: Borders, Borderlands and Theory: An Introduction." *Geopolitics* 16 (1): 1–6. https://doi.org/10.1080/14650045.2010.493765.

Buhaug, Halvard, and Jan Ketil Rod. 2006. "Local Determinants of African Civil Wars, 1970–2001." *Political Geography* 25 (3): 315–335. https://doi.org/10.1016/j.polgeo.2006.02.005.

Burke, Jason. 2017. "Islamist attack kills at least 15 UN peacekeepers and five soldiers in DRC." *The Guardian*, December 8, 2017. Accessed August 15, 2020. https://www.theguardian.com/world/2017/dec/08/peacekeepers-killed-in-attack-on-un-base-in-dr-congo.

Callaghy, Thomas. 1984. *The State-Society Struggle: Zaire in Comparative Perspective.* New York: Columbia University Press.

Callimachi, Rukmini. 2019. "ISIS, After Laying Groundwork, Gains Toehold in Congo." *The New York Times*, April 20, 2019. Accessed August 15, 2020. https://www.nytimes.com/2019/04/20/world/africa/isis-attack-congo.html.

Candland, Tara, et al. "The Islamic State in Congo." *The George Washington University Program on Extremism*, March 2021. Accessed June 23, 2021. https://extremism.gwu.edu/sites/g/files/zaxdzs2191/f/The%20Islamic%20State%20in%20Congo%20English.pdf.

Carayannis, Tatiana. 2003. "The Complex Wars of the Congo: Towards a New Analytic Approach." *Journal of Asian and African Studies* 38 (2-3): 232–255. https://doi.org/10.1177/002190960303800206.

Carla, Andrea. 2005. "Community Security: Letters from Bosnia: A Theoretical Analysis and its Application to the Case of Bosnia-Herzegovina." *Peace, Conflict and Development* 7 (7): 217–250. Accessed August 13, 2020. https://pdfs.semanticscholar.org/cf07/66b7f8c5c962a881b5823675bd7bc55cf260.pdf?_ga=2.70791124.512090655.1597362491-73293978.1597013406.

Carr Center for Human Rights. 2007. *Children in Conflict: Eradicating the Child Soldier Doctrine.* Harvard University. Accessed August 14, 2020. http://www.operationspaix.net/DATA/DOCUMENT/5627~v~_Children_in_Conflict_Eradicating_the_Child_Soldier_Doctrine.pdf.

Cassanelli, Lee. 2010. "The Opportunistic Economics of the Kenya-Somali Borderland in Historical Perspective." In *Borders and Borderlands as Resources in the Horn of Africa*, edited by Feyissa, Dereje, and Markus Virgil Hoehne, 133–150. Oxford: James Currey.

Chabal, Patrick, and Jean-Pascal Daloz. 1999. *Africa Works: Disorder as a Political Instrument.* Oxford: James Currey.

Chan, Yuk Wah, and Brantly Womack. 2016. "Not Merely a Border: Borderland Governance, Development and Transborder Relations in Asia." *Asian Anthropology* 15 (2): 95–103. http://dx.doi.org/10.1080/1683478X.2016.1214352.

Chande, Abdin N. 2000. "Radicalism and Reform in East Africa," in *The History of Islam in Africa*, edited by Levtzion, Nehemia, and Randall L. Pouwels Athens: Ohio University Press.

Channel 4. 2011. "Congo: The Children Who Came Back From the Dead." *Unreported World* TV Broadcast. Accessed August 15, 2020. https://www.quicksilvermedia.tv/productions/congo-the-children-who-came-back-from-the-dead.

Checkel, Jeffrey T. 2013. "Transnational Dynamics of Civil War." In *Transnational Dynamics of Civil War*, edited by Checkel, Jeffrey T., 3–28. Cambridge: Cambridge University Press.

Chevallier, Romy, and Mari-Lise du Preez. 2012. "Timber Trade in Africa's Great Lakes: The Road from Beni, DRC to Kampala, Uganda." The South Africa Institute of International Affairs, July 15, 2012. Accessed August 9, 2020. https://saiia.org.za/research/timber-trade-in-africas-great-lakes-the-road-from-beni-drc-to-kampala-uganda/.

Chishweka, Gustave. 2006. *S.O.S. 'La Tronçonneuse': Une Menace Sérieuse de la Forêt Congolaise. La Tronçonneuse Actuelle Unité de Transformation du Bois à Beni-Ituri.* Beni: Great Lakes Human Rights Programme.

Chishweka, Gustave. 2007. *Déforestation Abusive en Région a Forte Explosion.* Beni: Great Lakes Human Rights Programme.

Clapham, Christopher. 1999. "Boundaries and States in the New African Order." In *Regionalisation in Africa: Integration and Disintegration*, edited by Bach, Daniel C., 53–66. Oxford: James Currey.

Clapham, Christopher. 2010. "Conclusion: Putting Back the Bigger Picture." In *Borders and Borderlands as Resources in the Horn of Africa*, edited by Feyissa, Dereje, and Markus Virgil Hoehne, 187–196. Oxford: James Currey.

Clark, John F. 2004. "Museveni's Adventure in the Congo War: Uganda's Vietnam?" In *The African Stakes of the Congo War*, edited by Clark, John F., 145–168. New York: Palgrave MacMillan.

Claude, Muhindo Sengenya. 2018. "Fighting fire with fire—DRC massacres breed 'self-defence' militias." *Southern Times Africa*, March 19, 2018. Accessed August 15, 2020. https://southerntimesafrica.com/site/news/fighting-fire-with-fire-drc-massacres-breed-self-defence-militias.

Conciliation Resources. 2017. "Bringing in the Margins: Peacebuilding and Transition in Borderlands." *Accord: An International Review of Peace Initiatives*. Accessed August 9, 2020. https://www.c-r.org/accord/bringing-margins.

Congo Research Group. 2017a. "Mass Killings in Beni Territory: Political Violence, Cover Ups, and Cooptation." Center on International Cooperation, September 2017. Accessed August 9, 2020. http://congoresearchgroup.org/wp-content/uploads/2017/09/CRG-Beni-2017-report-updated.pdf.

Congo Research Group. 2017b. "MONUSCO Suffers the Worst Attack in its History." Center on International Cooperation, December 10, 2018. Accessed August 15, 2020. http://congoresearchgroup.org/monusco-suffers-the-worst-attack-in-its-history/.

Congo Research Group. 2018a. "The Art of the Possible: MONUSCO's New Mandate." Center on International Cooperation, March 2018. Accessed August 9, 2020. http://congoresearchgroup.org/wp-content/uploads/2018/02/The-Art-of-the-Possible-MONUSCOs-New-Mandate-23Feb18.pdf.

Congo Research Group. 2018b. "Inside the ADF Rebellion: A Glimpse into the Life and Operations of a Secretive Jihadi Armed Group." Center on International Cooperation, November 2018. Accessed August 19, 2020. https://cic.nyu.edu/publications/Inside-the-ADF-Rebellion-A-Glimpse-into-the-Life-and-Operations-of-a-Secretive-Jihadi-Armed-Group.

Coplan, David. 2009. "From Empiricism to Theory in African Border Studies." Presented at the African Borderlands Research Network, Johannesburg.

Coplan, David. 2011. "Introduction: From Empiricism to Theory in African Border Studies." *Journal of Borderlands Studies* 25 (2): 1–5. https://doi.org/10.1080/08865655.2010.9695757.

Correspondent in East Africa. 1963. "Common Kings." *The Economist*, March 30, 1963.

Das, Debojyoti. 2014. "Understanding Margins, State Power, Space and Territory in the Naga Hills." *Journal of Borderlands Studies* 29 (1): 63–80.

Das, Veena, and Deborah Poole. 2004. "The State and Its Margins." In *Anthropology in the Margins of the State*, edited by Das, Veena, and Deborah Poole, 3–34. Santa Fe: School of American Research Press.

Day, Adam. 2017a. "The Best Defence is No Offence: Why Cuts to UN Troops in Congo Could be a Good Thing." United Nations University, May 15, 2017. Accessed August 15, 2020. https://unu.edu/publications/articles/why-cuts-to-un-troops-in-congo-could-be-good-thing.html.

Day, Adam. 2017b. "14 peacekeepers were killed in the Congo—UN response may make things worse." *The Hill*, December

26, 2017. Accessed August 15, 2020. https://ourworld.unu.edu/en/14-peacekeepers-were-killed-in-congo-un-response-may-make-things-worse.

De Temmerman, Els. 2007a. "ADF rebellion: guerrilla to urban terrorism." *The New Vision*, May 21, 2007.

De Temmerman, Els. 2007b. "Inside ADF: abductees tell harrowing tales." *The New Vision*, May 21, 2007.

De Waal, Alex. 2004. "The Politics of Destabilisation in the Horn, 1989–2001." In *Islamism and its Enemies in the Horn of Africa*, edited by De Waal, Alex, 182–230. Bloomington: Indiana University Press.

Debos, Marielle. 2008. "Fluid Loyalties in a Regional Crisis: Chadian 'Ex-Liberators' in the Central African Republic." *African Affairs* 107 (427): 225–241. https://doi.org/10.1093/afraf/adn004.

Deltenre, Damien, and Michel Liégeois. 2016. "Filling a Leaking Bathtub? Peacekeeping in Africa and the Challenge of Transnational Armed Rebellions." *African Security* 9 (1): 1–20. https://doi.org/10.1080/19392206.2016.1132902.

Diener, Alexander C., and Joshua Hagen. 2010a. "Conclusion: Borders in a Changing Global Context." In *Borderlines and Borderlands: Political Oddities at the Edge of the Nation-State*, edited by Diener, Alexander C., and Joshua Hagen, 189–194. Lanham: Rowman & Littlefield Publishing Group, Inc.

Diener, Alexander C., and Joshua Hagen. 2010b. "Introduction: Borders, Identity, and Geopolitics." In *Borderlines and Borderlands: Political Oddities at the Edge of the Nation-State*, edited by Diener, Alexander c., and Joshua Hagen, 1–14. Lanham: Rowman & Littlefield Publishing Group, Inc.

Dixon, Kamukama. 2004. "War and Conflicts in the Great Lakes Region: Conflict Prevention and Post-Conflict Reconstruction." In *Uganda Riding the Political Tiger: Security and the Wars in the Greater Lakes Region*, edited by Mukwaya, Aaron K., 37–50. Kampala: Makerere University Printery.

Dobler, Gregor, and Wolfgang Zeller. 2009. "Marginal Hotspots: African Border Boom Towns." Presented at the African Borderlands Research Network, Johannesburg.

Donnan, Hastings, and Dieter Haller. 2000. "Liminal No More: The Relevance of Borderland Studies." *Ethnologia Europaea: The Journal of European Ethnology* 30 (2): 7–22.

Doornbos, Martin. 1970. "Kumanya and Rwenzururu: Two Responses to Ethnic Inequality." In *Protest and Power in Black Africa*, edited by Rotberg, Robert I., and Ali A. Mazrui, 1088-1136. New York: Oxford University Press.

Doornbos, Martin. 1979. "Protest Movements in Western Uganda: Some Parallels and Contrasts." In *Ethnic Autonomy—Comparative Dynamics: The Americas, Europe, and the Developing World*, edited by Hall, Raymond L., 213-229. New York: Pergamon Press.

Doss, Alan. 2014. "In the Footsteps of Dr Bunche: The Congo, UN Peacekeeping and the Use of Force." *Journal of Strategic Studies* 37 (5): 703–735. https://doi.org/10.1080/01402390.2014.908284.

Dowd, Catriona. 2018. "Nigeria's Boko Haram: Local, National and Transnational Dynamics." In *African Border Disorders: Addressing Transnational Extremist*

Organizations, edited by Walther, Olivier J., and William F. S. Miles, 115-135. Oxon: Routledge.
Dowd, Catriona, and Clionadh Raleigh. 2013. "The Myth of Global Islamic Terrorism and Local Conflict in Mali and the Sahel." *African Affairs* 112 (448): 498–509. https://doi:10.1093/afraf/adt039.
DW. 2017. "Political instability fuels rebels in the DR Congo conflict, analyst says." *DW*, December 11, 2017. Accessed August 22, 2020. https://www.dw.com/en/political-instability-fuels-rebels-in-the-dr-congo-conflict-analyst-says/a-41745349.
Eilenberg, Michael. 2011. "Flouting the Law: Vigilante Justice and Regional Autonomy on the Indonesian Border." *Austrian Journal of South-East Asian Studies* 4 (2): 237–253. http://doi.10.4232/10.ASEAS-4-2-3.
Eilenberg, Michael. 2012. "The Confession of a Timber Baron: Patterns of Patronage on the Indonesian-Malaysian Border." *Identities: Global Studies in Culture and Power* 19 (2): 149–167. http://dx.doi.org/10.1080/1070289X.2012.672841.
Eilenberg, Michael. 2016. "A State of Fragmentation: Enacting Sovereignty and Citizenship at the Edge of the Indonesian State." *Development and Change* 47 (6): 1338–1360. https://DOI: 10.1111/dech.12272.
El Abdellaoui, Jamila. 2009. "Cleaning Out the Closet: Armed Groups in the Great Lakes Region." Institute for Security Studies, October 8, 2009. Accessed August 14, 2020. https://oldsite.issafrica.org/iss-today/cleaning-out-the-closet-armed-groups-in-the-great-lakes-region.
Epstein, Helen C. 2021. "The Bewildering Search for the Islamic State in the Congo: Will a Texas hedge fund drag the US into another dangerous quagmire?" *The Nation*, April 20, 2021. Accessed June 23, 2021. https://www.thenation.com/article/world/congo-bridgeway-adf/.
Ernst, Amy. 2010-2012. "The King Effect Blog." Accessed August 9, 2020. http://thekingeffect.blogspot.ca/.
Esiara, Kabona. 2006. "Ugandan army kills two rebel commanders near DRCongo border." *The Daily Monitor*, April 9, 2006.
Etengu, Nathan. 1996. "Mbale Tabliqs accused of recruiting rebels." *The New Vision*, January 29, 1996.
Evans, Rosalind. 2013. "The Perils of Being a Borderland People: On the Lhotshampas of Bhutan." In *Borderland Lives in Northern South Asia: Non-State Perspectives*, edited by Gellner, David N., 117–140. Durham: Duke University Press.
Facci, Serena. 2009. "Dances Across the Boundary: Banande and Bakonjo in the Twentieth Century." *Journal of Eastern African Studies* 3 (2): 350–366. https://doi.org/10.1080/17531050902972998.
Fahey, Dan. 2009. "Guns and Butter: Uganda's Involvement in Northeastern Congo 2003-2009." *L'Afrique des Grands Lacs Annuaire*: 343–370.
Fahey, Dan. 2010. "Researcher's Guide to Bunia, Beni, and Butembo (DR Congo)." Fahey, Dan. 2016. "Congo's 'Mr. X': The Man Who Fooled the UN." *World Policy Journal* 3 (2): 91–100. Accessed August 15, 2020. https://doi.org/10.1215/07402775-3642608.

Farrelly, Nicholas. 2013. "Nodes of Control in a South(east) Asian Borderland." In *Borderland Lives in Northern South Asia: Non-State Perspectives*, edited by Gellner, David N., 194–213. Durham: Duke University Press.

Feyissa, Dereje, and Markus Virgil Hoehne. 2010. "State Borders and Borderlands as Resources: An Analytical Framework." In *Borders and Borderlands as Resources in the Horn of Africa*, edited by Feyissa, Dereje, and Markus Virgil Hoehne, 1–26. Oxford: James Currey.

Finnström, Sverker. 2008. *Living with Bad Surroundings: War, History, and Everyday Moments in Northern Uganda*. Durham: Duke University Press.

Fisher, Jonathan. 2012. "Managing Donor Perceptions: Contextualizing Uganda's 2007 Intervention in Somalia." *African Affairs* 111 (444): 404–423. https://www.jstor.org/stable/41494509.

Fisher, Jonathan. 2013. "'Some More Reliable than Others': Image Management, Donor Perceptions and the Global War on Terror in East African Diplomacy." *Journal of Modern African Studies* 51 (1): 1–31. https://doi.org/10.1017/S0022278X12000535.

Fisher, Jonathan. 2014a. "Framing Kony: Uganda's War, Obama's Advisers and the Nature of 'Influence' in Western Foreign Policy Making." *Third World Quarterly* 35 (4): 686–704. http://dx.doi.org/10.1080/01436597.2014.924068.

Fisher, Jonathan. 2014b. "When it Pays to be a 'Fragile State': Uganda's Use and Abuse of a Dubious Concept." *Third World Quarterly* 35 (2): 316–322. https://doi.org/10.1080/01436597.2014.878493.

Fisher, Max. 2012. "The Soft Bigotry of Kony 2012." *The Atlantic*, March 8, 2012. Accessed June 23, 2021. https://www.theatlantic.com/international/archive/2012/03/the-soft-bigotry-of-kony-2012/254194/.

Flummerelt, Robert. 2020. "Gruesome attacks deepen instability in Congo's Ebola zone." *The New Humanitarian*, January 29, 2020. Accessed July 2, 2021. https://www.thenewhumanitarian.org/news-feature/2020/1/29/congo-beni-adf-allied-democratic-forces-ebola-un.

Flummerfelt, Robert and Judith Verwijen. 2021. "The US has placed sanctions on ISIS-DRC, but does the group even exist?" *African Arguments*, March 31, 2021. Accessed July 2, 2021. https://africanarguments.org/2021/03/the-us-has-placed-sanctions-on-isis-drc-but-does-this-group-even-exist/.

Flynn, Donna K. 1997. "'We are the Border': Identity, Exchange, and the State Along the Benin-Nigeria Border." *American Ethnologist* 24 (2): 311–330. Accessed August 13, 2020. http://www.jstor.com/stable/646753.

Forest, James. 2011. "Engaging Non-State Actors in Zones of Competing Governance." Presented at the International Studies Association, Montreal.

Forests Monitor. 2007. *The Timber Trade and Poverty Alleviation: Upper Great Lakes Region*. Cambridge: Forests Monitor.

Forno, Gianluca. 2008. "Marginalisation and Uprooting: The Basua Pygmies of the Bundibugyo District." In *Rwenzori: Histories and Cultures of an African Mountain*, edited by Pennacini, Cecilia, and Hermann Wittenberg, 301–317. Kampala: Fountain Publishers.

Garrett, Nicholas and Laura Seay. 2011. "Trade, Development and Peacebuilding in the African Great Lakes." *Accord: An International Review of Peace Initiatives* 22: 85–89. Accessed August 14, 2020. http://www.c-r.org/accord/cross-border-peacebuilding/trade-development-and-peacebuilding-african-great-lakes.

Geenen, Kristien. 2011. "How the People of Butembo (RDC) were Chosen to Embody 'the New Congo': Or What the Appearance of a Poster in a City's Public Places can Teach about its Social Tissue." *International Journal of Urban and Regional Research* 36 (3): 448–461. https://doi.org/10.1111/j.1468-2427.2011.01084.x.

Geenen, Kristien. 2016. "The Pursuit of Pleasurable Women in the War-Ridden City of Butembo, Eastern DR Congo." *Journal of Modern African Studies* 54 (2): 191–210. https://doi.org/10.1017/S0022278X1600001X.

Geenen, Sara. 2010. "The Gold Trade in Butembo." In *The Complexity of Resource Governance in a Context of State Fragility: The Case of Eastern DRC*, edited by Cuvelier, Jeroen, 21–25. London: International Alert.

Ghins, Léopold. 2019. "Fragility and Uneven Aid in the African Great Lakes." Africa at LSE Blog, March 19, 2019. Accessed August 15, 2020. https://blogs.lse.ac.uk/africaatlse/2019/03/19/fragility-and-uneven-aid-in-the-african-great-lakes/.

Giersch, C. Patterson. 2010. "Across Zomia with Merchants, Monks, and Musk: Process Geographies, Trade Networks, and the Inner-East-Southeast Asian Borderlands." *Journal of Global History* 5 (2): 215–239. https://doi.org/10.1017/S1740022810000069.

Giroux, Jennifer, David Lanz, and Damiano Sguaitamatti. 2009. "The Tormented Triangle: The Regionalisation of Conflict in Sudan, Chad and the Central African Republic." Crisis States Research Centre, April 2009. Accessed August 14, 2020. https://css.ethz.ch/content/dam/ethz/special-interest/gess/cis/center-for-securities-studies/pdfs/The-Tormented-Triangle.pdf.

Gleditsch, Kristian Skrede. 2007. "Transnational Dimensions of Civil War." *Journal of Peace Research* 44 (3): 293–309. Accessed August 13, 2020. http://www.jstor.com/stable/27640512.

Goodhand, Jonathan. 2005a. "Bringing the Borderlands Back In: A Commentary on 'Selfish Determination.'" *Ethnopolitics* 4 (1): 94–97. Accessed August 13, 2020. https://eprints.soas.ac.uk/2098/.

Goodhand, Jonathan. 2005b. "Frontiers and Wars: the Opium Economy in Afghanistan." *Journal of Agrarian Change* 5 (2): 191–216. https://doi.org/10.1111/j.1471-0366.2005.00099.x.

Goodhand, Jonathan. 2009a. "Bandits, Borderlands and Opium Wars: Afghan State-Building Viewed from the Margins." Danish Institute for International Studies. Accessed August 14, 2020. https://www.files.ethz.ch/isn/110437/WP2009-26_bandits_borderlands_opiumwars.pdf.

Goodhand, Jonathan. 2009b. "War, Peace and the Places in Between: Why Borderlands are Central." In *Whose Peace? Critical Perspectives on the Political Economy of Peacebuilding*, edited by Pugh, Michael, Neil Cooper, and Mandy Turner, 225-244. Houndmills: Palgrave MacMillan.

Goodhand, Jonathan. 2018. "The Centrality of Margins: The Political Economy of Conflict and Development in Borderlands." Working Paper 2, September 2018.

Accessed August 9, 2020. http://www.borderlandsasia.org/uploads/1579261490_The%20Centrality%20of%20the%20Margins.pdf.

Gould, Lauren M. "The Politics of Portrayal in Violent Conflict: The Case of the Kony 2012 Campaign." *Alternatives: Global, Local, Political* 39 (4): 207–230.

Grant, Andrew J. 2008. "Informal Cross-Border Micro-Regionalism in West Africa: The Case of the Parrot's Beak." In *Afro-Regions: The Dynamics of Cross-Border Micro-Regionalism in Africa*, edited by Soderbaum, Fredrick, and Ian Taylor, 105–120. Stockholm: Elanders Sverige AB.

Gras, Romain. 2021. "Is the Islamic State really operating in eastern DRC?" *The Africa Report*, March 22, 2021. Accessed June 17, 2021. https://www.theafricareport.com/73449/is-the-islamic-state-really-operating-in-eastern-drc/.

Griffiths, Ieuan. 1996. "Permeable Boundaries in Africa." In *African Boundaries: Barriers, Conduits and Opportunities*, edited by Nugent, Paul, and Anthony I. Asiwaju, 68–83. London: Pinter.

Group of Experts on the Democratic Republic of the Congo. 2014. "Midterm Report of the Group of Experts (2014)." S/2014/428, June 25, 2014. Accessed August 15, 2020. https://www.undocs.org/S/2014/428.

Group of Experts on the Democratic Republic of the Congo. 2015. "Final Report of the Group of Experts (2014)." S/2015/19, January 12, 2015. Accessed August 15, 2020. https://www.undocs.org/S/2015/19.

Group of Experts on the Democratic Republic of the Congo. 2016. "Final Report of the Group of Experts (2015)." S/2016/466, May 23, 2016. Accessed August 15, 2020. https://www.undocs.org/S/2016/466.

Group of Experts on the Democratic Republic of the Congo. 2016. "Midterm Report of the Group of Experts (2016)." S/2016/1102, December 28, 2016. Accessed August 15, 2020. https://www.undocs.org/S/2016/1102.

Group of Experts on the Democratic Republic of the Congo. 2017. "Final Report of the Group of Experts (2016)." S/2017/672, August 10, 2017. Accessed August 15, 2020. https://www.undocs.org/S/2017/672/Rev.1.

Group of Experts on the Democratic Republic of the Congo. 2018. "Final Report of the Group of Experts (2017)." S/2018/531, June 4, 2018. Accessed August 15, 2020. https://www.undocs.org/S/2018/531.

Group of Experts on the Democratic Republic of the Congo. 2018. "Midterm Report of the Group of Experts (2018)." S/2018/1133, December 18, 2018. Accessed August 15, 2020. https://www.undocs.org/S/2018/1133.

Group of Experts on the Democratic Republic of the Congo. 2019. "Final Report of the Group of Experts (2018)." S/2019/469, June 7, 2019. Accessed August 15, 2020. https://undocs.org/S/2019/469.

Group of Experts on the Democratic Republic of the Congo. 2020. "Final Report of the Group of Experts (2019)." S/2020/482, June 2, 2020. Accessed August 15, 2020. https://www.undocs.org/S/2020/482.

Group of Experts on the Democratic Republic of the Congo. 2020. "Midterm Report of the Group of Experts (2020)." S/2020/1283, December 23, 2020. Accessed June 18, 2021. https://www.undocs.org/S/2020/1283.

Group of Experts on the Democratic Republic of the Congo. 2021. "Final Reports of the Group of Experts (2020)." S/2021/560, June 10, 2021. Accessed June 18, 2021. https://www.undocs.org/en/S/2021/560

Hagmann, Tobias, and Benedikt Korf. 2009. "Revisiting the African Frontier." Presented at the AEGIS European Conference on African Studies, Leipzig.

Hale, Aaron. 2010. "Weathering and Taming the Storm in 'Hard Times': The Case of Nande Economic Influence and Power in North Kivu, DRC." Presented at the American Political Science Association, Washington.

Heathershaw, John, and Daniel Lambach. 2008. "Introduction: Post-Conflict Spaces and Approaches to Statebuilding." *Journal of Intervention and Statebuilding* 2 (3): 269–289. https://doi.org/10.1080/17502970802436296.

Hellyer, Caroline. 2014. "Congo/Uganda: high profile military operations against ADF will not rebuild local stability." *African Arguments*, October 16, 2014. Accessed August 15, 2020. https://africanarguments.org/2014/10/16/congouganda-high-profile-military-operations-against-adf-will-not-rebuild-local-stability-by-caroline-hellyer/.

Hentz, James L. 2009. "War, Westphalia, and Africa: War Across States and the DRC Badlands." Presented at the International Studies Association, New York.

Herbst, Jeffrey. 2000. *States and Power in Africa: Comparative Lessons in Authority and Control*. Princeton: Princeton University Press.

Hinks, Arthur R. 1921. "Notes on the Technique of Boundary Delimitation." *The Geographical Journal* 58 (6): 417–443. Accessed August 13, 2020. http://www.jstor.com/stable/1781719.

Hoehne, Markus Virgil, and Dereje Feyissa. 2013. "Centering Borders and Borderlands: The Evidence from Africa." In *Violence on the Margins: States, Conflict, and Borderlands*, edited by Korf, Benedikt, and Timothy Raeymaekers, 55–86. New York: Palgrave Macmillan.

Horstmann, Alexander. 2014. "Stretching the Border: Confinement, Mobility and the Refugee Public Among Karen Refugees in Thailand and Burma." *Journal of Borderlands Studies* 29 (1): 47–61.

Horstmann, Alexander, and Reed L. Wadley. 2006. "Introduction: Centering the Margin in Southeast Asia." In *Centering the Margin: Agency and Narrative in Southeast Asian Borderlands*, edited by Horstmann, Alexander, and Reed L. Wadley, 1–26. New York: Berghahn Books.

Hovil, Lucy. 2003. *Displacement in Bundibugyo District: A Situation Analysis*. Kampala: Makerere University.

Hovil, Lucy, and Eric Werker. 2005. "Portrait of a Failed Rebellion: An Account of Rational, Sub-Optimal Violence in Western Uganda." *Rationality and Society* 17 (5): 5–34. https://doi.org/10.1177/1043463105051775.

Hovil, Lucy, and Zachary Lomo. 2005. *Whose Justice?: Perceptions of Uganda's Amnesty Act 2000: The Potential for Conflict Resolution and Long-Term Reconciliation*. Kampala: Makerere University.

Hultman, Lisa. 2007. "Battle Losses and Rebel Violence: Raising the Costs for Fighting." *Terrorism and Political Violence* 19 (2): 205–222. https://doi.org/10.1080/09546550701246866.

Human Rights Watch. 1999. *Hostile to Democracy: The Movement System and Political Repression in Uganda*. New York: Human Rights Watch.

Human Rights Watch. 2001. *Uganda in Eastern DRC: Fueling Political and Ethnic Strife*.

Human Rights Watch, March 1, 2001. Accessed June 20, 2021. https://www.hrw.org/report/2001/03/01/uganda-eastern-drc/fueling-politcal-and-ethnic-strife.

Human Rights Watch. 2009. "Open Secret: Illegal Detention and Torture by the Joint Anti-Terrorism Task Force in Uganda." Human Rights Watch, April 8, 2009. Accessed May 31, 2021. https://www.hrw.org/report/2009/04/08/open-secret/illegal-detention-and-torture-joint-anti-terrorism-task-force-uganda.

Human Rights Watch. 2014. "Uganda: Violence, Reprisals in Western Region." Human Rights Watch, November 5, 2014. Accessed August 15, 2020. https://www.hrw.org/news/2014/11/05/uganda-violence-reprisals-western-region.

Hüsken, Thomas. 2009. "The Neo-Tribal Competitive Order in the Borderland of Egypt and Libya." Presented at the African Borderlands Research Network, Johannesburg.

Idler, Annette. 2016. "Securing Peace in the Borderlands: A Post-Agreement Strategy for Colombia." University of Oxford: Department of Politics & International Relations, August 2016. Accessed August 9, 2020. https://www.politics.ox.ac.uk/materials/publications/15409/securing-peace-in-the-borderlands-colombia.pdf.

Idler, Annette. 2018. "Preventing Conflict Upstream: Impunity and Illicit Governance Across Colombia's Borders." *Defence Studies* 18 (1): 58–75. https://doi.org/10.1080/14702436.2017.1421859.

Idler, Annette, and James J. F. Forest. 2015. "Behavioral Patterns Among (Violent) Non-State Actors: A Study of Complimentary Governance." *Stability: International Journal of Security & Development* 4 (1): 1–19. https://DOI: http://dx.doi.org/10.5334/sta.er.

Information Counselling and Referral Services. 2008. "Preliminary Analysis: Reporter Profiling from the Amnesty Commission of Uganda." Information Counselling and Referral Services Database, November 14, 2008. https://reliefweb.int/sites/reliefweb.int/files/resources/DB6D36C252A6579C4925767100235728-Full_Report.pdf.

International Court of Justice. December 19, 2005. "Case Concerning Armed Activities on the Territory of the Congo (Democratic Republic of the Congo v. Uganda)." Accessed August 14, 2020. https://www.icj-cij.org/files/case-related/116/116-20051219-JUD-01-00-EN.pdf.

International Crisis Group. 1998. "North Kivu, Into the Quagmire? An Overview of the Current Crisis in North Kivu." International Crisis Group, August 13, 1998. Accessed August 14, 2020. https://www.crisisgroup.org/africa/central-africa/democratic-republic-congo/north-kivu-quagmire-overview-current-crisis-north-kivu.

International Crisis Group. 2019. "A New Approach for the UN to Stabilise the DR Congo." International Crisis Group, December 4, 2019. Accessed July 2, 2021. https://www.crisisgroup.org/africa/central-africa/democratic-republic-congo/b148-new-approach-un-stabilise-dr-congo.

International Crisis Group. 2021. "Understanding the New U.S. Terrorism Designations in Africa." International Crisis Group, March 18, 2021. Accessed July, 2, 2021. https://www.crisisgroup.org/africa/understanding-new-us-terrorism-designations-africa.

International Organization for Migration. 2019a. "Uganda—Flow Monitoring Dashboard: Uganda/DRC Border (7-21 December 2018)," January 2, 2019. Accessed August 15, 2020. https://migration.iom.int/reports/uganda-%E2%80%94-flow-monitoring-dashboard-ugandadrc-border-7%E2%80%9421-december-2018.

International Organization for Migration. 2019b. "Uganda—Flow Monitoring Dashboard: Uganda/DRC Border (1-30 March 2019)," April 24, 2019. Accessed August 15, 2020. https://migration.iom.int/reports/uganda-%E2%80%94-flow-monitoring-dashboard-ugandadrc-border-1-30-march-2019.

International Organization for Migration. 2019c. "Uganda—Flow Monitoring Dashboard: Uganda/DRC Border (1-30 April 2019)," May 14, 2019. Accessed August 15, 2020. https://dtm.iom.int/reports/uganda-%E2%80%94-flow-monitoring-dashboard-ugandadrc-border-1-30-april-2019.

IRIN News. 1999. "UGANDA: IRIN Special Report on the ADF rebellion." *The New Humanitarian*, December 8, 1999. Accessed August 14, 2020. https://www.thenewhumanitarian.org/report/11082/uganda-irin-special-report-adf-rebellion.

IRIN News. 2000. "UGANDA: Army targeting rebel hideouts in DRC." *The New Humanitarian*, January 25, 2000. Accessed August 14, 2020. https://www.thenewhumanitarian.org/report/11924/uganda-army-targeting-rebel-hideouts-drc.

IRIN News. 2004. "DRC-Uganda: Kampala deploys troops along border with Congo." *The New Humanitarian*, December 1, 2004. Accessed August 14, 2020. https://www.thenewhumanitarian.org/report/52281/drc-uganda-kampala-deploys-troops-along-border-congo.

IRIN. 2005. "DRC-Uganda: Disarm LRA rebels, Museveni tells Kinshasa and MONUC." *The New Humanitarian*, September 30, 2005. Accessed August 14, 2020. http://www.irinnews.org/Report/56540/DRC-UGANDA-Disarm-LRA-rebels-Museveni-tells-Kinshasa-and-MONUC.

IRIN. 2006a. "DRC: Security concerns in a 'democracy without democrats.'" *The New Humanitarian*, March 16, 2006. Accessed August 14, 2020. http://www.irinnews.org/Report/58444/DRC-Security-concerns-in-a-democracy-without-democrats.

IRIN. 2006b. "DRC: Ugandan rebels dislodged, but civilians not returning home." *The New Humanitarian*, May 26, 2006. Accessed August 14, 2020. https://www.thenewhumanitarian.org/report/59132/drc-ugandan-rebels-dislodged-civilians-not-returning-home.

IRIN. 2010. "DRC: when thousands suddenly take flight...." *The New Humanitarian*, July 15, 2010. Accessed August 14, 2020. http://www.irinnews.org/Report/89844/DRC-When-thousands-suddenly-take-flight.

Jackson, Robert, and Carl Rosberg. 1982. "Why Africa's Weak States Persist: The Empirical and the Juridical in Statehood." *World Politics* 33 (1): 1–24. Accessed August 13, 2020. https://www.jstor.org/stable/2010277?seq=1#metadata_info_tab_contents.

Jackson, Stephen. 2006. "Borderlands and the Transformation of War Economies: Lessons from the DR Congo." *Conflict, Security and Development* 6 (3): 425–447. https://doi.org/10.1080/14678800600933621.

Jackson, Stephen. 2009. "Potential Difference: Internal Borderlands in Africa." In *Whose Peace? Critical Perspectives on the Political Economy of Peacebuilding*, edited by Pugh, Michael, Neil Cooper, and Mandy Turner, 266–283. Houndmills: Palgrave MacMillan.

Jamboree, Walemba Eric. "Rebel scare grips Bundibugyo." *The Monitor*, March 29, 1995.

Jarvis, Anthony P., and Joseph A. Camilleri. 1995. "Locating the State." In *The State in Transition: Reimagining Political Space*, edited by Camilleri, Joseph A., Anthony P. Jarvis, and Albert J. Paolini, 3–20. Boulder: Lynne Rienner Publishers.

Jobbins, Michael. 2008. "Local Peace in Civil War: The Case of Butembo in Eastern DRC." Master's thesis, Georgetown University.

Jones, Reece. 2011. "Spaces of Refusal: Rethinking Sovereign Power and Resistance at the Border." *Annals of the Association of American Geographers* 102 (3): 1–15. http://dx.doi.org/10.1080/00045608.2011.600193.

Jourdan, Luca. 2008. "Ambiguous Borders: The Case of Rwenzori." In *Rwenzori: Histories and Cultures of an African Mountain*, edited by Pennacini, Cecilia, and Hermann Wittenberg, 285–300. Kampala: Fountain Publishers.

Justus, Souza. 1999. "150 ADF attack trading centre." *The Monitor*, December 24, 1999.

Kabamba, Patience S. 2008. "Trading on War: New Forms of Life in the Debris of the State." PhD thesis, Columbia University.

Kabarole Research and Resource Centre. 2002/2003. *The Effect of Trauma on the Resettlement of Internally Displaced People in Bwamba County, Bundibugyo District (Western-Uganda)*. Fort Portal: Kabarole Research and Resource Centre.

Kabarole Research and Resource Centre. 2004. *Trauma Research Report. Bundibugyo District*. Fort Portal: Kabarole Research and Resource Centre.

Kahindo, Jeanne d'Arc. 2018a. Beni: Así se disfrazan los de las FARDC en ADF." *Beni Lubero Online*, June 18, 2018. Accessed June 24, 2021. https://benilubero.com/page/3/?s=ADF.

Kahindo, Jeanne d'Arc. 2018b. "Nouvelles preuves scandaleuses que les ADF à Beni ne sont que des FARDC se déguisant en rebelles. . . ." *Beni Lubero Online*, September 13, 2018. Accessed June 24, 2021. https://benilubero.com/nouvelles-preuves-scandaleuses-que-les-adf-a-beni-ne-sont-que-des-fardc-se-deguisant-en-rebelles/.

Kakande, John. 1997. "Army nets Zaire captain—Mbabazi." *The New Vision*, June 26, 1997.

Kakande, John. 1998. "ADF releases manifesto." *The New Vision*, June 19, 1998.

Kalema, Andrew Ndawula. 1997. "A personal account of a survivor of the invasions: How I escaped the Bundibugyo attack." *The Sunday Vision*, June 22, 1997.

Kalir, Barak, Malini Sur, and Willem Van Schendel. 2012. "Introduction: Mobile Practices and Regimes of Permissiveness." In *Transnational Flows and Permissive*

Polities: Ethnographies of Human Mobilities in Asia, edited by Kalir, Barak, and Malini Sur, 11–26. Amsterdam: Amsterdam University Press.

Kalyvas, Stathis. 2003. "The Ontology of 'Political Violence': Action and Identity in Civil Wars." *Perspective on Politics* 1 (3): 475–494. Accessed August 14, 2020. http://www.jstor.com/stable/3688707.

Kalyvas, Stathis. 2004. "The Urban Bias in Research on Civil Wars." *Security Studies* 13 (3): 1–31. https://doi.org/10.1080/09636410490914022.

Kalyvas, Stathis. 2006. *The Logic of Violence in Civil War*. New York: Cambridge University Press.

Kananura, Stephen K. 2005. "The Ideological Question in Uganda as a Primary Aspect of Internal Conflict." In *Uganda's Fundamental Change: Domestics and External Dynamics of Conflicts and Development*, edited by Mukwaya, Aaron K. Kampala: Makerere University Printery.

Kantor, Ana, and Mariam Persson. 2011. "Liberian Vigilantes: Informal Security Provision on the Margins of Security Sector Reform." In *The Politics of Security Sector Reform: Challenges and Opportunities for the European Union's Global Role*, edited by Ekengren, Magnus, and Greg Simons, 273–304. Farnham: Ashgate Publishing Limited.

Kanyeihamba, George W. 1998. *Reflections on the Muslim Leadership Question in Uganda*. Kampala: Fountain Press.

Karugaba, Michael. 1996. "POWS implicate Zairian govt in Kasese war." *The Monitor*, November 21, 1996.

Karugaba, Michael. 1997. "Bashir, defence minister aiding rebels—Dr. Kiyonga." *The Monitor*, January 11, 1997.

Karugaba, Michael. 2001. "Mobutu gave us mines." *The Monitor*, September 21, 2001.

Karugaba, Michael. 2007. "Uganda: army chief says ADF rebels active in DRCongo." *The Daily Monitor*, March 13, 2007.

Kasfir, Nelson. 1976. *The Shrinking Political Arena: Participation and Ethnicity in African Politics, with a Case Study of Uganda*. Berkeley: University of California Press.

Kassimir, Ronald, and Robert Latham. 2001. "Toward a New Research Agenda." In *Intervention and Transnationalism in Africa*, edited by Callaghy, Thomas, Ronald Kassimir, and Robert Latham, 267–278. Cambridge: Cambridge University Press.

Kavanagh, Michael J. 2010. "Congo Army Clashes With Ugandan Rebels Displace 90,000 Civilians, UN Says." *Bloomberg BusinessWeek*, July 30, 2010. Accessed August 14, 2020. https://www.bloomberg.com/news/articles/2010-07-30/congo-army-clashes-with-ugandan-rebels-displace-90-000-civilians-un-says.

Keen, David. 2012. *Useful Enemies: When Waging Wars is More Important than Winning Them*. New Haven: Yale University Press.

King, Charles. 2004. "The Micropolitics of Social Violence." *World Politics* 56 (3): 431–455. Accessed August 14, 2020. http://www.jstor.com/stable/25054266.

Kiro, Merveilles. 2019. "'L'armée congolaise doit changer toutes ses stratégies face aux ADF enfin de les vaincre': Nicaise Kibel'bel." *Politico*, March 14, 2019. Accessed August 15, 2020. https://www.politico.cd/actualite/grands-lacs/2019/03/14/

larmee-congolaise-doit-changer-toutes-ses-strategies-face-aux-adf-enfin-de-les-vaincre-nicaise-kibelbel.html/35356/.

Kivu Security Tracker. "Monthly Report: December 2017." Accessed August 10, 2020. https://kivusecurity.org/reports.

Klein, Diana. 2011. "Funding War or Facilitating Peace?: Cross-Border Trade and Natural Resources." *Accord: An International Review of Peace Initiatives* 22: 77–80. Accessed August 14, 2020. http://www.c-r.org/accord/cross-border-peacebuilding/section-introduction-building-peace-below-state-cross-border-0.

Koen, Vlassenroot, Sandrine Perrot, and Jeroen Cuvelier. 2012. "Doing Business Out of War. An Analysis of the UPDF's Presence in the Democratic Republic of Congo." *Journal of Eastern African Studies* 6 (1): 2–21. https://doi.org/10.1080/17531055.2012.664701.

Kopytoff, Igor. 1987. *The African Frontier: The Reproduction of Traditional African Societies*. Bloomington: Indiana University Press.

Korf, Benedikt, Tobias Hagmann, and Rony Emmenegger. 2015. "Re-Spacing African Drylands: Territorialisation, Sedentarization and Indigenous Commodification in the Ethiopian Pastoral Frontier." *The Journal of Peasant Studies* 42 (5): 881–901. http://dx.doi.org/10.1080/03066150.2015.1006628.

Kramer, Mario. 2006. "Dynamics of Violence in KwaZulu-Natal, South Africa: Relations Between Centre and Periphery." Presented at the Annual Graduate Student Conference on Order, Conflict and Violence, New Haven.

Kwiravusa, Elie. 2019. "Le Cercle Vicieux de L'Insecurite au Grand Nord: Facteurs Politiques, Economiques et Socio-Culturels de la Crise de Beni." Suluhu Blog, April 2019. Accessed August 19, 2020. https://ethuin.files.wordpress.com/2019/05/swp-elie-kwiravusa-final.pdf.

Kyambogo University. 2002. *The Impact of a Hostile Environment on Children Living in Camps for Internally Displaced Persons in Bundibugyo District*. Kampala: Kyambogo University.

Kyankya, Sarah Mirembe. 1997. "Rebels threaten to attack 'any time.'" *The Crusader*, June 21, 1997.

Kyeyune, Moses. 2020. "Defence plans to spend Shs3 trillion from June." *Daily Monitor*, March 31, 2020. Accessed August 15, 2020. https://www.monitor.co.ug/News/National/Defence-spend-Shs3-trillion-June-domestic-arrears-Mwesige/688334-5510008-nssa72z/index.html.

Lamloum, Ola. 2016. "Marginalisation, Insecurity and Uncertainty on the Tunisian-Libyan Border: Ben Guerdane and Dhehiba from the Perspective of their Inhabitants." International Alert, December 2016. Accessed August 9, 2020. https://www.international-alert.org/publications/marginalisation-insecurity-and-uncertainty-tunisian-libyan-border.

Lauvergnier, Chloé. 2018. "Deadly attacks in DR Congo: 'The army always comes too late.'" *France 24*, September 27, 2018. Accessed August 15, 2020. https://observers.france24.com/en/20180927-deadly-attack-congo-army-beni-kivu.

Lee, Raymond M. 1995. *Dangerous Fieldwork*. Thousand Oaks: Sage Publications Incorporated.

Leenders, Reinoud. 2007. "Regional Conflict Formations: Is the Middle East Next?" *Third World Quarterly* 28 (5): 959–982. Accessed August 13, 2020. http://www.jstor.com/stable/20454974.

Lehtinen, Terhi. 2008. "'At the Gates of El Dorado': Micro-Dynamics in the Transnational Border Area Between Northern Morocco and Europe." In *Afro-Regions: The Dynamics of Cross-Border Micro-Regionalism in Africa*, edited by Soderbaum, Fredrick, and Ian Taylor, 121-135. Stockholm: Elanders Sverige AB.

Leni, Xanthia. 2019. "2016 Rwenzururu Kingdom attack: MPs want justice for Kasese massacre." *PML Daily*, November 26, 2019. Accessed August 24, 2020. https://www.pmldaily.com/news/2019/11/2016-rwenzururu-kingdom-attack-mps-want-justice-for-kasese-massacre.html.

Lind, Jeremy. 2015. "Understanding Insurgent Margins in Kenya, Nigeria and Mali." *Institute of Development Studies*, March 2015. Accessed August 9, 2020. https://opendocs.ids.ac.uk/opendocs/handle/20.500.12413/6013.

Lind, Jeremy. 2018. "Devolution, Shifting Centre-Periphery Relationships and Conflict in Northern Kenya." *Political Geography* 63: 135–147. http://dx.doi.org/10.1016/j.polgeo.2017.06.004.

Lombard, Louisa. 2012. "Raiding Sovereignty in Central African Borderlands." PhD thesis, Duke University. Accessed August 9, 2020. https://dukespace.lib.duke.edu/dspace/handle/10161/5861.

Long, James D. 2005. "Citizens and Insurgents: Mobilisation in the Politics of Rebellion." Presented at the International Studies Association, Honolulu.

Lucassen, Leo, Wim Willems, and Annemarie Cottaar. 1998. *Gypsies and Other Itinerant Groups: A Socio-Historical Approach*. New York: St. Martin's Press.

Lukinga, Christian. 2021. "État de siège à Beni-Ituri: Un fiasco bien planifé." *Beni Lubero Online*, June 1, 2021. Accessed June 24, 2021. https://benilubero.com/?s=kinyatsi.

Lwamba, Alfred. 2011a. "Attaque de la ville de Beni le 06 decembre 2011, un jeu du pouvoir?" *Journal Le Millénaire*.

Lwamba, Alfred. 2011b. "Toujours et Encore la Présence Inquiétante des ADF-NALU." *Journal Le Millénaire*.

MacGaffey, Janet. 1987. *Entrepreneurs and Parasites. The Struggle for Indigenous Capitalism in Zaire*. Cambridge: Cambridge University Press.

MacGaffey, Janet, and Remy Bazenguissa-Ganga. 1999. "Personal Networks and Trans-Frontier Trade: Zairian and Congolese Migrants." In *Regionalisation in Africa: Integration and Disintegration*, edited by Bach, Daniel C., 179–188. Oxford: James Currey.

Magezi, M. W., T. E. Nyakango, and M. K. Aganatia. 2004. *The People of the Rwenzoris: The Bayira (Bakonjo/Banande) and Their Culture*. Cologne: Rudiger Koppe Verlag.

Mamdani, Mahmood. 1996. *Citizen and Subject: Contemporary Africa and the Legacy of Late Colonialism*. Princeton: Princeton University Press.

Martinez, Oscar J. 1994. *Border People: Life and Society in the U.S.-Mexico Borderlands*. Tucson: University of Arizona Press.

Matfess, Hilary. 2019. "In Africa, All Jihad is Local." *Foreign Policy*, May 16, 2019. Accessed August 22, 2020. https://foreignpolicy.com/2019/05/16/in-africa-all-jihad-is-local/.

Mathur, Nayanika. 2013. "Naturalizing the Himalaya-as-Border in Uttarakhand." In *Borderland Lives in Northern South Asia: Non-State Perspectives*, edited by Gellner, David N., 72–93. Durham: Duke University Press.

Mathys, Gillian. 2009. "Doing Everything Twice: Methodological and Practical Problems of Doing Borderland Research (From a Historical Perspective)." Presented at the African Borderlands Research Network, Johannesburg.

Matsiko, Grace. 1998. "Why UPDF has not wiped out the ADF." *The New Vision*, October 6, 1998.

Matsiko, Grace. 2007. "Ugandan army intercepts rebel ADF arms on Lake Victoria." *The Daily Monitor*, December 29, 2007.

Matsiko, Grace, and John Thawite. 1998. "The genesis of ADF rebellion." *The New Vision*, October 5, 1998.

Mattheis, Frank, Luca Raineri, and Alessandra Russo. 2019. *Fringe Regionalism: When Peripheries Become Regions*. Cham: Palgrave Macmillan.

Mbabazi, Hannington. 1996. "More heavy fighting in Kasese." *The Monitor*, November 15, 1996.

Mbabazi, Hannington, and Michael Karugaba. 1997. "Gov't, rebels fight on for Bundibugyo." *The Monitor*, June 19, 1997.

Mbalibulha, Baluku Stanley. 2008a. "Rwenzori, A Bridge of Cultures." In *Rwenzori: Histories and Cultures of an African Mountain*, edited by Pennacini, Cecilia, and Hermann Wittenberg, 98–105. Kampala: Fountain Publishers.

Mbalibulha, Baluku Stanley. 2008b. "The Dynamics of Ethno-Political Relations in the Rwenzori Region, 1900-2000." Master's thesis, Makerere University.

Mbembe, Achille. 2000. "At the Edge of the World: Boundaries, Territoriality, and Sovereignty in Africa." *Public Culture* 12 (1): 259–284. https://doi.org/10.1215/08992363-12-1-259.

McGregor, Andrew. 2007. "Oil and Jihad in Central Africa: The Rise and Fall of Uganda's ADF." *Terrorism Monitor* 5 (24). Accessed August 14, 2020. https://jamestown.org/program/oil-and-jihad-in-central-africa-the-rise-and-fall-of-ugandas-adf/.

McKinnon, John, and Jean Michaud. 2000. "Introduction: Montagnard Domain in the South-East Asian Massif." In *Turbulent Times and Enduring Peoples: Mountain Minorities in the South-East Asian Massif*, edited by Michaud, Jean, 1–25. Richmond: Curzon Press.

Medard, Henri. 2009. "Building and Transgressing Borders in the Great Lakes Region of East Africa." *Journal of Eastern African Studies* 3 (2): 275–283. https://doi.org/10.1080/17531050902972709.

Meehan, Patrick. 2015. "Fortifying or Fragmenting the State? The Political Economy of the Opium/Heroin Trade in Shan State, Myanmar, 1988-2013." *Critical Asian Studies* 47 (2): 253–282. https://doi.org/10.1080/14672715.2015.1041280.

Meehan, Patrick, and Sharri Plonski. 2017. "Brokering the Margins: A Review of Concepts and Methods." SOAS and University of Bath, February 2017. Accessed August 9, 2020. https://eprints.soas.ac.uk/25820/1/1488349944_BROKERING%20

THE%20MARGINS%20-%20Patrick%2BMeehan%20and%20Sharri%20Plonski%20February%202017.pdf.
Menkhaus, Ken. 2007. "Constraints and Opportunities in Ungoverned Spaces." In *Denial of Sanctuary: Understanding Terrorist Safe Havens*, edited by Innes, Michael, 67–82. Westport: Praeger Security International.
Merkx, Jozef. 2002. "Refugee Identities and Relief in an African Borderland: A Study of Northern Uganda and Southern Sudan." *Refugee Survey Quarterly* 21 (1 and 2): 113–146. Accessed August 13, 2020. http://southsudanhumanitarianproject.com/wp-content/uploads/sites/21/formidable/Merkx-2002-Refugee-Identities-and-Relief-in-An-African-Borderland-A-study-of-Northern-Uganda-and-Southern-Sudan.pdf.
Michaud, Jean. 2010. "Editorial—Zomia and Beyond." *Journal of Global History* 5 (2): 187–214. https://doi.org/10.1017/S1740022810000057.
Migdal, Joel S. 2004. "Mental Maps and Virtual Checkpoints: Struggles to Construct and Maintain State and Social Boundaries." In *Boundaries and Belonging: States and Societies in the Struggle to Shape Identities and Local Practices*, edited by Migdal, Joel S., 3–26. Cambridge: Cambridge University Press.
Miles, William F. S. 2005. "Development, Not Division: Local Versus External Perceptions of the Niger-Nigeria Boundary." *Journal of Modern African Studies* 43 (2): 297–320. https://doi.org/10.1017/S0022278X05000844.
Miles, William F. S. 2015. "Postcolonial Borderland Legacies of Anglo-French Partition in West Africa." *African Studies Review* 58 (3): 191–213. https://doi:10.1017/asr.2015.71.
Mkandawire, Thandika. 2002. "The Terrible Toll of Post-Colonial 'Rebel Movements' in Africa: Towards an Explanation of the Violence against the Peasantry." *The Journal of Modern African Studies* 40 (2): 181–215. Accessed August 13, 2020. http://www.jstor.com/stable/3876277.
MONUSCO. 2016. "Press Statement of MONUSCO Regarding Operations Against Armed Groups in Eastern Democratic Republic of the Congo." MONUSCO, February 3, 2016. Accessed August 15, 2020. https://monusco.unmissions.org/en/press-statement-monusco-regarding-operations-against-armed-groups-eastern-democratic-republic-congo.
Morehouse, Barbara J. 2004. "Theoretical Approaches to Border Spaces and Identities." In *Challenged Borderlands: Transcending Political and Cultural Boundaries*, edited by Pavlakovich-Kochi, Vera, Barbara J. Morehouse, and Doris Wastl-Walter, 19–40. Aldershot: Ashgate Publishing Limited.
Mosley, Jason, and Elizabeth E. Watson. 2016. "Frontier Transformations: Development Visions, Spaces and Processes in Northern Kenya and Southern Ethiopia." *Journal of Eastern African Studies* 10 (3): 452–475. https://doi.org/10.1080/17531055.2016.1266199.
Mugabe, Faustin. 2016. "Tracing ethnic conflicts in the Rwenzori." *Daily Monitor*, March 20, 2016. Accessed August 15, 2020. https://www.monitor.co.ug/Magazines/PeoplePower/689844-3124160-5n7olm/index.html.
Mugabi, Frank. 2008. "Congo–Kinshasa: MONUC Calls for Joint Effort on Rebels." *The New Vision*, October 9, 2008.

Mugerwa, Francis. 2007. "Uganda tightens security along border with DRCongo." *The New Vision*, May 4, 2007.

Mugerwa, Francis. 2008. "Army cracks down on ADF collaborators in western Uganda." *The Monitor*, January 21, 2008.

Mugisa, Anne. 2008. "ADF Rebels Regrouping in Eastern Congo." *The New Vision*, July 18, 2008.

Mugisa, Joseph. 1999a. "LRA, ADF fighting proxy war—Museveni." *The Monitor*, April 27, 1999.

Mugisa, Joseph. 1999b. "Only 500 ADF are left—Museveni." *The Monitor*, July 8, 1999.

Muhame, Giles. 2012. "Investigation: Inside Rebel Activities in Uganda, Congo." *Chimp Reports*, March 12, 2012.

Muhanga, Kyomuhendo. 1999a. "Mai Mai join ADF in west." *The New Vision*, December 1, 1999.

Muhanga, Kyomuhendo. 1999b. "UPDF overruns ADF Congo camps." *The New Vision*, August 7, 1999.

Muhangi, Javan K. 2004. "International Humanitarian Law and its Application in a Situation of Internal Armed Conflict: A Case of ADF Armed Rebellion in Uganda." Master's thesis, Makerere University.

Muhangi, Jossy. 1996. "Tabliq invaders came from Iganga." *The New Vision*, November 21, 1996.

Muhumuza, Rodney. 2012. "Resurgent ADF threatens stability in Great Lakes Region." *Think Africa Press*, January 17, 2012.

Mulenga, Laura. 1996. "Death from the west." *The Crusader*, November 26, 1996.

Mulera, Muniini K. 1998. "LRA, ADF: What's there to talk?" *The Monitor*, June 15, 1998.

Mulingwa, Rogers. 1998. "Call back your ADF children, Minister Isoke tells Baganda." *The Monitor*, October 7, 1998.

Mumbere, Vumilia. 2010. "Poursuite des combats dans le territoire de Beni: le leadership politique Nande pris à son propre piège." *Congo Forum*, August 1, 2010. Accessed August 14, 2020. https://www.congoforum.be/fr/2010/08/01-08-10-le-millnaire-poursuite-des-combats-dans-le-territoire-de-beni-le-leadership-politique-nande-pris-son-propre-piege/.

Muranga, Manuel J. K. 2008. "Coping with Babel Around the Mountains of the Moon: A Case for Multilingual Patriotism in Uganda and Africa." In *Rwenzori: Histories and Cultures of an African Mountain*, edited by Pennacini, Cecilia, and Hermann Wittenberg, 341–366. Kampala: Fountain Publishers.

Murdoch, James C., and Todd Sandler. 2002. "Economic Growth, Civil Wars, and Spatial Spillovers." *The Journal of Conflict Resolution* 46 (1): 91–110. https://doi.org/10.1177/0022002702046001006.

Mwanawavene, Roger Kasereka. 2010. "Dynamiques Locales et Pressions Extérieures dans la Conflictualité Armée au Nord-Kivu: Cas des Territoires de Beni-Lubero." PhD thesis, Ghent University.

Mwanawavene, Roger Kasereka, Nestor Bauma Baheteet, and Charles Nasibu Bilali. 2006. "Trafics d'Armes: Enquête de Terrain au Kivu

(RDC)." GRIP, August 1, 2006. Accessed August 14, 2020. https://grip.org/trafics-darmes-enquete-de-terrain-au-kivu-rdc/.

Mwenda, Andrew M. 1999. "ADF attack leaves Museveni's Congo policy in tatters." *The Monitor*, December 18, 1999.

Mwenda, Andrew M. 2010a. "Security find new clues on the terror attacks." *The Independent*, July 25, 2010.

Mwenda, Andrew M. 2010b. "Uganda: Terror in Kampala." *The Independent*, July 18, 2010.

Mwesigwa, Alon. 2018. "19 assassinations: Gen Kayihura pins 10 on ADF." *The Observer*, September 19, 2018. Accessed August 15, 2020. Accessed August 15, 2020. https://observer.ug/news/headlines/58711-19-assassinations-gen-kayihura-pins-10-on-adf.

Namutebi, Joyce. 2000. "Baganda, Basoga dominate ADF—Kavuma." *The New Vision*, January 4, 2000.

Nantulya, Paul. 2001. "Exclusion, Identity and Armed Conflict: A Historical Survey of the Politics of Confrontation in Uganda with Special Reference to the Independence Era." Presented at the Politics of Identity and Exclusion in Africa: From Violent Confrontation to Peaceful Cooperation, Pretoria.

Nelson, Jack E. 1982. *Christian Missionizing and Social Transformation: A History of Conflict and Change in Eastern Zaire*. New York: Praeger.

Newman, David. 2009. "Contemporary Research Agendas in Border Studies: An Overview." Presented at the African Borderlands Research Network, Johannesburg.

Newman, David. 2011. "Contemporary Research Agendas in Border Studies: An Overview." In *The Ashgate Research Companion to Border Studies*, edited by Wastl-Walter, Doris, 33–48. New York: Routledge.

Newman, David, and Anssi Paasi. 1998. "Fences and Neighbours in the Postmodern World: Boundary Narratives in Political Geography." *Progress in Human Geography* 22 (2): 186–207. https://doi.org/10.1191/030913298666039113.

Ngwato, Tara Polzer, and Jacob Akech. 2009. "Between State and Society—Local Government in South African and Kenyan Border Districts." Presented at the African Borderlands Research Network, Johannesburg.

Ninsiima, Enid. 2014. "New rebel group sets up base in Rwenzori." *Daily Monitor*, October 16, 2014. Accessed August 15, 2020. https://www.monitor.co.ug/News/National/New-rebel-group-sets-up-base-in-Rwenzori/688334-2488148-k3man4z/index.html.

Nkuutu, Fred. 2003. *Situation Analysis of Kasese and Bundibugyo*. Kampala: International Rescue Committee.

Northrup, David. 1998. "A Church in Search of a State: Catholic Missions in Eastern Zaïre, 1879–1930." *Journal of Church and State* 30 (2): 309–319.

Nossiter, Adam. 2012. "In Nigeria, a Deadly Group's Rage Has Local Roots." *The New York Times*, February 25, 2012. Accessed August 15, 2020. https://www.nytimes.com/2012/02/26/world/africa/in-northern-nigeria-boko-haram-stirs-fear-and-sympathy.html.

Nsobya, Abdulhakim. 2015-2016. "Uganda's Militant Islamic Movement ADF: A Historical Analysis." *The Annual Review of Islam in Africa* 12/13: 30–39.

Ntambirweki, Pelucy. 2001. *Assessment of the Orphan Situation in Bundibugyo District*. Kampala: UNICEF.

Nugent, Paul. 1996. "Arbitrary Lines and the People's Minds: A Dissenting View on Colonial Boundaries in West Africa." In *African Boundaries: Barriers, Conduits and Opportunities*, edited by Nugent, Paul, and Anthony I. Asiwaju, 35–67. London: Pinter.

Nugent, Paul. 2002. *Smugglers, Secessionists and Loyal Citizens of the Ghana-Togo Frontier: The Lie of the Borderlands Since 1914*. Athens: Ohio University Press.

Nugent, Paul, and Anthony I. Asiwaju. 1996a. "Conclusion: The Future of African Boundaries." In *African Boundaries: Barriers, Conduits and Opportunities*, edited by Nugent, Paul, and Anthony I. Asiwaju, 266–272. London: Pinter.

Nugent, Paul and Anthony I. Asiwaju. 1996b. "Introduction: The Paradox of African Boundaries." In *African Boundaries: Barriers, Conduits and Opportunities*, edited by Nugent, Paul, and Anthony I. Asiwaju, 1–14. London: Pinter.

Nzinjah, John. 1992. "Kasese Insecurity: Historical View." *The New Vision*, September 24, 1992.

Nzinjah, John. 1995. "Former Rwenzururu bandit dies in Zaire." *The New Vision*, July 13, 1995.

Nzinjah, John. 1997a. "Army controls strategic heights." *The New Vision*, February 15, 1997.

Nzinjah, John. 1997b. "Sudan aircraft drops ADF arms." *The New Vision*, November 14, 1997.

Nzinjah, John. 1998. "ADF commanders surrender." *The New Vision*, December 8, 1998.

Nzinjah, John, and John Thawite. 1998. "ADF raze Kasese market." *The New Vision*, September 19, 1998.

Nzinja, John, and Mwine Mugisha. 1994. "Rwanda militia, NALU plan to attack Uganda." *The New Vision*, October 19, 1994.

Ochieng, Henry. 1998. "LRA, ADF, WNBF, NFA join forces." *The Monitor*, October 3, 1998.

O'Dwyer, Laura. 2019. "Are They or Aren't They? The Contested Alignment Between A.D.F. and I.S.I.S. in Democratic Republic of Congo." The Organization for World Peace, May 29, 2019. Accessed August 15, 2020. https://theowp.org/reports/are-they-or-arent-they-the-contested-alignment-between-a-d-f-and-i-s-i-s-in-democratic-republic-of-congo/.

Oftedal, Emilie. 2013. "Boko Haram: A Transnational Phenomenon?" Master's thesis, University of Oslo. Accessed August 9, 2020. https://www.duo.uio.no/bitstream/handle/10852/36925/OftedalxMaster.pdf.

Okee, Dusman A. 1999. "ADF denies Rwanda, to fight in DR Congo." *The Monitor*, September 25, 1999.

Okello, Felix Warom. 2011. "Uganda: Arrest of Two Heightens Claims of ADF Regrouping." *The Monitor*, March 30, 2011.

Oliver, Mario. 2021. "Democratic Republic of the Congo: 'We are in a state of utter misery.'" *Aid to the Church in Need*, May 17, 2021.

Accessed June 20, 2021. https://www.churchinneed.org/democratic-republic-of-the-congo-we-are-in-a-state-of-utter-misery/.

Omach, Paul. 2009. "Democratization and Conflict Resolution in Uganda." *Les Cahiers d'Afrique de l'Est* 41: 1–20. Accessed August 14, 2020. https://journals.openedition.org/eastafrica/576.

Onah, Emmanuel Ikechi. 2015. "The Role of Trans-Border ethnic Groups in Intra-State and Inter-State Conflict in Africa." *Journal of Borderlands Studies* 30 (1): 85–95: https://doi.org/10.1080/08865655.2015.1012734.

Oteng, Eric. 2018. "Museveni accuses UN, DRC of harbouring ADF rebels." *Africa News*, June 6, 2018. Accessed August 15, 2020. https://www.africanews.com/2018/06/06/museveni-accuses-un-drc-of-harbouring-adf-rebels/.

Otunnu, Ogenga. 2004. "Uganda as a Regional Actor in the Zairian War." In *War and Peace in Zaire/Congo: Analysing and Evaluating Intervention, 1996–1997*, edited by Adelman, Howard, and Govind C. Rao, 31–84. Trenton: Africa World Press Inc.

Oxfam. 2018a. "DRC: The World's First Ebola Outbreak Inside a Conflict." Oxfam, August 8, 2018. Accessed August 15, 2020. https://policy-practice.oxfam.org.uk/publications/the-ebola-outbreak-in-drc-strengthening-the-response-620555.

Oxfam. 2018b. "The Ebola Outbreak in DRC: Strengthening the response in Beni, DRC by putting communities at the centre." Oxfam, October 8, 2018. Accessed August 15, 2020. https://policy-practice.oxfam.org.uk/publications/the-ebola-outbreak-in-drc-strengthening-the-response-620555.

Paasi, Anssi. 2011. "A Border Theory: An Unattainable Dream or a Realistic Aim for Border Scholars?" In *The Ashgate Research Companion to Border Studies*, edited by Wastl-Walter, Doris, 11–32. New York: Routledge.

Parker, Melissa, Tim Allen, Georgina Pearson, Nichola Peach, Rachel Flynn, and Nicholas Rees. 2012. "Border Parasites: Schistosomisais Among Uganda's Fisherfolk." *Journal of Eastern African Studies* 6 (1): 98–123. https://doi.org/10.1080/17531055.2012.664706.

Pennacini, Cecilia. 2008. "The Rwenzori Ethnic 'Puzzle.'" In *Rwenzori: Histories and Cultures of an African Mountain*, edited by Cecilia Pennacini, and Hermann Wittenberg, 59–97. Kampala: Fountain Publishers.

Persson, Mariam. 2012. "Demobilized or Remobilized? Lingering Rebel Structures in Post-War Liberia." In *African Conflicts and Informal Power: Big Men and Networks*, edited by Utas, Mats, 101–118. Uppsala: Zed Books.

Peterson, Derek. 2009. "States of Mind: Political History and the Rwenzururu Kingdom in Western Uganda." In *Recasting the Past: History Writing and Political Work in Modern Africa*, edited by Peterson, Derek, and Giacomo Macola, 171–190. Athens: Ohio University Press.

Piliavsky, Anastasia. 2013. "Borders without Borderlands: On the Social Reproduction of State Demarcation in Rajasthan." In Borderland Lives in Northern South Asia: Non-State Perspectives, edited by Gellner, David N., 24–46. Durham: Duke University Press.

Pinos, Jaume Castan. 2018. "Terror, Territory and Statehood from Al Qaeda to the Islamic State." In *African Border Disorders: Addressing Transnational Extremist*

Organizations, edited by Walther, Olivier J., and William F. S. Miles, 153–169. Oxon: Routledge.

Pole Institute. 2010. "Guerrillas in the Mist: The Congolese Experience of the FDLR War in Eastern Congo and the Role of the International Community." *Pole Institute*, February 2010. Accessed August 14, 2020. http://www.pole-institute.org/sites/default/files/pole-fdlr-english.pdf.

Pollard, Sidney. 1997. *Marginal Europe: The Contribution of Marginal Lands Since the Middle Ages*. Oxford: Clarendon Press, 1997.

Postings, Robert. 2018. "The tentative ties between the Allied Democratic Forces and ISIS." *The Defense Post*, December 4, 2018. Accessed August 15, 2020. https://www.thedefensepost.com/2018/12/04/tentative-ties-allied-democratic-forces-isis-dr-congo/.

Prunier, Gérard. 1997. "The Geopolitical Situation in the Great Lakes Area in Light of the Kivu Crisis." *Refugee Survey Quarterly* 16 (1): 1–25. https://doi.org/10.1093/rsq/16.1.1-b.

Prunier, Gérard. 1999. "L'Ouganda et les Guerres Congolaises." *Politique Africaine* 75: 43–59. Accessed August 13, 2020. https://pdfs.semanticscholar.org/3241/0ef4c01234b6313a50ee79c9864633f593d5.pdf?_ga=2.146737264.512090655.1597362491-73293978.1597013406.

Prunier, Gérard. 2004. "Rebel Movements and Proxy Warfare: Uganda, Sudan and the Congo (1986-99)." *African Affairs* 103 (412): 359–383. https://doi.org/10.1093/afraf/adh050.

Prunier, Gérard. 2009. *From Genocide to Continental War: The 'Congolese' Conflict and the Crisis of Contemporary Africa*. London: Hurst and Company.

Radio France Internationale. 2005. "DRCongo: UN mission calls for further patrols to 'ensure total security' in east." *Radio France Internationale*, December 28, 2005.

Radio Okapi. 2011. "Beni: un an après l'attaque de l'ADF/Nalu, la société civile exige réparation." *Radio Okapi*, June 29, 2011. Accessed August 14, 2020. https://www.radiookapi.net/actualite/2011/06/29/beni-un-an-apres-lattaque-de-l%25e2%2580%2599adfnalu-la-societe-civile-exige-reparation.

Radio Okapi. 2012a. "Beni: la Monusco se réserve le droit de répliquer face aux tirs de ses hélicoptèrs par les rebelles ADF/Nalu." *Radio Okapi*, March 22, 2012. Accessed August 14, 2020. http://radiookapi.net/actualite/2012/03/22/beni-la-monusco-se-reserve-le-droit-de-repliquer-face-aux-tirs-de-ses-helicopteres-par-les-rebelles-adfnalu/.

Radio Okapi. 2012b. "Beni: la société civile dénonce l'insécurité persistant." *Radio Okapi*, January 30, 2012. Accessed August 14, 2020. https://www.radiookapi.net/regions/nord-kivu/2012/05/26/beni-la-societe-civile-denonce-la-persistance-de-linsecurite.

Radio Okapi. 2012c. "Nord-Kivu: la Monusco insiste sur la nécessité de protéger les civils lors des opérations contre les rebelles ADF/Nalu." *Radio Okapi*, March 27, 2012. Accessed August 14, 2020. https://www.radiookapi.net/actualite/2012/03/27/nord-kivu-la-monusco-insiste-sur-la-necessite-de-proteger-les-civils-lors-des-operations-contre-les-rebelles-adfnalu/.

Radio Okapi. 2012d. "Nord-Kivu: les FARDC tuent 13 rebelles des ADF-Nalu à Mukoko." *Radio Okapi*, January 19, 2012. Accessed August 14, 2020. http://radiookapi.net/actualite/2012/01/19/nord-kivu-les-fardc-tuent-13-rebelles-des-adf-nalu-mukoko/.

Radio Okapi. 2012e. "Nouveax affrontements entre FARDC et ADF/Nalu à Beni." *Radio Okapi*, March 29, 2012. Accessed August 14, 2020. http://radiookapi.net/actualite/2012/03/29/nouveaux-affrontements-entre-fardc-adfnalu-beni/.

Radio Okapi. 2018a. "Beni: la commune de Rwenzori quasi désertée par la population." *Radio Okapi*, October 4, 2018. Accessed August 10, 2020. https://www.radiookapi.net/2018/10/04/actualite/securite/beni-la-commune-de-rwenzori-quasi-desertee-par-la-population.

Radio Okapi. 2018b. "Beni: une coalition des ADF et Maï Maï attaque deux positions de l'armée, huit morts." *Radio Okapi*, July 5, 2018. Accessed August 10, 2020. https://www.radiookapi.net/2018/07/05/actualite/securite/beni-une-coalition-des-adf-et-mai-mai-attaque-deux-positions-de-larmee.

Radio Okapi. 2018c. "Capitaine Mak Hazukay: Le territoire de Beni fait face au terrorisme des ADF commandés par les ougandais." *Radio Okapi*, September 23, 2018. Accessed August 10, 2020. https://www.radiookapi.net/2018/09/23/actualite/securite/capitaine-mak-hazukay-le-territoire-de-beni-fait-face-au-terrorisme.

Radio Okapi. 2019a. "Nouvelle manifestation des jeunes et sit-in devant le Quartier général de la MONUSCO à Beni." *Radio Okapi*, November 22, 2019. Accessed August 21, 2020. https://www.radiookapi.net/2019/11/22/actualite/securite/nouvelle-manifestation-des-jeunes-et-sit-devant-le-quartier-general-de.

Radio Okapi. 2019b. "Leïla Zerrougui: On ne peut pas réussir à protéger la population si on deviant nous même une cible." *Radio Okapi*, November 26, 2019. Accessed August 21, 2020. https://www.radiookapi.net/2019/11/26/actualite/securite/leila-zerrougui-ne-peut-pas-reussir-proteger-la-population-si-devient.

Radio Okapi. 2021a. "Beni: les jeunes demandent à Félix Tshisekedi un audit des opérations Sokola 1." *Radio Okapi*, June 17, 2021. Accessed June 24, 2021. https://www.radiookapi.net/2021/06/17/actualite/securite/beni-les-jeunes-demandent-felix-tshisekedi-un-audit-des-operations.

Radio Okapi. 2021b. "Prolongation de l'état de siege: la société civile demande une évaluation des premières opérations." *Radio Okapi*, June 22, 2021. Accessed June 24, 2021. https://www.radiookapi.net/2021/06/22/actualite/securite/prolongation-de-letat-de-siege-la-societe-civile-demande-une.

Radio Uganda. 2007. "Army spokesman says 'ADF rebels have no capacity to control any part of Uganda.'" *Radio Uganda*, May 7, 2007.

Radvanyi, Jean, and Shakhmardan S. Muduyev. 2007. "Challenges Facing the Mountain Peoples of the Caucasus." *Eurasian Geography and Economics* 48 (2): 157–177. https://doi.org/10.2747/1538-7216.48.2.157.

Raeymaekers, Timothy. 2007. "The Power of Protection: Governance and Transborder Trade on the Congo–Ugandan Frontier." PhD thesis, Ghent University.

Raeymaekers, Timothy. 2009a. "The Central Margins: Congo's Transborder Economy and State-Making in the Borderlands." Danish Institute for International Studies. Accessed August 14, 2020. https://www.files.ethz.ch/isn/110436/WP2009-25_state_making_Congo_Raeymaekers.pdf.

Raeymaekers, Timothy. 2009b. "The Silent Encroachment of the Frontier: A Politics of Transborder Trade in the Semliki Valley (Congo–Uganda)." *Political Geography* 28 (1): 55–65. https://doi.org/10.1016/j.polgeo.2008.12.008.

Raeymaekers, Timothy. 2011. "Forced Displacement and Youth Employment in the Aftermath of the Congo War: From Making a Living to Making a Life." Microcon, January 2011. Accessed August 14, 2020. https://www.future-agricultures.org/wp-content/uploads/pdf-archive/RWP38_TR.pdf.

Raeymaekers, Timothy, and Luca Jourdan. 2009. "Economic Opportunities and Local Governance on an African Frontier: The Case of the Semliki Basin (Congo–Uganda)." *Journal of Eastern African Studies* 3 (2): 317–332. https://doi.org/10.1080/17531050902972964.

Raeymaekers, Timothy, et al. 2010. "Background: Violence in the Borderlands." Presented at the Bringing the Margins Back In: War Making and State Making in the Borderlands Workshop, Ghent.

Ramsbotham, Alexander, and I. William Zartman. 2011. "Introduction." *Accord: An International Review of Peace Initiatives* 22: 5. Accessed August 14, 2020. http://www.c-r.org/accord/cross-border-peacebuilding/introduction.

Remotti, Francesco. 2008. "Banana Groves and Tree Tombs: 'Disappearing' or 'Remaining' Among the Banande of Northern Kivu (Eastern Democratic Republic of the Congo)." In *Rwenzori: Histories and Cultures of an African Mountain*, edited by Pennacini, Cecilia, and Hermann Wittenberg, 169–199. Kampala: Fountain Publishers.

Reuss, Anna, and Kristof Titeca. 2016. "Beyond Ethnicity: The Violence in Western Uganda and Rwenzori's 99 Problems." *Review of African Political Economy* 44 (151): 131–141. https://doi.org/10.1080/03056244.2016.1270928.

Reuters. 2011. "Eleven family members found dead after Congo kidnap." *Reuters*, February 14, 2011. Accessed August 14, 2020. http://af.reuters.com/article/topNews/idAFJOE71D0KE20110214.

Reuters. 2014. "Congo crowd kills man, eats him after militant massacres: witnesses." *Reuters*, October 31, 2014. Accessed August 15, 2020. https://www.reuters.com/article/us-congodemocratic-rebels/congo-crowd-kills-man-eats-him-after-militant-massacres-witnesses-idUSKBN0IK1RN20141031.

Richards, Paul. 1996. *Fighting for the Rain Forest: War, Youth and Resources in Sierra Leone*. Oxford: James Currey.

Rokhideh, Maryam. 2021. "Leveraging the Peacebuilding Potential of Cross-border Trader Networks in Sub-Saharan Africa." *Resolve*, July 1, 2021. Accessed July 2, 2021. https://www.resolvenet.org/research/leveraging-peacebuilding-potential-cross-border-trader-networks-sub-saharan-africa.

Romkema, Hans. 2007. "Opportunities and Constraints for the Disarmament and Repatriation of Foreign Armed Groups in the Democratic Republic of Congo: The Cases of the FDLR, FNL, and ADF/NALU." The World Bank, June 2007. Accessed August 14, 2020. http://www.operationspaix.net/DATA/DOCUMENT/5459~v~Opportunities_and_Constraints_for_the_Disarmament___Repatriation_of_Foreign_Armed_Groups_in_the_Democratic_Republic_of_Congo.pdf.

Romo, Harriett, and Raquel R. Marquez. 2010. "Who's Who Across the U.S.-Mexican Border: Identities in Transition." In *Understanding Life in the Borderlands: Boundaries in Depth and in Motion*, edited by Zartman, I. William, 217–234. Athens: University of Georgia Press.

Ron, James. 2003. *Frontiers and Ghettos: State Violence in Serbia and Israel*. Berkeley: University of California Press.

Rubin, Barnett R., Andrea Armstrong, and Gloria Ntegeye. 2001. "Draft Discussion Paper I: Conceptual Overview of the Origin, Structure, and Dynamics of Regional Conflict." Presented at the conference organized by the Africa Peace Forum and Center on International Cooperation, Nairobi. Rubongoya, Joshua B. 1995. "The Bakonjo-Baamba and Uganda: Colonial and Postcolonial Integration and Ethnocide." *Studies in Conflict and Terrorism* 18 (2): 75–92. https://doi.org/10.1080/10576109508435970.

Ruhunda, Alex, et al. "The Civil Peace Mission in Western Uganda—Baseline Survey Findings." Fort Portal: Kabarole Research and Resource Centre. Sadler, James Hayes, Hesketh Bell, Mr. Freshfield, E. M. Jack, Mr. Wollaston, Captain Behrens, Mr. Fisher, and Colonel Close. 1909. "Survey and Exploration in the Ruwenzori and Lake Region, Central Africa: Discussion." *The Geographical Journal* 34 (2): 153–156. Accessed August 14, 2020. https://www.jstor.org/stable/1777817.

Salehyan, Idean. 2007. "Transnational Rebels: Neighbouring States as Sanctuary for Rebel Groups." *World Politics* 59 (2): 217–242. Accessed August 13, 2020. http://www.jstor.com/stable/40060187.

Scorgie, Lindsay. 2011. "Peripheral Pariah or Regional Rebel? The Allied Democratic Forces in the Uganda / Congo Borderland." *The Round Table* 100 (412): 79–93.

Scorgie, Lindsay. 2013. "Prominent Peripheries: The Role of Borderlands in Central Africa's Regionalized Conflict." *Journal of Critical African Studies* 5 (1): 32–47.

Scorgie, Lindsay. 2015a. "Economic Survival and Borderland Rebellion: The Case of the Allied Democratic Forces on the Uganda-Congo Border." *The Journal of the Middle East and Africa* 6 (2): 191–213.

Scorgie, Lindsay. 2015b. "Militant Islamists or Borderland Dissidents? An Exploration into the Allied Democratic Forces' Recruitment Practices and Constitution." *Journal of Modern African Studies* 53 (1): 1–25.

Scorgie, Lindsay. 2015c. "State Borders in Africa." In *Introduction to Border Studies*, edited by Sevastianov, Sergei V., Jussi P. Laine, and Anton A. Kireev, 284–304. Vladivostok: Dalnauka.

Scott, James C. 1998. *Seeing Like a State: How Certain Schemes to Improve the Human Condition Have Failed*. New Haven: Yale University Press.

Scott, James C. 2009. *The Art of Not Being Governed: An Anarchist History of Upland Southeast Asia*. New Haven: Yale University Press.

Sematumba, Onesphore. 2016. "Derniers développements et analyses du conflit dans la Région des Grands Lacs." Pole Institute, October 4, 2016. Accessed August 15, 2020. http://www.pole-institute.org/analyses/derniers-d%C3%A9veloppements-et-analyses-du-conflit-dans-la-r%C3%A9gion-des-grands-lacs.

Sentongo, Michael. 1997. "ADF was groomed in Sudan." *The New Vision*, September 13, 1997.

Shaw, Timothy M. 2003. "Regional Dimensions of Conflict and Peace-Building in Contemporary Africa." *Journal of International Development* 15: 487–498. https://doi.org/10.1002/jid.998.

Sheikh, Fawzia. 2005. "New danger from Ugandan rebel group?" Institute for War and Peace Reporting, June 6, 2005. Accessed August 14, 2020. https://iwpr.net/global-voices/new-danger-from-ugandan-rebel-group-0.

Shneiderman, Sara. 2010. "Are the Central Himalayas in Zomia? Some Scholarly and Political Considerations Across Time and Space." *Journal of Global History* 5 (2): 289–312. https://doi.org/10.1017/S1740022810000094.

Simala, Kenneth I., and Maurice Amutabi. 2005. "Small Arms, Cattle Raiding, and Borderlands: The Ilemi Triangle." In *Illicit Flows and Criminal Things: States, Borders, and the Other Side of Globalisation*, edited by Van Schendel, Willem, and Itty Abraham, 201–226. Bloomington: Indiana University Press.

Smucker, Philip, and Faye Bowers. 2003. "Iraq Regime Linked to Terror Group: Secret Iraqi Files Detail Contacts with Africa Group Linked to Al Qaeda." *The Christian Science Monitor*, April 18, 2003. Accessed August 14, 2020. https://www.csmonitor.com/2003/0418/p01s04-woiq.html.

Social Science in Humanitarian Action. 2018. "Uganda-DRC cross-border dynamics." Social Science in Humanitarian Action, December 15, 2018. Accessed August 15, 2020. https://reliefweb.int/report/democratic-republic-congo/uganda-drc-cross-border-dynamics.

Soguk, Nevzat. 2008. "Transversal Communication, Diaspora, and the Euro-Kurds." *Review of International Studies* 34 (S1): 173–192. Accessed August 13, 2020. http://www.jstor.com/stable/20542756.

Soguk, Nevzat, and Geoffrey Whitehall. 1999. "Wandering Grounds: Transversality, Identity, Territoriality, and Movement." *Millennium: Journal of International Studies* 28 (3): 675–698. https://doi.org/10.1177/03058298990280030301.

Sole, Marcellin. 2011. "Menace des rebelles ADF: l'intelligence géographique de l'Est de la RDC récupérée par les services occidentaux." *Journal Le Millénaire*. Accessed August 14, 2020. http://lemillenaireinfoplus.e-monsite.com/pages/est-de-la-rdc/menace-des-rebelles-adf.html.

Southall, Aidan. 1996. "Isolation and Underdevelopment: Periphery and Centre." In *Developing Uganda*, edited by Hansen, Holger Bernt, and Michael Twaddle. Oxford: James Currey.

Spittaels, Steven, and Filip Hilgert. 2008. "Mapping Conflict Motives: Eastern DRC." International Peace Information Service, March 4, 2008. Accessed August 14, 2020. https://ipisresearch.be/publication/mapping-conflict-motives-eastern-drc/.

Sserwanga, Moses. 1995. "20 rebels killed in Bundibugyo." *The New Vision*, March 17, 1995.

Sserwanga, Moses. 1997. "Civilians flee from Bundibugyo fighting." *The New Vision*, June 18, 1997.

Sserwanga, Moses. 1998a. "16 ADF killed in Congo." *The New Vision*, September 15, 1998.

Sserwanga, Moses. 1998b. "ADF 'feast on captives.'" *The New Vision*, April 4, 1998.

Sserwanga, Moses. 1998c. "Security raised at Congo border." *The New Vision*, May 1, 1998.
Sserwanga, Moses. 1999a. "ADF men flee UPDF offensive." *The New Vision*, May 19, 1999.
Sserwanga, Moses. 1999b. "The killing fields of Bundibugyo." *The New Vision*, April 26, 1999.
Sserwanga, Moses, and John Nzinjah. 1996a. "1000 troops fight rebels in Rwenzori." *The New Vision*, December 12, 1996.
Sserwanga, Moses, and John Nzinjah. 1996b. "Invaders planned Islamic state." *The New Vision*, November 21, 1996. Sserwanga, Moses, and John Nzinjah. 1997. "Rebels split in two." *The New Vision*, January 24, 1997.
Sserwanga, Moses, and John Nzinja. 2000. "ADF rebels no big deal, says Museveni." *The New Vision*, February 16, 2000.
Sserwanga, Moses, John Nzinjah, and Alfred Wasike. 1996. "Zairian troops invade Uganda." *The New Vision*, November 14, 1996.
Stacey, Tom. 2003. *Tribe: The Hidden History of the Mountain of the Moon*. London: Stacey International.
Staff Writers. 1989. "Rebels Plan Offensive on Fort Portal." *The Independent Observer*, August 24, 1989.
Staff Writers. 1996. "Border Brothers: As Zaire's Conflict Spreads, Kampala is Now Fighting or Backing Rebels on Three Borders." *Africa Confidential* 37 (25): 2–3. Accessed August 14, 2020. https://www.africa-confidential.com/article-preview/id/11226/Border_brothers.
Staff Writers. 1997. "Avoid vendettas!" *The New Vision*, October 18, 1997.
Staff Writers. 1999. "Call off the dogs of war." *The Economist*. 11 December.
Staff Writers. 2010. "Uganda's rebels seen behind border killing." *TerraDaily*, July 28, 2010. Accessed August 14, 2020. https://www.terradaily.com/reports/Ugandas_rebels_seen_behind_border_killing_999.html.
Stea, David, Jamie Zech, and Melissa Gray. 2010. "Change and Non-Change in the U.S.-Mexican Borderlands after NAFTA." In *Understanding Life in the Borderlands: Boundaries in Depth and in Motion*, edited by Zartman, I. William, 105–132. Athens: University of Georgia Press.
Stearns, Jason. 2010a. "x Blog." July 27, 2010. Accessed August 9, 2020. http://congosiasa.blogspot.ca/2010/07/congo-enters-axis-of-evil.html.
Stearns, Jason. 2010b. "Next Challenge for Congo: International Terrorism." *The Christian Science Monitor*, July 28, 2010. Accessed August 14, 2020. https://www.csmonitor.com/World/Africa/Africa-Monitor/2010/0728/Next-challenge-for-Congo-International-terrorism.
Stearns, Jason. 2011. *Dancing in the Glory of Monsters: The Collapse of the Congo and the Great War of Africa*. New York: Public Affairs.
Stearns, Jason. 2012. "Congo Siasa Blog." February 9, 2012. Accessed August 9, 2020. http://congosiasa.blogspot.com/search?updated-max=2012-02-12T11:35:00-08:00&max-results=7.
Steinhart, Edward I. 1999. *Conflict and Collaboration in the Kingdoms of Western Uganda, 1890–1907*. Kampala: Fountain Publishers Ltd.

Struck, Bernhard. 1910. "On the Ethnographic Nomenclature of the Uganda-Congo Border." *Journal of the Royal African Society* 9 (35): 275–288. https://doi.org/10.1093/oxfordjournals.afraf.a098938.

Studdard, Kaysie. 2004. "War Economies in a Regional Context: Overcoming the Challenges of Transformation." International Peace Academy, March 2004. Accessed August 14, 2020. https://www.ipinst.org/wp-content/uploads/publications/wareconomies.pdf.

Sturgeon, Janet. 2005. *Border Landscapes: The Politics of Akha Land Use in China and Thailand*. Seattle: University of Washington Press.

Sweet, Rachel. 2015. "Guest Blog: Politics and Business Intersect in String of North Kivu Killings." Congo Research Group, Center on International Cooperation, January 6, 2015. Accessed August 15, 2020. http://congoresearchgroup.org/guest-blog-politics-and-business/.

Sweet, Rachel. 2019. "Militating the Peace: UN Intervention Against Congo's 'Terrorist' Rebels." Lawfare Institute, June 2, 2019. Accessed August 15, 2020. https://www.lawfareblog.com/militarizing-peace-un-intervention-against-congos-terrorist-rebels.

Syahuka-Muhindo, Arthur. 1991. *The Rwenzururu Movement and the Democratic Struggle.* Kampala: Centre for Basic Research.

Syahuka-Muhindo, Arthur. 2008. "Migrations and Social Formation in the Rwenzori Region." In *Rwenzori: Histories and Cultures of an African Mountain*, edited by Pennacini, Cecilia, and Hermann Wittenberg, 18-58. Kampala: Fountain Publishers.

Tangseefa, Decha. 2003. "Flight to/through 'the Door': Imperceptible Naked-Karens and the Thai-Burmese In-Between Spaces." Presented at the International Convention of Asian Scholars, Singapore.

Tarrow, Sidney. 2007. "Book Review Essay: Inside Insurgencies: Politics and Violence in an Age of Civil War." *Perspectives on Politics* 5 (3): 587–600. https://doi.org/10.1017/S1537592707071575.

Taylor, Ian. 2003. "Conflict in Central Africa: Clandestine Networks and Regional/Global Configurations." *Review of African Political Economy* 30 (95): 45–55. Accessed August 13, 2020. http://www.jstor.com/stable/4006738.

Terdman, Moshe. 2006. "Tabliqi Groups in Uganda—The Allied Democratic Forces." *Islam in Africa Newsletter* 1 (4). Thakur, Monika. 2008. "Demilitarising Militias in the Kivus (eastern Democratic Republic of Congo)." *African Security Review* 17 (1): 52–67. https://doi.org/10.1080/10246029.2008.9627459.

Thawite, John. 2000. "Benz spills ADF secrets." *Sunday Vision*, December 31, 2000.

The Economist. 2013. "Afrighanistan?" *The Economist*, January 26, 2013. Accessed August 15, 2020. https://www.economist.com/leaders/2013/01/26/afrighanistan.

The Independent Team. 2009b. "Sudan government trains ADF rebels." *The Independent*, April 7, 2009.

The Independent Team. 2010a. "ADF dispatches urban terror squad." *The Independent*, November 16, 2010.

The Independent Team. 2010b. "ADF rebels intensify recruitment in Iganga." *The Independent*, December 7, 2010.

The Independent Team. 2010c. "ADF sets up tactical base in Kasokoso in Kampala." *The* Independent, November 9, 2010.

The Independent Team. 2010d. "Intelligence track ADF communication." *The Independent*, August 2, 2010.

The New Humanitarian. 2015. "A counterinsurgency failure in eastern Congo." *The New Humanitarian*, September 11, 2015. Accessed August 15, 2020. https://www.thenewhumanitarian.org/news/2015/09/11/counterinsurgency-failure-eastern-congo.

Tilouine, Joan. 2017. "La menace djihadiste dans l'est de la RDC est une pure invention." *Le Monde Afrique*, March 6, 2017. Accessed August 15, 2020. https://www.lemonde.fr/afrique/article/2017/03/06/la-menace-djihadiste-a-l-est-de-la-rdc-est-une-pure-invention_5090023_3212.html.

Titeca, Kristof. 2009a. "The Changing Cross-Border Trade Dynamics Between North-Western Uganda, North-Eastern Congo and Southern Sudan." Crisis States Research Centre. Accessed August 14, 2020. http://eprints.lse.ac.uk/28477/1/WP63.2.pdf.

Titeca, Kristof. 2009b. "The 'Masai' and Miraa: Public Authority, Vigilance and Criminality in a Ugandan Border Town." *Journal of Modern African Studies* 47 (2): 291–317. https://doi.org/10.1017/S0022278X0900384X.

Titeca, Kristof. 2016. "Jihadis in Congo? Probably not." *The Washington Post*, September 27, 2016. Accessed August 15, 2020. https://www.washingtonpost.com/news/monkey-cage/wp/2016/09/27/heres-why-its-a-problem-that-congos-un-peacekeeping-force-is-blaming-international-jihadis-for-these-killings-and-attacks/.

Titeca, Kristof, and Ronald R. Atkinson. 2014. "Why is the US hunting for Joseph Kony?" *Al Jazeera*, May 11, 2014. Accessed June 23, 2021. https://www.aljazeera.com/opinions/2014/5/11/why-is-the-us-hunting-for-joseph-kony.

Titeca, Kristof, and Theophile Costeur. 2015. "An LRA for Everyone: How Different Actors Frame the Lord's Resistance Army." *African Affairs* 114 (454): 92–114.

Titeca, Kristof, and Daniel Fahey. 2016. "The Many Faces of a Rebel Group: The Allied Democratic Forces in the Democratic Republic of Congo." *International Affairs* 92 (5): 1189–1206. https://doi.org/10.1111/1468-2346.12703.

Titeca, Kristof, and Koen Vlassenroot. 2012. "Rebels Without Borders in the Rwenzori Borderland? A Biography of the Allied Democratic Forces." *Journal of Eastern African Studies* 6 (1): 154–176. https://doi.org/10.1080/17531055.2012.664708.

Tsongo, Eric. 2021. "Est du Congo: Ce sont des M23, pas des ADF." *fBeni Lubero Online*, January 7, 2021. Accessed June 24, 2021. https://benilubero.com/est-du-congo-ce-sont-des-m23-pas-des-adf/.

Tumwine, Henry, and Kyomuhendo Muhanga. 1997. "Bundibugyo rebels burn people alive." *The New Vision*, June 24, 1997.

Tusasirwe, Benson. 1996. "Uganda's worst case scenario." *The New Vision*, November 21, 1996.

Tusiime, Columbus. 2008. "ADF recruits in DR Congo." *The New Vision*, April 21, 2008.

Uganda. Human Rights Commission. 2001. "2000-2001 Annual Report." Kampala: Uganda Human Rights Commission.

Uganda. Human Rights Commission. 2005. "2005 Annual Report." Kampala: Uganda Human Rights Commission.

Uganda. Human Rights Commission. 2006. "2006 Annual Report." Kampala: Uganda Human Rights Commission.

Uganda. Parliament. Session Records June 2, 1999. Kampala: Parliament of Uganda Library.

Uganda. Parliament. Session Records July 14, 1999. Kampala: Parliament of Uganda Library.

Uganda. Parliament. Session Records July 15, 1999. Kampala: Parliament of Uganda Library.

Uganda. Parliament. Session Records July 22, 1999. Kampala: Parliament of Uganda Library.

Uganda. Parliament. Session Records September 20, 1999. Kampala: Parliament of Uganda Library.

Uganda. Parliament. Session Records July 13, 2000. Kampala: Parliament of Uganda Library.

Uganda. Parliament. Session Records July 27, 2001. Kampala: Parliament of Uganda Library.

Uganda. Parliament. Session Records April 29, 2003. Kampala: Parliament of Uganda Library.

United Nations Meetings Coverage and Press Releases. 2001. "Secretary-General Evokes Promise Inherent in Launch of African Union." SG/SM/7884-AFR/331, July 9, 2001. Accessed September 25, 2020. https://www.un.org/press/en/2001/sgsm7884.doc.htm.

United Nations Office of the High Commissioner for Human Rights (OHCHR). 2010. "Report of the Mapping Exercise Documenting the Most Serious Violations of Human Rights and International Humanitarian Law Committed Within the Territory of the Democratic Republic of the Congo Between March 1993 and June 2003." OHCHR, August 2010. Accessed August 14, 2020. https://www.refworld.org/docid/4ca99bc22.html.

U.S. Department of State. 2021. "State Department Terrorist Designations of ISIS Affiliates and Leaders in the Democratic Republic of the Congo and Mozambique." *U.S. Department of State*, March 10, 2021. Accessed June 17, 2021. https://www.state.gov/state-department-terrorist-designations-of-isis-affiliates-and-leaders-in-the-democratic-republic-of-the-congo-and-mozambique/

Van Acker, Frank. 2000. "Ethnicity and Institutional Reform: A Case of Ugandan Exceptionalism?" In *Politics of Identity and Economics of Conflict in the Great Lakes Region*, edited by Doom, Ruddy, and Jan Gorus, 149–173. Brussels: VUB University Press.

Van Acker, Frank, and Koen Vlassenroot. 2001. "Les 'Mai-Mai' et les Fonctions de la Violence Milicienne dans l'Est du Congo." *Politique Africaine* 4 (84): 103–116. Accessed August 13, 2020. https://www.cairn.info/revue-politique-africaine-2001-4-page-103.htm.

Van Schendel, Willem. 2005. "Spaces of Engagement: How Borderlands, Illicit Flows, and Territorial States Interlock." In *Illicit Flows and Criminal Things:*

States, Borders, and the Other Side of Globalisation, edited by Van Schendel, Willem, and Itty Abraham, 38–68. Bloomington: Indiana University Press.

Van Schendel, Willem, and Erik de Maaker. 2014. "Asian Borderlands: Introducing their Permeability, Strategic Uses and Meanings." *Journal of Borderlands Studies* 29 (1): 3–9. https://doi.org/10.1080/08865655.2014.892689.

Verweijen, Judith. 2016. "Stable Instability: Political Settlements and Armed Groups in the Congo." Rift Valley Institute. Accessed August 10, 2020. https://riftvalley.net/publication/stable-instability.

Verweijen, Judith, and Claude Iguma Wakenge. 2015. "Understanding Armed Group Proliferation in the Eastern Congo." Rift Valley Institute, December 2015. Accessed August 15, 2020. https://riftvalley.net/publication/understanding-armed-group-proliferation-eastern-congo.

Vignal, Leila. 2017. "The Changing Borders and Borderlands of Syria in a Time of Conflict." *International Affairs* 93 (4): 809–827. https://doi.org/10.1093/ia/iix113.

Vision Reporter. 1992. "RCs quiz envoy." *The New Vision*, August 27, 1992.

Vision Reporter. 2015. "Muslim Clerics' murder suspects linked to ADF." *The New Vision*, January 13, 2015. Accessed August 15, 2020. https://www.newvision.co.ug/news/1318872/muslim-clerics-murder-suspects-linked-adf.

Vlassenroot, Koen, and Hans Romkema. 2002. "The Emergence of a New Order? Resources and War in Eastern Congo." *The Journal of Humanitarian Assistance*: 1-12. Accessed August 13, 2020. http://hdl.handle.net/1854/LU-159674.

Vogel, Christoph, and Jason K. Stearns. 2018. "Kivu's Intractable Security Conundrum, Revisited." *African Affairs* 117 (469): 695–707. https://doi.org/10.1093/afraf/ady033.

Volk, Lucia. 2009. "Martyrs at the Margins: The Politics of Neglect in Lebanon's Borderlands." *Middle Eastern Studies* 45 (2): 263–282. https://doi.org/10.1080/00263200802697365.

Vorrath, Judith. 2007. "African Borderlands: Below, Beyond or Against the State?" Presented at the International Studies Association, Chicago.

Vorrath, Judith. 2010. "On the Margin of Statehood? State-Society Relations in African Borderlands." In *Understanding Life in the Borderlands: Boundaries in Depth and in Motion*, edited by Zartman, I. William, 85–104. Athens: University of Georgia Press.

Vwakyanakazi, Mukohya. 1991. "Import and Export in the Second Economy in North Kivu." In *The Real Economy of Zaire: The Contribution of Smuggling and Other Unofficial Activities to National Wealth*, edited by MacGaffey, Janet, 43–54. Philadelphia: University of Pennsylvania Press.

Wakabi, Wairagala. 2005. "DRC and Uganda army to destroy rebel camps." *The East African*, February 21, 2005.

Walther, Oliver J., and William F. S. Miles. 2018. "Introduction: States, Borders and Political Violence in Africa." In *African Border Disorders: Addressing Transnational Extremist Organizations*, edited by Walther, Olivier J., and William F. S. Miles, 1–14. Oxon: Routledge.

Wamboka, Nabusayi L. 1998. "Rebels succeeded in one motive: to instil terror among people." *The Monitor*, June 24, 1998.

Wasike, Alfred. 2005. "ADF reorganises in eastern DRC." *The New Vision*, February 27, 2005.

Wastl-Walter, Doris. 2011. "Introduction." In *The Ashgate Research Companion to Border Studies*, edited by Wastl-Walter, Doris, 1–10. New York: Routledge.

Weeraratne, Suranjan, and Sterling Recker. 2018. "The Isolated Islamists: The Case of the Allied Democratic Forces in the Ugandan-Congolese Borderland." *Terrorism and Political Violence* 30 (1): 22–46. https://doi.org/10.1080/09546553.2016.1139577.

Weinstein, Jeremy M. 2007. *Inside Rebellion: The Politics of Insurgent Violence*. New York: Cambridge University Press.

Weis, Toni. 2009. "Precarious Statehood: Understanding Regional Conflict in the Horn of Africa and Beyond." *Human Security Journal* 8: 57–72.

West, Sunguta. 2019. "Has Islamic State Really Entered the Congo and is an IS Province There a Gamble?" *Terrorism Monitor* 17 (11). Accessed August 15, 2020. https://jamestown.org/program/has-islamic-state-really-entered-the-congo-and-is-an-is-province-there-a-gamble/.

Whitaker, Beth Elise. 2010. "Compliance Among Weak States: Africa and the Counter-Terrorism Regime." *Review of International Studies* 36 (3): 639–662. https://www.jstor.org/stable/40783289.

Whitehouse, Bruce. 2018. "Public Perceptions of Violent Extremism in Mali." In *African Border Disorders: Addressing Transnational Extremist Organizations*, edited by Walther, Olivier J., and William F. S. Miles, 170–186. Oxon: Routledge.

Wilson, Thomas M., and Hastings Donnan. 1998. *Border Identities: Nation and State at International Frontiers*. Cambridge: Cambridge University Press.

Womakuyu, Frederick. 2010. "Bundibugyo in fear over rumours of ADF regrouping in DR Congo." *The New Vision*, April 7, 2010.

Wood, Elisabeth. 2003. *Insurgent Collective Action and Civil War in El Salvador*. New York: Cambridge University Press.

Wood, Elisabeth. 2013. "Transnational Dynamics of Civil War: Where Do We Go From Here?" In *Transnational Dynamics of Civil War*, edited by Checkel, Jeffrey T., 231–258. Cambridge: Cambridge University Press.

World Bank. 2009. *DDR in the Democratic Republic of Congo: Program Update*. Washington: World Bank.

Xinhua. 2007. "Xinjua told: Ugandan army kills 4 ADF rebels in west Kampala." *Xinhua*, April 4, 2007. http://www.xinhuanet.com/english/2017-12/25/c_136851430.htm.

Zartman, I. William. 2010. "Introduction: Identity, Movement, and Response." In *Understanding Life in the Borderlands: Boundaries in Depth and in Motion*, edited by William I. Zartman, 1-20. Athens: University of Georgia Press.

Zeller, Wolfgang. 2010. "Illicit Resource Flows in Sugango: Making War and Profit in the Border Triangle of Sudan, Uganda and Congo–DRC." In *Exploring the Security-Development Nexus: Perspectives from Nepal, Northern Uganda and 'Sugango,'* edited by Alava, Henni, 111–129. Helsinki: Ministry for Foreign Affairs of Finland.

Zhurzhenko, Tatiana. 2011. "Borders and Memory." In *The Ashgate Research Companion to Border Studies*, edited by Wastl-Walter, Doris, 63–84. New York: Routledge.

MONUSCO DOCUMENTS

MONUSCO Document One
MONUSCO interview briefing note. Note is titled "Kampala Mission" and written on 19 February 2010.
MONUSCO Document Two
Letter written by the ADF, addressed to the Mayor of Beni, North Kivu, Congo. Letter is titled "Zone Operationnelle des ADF/NALU dans le Rwenzori", and written on 20 February 2011.
MONUSCO Document Three
Letter written by the ADF, to the Congolese population in the Grand Nord of North Kivu, Congo. Letter is titled "Message to Congolese", and written on 2 July 2010 (Unofficial English translation by UN).
MONUSCO Document Four
MONUSCO DDRRR debriefing note. Note is titled "Col. Bwonadeke Winny (Safari Kitobi Ismael) aka Jaguar", and written on 19 July 2010.
MONUSCO Document Five
MONUSCO DDRRR debriefing note, compiled and drafted by Mwitiravali Sikuli. Note is titled "Fiche Synthese d'Interview de Kasereka Kitambala, RDC ADF/NALU", and written on 24 February 2010.
MONUSCO Document Six
MONUSCO interrogation report for ADF suspect. Report is titled "Abdallah Bikumbi", and date is unspecified.
MONUSCO Document Seven
MONUSCO DDRRR document. Document is titled "Ex-Combatant's Interview Form", and written on 9 February 2010.
MONUSCO Document Eight
MONUSCO DDRRR document. Document is untitled, but is a "case study" of the debriefing of four ADF boys, which took place between 17-21 February 2012.
MONUSCO Document Nine
MONUSCO DDRRR debriefing note. Note is titled "Interview of Eritier Vakalani, a Congolese Ex-Combatant from ADF/NALU Group", and written on 18 November 2009.
MONUSCO Document Ten
MONUSCO Interview Document. Document is titled "Interview of Kambale Idi Musa: Congolese ADF", and date is unspecified.
MONUSCO Document Eleven
MONUSCO DDRRR debriefing note. Note is untitled, but is a debriefing report on Kambale Kitambala (aka Afande Mulozi) Nzalamingi, and written on 22 December 2010.

MONUSCO Document Twelve
MONUSCO DDRRR debriefing note. Note is titled "Interview Report of ADF CAAGs", and written in April 2010.
MONUSCO Document Thirteen
MONUSCO DDRRR debriefing note. Note is titled "Kasereka Kitambala Second Interview", and written on 25 February 2010.
MONUSCO Document Fourteen
MONUSCO DDRRR debriefing note, compiled and drafted by Gertrude Buhendwa. Document is titled "Interview Form of Mumbere Sylvain, RDC ADF/NALU", and written on 24 March 2010.
MONUSCO Document Fifteen
MONUSCO DDRRR debriefing note. Note is titled "Identification Form Ugandan Ex-Combatant for Muhammad Ismael", and written on 8 July 2011.
MONUSCO Document Sixteen
MONUSCO DDRRR debriefing note. Note is titled "Report of the Interview with Congolese ADF/NALU", and written on 17 July 1999.
MONUSCO Document Seventeen
MONUSCO fieldwork document. Document is titled "Special ADF Analysis: Post-Field Visit Report: Beni (14-19 March 2012)", and date is unspecified.
MONUSCO Document Eighteen
MONUSCO ADF assessment document. Document is titled "ADF Overview", and written on 25 March 2010.
MONUSCO Document Nineteen
MONUSCO ADF structure document. Document is titled "ADF Structure", and written on 10 October 2010.
MONUSCO Document Twenty
Transcript of voice recording by ADF leader, Jamil Mukulu. Document is titled "Lubumbashi Statement of Commitment to Peace Talks From Jamil Mukulu—Commander Allied Democratic Forces", and recorded on 14 November 2008.

INTERVIEWS

Every interview entry includes three pieces of data:
Interviewee's place of occupation (and/or occupation itself in some cases, where relevant)
Interviewee's occupation (title and/or place of work)
Date of interview
Location of interview (including village/town/city/district, and country)
A. Individual Interviews (informal interviews, email interviews, and telephone interviews are specifically denoted as such)
Interview One
Uganda—Great Lakes Programme, International Alert; 18 August 2010; International Alert offices, Kampala, Uganda.
Interview Two

Youth Education Services Uganda; 30 April 2010; Youth Education Services Uganda offices, Fort Portal, Uganda.
Interview Three
WFP; 22 April 2010; WFP offices, Kampala, Uganda.
Interview Four
UNHCR Representation in Uganda; 24 January 2011; UNHCR Representation in Uganda offices, Kampala, Uganda.
Interview Five
OCHA; 23 August 2011; OCHA offices, Beni, Congo.
Interview Six
Reverend and Journalist, Voice of Tooro Radio Station; 11 May 2010; Voice of Tooro Radio Station offices, Fort Portal, Uganda.
Interview Seven
Reverend and local conflict resolution expert in North Kivu; 30 August 2011; L'Auberge Hotel, Butembo, Congo.
Interview Eight
Search for Common Ground; 16 September 2011; Search for Common Ground offices, Goma, Congo.
Interview Nine
MONUSCO East Division, Goma, MONUSCO; 1 February 2011; N/A (Email).
Interview Ten
Graduate Student, Mountains of the Moon University; 3 May 2010; Mountains of the Moon University offices, Fort Portal, Uganda.
Interview Eleven
CARE International; 24 August 2010; CARE International offices, Kampala, Uganda.
Interview Twelve
Agape; 31 January 2011; The Boma, Entebbe, Uganda.
Interview Thirteen
Kasese local government; 6 September 2010; Deputy RDC's office, Kasese, Uganda.
Interview Fourteen
Direction Générale de Migration (DGM) Butembo; 29 August 2011; DGM Butembo's office, Butembo, North Kivu.
Interview Fifteen
MONUSCO Kampala Liaison Office; 24 January 2011; MONUSCO Kampala Liaison Office, Kampala, Uganda.
Interview Sixteen
International Committee of the Red Cross (ICRC) offices; 21 April 2010; ICRC, Kampala, Uganda.
Interview Seventeen
Fédération des Enterprises du Congo (FEC); 29 August 2011; FEC Butembo offices, Butembo, Congo.
Interview Eighteen
Action Aid; 1 May 2010; Gardens Restaurant, Fort Portal, Uganda.
Interview Nineteen

Adventist Development and Relief Agency; 21 August 2011; Hotel la Référence Plus, Beni, Congo.
Interview Twenty
Belgian Development Agency; 27 April 2010; Belgian Development Agency offices, Kampala, Uganda.
Interview Twenty-One
Norwegian Refugee Council; 15 February 2011; N/A (Email).
Interview Twenty-Two
IOM; 26 April 2010; IOM offices, Kampala, Uganda.
Interview Twenty-Three
Pole Institute; 23 August 2010; N/A (Email).
Interview Twenty-Four
Translator/Fixer; Various dates throughout August and September 2011; Various locations throughout North Kivu, Congo.
Interview Twenty-Five
News Editor, *The New Vision*; 19 April 2010; *The New Vision* offices, Kampala, Uganda.
Interview Twenty-Six
Amnesty Commission, Western District; 13 May 2010; Amnesty Commission, Western District offices, Kasese, Uganda.
Interview Twenty-Seven
Give Me A Chance; 25 November 2009; Give Me A Chance offices, Kampala, Uganda.
Interview Twenty-Eight
Banyabindi community leader; 6 September 2010; Yasin Tumwine's home, Kasese, Uganda.
Interview Twenty-Nine
Ministry of Defence/JATT; 18 August 2010; Phase Two Restaurant, Kampala, Uganda.
Interview Thirty
Amnesty Commission, Central District; 1 February 2011; N/A (Email).
Interview Thirty-One
Amnesty Commission, Central District; 13 August 2010; Amnesty Commission, Central District offices, Kampala, Uganda.
Interview Thirty-Two
Rwenzori Forum for Peace and Justice; 8 May 2010; Mountains of the Moon University offices, Fort Portal, Uganda.
Interview Thirty-Three
Centre d'Accompagnement des Autochtones Pygmies et Minoritaires Vulnérables; 20 August 2011; Hotel la Référence Plus, Beni, Congo.
Interview Thirty-Four
MONUSCO Kampala Liaison Office; 20 April 2010; MONUSCO Kampala Liaison Office, Kampala, Uganda.
Interview Thirty-Five
International Crisis Group; 29 June 2012; N/A (Telephone).

Interview Thirty-Six
Kasese local government; 13 May 2010; Kasese local government offices, Kasese, Uganda.
Interview Thirty-Seven
Journalist, Radio Okapi; 26 August 2011; MONUSCO Butembo Base offices, Butembo, Congo.
Interview Thirty-Eight
Researcher and Lecturer, Mountains of the Moon University; 30 April 2010; Mountains of the Moon University offices, Fort Portal, Uganda.
Interview Thirty-Nine
Kabarole Research and Resource Centre; 4 May 2010; Kabarole Research and Resource Centre offices, Fort Portal, Uganda.
Interview Forty
Caritas; 6 May 2010; Virika Cathedral offices, Fort Portal, Uganda.
Interview Forty-One
Sub-Dean, Kabarole Cathedral; 7 May 2010; Musobozi's home, Fort Portal, Uganda.
Interview Forty-Two
Tour Guide, Kabarole Tours and Safari Ltd.; 2 May 2010; Rwenzori Mountains, (western) Uganda (Informal—took place during a two day hike through mountainous former ADF territory).
Interview Forty-Three
Former ADF member; 16 May 2010; Local park, Kasese, Uganda.
Interview Forty-Four
Movement Control, MONUSCO; 16 September 2011; Linda Hotel, Goma, Congo.
Interview Forty-Five
Rwenzori Peace Bridge of Reconciliation; 9 September 2010; Rwenzori Peace Bridge of Reconciliation offices, Kasese, Uganda.
Interview Forty-Six
Agape; 12 May 2010; Agape offices, Kasese, Uganda.
Interview Forty-Seven
UNHCR Ghana; 26 August 2010; N/A (Email).
Interview Forty-Eight
DFID; 27 January 2011; DFID offices, Kampala, Uganda.
Interview Forty-Nine
Kasese local government; 6 September 2010; RDC's office, Kasese, Uganda.
Interview Fifty
UNDP; 13 September 2011; UNDP offices, Goma, Congo.
Interview Fifty-One
Amnesty Commission, Beni Liaison Office; 6 September 2011; Amnesty Commission, Beni Liaison Office, Beni, Congo.
Interview Fifty-Two
Saferworld; 20 January 2011; Saferworld offices, Kampala, Uganda.
Interview Fifty-Three
MONUSCO Beni Base; 22 August 2011; MONUSCO Beni Base offices, Beni, Congo.

Interview Fifty-Four
MONUSCO Butembo Base; 26 August 2011; MONUSCO Butembo Base offices, Butembo, Congo.
Interview Fifty-Five
Solidarités International; 13 September 2011; Solidarités International offices, Goma, Congo.
Interview Fifty-Six
Pole Institute; 20 August 2010; N/A (Email).
Interview Fifty-Seven
Manager, Kabarole Tours and Safari Ltd.; 28 April 2010; Kabarole Tours and Safari Ltd. headquarters, Fort Portal, Uganda (Informal).
Interview Fifty-Eight
Student, Uganda Martyrs University; 21 January 2011; Munyonyo, Kampala, Uganda.
Interview Fifty-Nine
Centre for Basic Research; 15 April 2010; Centre for Basic Research headquarters, Kampala, Uganda (Informal).
Interview Sixty
NAYODE; 1, 6, and 13 September 2010; NAYODE offices and various locations throughout Kasese, Uganda.
Interview Sixty-One
Parents Concern; 16 September 2010; Parents Concern offices, Fort Portal, Uganda.
Interview Sixty-Two
Taxicab driver; Various dates throughout August and September 2010; Various locations throughout western Uganda (Informal).
Interview Sixty-Three
MONUSCO; 24 August 2011; MONUSCO offices, Beni, Congo.
B. Focus Group Interviews (where names are not provided, the number of participants in the focus group interview is noted)
Interview Sixty-Four
Agape members and survivors of ADF violence (fifteen); 15 September 2010; Agape offices, Kasese, Uganda.
Interview Sixty-Five
Bakonjo Joint Cooperative staff members; 16 September 2010; Bakonjo Joint Cooperative offices, Kyarumba village, (western) Uganda.
Interview Sixty-Six
Bukana Rural Development Association staff members (six); 12 May 2010; Kirembo village, (western) Uganda.
Interview Sixty-Seven
Centre d'Accompagnement des Autochthones Pygmées et Minoritaires Vulnérables staff members (five); 20 August 2011; Hotel la Référence Plus, Beni, Congo.
Interview Sixty-Eight
CRC staff members (five); 24 August 2011; CRC offices, Beni, Congo.
Interview Sixty-Nine
FAO staff members (three); 22 August 2011; FAO offices, Beni, Congo.
Interview Seventy

Former ADF members (five), accompanied and translated by Amnesty Commission, Western District; 4 September 2010; Community courtroom building in Kisinga village, (western) Uganda.

Interview Seventy-One

Former ADF members (five), accompanied and translated by Amnesty Commission, Western District; 4 September 2010; Community meeting point in a village outside of Bwera, (western) Uganda.

Interview Seventy-Two

Former ADF members (four), accompanied and translated by Amnesty Commission, Western District; 5 September 2010; Community meeting point in a village outside of Bwera, (western) Uganda.

Interview Seventy-Three

Former ADF members (four), accompanied and translated by Amnesty Commission, Western District; 5 September 2010; Community meeting point in a village outside of Bwera, (western) Uganda.

Interview Seventy-Four

Former ADF members (eight), accompanied and translated by Amnesty Commission, Western District; 16 May 2010; Pan Afrique Hotel, Bwera, (western) Uganda.

Interview Seventy-Five

Former ADF members (three), accompanied and translated by Amnesty Commission, Western District; 16 May 2010; Pan Afrique Hotel, Bwera, (western) Uganda.

Interview Seventy-Six

IWDP staff members; 26 August 2010; IWDP offices, Fort Portal, Uganda.

Interview Seventy-Seven

Rwenzururu Kingdom Cabinet staff; 13 September 2010; Rwenzururu Kingdom Cabinet offices, Kasese, Uganda.

Interview Seventy-Eight

Uganda Technical College Kichwamba staff members (six); 27 August 2010; Uganda Technical College Kichwamba offices and classrooms, Kichwamba, (western) Uganda.

Interview Seventy-Nine

UNICEF staff members; 27 April 2010; UNICEF offices, Kampala, Uganda

C. Interview and Source Data Collected by Others

Interview Eighty

Personal interview notes from American associate professor and researcher—"ADF ex combatant interviews"; Associate Professor, Harvard University; Acquired from source on 28 January 2011; N/A.

Interview Eighty-One

Personal interview notes from American associate professor and researcher—"ADF Printed Material"; Associate Professor, Harvard University; Acquired from source on 28 January 2011; N/A.

Index

Abdoulhakim, Sachimbi, 154
abduction, 237n16
actors: in Beni massacres, 224–25; in borderlands, 118–19; Mai Mai militias as, 24n13; national, 9; NGOs as, 50, 103; non-state, 53; political, 24n12; transnational, 54–55; violence by, 51, 58
ADF. *See* Allied Democratic Forces
Afghanistan, 241; conflict in, 33–34; Pakistan and, 56; Pashtun tribes in, 39; Taliban in, 13–14
Africa. *See specific topics*
African Union Mission in Somalia, 155
Akech, Jacob, 37
Ali, Lyavala, 127–28
Ali, Moses, 109
Aliker, Martin, 133
alliances, 158–59, 162–63, 199n28
Allied Democratic Forces (ADF): for Africa, 206–9; alliances with, 162–63; amnesty with, 247n2; Beni massacres for, 221–24; borderlands grievances for, 140–44; branding by, 224–25; business networks for, 233–34; business practices of, 171–76; children for, 159–62; civilian collaboration for, 144–48, 191–97; for civil war, 14; conflict with, 217–19, 247n1; for Congo, 25n19, 198n8; crime by, 169–70; for DDRRR, 115, 135, 153–54, 164–66; economics of, 231–33; for FARDC, 172; globalization for, 201–4, 242–45; for government, 178–83; history of, 1–5, 101–7; identity of, 226; information for, 116–19, 163–68; internal factions in, 135–37; ISIS and, 204–6, 209–12; Islam for, 105, 229–31; LRA compared to, 118; Mai Mai militias for, 190; material resources for, 120–23, 169–71; membership in, 226–27; for Mobutu, 149n5; NALU for, 107–11, 119, 123–27, 131, 136–40, 157–59; Nande for, 114, 196; negotiations with, 198n17; political geography factors for, 188–90; in politics, 127–31, 149n7; recruitment for, 110–15, 152–57, 197n5, 227–29; reputation of, 214–15; resiliency of, 5–6; Rwenzori borderland for, 17–18, 68–69, 97, 108–9, 151, 239–40, 246–47; scholarship on, 10–12, 18–21, 133–34; Sudan for, 130–31; Tabliqs for, 11; tactics by, 185–88; territorial control practices of, 176–78; torture by, 198n9; trade for, 235–36; training

293

for, 169–71; Uganda before, 66; for UN, 2, 163–66; for UPDF, 146–47, 186; violence by, 105–6, 132–35, 183–84, 212–14; in Western Uganda, 219–21
Amba, 75–76, 98n5
Amin, Idi, 109, 148n3
amnesty, with ADF, 247n2
Amnesty Act, 117, 143
Anderson, Malcolm, 60n7
Annan, Kofi, 6–7
Asia, 38–41, 92–93
Azarya, Victor, 40

Bagenda, Emmanuel, 126
Bakonjo Life History Research Association, 73–75
Bal, Ellen, 36
Baluku, Musa Seka, 202, 237n6
Bamba, 72, 98n7
Bamukoko, Saambili, 175
Bamuturaki, Jackie Sharon, 72
Bangladesh, 122
Bantariza, Shaban, 114
barbarians, 63n39
Baud, Michiel, 34
Bauma, Lucien, 202
Bazenguissa-Ganga, Remy, 48
Bazira, Amon, 81, 107–8
BBC News, 214
Belgium, 84, 95, 99n7, 99n20
Bell, Hesketh, 67
Bel'Oka, Nicaise Kibel, 227
Beni massacres, 205, 216–17, 221–25
Berlin Conference, 31, 35, 67
Bleiker, Roland, 9
BLHRA. *See* Bakonjo Life History Research Association
Boko Haram, 52, 205, 213, 214–15
borderlands: actors in, 118–19; borderland conceptual framework, 27–30; conflict in, 29–35, 147–48; conflict management in, 239–42; consolidated, 77–83, 90–97; as contested economic space, 57–60; as contested political space, 49–54; as contested social space, 54–57; disenfranchisement in, 111–13, 159–62; economics in, 45–49, 62n27; FARDC in, 162–63, 215–17; grievances, 140–44; identity in, 60, 62n26, 148; in Latin America, 53; monopolies in, 124–26; for Nande, 67, 174; in political science, 29–30; politics in, 35–41, 71–72, 88; rough terrain in, 62n34; safety in, 86–87; scholarship on, 245–47; smuggling in, 92; society in, 41–45, 178–79, 226–27; territorial accessibility in, 126–27; trade in, 62n29, 85–86, 181–82; for Uganda, 198n14; UPDF in, 140–41, 149n11; violence in, 245. *See also specific topics*
boundary activation, 56
Brazil, 246
bribery, 46
Britain, 69–70, 73, 98n9, 99n20
British East Africa Company, 67
Bronson, Bennet, 58
Buhaug, Halvard, 50
Bulumosi, Donat, 174
Burundi, 85, 155–56
Busiinge, Christopher, 72
business networks, 233–34

Cameroon, 52
Cassanelli, Lee, 47
Central Africa. *See specific topics*
Central African Republic, 7, 51
Chad, 7, 52
Chambugong, Timour Claquin, 36
Charles, Bakkabulindi, 142
Chazan, Naomi, 40
children, 154, 205–6; for ADF, 159–62; in Mai Mai militias, 163, 228; rebel conflict for, 211–12; recruitment of, 161–62, 166–67; for Tabliqs, 230; women and, 191–92, 221–24
China, 37, 42–43, 246

Christians, 104–5, 148n1, 156, 211, 214, 242–43
civilians: adaptation by, 49; alliances for, 199n28; collaboration by, 144–48, 191–97; elitism for, 89–90; FARDC for, 193–95, 237n9; military for, 61n15; Nande, 81; politics for, 15–16, 24n11; rebel conflict for, 18–19, 185–86; social justice for, 57–58; trust from, 55–56; violence for, 4, 134; war for, 14–15, 54–55
CNDP. *See* Congrès National pour la Défense du Peuple
coffee, 93–94
collaboration, by civilians, 144–48, 191–97
Collier, Paul, 7
Colombia, 53, 55, 246
colonialism: Britain in, 69–70; colonial marginalization, 68–72, 84–87; for Congo, 83; nationalism in, 98n11; post-colonial peripherality, 72–77, 87–90; religion in, 95; trade in, 91
conflict: with ADF, 217–19, 247n1; in Afghanistan, 33–34; in Asia, 38–39; borderland analytical frameworks for, 20–21; in borderlands, 29–35, 147–48; in Congo, 1–3, 113–15; entrepreneurs, 59–60; from ethnicity, 86; FARDC in, 152, 171, 179; FDLR in, 164; from geography, 57; in Grand Nord, 3–4; with Islam, 3–5; for Kampala, 140–44; in Lebanon, 37–38; liminality in, 33–35, 59–60; management, 239–42; in Middle East, 245–46; network war approaches for, 8–12; for NGOs, 18; RCF, 8–9; rebel, 12–18; in Rwenzori borderland, 65–66; scholarship on, 20–21, 30–33; Tabliqs in, 139–40; for UN, 6–8; in Zaire, 133. *See also* rebel conflict
Congo: ADF for, 25n19, 198n8; for Bakonjo Life History Research Association, 75; CNDP for, 158–59; colonialism for, 83; colonial marginalization in, 84–87; conflict in, 1–3, 113–15; Congolization, 167; consolidated borderlands in, 90–97; for DDRRR, 166–67, 197n3; economics in, 160; election fraud in, 228; FDLR in, 187; First Congo War, 23n5, 113, 149n5; government of, 194, 211; ISIS in, 229–30; Islam in, 10–11, 104–5, 155–56, 165; jihadism in, 204–6; leadership in, 175; military in, 3–4; Mobutu for, 131; NALU in, 81–82, 102; for Nande, 75, 159–60; post-colonial peripherality in, 87–90; rebel conflict in, 138–39, 166–67, 183–84, 199n23, 201–2, 215–17; for regional governments, 206–7; Rwanda and, 17, 23n5; Rwenzori borderland for, 22, 187; Second Congo War, 113–14, 237n14; timber from, 236, 238n24; trade with, 129; Uganda and, 11–13, 18–20, 25n15, 66–68, 75–77, 87, 92, 107–8, 124–25, 133, 149n11, 151, 160–61, 176, 191, 232–34, 243–45; for UN, 165, 170, 174; UPDF in, 149n15; violence in, 5–6; Zaire and, 43, 120, 127. *See also specific topics*
Congo Research Group (CRG), 206, 210, 222–23, 226, 229
Congrès National pour la Défense du Peuple (CNDP), 4, 158–59, 179
consolidated borderlands, 77–83, 90–97
contested economic space, 57–60
contested political space, 49–54
contested social space, 54–57
Correlates of War (COW) data, 32–33
Côte d'Ivoire, 8
COW data. *See* Correlates of War data
CRG. *See* Congo Research Group
crime: by ADF, 169–70; Kangbayi Beni prison, 227–28; looting, 235–36; politics of, 54; smuggling as, 57–58; in South Africa, 55–56
cross-border frameworks, 10–11

cultural identity, 98n4, 211
cultural values, 44–45

Davis, Sedgewick, 205–6
DDRRR. *See* Disarmament, Demobilization, Repatriation, Reintegration, and Resettlement
deep territorialization, 43
Democratic Forces for the Liberation of Rwanda (FDLR): in conflict, 164; in Congo, 187; FARDC and, 199n23; LRA compared to, 244; for MONUSCO, 212–13; recruitment for, 190; society for, 196
Democratic Republic of Congo. *See* Congo
Disarmament, Demobilization, Repatriation, Reintegration, and Resettlement (DDRRR): ADF for, 115, 135, 153–54, 164–66; Congo for, 166–67, 197n3; information from, 104–5; rebel conflict for, 160, 162, 174, 189–90; war for, 240
disenfranchisement, 111–13, 159–62
distinct population concept, 42
Donnan, Hastings, 20
Dowd, Catriona, 53

Eastern Congo: colonial marginalization in, 84–87; consolidated borderlands in, 90–97; post-colonial peripherality in, 87–90
Ebola, 233
economics: of ADF, 231–33; in borderlands, 45–49, 62n27; of business practices, 171–76; in Congo, 160; contested economic space, 57–60; of elitism, 106–7; of FARDC, 237n8; in Grand Nord, 176–78; of Konjo, 175; of Mai Mai militias, 164; migration for, 93; of NALU, 126; for Nande, 90–94, 99n20; in politics, 89–90; of rebel conflict, 176, 182–83; in recruitment, 160–61, 168; for society, 75–76; in Uganda, 123–24; in war, 58–59
Ecuador, 53
edge effects, 58
elitism, 89–90, 106–7
El Salvador, 14–15
entrepreneurs, conflict, 59–60
Ethiopia, 35–36
ethnicity, 86
Europe, 36, 60n7, 67–68

FAO. *See* Food and Agriculture Organization
FARDC. *See* Forces Armées de la République Démocratique du Congo
farming, 211–12, 235–36
FDLR. *See* Democratic Forces for the Liberation of Rwanda
FIB. *See* Force Intervention Brigade
First Congo War, 23n5, 113, 149n5
fisherfolk, 36–37
food, 130, 173, 234
Food and Agriculture Organization (FAO), 194
Force Intervention Brigade (FIB), 217–18
Forces Armées de la République Démocratique du Congo (FARDC), 2, 4; ADF for, 172; in borderlands, 162–63, 215–17; for civilians, 193–95, 237n9; in conflict, 152, 171, 179; economics of, 237n8; FDLR and, 199n23; IDP camps for, 191–92; information for, 195; labor camps by, 199n27; for MONUSCO, 215–19, 235; Operation Rwenzori for, 159, 189; reputation of, 221–24; timber for, 198n14; for Uganda, 180; for UN, 185–88, 192–93, 201–4, 244; war with, 211–12
Forno, Gianluca, 69
France, 53
frontiers. *See* borderlands

gangs, 132

Gellner, Ernest, 39
Ghana, 60n8
Ghins, Léopold, 218–19
globalization: for ADF, 201–4, 242–45; human rights in, 237n13; of jihadism, 210–11; of terrorism, 122–23, 214–15; of trade, 95–96
gold mining, 84, 93–94, 161, 174, 182, 234
Goodhand, Jonathan, 32
government: ADF for, 178–83; Boko Haram for, 52; of Congo, 194, 211; infrastructure of, 116–19; mediated governance, 99n15; policy, 45–46; in rebel conflict, 163–68; regional, 206–9; social justice for, 55–56; of Uganda, 127, 134–35, 152–53; ungoverned spaces, 61n16; violence by, 59
Grand Nord, 23n4, 198n15, 237n14, 238n20; conflict in, 3–4; economics in, 176–78; logging in, 174–75; military in, 159; for Nande, 227; networks in, 179–80; for NGOs, 194; society, 168, 173
grey zones, 17
Griffiths, Ieuan, 47
guerrilla warfare, 188–89
Guterres, Antonio, 217
Gypsies, 62n20

Hagmann, Tobias, 33
Haller, Dieter, 20
Herbst, Jeffrey, 35
Hezbollah, 205, 213
Hinks, Arthur R., 65
history: of ADF, 1–5, 101–7; of Berlin Conference, 35; of Ethiopia, 35–36; of Islam, 51–52; of Konjo, 23n3, 69–70; of LRA, 55; of Nande, 83–87; of rebel conflict, 5–6; of Rwenzori borderland, 11, 60, 110–11; of trade routes, 48; of Uganda, 22n2, 65–68; of Zaire, 94
Hoeffler, Anke, 7

hot spots, 245–46
Hovil, Lucy, 105
human rights: in globalization, 237n13; in IDP camps, 150n19; IWDP for, 135; NGOs for, 161–62; in rebel conflict, 112–13, 129, 143–44; in Uganda, 183–84, 219–20; violence for, 25n18
Hussein, Saddam, 122
Hutu, 17, 23n5, 24n13, 109

identity: of ADF, 226; in borderlands, 60, 62n26, 148; cultural, 98n4, 211; Nande, 84–85, 96; politics, 43–44; power with, 50; in Rwenzori borderland, 75–76; with terrorism, 51
IDP camps. See internally displaced person's camps
immigration, 46, 85
income, 171–76
India, 246
indiscriminate violence, 17
Indonesia, 44
information, 104–5, 116–19, 126–27, 163–68, 186–87, 195
infrastructure, 50–51, 92, 116–19
Integrated Women Development Program (IWDP), 135
internally displaced person's (IDP) camps, 3, 143–44, 150n19, 191–92, 193, 199n22
international intervention, 58
International Organization of Migration (IOM), 181, 232–33
Invisible Children, 205–6
IOM. See International Organization of Migration
ISIS. See Islamic State of Iraq and the Levant
"ISIS, After Laying Groundwork, Gains Toehold in Congo" (*New York Times*), 204–5
Islam: for ADF, 105, 229–31; Amin for, 148n3; attacks against, 208; for Christians, 104–5, 148n1, 242–43;

conflict with, 3–5; in Congo, 10–11, 104–5, 155–56, 165; conversion to, 108; history of, 51–52; jihadism for, 156; marginality for, 51; networks, 110; recruitment for, 156; reputation of, 156–57, 192; Al-Shabaab for, 169; Sharia Law, 210–11; for society, 122–23; in Sudan, 131; for Tabliqs, 197n4; terrorism for, 4–6, 52–53, 102–3, 152, 154–55; in Uganda, 10, 101, 122, 148n1, 149n4, 153–54, 167–68; violence by, 195, 215, 242; for women, 197n7
Islamic State of Iraq and the Levant (ISIS), 204–6, 209–12, 229–30, 242
IWDP. *See* Integrated Women Development Program

JATT. *See* Joint Anti-Terrorism Taskforce
jihadism, 51; for Christians, 214; in Congo, 204–6; globalization of, 210–11; for Islam, 156; for Mukulu, 153–54; by Al-Shabaab, 242; for Tabliqs, 102
Joint Anti-Terrorism Taskforce (JATT), 154–55, 164–65, 169, 177, 183–84, 206
Jonathan, Goodluck, 52–53
Joseph, Ali, 156

Kabanda, Yusuf, 108, 116
Kabila, Joseph, 88, 128–29, 149n15, 201–2, 207, 233
Kamango zone, 178
Kampala (Uganda), 140–44
Kangbayi Beni prison, 227–28
Kasada, Amisi, 165
Kasada, Costa, 165
Kasagama, Daudi, 70
Kasfir, Nelson, 98n7
Kashmir, 246
Kavota, Omar, 193
Kaweesi, Andrew Felix, 208
Kayihura, Kale, 184

Kazini, James, 143
Kekedo, Suleiman, 154
Kenya, 92, 229
Keranio, Kiso, 170
kidnapping, 165
Kigozi, Hamza, 165
Kinyamusitu, Richard, 78
Kisokeranio, Fenahasi, 108
Kiyonga, Crispus, 102
Klein, Diana, 59
Koko (sheikh), 230
Konjo: Amba for, 75–76; Bakonjo Life History Research Association for, 73; economics of, 175; history of, 23n3, 69–70; NALU for, 78–83; Nande and, 66–67, 85–86, 107, 124, 127, 137, 168, 175, 182; networks, 110–11; Rwenzori borderland for, 77–78, 157–58; self-induced exile for, 71; society for, 68, 98n12, 173; Toro and, 69–73, 79, 87, 98n6, 98n8; trade with, 92–94
Kony, Joseph, 119, 121, 133, 135, 205
Korf, Benedikt, 33
Kwiravusa, Elie, 232
Kyambalangu, Kassim, 165

labor camps, 199n27
Lakwena, Alice, 16
landscape plasticity, 42
language, 41–42, 73–74
Latin America, 53
Lebanon, 37–38
Leopold (king), 95
Liberia, 8
Libya, 46
liminality: in Africa, 48–49; in conflict, 33–35, 59–60; for LRA, 115; for policy, 42; for rebel conflict, 79–81; of Rwenzori borderland, 12, 151, 196–97
Lind, Jeremy, 51
Long, James D., 14
looting, 235–36

Lord's Resistance Army (LRA), 3, 16; ADF compared to, 118; FDLR compared to, 244; history of, 55; liminality for, 115; with military, 132–33; for Museveni, 145; in rebel conflict, 196; recruitment of, 162–63; reputation of, 153; Uganda for, 241; with UPDF, 140
Lugard, Frederick D., 70
Lusaka Ceasefire Agreement, 153
Luyamuzi, Ken, 141–43

MacGaffey, Janet, 48
Magara, Badru, 165
Mai Mai militias: as actors, 24n13; for ADF, 190; children in, 163, 228; economics of, 164; networks with, 114–15; support for, 223–24; violence by, 136
Malaysia, 44
Mali, 53, 61n15
Malkki, Liisa, 9
Manaki, Mao, 174
marginality: in borderland conceptual framework, 29–30; colonial marginalization, 68–72, 84–87; for Islam, 51; for Konjo, 66–67; for Nande, 88–89; politics of, 61n13; for Tabliqs, 103; trade for, 96–97; in Uganda, 49–50
Martinez, Oscar J., 33
material resources, 120–23, 127–31, 169–71
Mauritania, 53
Mbangu, Marcel, 203
McGregor, Andrew, 103
Médard, Frédéric, 185
mediated governance, 99n15
Mende, Lambert, 187
Merkx, Jozef, 50
meta-narratives, 50, 72, 76–78, 82, 119, 168
micro-political perspectives, 12–18
Middle East, 122, 245–46
migration, 93, 103–4, 181, 232–33

Miles, William F. S., 45
military: allies, 37–38; for civilians, 61n15; in Congo, 3–4; in Grand Nord, 159; LRA with, 132–33; network war approaches for, 6–8; politics of, 244–45; in rebel conflict, 74–75, 109, 114–15, 120–21, 137; in Syria, 53–54; for trade, 58–59; in Uganda, 1–5; UPDF as, 118
missionaries, 95, 99n20
Mission de l'Organization des Nations Uniesen République Démocratique du Congo (MONUSCO), 2, 4, 19–20, 188, 202; FARDC for, 215–19, 235; rebel conflict for, 22, 104–5, 161–62, 186, 212–13, 243–44. See also Disarmament, Demobilization, Repatriation, Reintegration, and Resettlement
Mkandawire, Thandika, 17
Mobutu, Joseph, 88–89, 127–28, 131, 149n5
monopolies, 124–26
MONUSCO. See Mission de l'Organization des Nations Uniesen République Démocratique du Congo
Mozambique, 44
Mugira, James, 122, 184
Mukirane, Isaya, 73–75, 77
Mukirania, Christina, 220–21
Mukulu, Jamil, 102, 106, 116, 202; jihadism for, 153–54; Kony with, 133; leadership of, 149n4; reputation of, 164–65
Mulele Rebellion, 75, 91
Mulima, Ali Bwambale, 146–47
Mumbere, Charles Wesley, 77, 110–11, 158
Museveni, Yoweri: information for, 186–87; LRA for, 145; policy of, 81, 99, 106–7, 180–81; power for, 102–4; propaganda by, 134–35; rebel conflict for, 133; reputation of, 109, 112, 142–43, 149n9, 208–9;

Rwenzori borderland for, 220–21; terrorism for, 207–8
Muslims. *See* Islam
Myanmar, 59

Nairobi Agreement, 10
NALU. *See* National Army for the Liberation of Uganda
Nande: for ADF, 114, 196; alliances with, 158–59; borderlands for, 67, 174; civilians, 81; Congo for, 75, 159–60; economics for, 90–94, 99n20; Grand Nord for, 227; history of, 83–87; identity, 84–85, 96; Kabila for, 233; kidnapping of, 165; Konjo and, 66–67, 85–86, 107, 124, 127, 137, 168, 175, 182; leadership for, 158; marginality for, 88–89; for NALU, 171–72; politics for, 94–95; Rwanda for, 90; society for, 95–96; trade for, 96–97, 176; Uganda for, 70
Nasser, Bekkah Abdul, 122
national actors, 9
National Army for the Liberation of Uganda (NALU), 3, 78–83; for ADF, 107–11, 119, 123–27, 131, 136–40, 157–59; in Congo, 81–82, 102; economics of, 126; leadership for, 106, 169–70; Nande for, 171–72
nationalism, 54, 98n11
Ndala, Mamadou, 213
negotiations, 198n17
Nepal, 42–43
nepotism, 106–7
networks: in Africa, 164–65, 171–72; business, 233–34; in Grand Nord, 179–80; Konjo, 110–11; with Mai Mai militias, 114–15; network war approaches, 6–12
New Barbarism, 24n14
New York Times, 204–5
NGOs. *See* nongovernmental organizations
Ngwato, Tara Polzer, 37
Nigeria, 43, 45–46, 52–53, 215

nongovernmental organizations (NGOs): as actors, 50, 103; conflict for, 18; Grand Nord for, 194; for human rights, 161–62; Rwenzori borderland for, 76–77; for scholarship, 25n20; UN with, 183
non-state actors, 53
Nsibambi, Apolo, 133
Nugent, Paul, 30–31
Nyamwisi, Mbusa, 225

Obote, Milton, II, 77
Ongwen, Dominique, 115
Operation North Night Final, 185–88, 197, 243–44
Operation Rwenzori, 173, 185–86, 188, 244; for FARDC, 159, 189; for Grand Nord, 198n15; IDP camps before, 199n22; for rebel conflict, 195–96; refugees from, 192–93; for UN, 187

Pakistan, 56, 122, 246
Paluku, Julien, 225
Pashtun tribes, 39
Peterson, Derek, 15
policy, 42, 45–46, 72–73; in Europe, 67–68; of Museveni, 81, 99, 106–7, 180–81; by UN, 240–41
politics: ADF in, 127–31, 149n7; borderland, 35–41, 71–72, 88; in China, 246; for civilians, 15–16, 24n11; contested political space, 49–54; of crime, 54; of cross-border frameworks, 10–11; economics in, 89–90; identity, 43–44; of infrastructure, 50–51; of marginality, 61n13; meta-narratives in, 50, 72, 76–78, 82, 119, 168; of military, 244–45; for Nande, 94–95; nepotism in, 106–7; in Nigeria, 52–53; political actors, 24n12; political geography factors, 188–90; political science, 29–30; of power, 112; of RCF, 8; of rebel conflict, 8–9,

132–33, 153; of religion, 148n1; of Rwenzori borderland, 1–2; social, 49–50; on social media, 236n1; of terrorism, 4–5; of trade, 94–95; of war, 6–7; zero-sum, 45
Pollard, Sidney, 36
Poole, Lauren, 206
post-colonial peripherality, 72–77, 87–90
power, 50, 102–4, 112–13
propaganda, 134–35
property rights, 38
Prunier, Gérard, 43

Al Qaeda, 4, 52, 181, 205, 209, 213
Al Qaeda in Islamic Maghreb, 51–53

quasi-states, 61n12

Raleigh, Clionadh, 53
rape, 226
RCF. *See* Regional Conflict Formations
rebel conflict, 12–18; agency in, 30; for Boko Haram, 214–15; for children, 211–12; for civilians, 18–19, 185–86; in Colombia, 53; in Congo, 138–39, 166–67, 183–84, 199n23, 201–2, 215–17; for DDRRR, 160, 162, 174, 189–90; economics of, 176, 182–83; food during, 130; government in, 163–68; history of, 5–6; hot spots for, 245–46; human rights in, 112–13, 129, 143–44; leadership in, 3; liminality for, 79–81; LRA in, 196; military in, 74–75, 109, 114–15, 120–21, 137; for MONUSCO, 22, 104–5, 161–62, 186, 212–13, 243–44; Operation Rwenzori for, 195–96; organization in, 116–19; politics of, 8–9, 132–33, 153; retention in, 152–57; scholarship on, 15; smuggling in, 90; for society, 78, 129–30; terrorism in, 1–2; for UPDF, 135–36, 139, 144–45, 204; victims of, 16–17; violence in, 101–2, 107–8, 172–73; as war, 7–8
recruitment: for ADF, 110–15, 152–57, 197n5, 227–29; of children, 161–62, 166–67; by Christians, 156; economics in, 160–61, 168; for FDLR, 190; for Islam, 156; of LRA, 162–63; from Nigeria, 215
refugees, 63n36, 192–93
Regional Conflict Formations (RCF), 8–9
regional governments, 206–9
religion, 95, 99n20, 148n1. *See also* Christians; Islam
resources, 120–23, 125–31, 169–71
retention, in rebel conflict, 152–57
Rod, Jan Ketil, 50

al-Rubdie, Fallah Hassan, 122

Ruhorimbere, Eric, 192
Rukwango, David, 165
Russia, 246
Rwanda, 17, 23n5, 24n13, 85, 90, 109. *See also* Democratic Forces for the Liberation of Rwanda
Rwenzori borderland: for ADF, 17–18, 68–69, 97, 108–9, 151, 239–40, 246–47; conflict in, 65–66; for Congo, 22, 187; geography of, 105, 118, 138; history of, 11, 60, 110–11; identity in, 75–76; for Konjo, 77–78, 157–58; language in, 73–74; liminality of, 12, 151, 196–97; for Museveni, 220–21; for NGOs, 76–77; politics of, 1–2; Rwenzururu Freedom Movement, 78–83; Rwenzururu Movement, 73–77, 81–82, 108, 111, 136; society in, 182–83; timber in, 174–75; for Uganda, 20–21; violence in, 219–20; weapons in, 180. *See also* Operation Rwenzori; Western Uganda

Salehyan, Idean, 8–9
scarcity, of resources, 125–26

scholarship: on ADF, 10–12, 18–21, 133–34; on agency, 30; borderland conceptual framework for, 27–29; on borderlands, 245–47; boundary activation in, 56; on civil war, 16; on conflict, 20–21, 30–33; COW data for, 32–33; CRG for, 206, 210, 222–23, 226, 229; MONUSCO for, 19–20; NGOs for, 25n20; RCF theory, 9; on rebel conflict, 15; on religion, 99n20; urban bias in, 24n9
Second Congo War, 113–14, 237n14
security, 63n37
Seko, Mobutu Sese, 82, 115
self-induced exile, 71

Al-Shabaab, 51–52, 169, 181, 207; jihadism by, 242; reputation of, 155, 205, 213; terrorism by, 183

Shabe people, 43
Sharia Law, 210–11
shatter-zones, 39, 61n19
Shneiderman, Sara, 42–43
Sierra Leone, 8
smuggling, 47, 57–58, 63n37, 90, 92
social justice, 55–58
social media, 236n1
society: in borderlands, 41–45, 178–79, 226–27; contested social space, 54–57; economics for, 75–76; ethnicity in, 86; for FDLR, 196; Grand Nord, 168, 173; Islam for, 122–23; for Konjo, 68, 98n12, 173; language for, 41–42; for Nande, 95–96; rebel conflict for, 78, 129–30; in Rwenzori borderland, 182–83; social politics, 49–50; social relationships, 56; trade in, 47–48; of Uganda, 109
Somalia, 155, 208
South Africa, 44, 55–56
SPLA. *See* Sudan People's Liberation Army
Stearns, Jason, 87–88

Steinhart, Edward I., 67
Sudan: for ADF, 130–31; for borderland analytical frameworks, 12–13; Chad and, 7; Islam in, 131; Kenya and, 92; Mobutu, 128; SPLA, 5, 10, 170; in terrorism, 104; Uganda and, 5, 102–3, 120–23
Sudan-Chad-Central African Republic corridor, 30
Sudan People's Liberation Army (SPLA), 5, 10, 170
suffer-manage techniques, 40
supplies, 171–76
Swaziland, 44
Syria, 53–54

Tabliqs, 102–4; for ADF, 11; children for, 230; in conflict, 139–40; Islam for, 197n4; reputation of, 121–23; for Uganda, 6
tactics, 185–89
Taliban, 13–14, 205, 213
Tangseefa, Decha, 32
taxation, 72, 98n9
Terdman, Moshe, 103
territorial accessibility, 126–27
territorial control practices, 176–78
territorialization, 43
territory management, 171–76
terrorism: ADF related to, 203–4; globalization of, 122–23, 214–15; identity with, 51; by ISIS, 204–6, 242; for Islam, 4–6, 52–53, 102–3, 152, 154–55; for JATT, 154–55, 164–65, 169, 177, 183–84, 206; in Middle East, 122; for Museveni, 207–8; politics of, 4–5; Al Qaeda in, 4; in rebel conflict, 1–2; by Al-Shabaab, 183; Sudan in, 104; by Taliban, 13–14; Taliban in, 213; terrorist exclusion list, 181; in Uganda, 184; for UN, 210; for US, 154, 181, 208. *See also* jihadism
Thangmi culture, 42–43
Tibet, 37, 42–43, 246

Tilly, Charles, 56
timber, 174–75, 198n14, 236, 238n24
Titeca, Kristof, 116
Togo, 60n8
Toro, 69–73, 79, 87, 98n6, 98n8
torture, 198n9
trade: for ADF, 235–36; in borderlands, 62n29, 85–86, 181–82; in colonialism, 91; with Congo, 129; globalization of, 95–96; immigration and, 46; infrastructure for, 92; with Konjo, 92–94; for marginality, 96–97; military for, 58–59; for Nande, 96–97, 176; politics of, 94–95; in society, 47–48; timber, 175; violence in, 55, 180
training, for ADF, 169–71
transnational actors, 54–55
Tshisekedi, Félix, 202, 207
Tunisia, 46
Tusasirwe, Benson, 109

Uganda: before ADF, 66; Amnesty Act, 117, 143; Berlin Conference for, 67; borderlands for, 198n14; colonial marginalization in, 68–72; Congo and, 11–13, 18–20, 25n15, 66–68, 75–77, 87, 92, 107–8, 124–25, 133, 149n11, 151, 160–61, 176, 191, 232–34, 243–45; consolidated borderlands in, 77–83; economics in, 123–24; FARDC for, 180; First Congo War for, 149n5; fisherfolk in, 36–37; gangs in, 132; geography of, 99n13; government of, 127, 134–35, 152–53; history of, 22n2, 65–68; human rights in, 183–84, 219–20; IDP camps in, 3; Islam in, 10, 101, 122, 148n1, 149n4, 153–54, 167–68; Kabila for, 149n15; Kampala, 140–44; for LRA, 241; marginality in, 49–50; material resources in, 127–31; military in, 1–5; for Nande, 70; post-colonial peripherality in, 72–77; for regional governments, 207–9; Rwenzori borderland for, 20–21; society of, 109; Sudan and, 5, 102–3, 120–23; Tabliqs for, 6; terrorism in, 184; Uganda National Rescue Front, 109; WNBF rebel group in, 104; women in, 226; Zaire and, 6, 80–81, 109. *See also specific topics*
Uganda National Liberation Army (UNLA), 77
"The Ugandan Rebels Working with IS in DR Congo" (*BBC News*), 214
Uganda People's Defense Force (UPDF), 2–3, 105–6, 113–14; ADF for, 146–47, 186; in borderlands, 140–41, 149n11; in Congo, 149n15; for IDP camps, 143–44; LRA with, 140; as military, 118; rebel conflict for, 135–36, 139, 144–45, 204; violence by, 142
UK. *See* United Kingdom
Ukraine, 246
UN. *See* United Nations
ungoverned spaces, 61n16
United Kingdom (UK), 122, 164, 208
United Nations (UN), 183; ADF for, 2, 163–66; conflict for, 6–8; Congo for, 165, 170, 174; FARDC for, 185–88, 192–93, 201–4, 244; Operation Rwenzori for, 187; policy by, 240–41; terrorism for, 210
United States (US), 122, 154, 181, 207, 208
UNLA. *See* Uganda National Liberation Army
UPDF. *See* Uganda People's Defense Force
urban bias, 24n9
US. *See* United States

Van Schendel, Willem, 34
Venezuela, 53
victims, 16–17, 61n9
violence: by actors, 51, 58; by ADF, 105–6, 132–35, 183–84, 212–14; in Beni massacres, 216–17, 221–22; in

borderland analytical frameworks, 12; in borderlands, 245; in Central African Republic, 7, 51; for civilians, 4, 134; in Congo, 5–6; in Côte d'Ivoire, 8; by government, 59; for human rights, 25n18; in IDP camps, 193; indiscriminate, 17; by Islam, 195, 215, 242; by Mai Mai militias, 136; mobilization of, 90; from nationalism, 54; nature of, 135–37; New Barbarism, 24n14; by non-state actors, 53; power from, 113; rape, 226; in rebel conflict, 101–2, 107–8, 172–73; in Rwenzori borderland, 219–20; torture, 198n9; in trade, 55, 180; by UPDF, 142; against women, 166
Vlassenroot, Koen, 116

Wapakhabulo, James, 120
war, 6–8, 14–15, 28, 54–55, 240; economics in, 58–59; with FARDC, 211–12. *See also specific topics*
weapons, 180
Western Uganda: ADF in, 219–21; colonial marginalization in, 68–72; consolidated borderlands in, 77–83; post-colonial peripherality in, 72–77
West Nile Bank Front (WNBF) rebel group, 104, 109
women: abduction of, 237n16; children and, 191–92, 221–24; Islam for, 197n7; in Uganda, 226; violence against, 166
Wood, Elisabeth, 14–15

Yira people, 68

Zaire, 94, 133; Congo and, 43, 120, 127; Uganda and, 6, 80–81, 109. *See also* Congo
Zartman, William I., 27
zero-sum politics, 45
Zomian spaces, 38–41, 62n28

About the Author

Lindsay Scorgie is Assistant Professor of Political Science at Huron College, Western University. Her teaching and research focuses on conflict in non-state spaces, borderland politics, and most recently on the intersection of genocide denial and Dark Tourism. She holds a PhD from the University of Cambridge, MSc from the London School of Economics, and BA (Hons) from the University of Toronto.

www.ingramcontent.com/pod-product-compliance
Lightning Source LLC
Chambersburg PA
CBHW032032300426
44117CB00009B/1029